Introduction to
Data Structures
with Pascal

Introduction to Data Structures with Pascal

Thomas L. Naps
Lawrence University

Bhagat Singh
University of Wisconsin Center System

WEST PUBLISHING COMPANY
St. Paul   New York   San Francisco   Los Angeles

Copyediting: Martha S. Knutson
Design: Lucy Lesiak
Typesetting: Rolin Graphics
Cover Design: Paul Kemp
Cover Photograph: Floyd Rollefstad, Laser Fantasy Productions

Library of Congress Cataloging-in-Publication Data

Naps, Thomas L.
  Introduction to data structures with PASCAL.

  Includes index.
  1. PASCAL (Computer program language) 2. Data
structures (Computer science) I. Singh, Bhagat,
1940-   . II. Title.
QA76.73.P2N37 1986   005.7'3   85-22582
ISBN 0-314-93207-0

To

Joyce and Rosemary

Contents

6

Tree Structures   142

APPENDICES

Preface

With the rapid evolution of computer science, the study of data structures has found its way into the undergraduate curriculum as early as the sophomore year. Moreover, an increasingly diverse collection of students is studying this subject. Once solely the domain of hard-core computer science majors, data structures is now taken by business, economics, engineering, and mathematics majors who wish to enhance their chosen discipline with a strong background in computer science. Texts that emphasize a highly rigorous mathematical approach to data structures no longer are appropriate for this growing number of heterogeneous students. In *Introduction to Data Structures with Pascal*, we attempt to satisfy the needs of this new group of students by providing a text that emphasizes implementing and evaluating data structures in practical situations and avoids relying on an overly theoretical approach. The text is designed for anyone who has had a solid programming background in Pascal. Such a background should include a detailed grasp of procedures, functions, parameter passing, and arrays. To a lesser extent, some prior work with records and files is desirable although these topics are developed as needed in the text itself.

Introduction to Data Structures with Pascal represents an alternative to our earlier pseudocode-based *Introduction to Data Structures*. The development of such an alternative was motivated by a near 50-50 split which we found among the reviewers of our efforts. Though these reviewers were essentially in agreement as to topics covered and the order in which they were presented, there was a pronounced and irresolvable split between those who believed in a pseudocode approach and those who felt that seeing algorithms in the familiar Pascal language would make concepts easier for students. It is to this latter group that this version of the text is addressed.

In addition to providing a Pascal-specific orientation, we have also expanded our coverage of important software engineering concepts to help students as they begin using data structures in larger programming projects. Sections on Program Design Considerations appear in each chapter. Some of these sections (notably those in Chapter 3, Chapter 7, and Chapter 11) deal with the development of complete large-scale programs which use the data structures studied up to that point. Others touch upon design issues which are then further expanded in the exercises and programming problems.

Three new appendices have also been added for those students of Pascal who may need a bit more general experience as well as a thorough treatment of data structures. Appendix C presents a description of those testing, verification, and debugging strategies that are so essential for students developing large-scale programs. Appendix B on formal analysis of algorithms presents the basics of this topic. We have chosen to treat this issue in a separate appendix because we want the book to retain its intuitive, implementation-oriented approach. Appendix A discusses how various versions of Pascal implement direct access files—a topic which we consider essential despite its absence from the Pascal standard. A "real world" proof of the essential nature of this topic is that virtually all widely used implementations of Pascal have included procedures for direct access files in their repetoires. Appropriate references to all of these appendices are made throughout the text, making it easy for the student to merge this additional material with specific data structures topics. Depending upon the curriculum at your institution, this increased emphasis upon software engineering issues and the coverage of advanced topics in a Pascal-specific fashion may in fact make the text suitable for an advanced course in programming, as described in the C.S. II Course Guidelines recommended by the recent ACM Curriculum Task Force for C.S. II.

Further changes from the pseudocode version are less oriented toward Pascal but instead induced by feedback we have been receiving from the field. Exercises have been added in each chapter. The thematic Wing-and-a-Prayer Airlines problems proved popular, so we have included two other thematic problem lines running throughout the text—the Fly-By-Night Credit Company and the Bay Area Brawlers Professional Football Club. In Chapter 5, we have expanded our discussion of recursion, offering a more gradual introduction to this difficult topic. Discussions of algorithm efficiency in the body of the text itself have been isolated in separate sections for greater emphasis and easier reference. Finally, new "In the World of Applications" boxes have been developed for Chapters 4, 7, and 9 to replace old ones which some readers felt lacked a "real world" flavor.

However, despite these changes, the two major goals of this text remain unchanged from the pseudocode version:

1. The student must acquire an understanding of the algorithms that manipulate various data structures.
2. The student must learn to select from among data structures for a given application.

Relative to this second goal, data structures could be considered the toolbox of the computer scientist or data processor. Many jobs can be accomplished in more than one way; the student who understands data structures thoroughly is able to match the tool to the job most effectively.

Understanding of data structures is enhanced by pictures. For this reason, we have made ours a graphically oriented book. Throughout the text, algorithms written in Pascal are enhanced by "graphic documentation" to clarify the responsibilities of various segments of code. Our experience as instructors of data structures has so often indicated that a student's question about how to do something can be answered by the simple dictum to "draw a picture." Data structures are, after all, the programmer's way of implementing certain types of mental images within the computer. Every segment of a program is in some way responsible for maintaining or altering that structural image. Can there be a better way to document that segment than to picture what it is intended to do? In a certain sense, this graphic orientation embodies the essence of data abstraction—that the student understand the data structure itself rather than memorize a particular algorithm or the details of a particular implementation.

The order of topics presented in the book is relatively flexible, although the first seven chapters represent a core of fundamental material that should be covered before moving on to any of the topics in Chapters 8 through 12. Chapter 1 lays the groundwork for the rest of the book by specifying a rationale for data structures and developing those advanced features of Pascal (including records and pointer variables) that will be used throughout. The first data structure discussed in detail is the linked list, presented in Chapter 2. Initial implementation of linked lists in this chapter is achieved through the use of arrays instead of Pascal's NEW and DISPOSE procedures to allow the student to actually trace through the implementation. In Chapter 3, we consider strings in detail as an example of an application in which pointers, indices, and linked lists can be used effectively. Chapter 4 presents two special types of lists: queues and stacks, and Chapter 5 follows up on this theme by looking at two critically important applications of stacks: the parsing of arithmetic expressions and recursion. Chapters 6 and 7 cover in detail what we consider to be the most versatile of all data structures—the tree. We discuss both binary and general trees, along with such variations as threading and height-balancing.

Although the first seven chapters of this book should be studied consecutively, there is considerable leeway in the order in which the remaining topics may be covered. Some instructors may find it possible to cover only selected topics from Chapters 8 through 12, and these chapters are connected loosely enough to allow picking and choosing. Chapter 8 fully describes multidimensional and sparse matrices, which serves as a convenient introduction to the adjacency matrix representation of graphs and networks, the topic of Chapter 9. Chapters 8 and 9 thus form a cohesive unit. However, it is possible to proceed directly from Chapter 7 to either Chapter 10 (Sorting) or Chapter 11 (Search Methods). Chapter 12, Data Structures and Data Management, presents a nice wrapup for a data structures course by describing how a variety of data structures can be applied in the areas of memory management and database management. Because not all instructors will find time in a semester to cover the material in Chapter 12, we have written it such that it lends itself to independent study. For those students going on into systems programming, the material in Chapter 12 on memory management algorithms used by operating systems should prove particularly valuable. For the more business-oriented student, the database management section is more suitable. The following flowchart summarizes the possible sequences in which chapters can be covered.

Additional features of the book include "In the World of Applications . . ." boxes, which emphasize how data structures are used in a variety of settings; chapter exercises and programming problems; a glossary; and an appendix of solutions to odd-numbered exercises. The Instructor's Manual provides useful hints on how to present the material in each chapter, solutions to even-numbered exercises, and additional ideas for programming problems and projects. Transparency masters that can be used to illustrate key concepts are available to adopters from the publisher. A list of figures from the text available as transparency masters is in the Instructor's Manual.

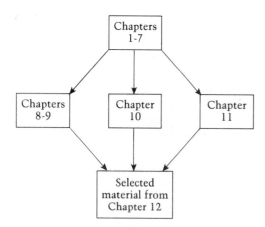

Acknowledgements

Although work on this text was greatly smoothed by the previous work we had done for the pseudocode version, a large number of people have nonetheless played key roles in its development. Of course, our students never cease to amaze us with the clever ideas and insights they continually offer. Jerry Westby, our editor, always had another (and another) innovative idea to try. Our work with production editor Peggy Adams and the staff at West Publishing proved to be a pleasure. Thanks go also to the large group of skilled reviewers who offered constructive criticism on our efforts:

John Rezac, Johnson County Community College
Andrew Bernat, University of Texas at El Paso
Michael Henry, West Virginia University
Charles Williams, Georgia State University
W. Bruce Croft, University of Massachusetts at Amherst
Robert Holloway, University of Wisconsin at Madison
Tamisra Sanyal, Monroe Community College
Martha Hansard, Georgia State University
Barent Johnson, University of Wisconsin at Oshkosh

Finally, our most sincere gratitude is directed to our wives and families. The warmth and freshness they provide keep our lives nicely unstructured.

1

Data Structures—An Overview

"The last thing that we find in making a book is to
know what we must put first."

BLAISE PASCAL (1623-1662)

1-1   Introductory Considerations

The essence of programming and contemporary data processing requires **efficient algorithms** for accessing the data both in main memory and on secondary storage devices. This efficiency is directly linked to the structure of the data being processed. You do not have to progress far into the study of computers to realize that only the most trivial applications allow data items to exist independently of each other. A data item that can be effectively linked to other data items takes on a meaning that transcends its individual content. For instance, a grade of "A" standing alone says very little. But a grade of "A" linked to a course title "Computer Science 480" which is in turn linked to the student "Mary Smith" takes on a much more significant meaning. A **data structure** is a way of organizing data that considers not only the items stored but also their relationship to each other.

A natural example is that of a **one-dimensional array** declared in a language like PASCAL:

```
TYPE INTARRAY = ARRAY [1..20] OF INTEGER;
    .
    .
    .


VAR M:INTARRAY;
    .
    .
    .

FOR I:=1 TO 20 DO
    READ(M[I]);
```

We are told by these statements that the structure M contains 20 elements, each one integer word in length. The first element is M[1], the 10th element is M[10], and so on. The segment of the PASCAL program given above will read numbers from the standard input and store them consecutively in M[1], M[2], . . ., M[20]. The 20 words of memory associated with the structure M are contiguous. Thus, the accessing of data in M is a function of how it is organized.

The **record** is another common type of data structure used in languages such as PL/1, COBOL, and Pascal. In this structure, logically related data items of different types are grouped together under one name. An example of a record as it may be coded in COBOL is:

```
01      STUDENT-REC.
        02    NAME          PIC   X(20).
        02    SEMESTER      PIC   99.
        02    EXAM-SCORE    PIC   9(3).
        02    GRADE         PIC   X.
```

Its equivalent in Pascal is:

```
STUDENTREC   =   RECORD
                     NAME : ARRAY [1..20] OF CHAR;
                     SEMESTER : INTEGER;
                     EXAMSCORE : INTEGER;
                     GRADE : CHAR
                 END;
```

These languages each contain sufficient data description techniques to allow algorithms to access all or part of such a record structure. The concept of a record is essential to numerous applications in computer science and data processing. The use of records in Pascal will be discussed in the latter part of this chapter.

Other more complex data structures such as stacks, queues, linked lists, trees, and graphs will be introduced as we progress. A general understanding of data structures is essential to developing efficient algorithms in virtually all phases of advanced data processing and computer science. For example, in the implementation of a database management system, the two most commonly used techniques are the **linked list** (chain pointer) and **inverted file** methods. A clear notion of the relative advantages and disadvantages of each technique is obviously crucial to those designing such a system. However, as the advertisement reproduced in Figure 1-1 indicates, the buyer of a database management system also must be aware of the data structures involved in its design to avoid making a costly wrong decision.

FIGURE 1-1   ADABAS database management advertisement appealing to the buyer's knowledge of inverted file and chain pointer data structures. (Reproduced courtesy of Software AG.)

The ability to make correct decisions is vital to anyone involved with computers. Such decisions typically involve the following general issues:

- The efficiency of a program with respect to its **run time.** Does it perform its task in a time allotment that does not detract from overall system performance?
- The efficiency of a program with respect to its **utilization of main memory and secondary storage** devices. Does it consume such resources in a fashion that makes its use impractical?
- The **developmental costs** of a program (or system of programs). Could a different approach to the problem significantly reduce the total person-hours invested in it?

Thorough knowledge of a programming language is *not* a sufficient base upon which to make these decisions. The study of data structures will expose you to a vast collection of tried and proven methods used in designing efficient programs. Thus, as you develop an awareness of data structures, you will begin to realize the considerations involved in large-scale software projects. Later chapters and their exercises will illustrate applications of various data structures in such diverse areas as:

- Compiler design
- Operating systems
- Database management systems
- Statistical analysis packages
- Numerical analysis
- Graphics
- Artificial intelligence
- Simulation
- Network analysis

When you examine the relative advantages and disadvantages of different types of data structures in such applications, you become acutely aware of an old computer adage: *You get nothing for nothing.* That is, in many applications, different types of data structures could be used to achieve the same end, and in such situations, the designer plays a game of tradeoffs. One data structure sacrifices memory compactness for speed; another utilizes memory efficiently but results in a slow run time. For each positive there seems to be a corresponding negative. No absolutely best data structure exists. Instead, designers must rely on their knowledge of the strong and weak points of various data structures to choose the one that best fits each application. These strengths and weaknesses will be fully discussed for each of the data structures we study.

1-2   Algorithms for Data Structures

Once a data structure has been chosen for a particular application, it is given life by the logical instructions that manipulate the related data items stored in it. Thus, a study of data structures is also necessarily a study of the **algorithms** that control them. Certain traits can be clearly identified as desirable in all such algorithms.

First, the algorithms must be expressed in a fashion that is completely *free of ambiguities*. Toward this end, the method we use to express algorithms must be formal enough to avoid the imprecision inherent in a natural language and yet flexible enough to allow us to focus on problem-oriented issues instead of syntactical considerations. To meet this two-fold goal, we will use the **Pascal** language. Its structured nature encourages clarity in the expression of algorithms. Moreover, because it is highly standardized across a variety of implementations, algorithms appearing in the book may easily be converted for machine-testing by the reader. Where appropriate, the initial statement of an algorithm may be made in a Pascal-like pseudocode prior to its formalization in actual Pascal. We stress that this text is intended to teach data structures, *not* Pascal. We assume a familiarity with the various control constructs, procedure/function conventions, and array declaration capabilities of the language. Some of the more advanced features of Pascal which we need for data structures algorithms will be introduced in the latter portion of this chapter.

Second, algorithms should be *efficient.* They should not unnecessarily use memory locations nor should they require an excessive number of logical operations. To analyze the efficiency of our algorithms, we will have to describe numerically the logical operations and memory that they require. Such a numerical analysis may tell us whether or not the algorithm is practical.

Third, algorithms should be *concise and compact* to facilitate **verification** of their correctness. Verification involves observing the performance of the algorithm with a carefully selected set of test cases. These test cases should attempt to cover all of the exceptional circumstances likely to be encountered by the algorithm. Just what these exceptional circumstances are will depend upon the data structure being manipulated. However, certain generic circumstances must be considered in verifying all algorithms manipulating data structures:

- Does the algorithm work when the data structure is empty? For instance, does the logic of the algorithm correctly allow data to be added to a structure that presently contains no data? Is an attempt to delete data from such a structure appropriately trapped?
- Does the algorithm work when the data structure is full?
- Does the algorithm work for all the possibilities that can occur between an empty structure and a full structure?

The need for conciseness in algorithms becomes obvious when you consider the problem of verifying their correctness. The more an algorithm attempts to do, the more possibilities must be considered in its verification. Hence, we will take the view that an algorithm should concern itself with one specific problem. Each algorithm is a logical **module** designed to handle a specific problem relative to a particular data structure. Such modules could be tied together by higher level algorithms which focus upon the connections between modules rather than the underlying data structures. However, our primary concern in this text will be with those algorithms that access the data structures. The interfacing of such modules into a complete system is appropriately studied in a course on systems analysis and design.

1-3   An Example of Algorithm Development in Pascal

Initial Version of Bubble Sort

To illustrate some of the general comments which were made in the previous section, let us trace the development of a sorting algorithm using Pascal. This will give us an opportunity to demonstrate how an algorithm can be refined to make it more efficient and to introduce several advanced features of Pascal which will be used throughout the remainder of the text. The task at hand is to sort a list of input names by alphabetical order. The algorithm chosen is called the **bubble sort.** This method has the advantage of being one of the easiest of all sorting algorithms to understand. Consequently, by Murphy's Law, it must be the least efficient. Chapter 10 will be devoted to a full discussion of more complex and efficient sorting methods. However, it is noteworthy that even an algorithm as simple as the bubble sort can be examined and refined to enhance the efficiency of both its run time and its memory utilization. The general idea of the bubble sort may be described as follows. Given a list of names stored in an array, pass through the array and compare adjacent pairs of names. Whenever two names are out of order with respect to each other, interchange them. The effect of such a pass through a list of names is illustrated in Figure 1-2. Notice that, after such a pass, we are assured that the list will have the name which comes last in alphabetical order in the final array position.

If one pass through an array of N names can guarantee that the name which comes last in alphabetical order is in the appropriate position, then slicing off the last element and passing through the remaining $N - 1$ entries using the same logic will guarantee that the name which comes second to last in alphabetical order is in its appropriate position. Repeating the process for a total of $N-1$ passes will eventually insure that all names are in their appropriate alphabetical position. In general, on the Ith pass through the array, $N - I$ pairwise

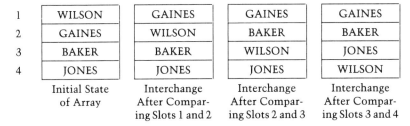

FIGURE 1-2 *First Pass Through Array Using Bubble Sort*

comparisons must be made. A complete Pascal program to demonstrate the bubble sort logic is given below. Notice that the sorting logic itself is isolated in a procedure BUBBLE1 which receives N, the number of entries to sort in the global array NAME. The program also illustrates the **graphic documentation** that will be used to enhance the clarity of Pascal algorithms throughout the book. The importance of using such graphic diagrams when working with data structures cannot be overemphasized. Data structures is a subject which will require that you translate your mental image of the way data is to be stored into a computer program. Frequently the best way to do this is to draw a picture of what you want to happen and then write the code to achieve it!

```
PROGRAM SORTDEMONSTRATION(INPUT, OUTPUT);

{BUBBLE SORT AN ARRAY OF NAMES}

  CONST
    ARRAYSIZE = 100;
    MAXNAMELEN = 20;

  TYPE
    NAMESTRING = PACKED ARRAY [1..MAXNAMELEN] OF CHAR;
    NAMETABLE = ARRAY [1..ARRAYSIZE] OF NAMESTRING;

  VAR
    NUMNAME, I: INTEGER;
    NAME: NAMETABLE;

  PROCEDURE BUBBLE1(N: INTEGER);

    VAR
      I, J: INTEGER;
      TEMP: NAMESTRING;
```

```
BEGIN
   FOR I := 1 TO N - 1 DO {NUMBER OF PASSES}
      FOR J := 1 TO N - I DO {NUMBER OF COMPARISONS ON ITH PASS}
         IF NAME[J] > NAME[J + 1] THEN
            BEGIN
            TEMP := NAME[J];
            NAME[J] := NAME[J + 1];
            NAME[J + 1] := TEMP
            END
   END; {BUBBLE1}

BEGIN {MAIN}
   WRITE('HOW MANY NAMES-->');
   READLN(NUMNAME);
   WRITELN('ENTER NAMES:');
   FOR I := 1 TO NUMNAME DO
      READLN(NAME[I]);
   BUBBLE1(NUMNAME);
   WRITELN;
   WRITELN('NOW PRINT IN ORDER');
   WRITELN;
   FOR I := 1 TO NUMNAME DO
      WRITELN(NAME[I])
END.
```

Sample Run:

```
HOW MANY NAMES-->4
ENTER NAMES:
SMITH
JONES
TYLER
HARRISON

NOW PRINT IN ORDER

HARRISON
JONES
SMITH
TYLER
```

Given this initial version of the bubble sort algorithm, we should now analyze its run time efficiency. One measure of this efficiency would be the number of comparisons which are required by the algorithm to sort a list of N names. Such an analysis proves to be quite easy. N−1 passes through the array are made. On the first pass, N−1 comparisons are made. This number decreases by one on each pass until, on the final pass, only one comparison is made. Thus, on the average, $N/2$ comparisons are made per pass through the array. The product $(N-1)*(N/2) = (N^2/2 -(N/2)$ is hence the total number of comparisons required for this version of the bubble sort. For large N, it is the N^2 term in this product which will tend to dominate any other terms in the expression. For example, if our list contains 100 names, the $N^2/2$ term mandates 5000 comparisons; the 50 that may be subtracted because of the $N/2$ term is trivial by comparison. We say that the efficiency of this version of the bubble sort is **proportional** to N^2, denoted $O(N^2)$. This proportionality notation will be used in analyzing the run time efficiency of algorithms throughout the text. A more formal mathematical presentation of such efficiency considerations for the bubble sort is presented in Appendix B.

Enhancing Efficiency of the Bubble Sort

The $O(N^2)$ efficiency of this bubble sort should clearly be a matter of some concern if our list of names is large. For instance, a list of 1000 names would require 500,000 comparisons. Operations of such magnitude can easily destroy the instantaneous response that beginning users of a computer system so naively expect. We will see in Chapter 10 that more powerful sorting methods can reduce this efficiency factor to $O(N*\log_2 N)$. However, we don't even need to wait that long to improve the efficiency of this algorithm for certain lists of names. Consider, for instance, the list of 10 names that appears below:

```
BAKER
CHARLES
DAGGETT
FOSTER
GAINES
MILLER
NEVILLE
PETERSON
SMITH
REYNOLDS
```

Our present version of the bubble sort algorithm will require on the order of 50 comparisons to sort this list. Yet, on the second pass through the list, it could be confirmed that all future passes will be fruitless in the sense of producing no further interchanges of names. We can make our bubble sort procedure smarter by introducing a boolean variable to control the outer loop. This boolean variable signals the end of the algorithm as soon as a pass through the array does not produce an interchange. The Pascal procedure BUBBLE2 illustrates this logic in full detail.

```
{ GLOBAL DECLARATIONS }

CONST
  ARRAYSIZE = 100;
  MAXNAMELEN = 20;

TYPE
  NAMESTRING = PACKED ARRAY [1..MAXNAMELEN] OF CHAR;
  NAMETABLE = ARRAY [1..ARRAYSIZE] OF NAMESTRING;

VAR
  NAME: NAMETABLE;

  {- - - - - - - - - - - - - - - - - - - - - - - - - - - - - - - - - - - - - - - - - - - - - - - -}

PROCEDURE BUBBLE2(N: INTEGER);

         {USE A BOOLEAN FLAG TO SHUT OFF LOOP WHEN NO INTERCHANGES
          ARE MADE, HENCE INCREASING RUN-TIME EFFICIENCY.}

  VAR
    I, J: INTEGER;
    TEMP: NAMESTRING;
    NOEXCHANGES: BOOLEAN;

  BEGIN
    I := 0;
    REPEAT {LOOP TO CONTROL PASSES THROUGH ARRAY}
      NOEXCHANGES := TRUE;
      I := I + 1;
      FOR J := 1 TO N - I DO {NUMBER OF COMPARISONS}
        IF NAME[J] > NAME[J + 1] THEN
          BEGIN
          TEMP := NAME[J];
          NAME[J] := NAME[J + 1];
          NAME[J + 1] := TEMP;
          NOEXCHANGES := FALSE
          END
    UNTIL (I = N - 1) OR NOEXCHANGES
  END; {BUBBLE2}
```

Two comments are in order regarding the procedure BUBBLE2. The first of these comments relates to a stylistic convention that we will frequently use. Since algorithms will generally be presented as procedures and not as complete programs, declarations which are intended to have meaning outside the procedure currently under consideration will merely be listed under the heading GLOBAL DECLARATIONS prior to the beginning of the procedure. Although this is not standard Pascal in the strictest sense, it is the way many implementations handle the problem of global variables which need to be accessed by separate external procedures.

The second comment relates to the run-time efficiency of our new algorithm. Have we enhanced its efficiency to the point where it is now better than a $O(N^2)$ algorithm? The answer to this question is, for most lists of names, "No". Only for those lists of names which are input in almost alphabetical order will our new algorithm offer a substantial improvement. Even for some cases in which the data is almost alphabetical to start with, the algorithm will behave in a very inefficient fashion. Consider, for instance, the list of names given below. What is the efficiency of BUBBLE2 for this nearly alphabetical list?

```
CHARLES
DAGGETT
FOSTER
GAINS
MILLER
NEVILLE
PETERSON
REYNOLDS
SMITH
BAKER
```

Using Pascal Record Declarations.   Our next version of the bubble sort is merely intended to illustrate how record declarations in Pascal can be used to enhance the clarity of algorithms. Let us suppose that the list we wish to alphabetize is a list of customer records which consist of the customer's name and address. The alphabetization of this list is to key on the customer name, which is stored in a 20-character memory location. The address, which is stored as a 60-character string, does not affect the order of alphabetization. How is this customer data to be stored? One solution would be to store the names and addresses in two parallel arrays — NAME and ADDRESS. Each time the algorithm called for the interchange of two names, we would also have to be sure to include the code necessary to interchange the corresponding two addresses. In many languages the parallel array solution to this problem is the only one available. However, Pascal offers its users a **record declaration,** which may be used to group together under one name heterogeneous data **fields** (NAME and ADDRESS in our particular example). Any Pascal textbook may be consulted for the syntax of a record declaration. We illustrate it here by GLOBAL TYPE and VAR declarations for the third version of our bubble sort algorithm, BUBBLE3.

```
{ GLOBAL DECLARATIONS }

CONST
  ARRAYSIZE = 100;
  MAXNAMELEN = 20;
  MAXADDRESSLEN = 60;

TYPE
  CUSTREC =
    RECORD
      NAME: PACKED ARRAY [1..MAXNAMELEN] OF CHAR;
      ADDRESS: PACKED ARRAY [1..MAXADDRESSLEN] OF CHAR
    END;

VAR
  CUSTLIST: ARRAY [1..ARRAYSIZE] OF CUSTREC;

  {- - - - - - - - - - - - - - - - - - - - - - - - - - - - - - - - - - - - - - - -}

PROCEDURE BUBBLE3(N: INTEGER);

        {USE BUBBLE SORT LOGIC TO SORT LIST OF NAMES AND ADDRESSES,
         KEYING ON NAME FIELD.}

  VAR
    I, J: INTEGER;
    TEMP: CUSTREC;
    NOEXCHANGES: BOOLEAN;

  BEGIN
    I := 0;
    REPEAT {LOOP TO CONTROL PASSES THROUGH ARRAY}
      NOEXCHANGES := TRUE;
      I := I + 1;
      FOR J := 1 TO N — I DO {NUMBER OF COMPARISONS}
        IF CUSTLIST[J].NAME > CUSTLIST[J + 1].NAME THEN
          BEGIN
          TEMP := CUSTLIST[J];  ─────────────────►
          CUSTLIST[J] := CUSTLIST[J + 1];
          CUSTLIST[J + 1] := TEMP;
          NOEXCHANGES := FALSE
          END
    UNTIL (I = N — 1) OR NOEXCHANGES
  END; {BUBBLE3}
```

	CUSTLIST	
	NAME	ADDRESS
	·	·
	·	·
J	NEWTON	N. 4TH ST.
J+1	HENDERSON	S. 9TH ST.
	·	·
	·	·
	·	·

Though comparison keys on NAME field,
entire records are interchanged

For the reader not familiar with Pascal record declarations, several comments are in order regarding this procedure. The TYPE declaration for CUSTREC establishes a record type with two distinct fields — NAME and ADDRESS. The VAR declaration for CUSTLIST then establishes an array, each of whose elements is a record of type of CUSTREC. Note that CUSTLIST is not two arrays; it is one array with elements which are records containing two fields. Also note that the record declaration gives us the capability of referring to an entire record, as in the line

```
TEMP := CUSTLIST(I);
```

or to an individual field within a given record, as in the line:

```
IF CUSTLIST(I).NAME > CUSTLIST(I+1).NAME THEN . . .
```

In the latter example, the dot separates the record designator CUSTLIST[I] from the field designator NAME. The dot notation is said to **qualify** the record.

We remark that the field ADDRESS could itself be broken down into separate STREET, CITY, STATE, and ZIP fields by another record description which would then allow us to refer to the address as a whole or to the individual fields within the address by additional "dot" qualification. Such multi-level record description will be unnecessary for the algorithms presented in this text and hence we shall not comment further upon it. The interested reader is again referred to an appropriate Pascal textbook.

A question of greater importance to our considerations is that of how the ability to declare a record containing distinct NAME and ADDRESS fields has improved the efficiency of our bubble sort algorithm. The answer to this question is, unfortunately, "Not at all". The parallel array approach would work equally well. Record declarations are more a cosmetic tool which enhance the readability of an algorithm but have no significant impact on efficiency. In fact, the efficiency of the BUBBLE3 procedure is significantly worse than that of BUBBLE1 and BUBBLE2 because, whether records or parallel arrays are used, we now must move 3 x 80 characters for each interchange instead of the 3 x 20 characters to be moved when only the name was involved. Hence a new measure of run-time efficiency emerges. We need to be concerned with not only the number of comparisons mandated by our sorting algorithm but also the amount of data that is moved between locations inside computer memory. This consideration is particularly important because, measured as elementary machine operations, the movement of one character is roughly equivalent in time to performing one comparison. Since one comparison may lead to the movement of 240 individual characters, perhaps the wise way to increase the efficiency of our algorithm would be to concentrate on how to reduce data movement instead of the number of comparisons. It is that task to which we now turn our attention.

Bubble Sort Implemented with Pointers.   So far our algorithms to sort data have implicitly assumed that the data is to be *physically* sorted, i.e., the data is to be arranged alphabetically in computer memory. Hence, the data in the first subscript of our CUSTLIST array is the name (and address) of the customer who comes first in alphabetical order, the data in the second subscript belongs to the customer who comes second, etc. However, if we are only interested in producing an alphabetical listing of the names and addresses of our customers, is it really necessary that the data be arranged in physically alphabetical fashion in computer memory? The answer is "No"; it is possible to step *logically* through the data in alphabetical order without physically arranging it in that order in memory. To do so we must use another array of **pointers.** These pointers keep track of the logical order of the data without requiring it to be physically moved. At the end of our sorting routine, POINTER[1] tells us the location of the name and address that should come first in our alphabetical listing; POINTER[2] contains the location of the customer record that should come second, and so on. The sorting algorithm itself uses the logic of the bubble sort to interchange pointers instead of interchanging actual data, i.e., names and addresses. The actual data never moves, remaining precisely where it was stored upon initial input. A fully coded Pascal program illustrating this method is given below. The sorting itself is isolated in the procedure PTRSORT1, which again receives the number of customer records to be sorted. The main program then illustrates how one may proceed through the customers in logically alphabetical order using the rearranged pointer array.

```
PROGRAM POINTERSORT(INPUT, OUTPUT);

        {LOGICALLY SORT AN ARRAY BY MANIPULATING POINTERS
         INSTEAD OF ACTUALLY MOVING DATA.}

  CONST
    ARRAYSIZE = 100;
    MAXNAMELEN = 20;
    MAXADDRESSLEN = 60;

  TYPE
    CUSTREC =
      RECORD
        NAME: PACKED ARRAY [1..MAXNAMELEN] OF CHAR;
        ADDRESS: PACKED ARRAY [1..MAXADDRESSLEN] OF CHAR
      END;
```

```
VAR
  CUSTLIST: ARRAY [1..ARRAYSIZE] OF CUSTREC;
  POINTER: ARRAY [1..ARRAYSIZE] OF INTEGER;
  I, NUMREC: INTEGER;

PROCEDURE PTRSORT1(N: INTEGER);

 {APPLY POINTER LOGIC TO LIST OF N RECORDS}

  VAR
    I, J, TEMP: INTEGER;
    NOEXCHANGES: BOOLEAN;

  BEGIN
    I := 0;
    REPEAT {LOOP TO CONTROL PASSES THROUGH ARRAY}
      NOEXCHANGES := TRUE;
      I := I + 1;
      FOR J := 1 TO N - I DO {NUMBER OF COMPARISONS}

        {THE NEXT LINE COMPARES NAMES BEING POINTED TO}

        IF CUSTLIST[POINTER[J]].NAME > CUSTLIST[POINTER[J + 1]].NAME
          THEN

        { BUT WILL ONLY EXCHANGE POINTERS }

          BEGIN
          TEMP := POINTER[J];
          POINTER[J] := POINTER[J + 1];
          POINTER[J + 1] := TEMP;
          NOEXCHANGES := FALSE
          END
    UNTIL (I = N - 1) OR NOEXCHANGES
  END; {PTRSORT1}
```

	POINTER	CUSTLIST	
		NAME	ADDRESS
		.	
		.	
		.	
	4	NEWTON	N. 4TH ST.
		.	
J	4	.	
J+1	89	.	
	89	HENDERSON	S. 9TH ST.
		.	
		.	
		.	

4 and 9 will be interchanged in POINTER array. No data moves in CUSTLIST.

```
BEGIN {MAIN}
  FOR I := 1 TO ARRAYSIZE DO
    POINTER[I] := I; {INITIALIZE POINTER ARRAY}
  WRITE('HOW MANY RECORDS-->');
  READLN(NUMREC);
  WRITELN('ENTER NAMES AND ADDRESSES ON SEPARATE LINES:');
  FOR I := 1 TO NUMREC DO
    BEGIN
    READLN(CUSTLIST[I].NAME);
    READLN(CUSTLIST[I].ADDRESS)
    END;
  PTRSORT1(NUMREC);
  WRITELN;
  WRITELN('NAMES HAVE NOW BEEN SORTED.');
  WRITELN;
  WRITELN('POINTER NAME                    ADDRESS');
  FOR I := 1 TO NUMREC DO
    WRITELN(POINTER[I]: 4, '     ', CUSTLIST[POINTER[I]].NAME,
            CUSTLIST[POINTER[I]].ADDRESS)
END.
```

Sample Run:

```
HOW MANY RECORDS-->4
ENTER NAMES AND ADDRESSES ON SEPARATE LINES:
SMITH
414 N 16TH ST
JONES
990 S 40TH ST
TYLER
553 E 12TH AVE
HARRISON
698 W 8TH AVE

NAMES HAVE NOW BEEN SORTED.

POINTER  NAME                 ADDRESS
    4    HARRISON             698 W 8TH AVE
    2    JONES                990 S 40TH ST
    1    SMITH                414 N 16TH ST
    3    TYLER                553 E 12TH AVE
```

It is essential at this point for the reader to trace through the pointer sort algorithm since we will be referring to it again in Chapter 2. Suppose, for example, that after the execution of the read loop given in the main program, we had arrays of customers and corresponding pointer values as indicated in Figure 1-3. After a return from the procedure PTRSORT1, the CUSTLIST array would be left untouched,

CUSTLIST

	NAME	ADDRESS		POINTER
1	MAXWELL CR	GRAND AVE. MILWAUKEE WI	1	1
2	BUCKNER QB	MAIN ST. BOSTON MA	2	2
3	LANIER BJ	STATE ST. CHICAGO IL	3	3
4	AARON HH	PEACHTREE ST. ATLANTA GA	4	4

FIGURE 1-3   CUSTLIST and POINTER arrays before PTRSORT1 called

but the POINTER array would be altered to appear as in Figure 1-4. If we follow in order the CUSTLIST subscripts given in the POINTER array of Figure 1-4, we obtain an alphabetical listing of the customers. Moreover, this logically alphabetical listing was achieved without ever having to move massive amounts of data, as was necessary in the procedure BUBBLE3.

Have we achieved this significant improvement in run-time efficiency without having to pay any price? Recall the adage, "You get nothing for nothing," cited earlier in this chapter. Of course we had to pay a price. Here the price was the additional memory required for the *data about data* which was stored in the array of pointers. This illustrates the memory vs. time tradeoff that continually recurs in the analysis of computer algorithms. The issue of memory utilization is one that we have not yet touched upon in our discussion of variations on the bubble sort. Even more serious than the memory required for pointers is the **static** nature of the CUSTLIST array which is used to store customer names and addresses. "Static" in this sense means that the array (of size 100) is declared at the time the program is compiled, and we are charged for 100 storage locations whether or not they are all used at run time. When we only have 50 customers to sort, 50% of the memory allocated for the array is being wasted. In the final demonstration program of this introductory chapter, we shall illustrate how the **dynamic memory allocation** feature of Pascal may be used to allow the programmer to claim only that amount of memory which is actually needed at run time.

CUSTLIST

	NAME	ADDRESS		POINTER
1	MAXWELL CR	GRAND AVE. MILWAUKEE WI	1	4
2	BUCKNER QB	MAIN ST. BOSTON MA	2	2
3	LANIER BJ	STATE ST. CHICAGO IL	3	3
4	AARON HH	PEACHTREE ST. ATLANTA GA	4	1

FIGURE 1-4   CUSTLIST and POINTER arrays after PTRSORT1

Pascal Pointer Variables and Dynamic Memory Management.   To understand dynamic memory management, we must first understand the configuration of memory when your program is loaded into it from an external file. As indicated in Figure 1-5, there are memory costs that must be paid in addition to the mere object code of your program. In particular, memory must have room to accomodate:

- Various operating system necessities
- A *stack* used by the operating system for subroutine processing (to be explained in Chapter 5)
- The object code of your program, i.e., the machine language version of your program's instructions
- Static data areas, i.e., the declared arrays and other variables used by your program

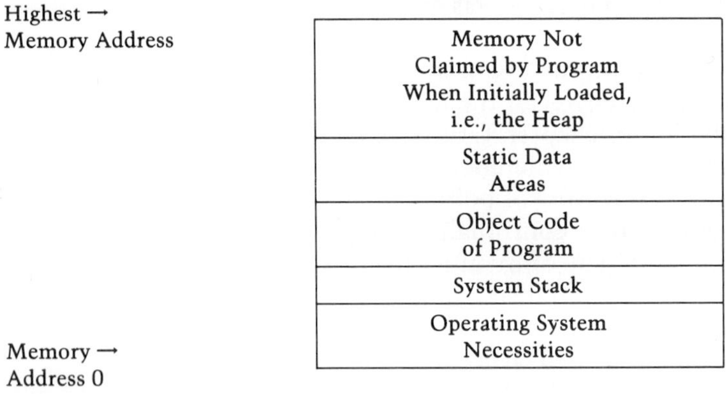

Highest →
Memory Address

Memory Not Claimed by Program When Initially Loaded, i.e., the Heap
Static Data Areas
Object Code of Program
System Stack
Operating System Necessities

Memory →
Address 0

FIGURE 1-5   Computer Memory Configuration for Typical Program

Notice that the four memory components listed above generally will not consume all of the available computer memory. What is left over is called the **heap.** Unless you have already used the dynamic memory allocation scheme of a language like Pascal, your programs until now have never been able to get at the heap and take advantage of it. With Pascal's **pointer variables,** all this changes. Given a record declaration, such as that for CUSTREC in our previous program, and a declaration for a pointer variable *to that type of record* via Pascal's up-arrow notation

```
TYPE PTRTOCUSTREC :^CUSTREC;
                 .
                 .
                 .

VAR  P : PTRTOCUSTREC;
```

we can get Pascal's **heap manager** to allocate segments of memory in the heap for records of this type *as our program runs.* The key is a supplied procedure **NEW,** which takes as its only argument a pointer variable such as P above and returns in P a pointer, i.e., a memory address, indicating the location within the heap where the heap manager has allocated space for the currently requested record. Several facts about the NEW procedure should be emphasized at this point:

- It is a *run time* request for memory. Unlike an array, you are not charged for the memory requested until you actually have something to store in it. Moreover, unlike static array declarations you are not charged for an excess of memory that you may not even need for this particular run of the program.
- After a call to NEW(P) for a suitably declared pointer variable P, P is a memory address. As such its actual value is of little concern to you. Suffice it to say that it is an address somewhere in the heap. How the heap manager was able to arrive at such an address remains a mystery for now but may become a bit clearer in the next chapter. The important point to note here is that, as a memory address, P's actual value is not important. In fact, Pascal won't even let you see what it is since a statement like WRITE(P) will result in a syntax error.
- What is important is that Pascal lets you manipulate these addresses in appropriate ways and lets you get at the *contents* of records which are stored at an address "pointed to" by a pointer variable such as P. To access the contents of such a dynamically allocated record, the up-arrow notation is again used. Hence Pˆ refers to the contents of the record at the address pointed to by P. Figure 1-6 illustrates this crucial difference between the address stored in a pointer variable P and the contents of the record stored at that address. Given P, fields within such a record may be examined by the usual dot qualification, i.e., Pˆ.NAME or Pˆ.ADDRESS.

These pointer variable concepts are illustrated in the final version of our sorting program which is given below. In this program, instead of allocating an array with space for 100 customer records, we merely allocate an array with space for 100 pointers. (Note that storing a memory address would require considerably less computer storage than an 80 character record.) Then, whenever a name and address is input, we call on NEW to allocate the necessary heap space to store the input data. The sort routine, PTRSORT2, now interchanges Pascal pointer variables instead of the integer array pointers that were manipulated in PTRSORT1. In this regard, it is important to note that Pascal pointers can be manipulated in the sense of participating in assignment statements; they just cannot be directly output. Finally,

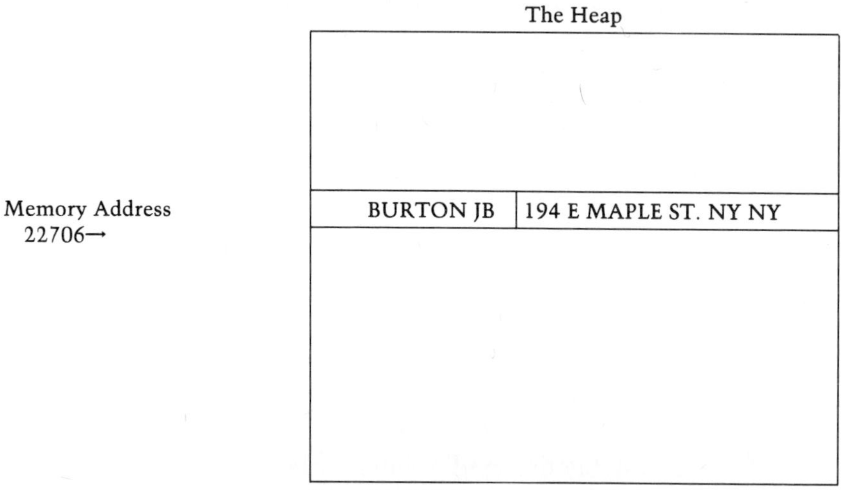

The Heap

BURTON JB	194 E MAPLE ST. NY NY

Memory Address
22706→

P itself is 22706, a memory address. P^ is the contents of the record at address 22706. Hence
P^.NAME is BURTON JB and P^.ADDRESS is 194 E
MAPLE ST. NY NY

FIGURE 1-6   The Difference Between P and P^.

after the pointers have been suitably rearranged by PTRSORT2, the main program follows them through the logically ordered names to print the customer list in alphabetical order. Figure 1-7 indicates the action of this program with some hypothetical memory address values for the pointer variables involved.

	POINTER	NAME	ADDRESS
1	86418	At location 70332: BUCKNER QB	MAIN ST. BOSTON MA
2	78414	At location 78414: LANIER BJ	STATE ST. CHICAGO IL
3	70332	At location 80396:AARON HH	PEACHTREE ST. ATLANTA GA
4	80396	At location 86418:MAXWELL CR	GRAND AVE. MILWAUKEE WI

Before PTRSORT2

POINTER

1	80396
2	70332
3	78414
4	86418

No Data in the Heap
Is Moved!

After PTRSORT2

FIGURE 1-7   Action Taken By PTRSORT2

```
PROGRAM POINTERSORT(INPUT, OUTPUT);

        {LOGICALLY SORT AN ARRAY BY MANIPULATING POINTERS
         INSTEAD OF ACTUALLY MOVING DATA. IN THIS VERSION, PASCAL
         DYNAMIC MEMORY ALLOCATION IS USED.}

  CONST
    ARRAYSIZE = 100;
    MAXNAMELEN = 20;
    MAXADDRESSLEN = 60;

  TYPE
    CUSTREC =
      RECORD
        NAME: PACKED ARRAY [1..MAXNAMELEN] OF CHAR;
        ADDRESS: PACKED ARRAY [1..MAXADDRESSLEN] OF CHAR
      END;
    PTRTOCUSTREC = ^CUSTREC;

  VAR
    POINTER: ARRAY [1..ARRAYSIZE] OF PTRTOCUSTREC;
    I, NUMREC: INTEGER;

  PROCEDURE PTRSORT2(N: INTEGER);

   {APPLY POINTER SORT LOGIC TO LIST OF N RECORDS}

    VAR
      I, J: INTEGER;
      TEMP: PTRTOCUSTREC;
      NOEXCHANGES: BOOLEAN;

    BEGIN
      I := 0;
      REPEAT {LOOP TO CONTROL PASSES THROUGH ARRAY}
        NOEXCHANGES := TRUE;
        I := I + 1;
        FOR J := 1 TO N - I DO {NUMBER OF COMPARISONS}

          {THE NEXT LINE COMPARES NAMES BEING POINTED TO}

          IF POINTER[J]^.NAME > POINTER[J + 1]^.NAME THEN

          { BUT WILL ONLY EXCHANGE POINTERS }
```

```
        BEGIN
        TEMP := POINTER[J];
        POINTER[J] := POINTER[J + 1];
        POINTER[J + 1] := TEMP;
        NOEXCHANGES := FALSE
        END
   UNTIL (I = N - 1) OR NOEXCHANGES
END; {PTRSORT2}
```

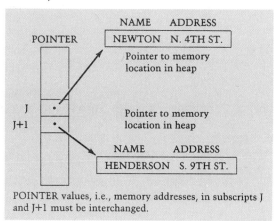

POINTER values, i.e., memory addresses, in subscripts J and J+1 must be interchanged.

```
BEGIN {MAIN}
  WRITE('HOW MANY RECORDS-->');
  READLN(NUMREC);
  WRITELN('ENTER NAMES AND ADDRESSES ON SEPARATE LINES:');
  FOR I := 1 TO NUMREC DO
    BEGIN
    NEW(POINTER[I]); {REQUEST HEAP SPACE}
    READLN(POINTER[I]^.NAME);
    READLN(POINTER[I]^.ADDRESS)
    END;
  PTRSORT2(NUMREC);
  WRITELN;
  WRITELN('NAMES HAVE NOW BEEN SORTED.');
  WRITELN;
  WRITELN('NAME                ADDRESS');
  FOR I := 1 TO NUMREC DO
    WRITELN(POINTER[I]^.NAME, POINTER[I]^.ADDRESS)
END.
```

Sample Run:

```
HOW MANY RECORDS-->4
ENTER NAMES AND ADDRESSES ON SEPARATE LINES:
SMITH
414 N 16TH ST
JONES
990 S 40TH ST
TYLER
553 E 12TH AVE
HARRISON
698 W 8TH AVE

NAMES HAVE NOW BEEN SORTED.

NAME                ADDRESS
HARRISON            698 W 8TH AVE
JONES               990 S 40TH ST
SMITH               414 N 16TH ST
TYLER               553 E 12TH AVE
```

In the World of Applications . . .

Daniel D. McCracken, well-known computer author and consultant, identified five commandments for program developers in an article entitled "Software in the 80's", which appeared in *Computerworld* on September 17th, 1980.

McCracken's Five Commandments for Developers

1. Don't solve any problem that has already been solved.
2. Don't solve any problem twice yourself.
3. Don't solve any problem that someone else can solve better and more efficiently.
4. Don't "solve" any "problem" that results in a net loss of time and resources in completing the application.
5. Summary of above: Don't work any harder than you have to, don't do any useless work, and don't do any work that has negative value.

How do McCracken's commandments relate to the subject of data structures? The techniques you will learn in this book represent a collection of "problems that have already been solved". At one time they were part of a general computer folklore that one never learned except by time-consuming, on-the-job experience. Today this *folklore* has come to be part of the documented knowledge we call *computer science*. It has become an essential part of what a prospective computer scientist is expected to know. Learn the techniques well! They can help you follow McCracken's commandments and devote your future efforts to solving new problems.

Courtesy of Daniel D. McCracken.

Program Design Considerations

The programs presented in this first chapter illustrate, on a small scale, the importance of approaching problems in a "divide-and-conquer" fashion. The essence of this approach is to divide a problem into small, more manageable, subordinate problems. A procedure, or module, is developed for each of these subordinate problems. The modules are then tested, verified, and debugged individually (see Appendix C.) Confident that each module achieves its specified task, we can then tie them together into a unified **software system**. The emphasis upon synthesizing a complete software system from isolated, well-defined components (many of which can be re-used in other systems) has spawned its own area of study within computer science—**software engineering**. Just as an electrical engineer constructs computer hardware from well-known, time-tested components, so can the software engineer build the software systems which drive the hardware.

One of the essential tools of the software engineer is the **modular structure chart**. Such a chart describing the structure of the final POINTERSORT program in this chapter appears in Figure 1-8.

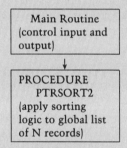

FIGURE 1-8   Modular structure chart for POINTERSORT program.

The relationship between the blocks in such a chart reflects the "boss-worker" hierarchy between the modules in a program. In the case of Figure 1-8, we immediately see that the structure of the entire program will have a main routine calling on PROCEDURE PTRSORT2, expecting it to appropriately sort N records. To a certain extent, the author of the main routine does not care how PTRSORT2 sorts the records, only that the records are sorted reliably when they are passed back to the calling module. The software engineer insists that each module in a system be **functionally cohesive**. That is, each should focus on achieving one particular predefined task without having side effects which may (surprisingly) influence what other modules in the same system are trying to accomplish.

By approaching the development of software systems in this manner, the software engineer is able to completely test and debug each module before integrating it into the entire system. The end result is a system which is less likely to fail. Hence, in the long run, the software engineering approach will actually save time. The time invested in initial planning should avoid the need for emergency patching once the system has been fully implemented.

SUMMARY

Perhaps the primary lesson of this initial chapter has been that the process of program development is one of successive refinement. Such refinement should be aimed at enhancing both the run-time and memory efficiency of the program. From our initial version of the bubble sort, BUBBLE1, we progressed to BUBBLE2, in which a Boolean flag was introduced to reduce the number of comparisons required for lists of names which were in nearly alphabetical form upon input. The refinements of PTRSORT1 and PTRSORT2 then allowed us respectively to avoid moving large amounts of data and to avoid pre-allocating space for storing customer records. The final version is as efficient as the general logic of the bubble sort algorithm will allow. Yet the process of refinement is never-ending, and to claim that we now have the most efficient version of the program is a falsehood. For instance, we shall see in Chapter 10 that other sorting algorithms combined with the pointer concept we have introduced here could greatly improve the run-time efficiency of the program. To improve the memory utilization, we shall study a technique in Chapter 2 which will not only do away with the need to pre-allocate space for customer records but will also not require us to pre-allocate the array of Pascal pointer variables that was needed in PTRSORT2. In Chapter 3, we will examine more efficient methods of storing the character strings which contain customer names and addresses. In our present version of the algorithm, we waste 30 characters of computer storage on blanks if the actual address is only 30 characters long. How can this padding with seemingly unnecessary blanks be eliminated? Hence the process of algorithm refinement involves continual re-examination of how the current algorithm meets the goals of the task at hand. The remainder of this book is devoted to helping you develop the skills needed to carry on this type of analytical examination.

KEY TERMS

Data Structure	Qualify
Array	Dot Notation
Algorithm	Pointer
Bubble Sort	Static Memory Allocation
Run-time Efficiency	Dynamic Memory Allocation
Memory Utilization Efficiency	Heap
Records	NEW
Fields	Pointer Variables

EXERCISES

1. Write a Pascal procedure which will check for the largest and the smallest entries in an integer array.
2. Write a Pascal procedure which will sum the entries in a real array.
3. Write a Pascal procedure which will reverse the order of the entries in an integer array.
4. Write a complete Pascal program to obtain the output
   $2/7 = .285714285714285714$

PROGRAMMING PROBLEMS

1. The Wing-and-a-Prayer Airlines Company maintains a fleet of four aircraft which are color-coded as Blue, Gold, Green and White. Passengers riding the Gold aircraft pay the highest for the quality of onboard service; the next lower category is the Green aircraft followed by Blue and then White. The airline is interested in maintaining a statistical breakdown of the number of passengers on each type of service. Write a complete Pascal program with proper record descriptions that will read a passenger datum and update accordingly the statistical information of the type of service that passenger requested.
2. The Fly-By-Night Credit Card Company is a growing enterprise interested in maintaining a large data file of records about their customers. Write a program in any high level language to create a file of customer records, each of which has the following format:

Character Position	Interpretation
1-9	Customer ID
10	First name initial
11	Middle name initial
12-20	Last name
21-44	Customer address broken down in street, city, and zip
45-51	Current balance
52-58	Past amount due
59-70	One letter code for each of 12 month payment history
71	One letter code for the income bracket
72	One letter code for the maximum credit allowed to the customer based on his payment history
73-78	Due date for payment
79-86	Date of birth
87-100	Special comments

Create a file of at least 1000 such records.

2

Linked Lists

"A chain is only as strong as its weakest link."

OLD PROVERB

2-1 Introductory Considerations

We are all familiar with the dynamics of waiting in a long line. When someone cuts into the middle of the line, there is a domino-like effect that forces everyone behind that person to move back. When someone in the middle of the line decides to leave the line, the reverse effect occurs; everyone behind the departed person is able to move ahead one slot. It is possible to draw an analogy between people waiting in a line and data items stored next to each other in computer memory. If the data items are arranged in some type of order and it becomes necessary to insert into or delete from the middle of the line, a considerable amount of **data movement** is involved. This data movement requires computer time and decreases program efficiency. The central motivation behind the **linked list** data structure is *to eliminate the data movement associated with insertions into and deletions from the middle of the list.*

2-2 Arrays

One of the most commonly used data structures is an **array**. Although we shall say a great deal about multi-dimensional arrays in a later chapter, we assume that you are familiar with the concept of a one-dimensional array. Also termed a **vector**, this type of array simply refers to a specific number of consecutive memory locations. This number is the size of the vector. A one-dimensional array of data items is thus the computer equivalent of the densely packed line of people. Note that in an array we have the ability to access *directly* any item in the list merely by specifying its position. Two, three, or higher dimensional arrays can be viewed for the time being as arrays of one dimensional arrays.

Arrays are often used for contiguous storage of data. For example, the FORTRAN array

```
DIMENSION M(10,15)
```

can be conveniently used to store 150 integer numbers in a contiguous structure that can be thought of as having 10 rows and 15 columns. Similarly the array declared in Pascal by

```
VAR X: ARRAY[1..120] OF STRING;
```

can be used to alphabetize a small list containing no more than 120 names. Once stored in an array, data can be accessed directly. For example, if we ask to examine the 40th name in our list of 120 names, we do not need to examine the first 39 names.

2-3   Linked Lists

A structure involved in many data processing activities is the **ordered list** of data items. Typical examples are alphabetical lists of names, a master payroll file containing information about employees in ascending order of social security number, or lists sorted by days of the year or chronologically sequenced events. Such a data set can be represented by a one-dimensional array in which the jth subscript corresponds to the jth item in the ordered list.

When such ordered lists contain a large number of entries, developing efficient means of updating them is a matter of great concern. In general, data processing activity pertaining to an ordered list involves:

1. **Accessing** the jth element of the list where, if n is the length of the list, then $1 \leq j \leq n$
2. **Inserting** a new element between positions j and (j + 1) in the list, while maintaining the correct order
3. **Deleting** the jth element from the list, while preserving the order of the list

If, for example, we have a list of student ID numbers in ascending order

$$(1121, \ 1125, \ 1172, \ 1180, \ 1195)$$

to which another ID, 1175, is to be added, then we want this list to remain in proper order:

$$(1121, \ 1125, \ 1172, \ 1175, \ 1180, \ 1195)$$

Similarly if an existing ID, such as 1125, is to be deleted from this new list, then the list should properly appear as

$$(1121, \ 1172, \ 1175, \ 1180, \ 1195)$$

upon completion.

Although small ordered lists can be implemented with ease using arrays, maintenance of longer ordered lists in this type of contiguous storage structure becomes very expensive because of the number of data items that must be moved for each operation. A quick look at the previous example should convince you that the tasks of inserting in and deleting from an ordered list containing thousands of data items require considerable data movement up and down the list. If, in a large company, the master list of employees arranged in ascending order by their social security number is updated frequently by insertions and deletions, then the array is a highly inefficient way of accomplishing such an update. What we need is a structure that *minimizes* such wholesale data movement.

In Chapter 1, we introduced a sorting method (called the POINTER SORT) that, *without physically moving the data to be sorted*, achieved sorting by merely rearranging the pointers to data items in a parallel array. By eliminating the necessity of interchanging character strings, the use of these pointers makes the sorting algorithm more efficient from the perspective of data movement and, consequently, run time. Note that at the same time, the algorithm becomes less efficient from the perspective of memory utilization because of the "data about data" maintained by the pointers. This trade-off between efficiency in run time and memory utilization must be weighed continually when you select data structures. Although a great deal more will be said about sorting techniques in a later chapter, the example of the POINTER SORT illustrates the frequently occurring principle that, if you can afford the memory overhead of storing data about data, then the run time efficiency often can be enhanced.

Like the array of pointers used in the pointer sort example, a **linked list** is a structure that leads to algorithms that minimize data movement as insertions and deletions occur in an ordered list. Each element—called a **node**—in a linked list contains not only a data field but also one pointer (in the sense of an address) to another node in the list. The pointer system in the linked list structure eliminates the need for wholesale movement of data in memory, because all that is needed to keep track of the position of a node in the list is to update the appropriate pointers. Thus, insertions, deletions, and extensions of the list become significantly more economical in processing time than they are in an array in which proper positioning of the data items up and down the list is mandatory. A linked list thus maintains data items in a **logical order** rather than in a **physical order**. In an abstract sense, we may define a linked list as a collection of logically ordered data nodes in which each node carries with it informtion about the position of the next (and possibly also the preceding) node in the list.

Singly Linked Lists

A **singly linked list** is a linked list in which each node contains only one link field pointing to the next node in the list. The first node in the list is pointed to by a HEAD pointer. The last node in the list has a link field containing a NULL flag indicating "end of list". Figures 2-1 and 2-2 show the physical and logical representations (respectively) of a linked list containing five data nodes arranged in alphabetical order. The physical representation in Figure 2-1 is an array of Pascal records to which you were introduced in Chapter 1. Again depending upon the language used, memory for such records could be allocated at compilation time (**static allocation**) or execution time (**dynamic allocation**) as used in Pascal.

We shall demonstrate the processing of a singly linked list by examining a procedure to find the numeric average of the value of data items stored in a linked list. The procedure itself must also determine the number N of nodes in the list in order to calculate the average. The procedure assumes that the list is not empty.

	DATA	LINK
1	FOSTER	5
2	SMITH	NULL
3	MILLER	2
4	ALLEN	1
5	LOCKE	3

HEAD: 4

FIGURE 2-1 Physical representation of a linked list.

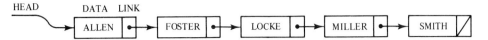

FIGURE 2-2 Logical representation of a linked list.

```
{Global declarations}

CONST
  K = 1000;
  NULL = 0;

TYPE
  ARR = ARRAY [1..K] OF INTEGER;
  DATA = ARRAY [1..K] OF REAL;

VAR
  HEAD, POINT: INTEGER;

PROCEDURE AVERAGE(VAR LINK: ARR);

  VAR
    AVE, SUM1: REAL;
    N: INTEGER;

  BEGIN
    POINT := HEAD;
    N := 0;
    SUM1 := 0;
    WHILE POINT <> NULL DO
      BEGIN
      SUM1 := SUM1 + DATA[POINT];
      N := N + 1;
      POINT := LINK[POINT]
      END;
    AVE := SUM1 / N;
    WRITELN('AVERAGE OF': 20, N: 4, 'DATA ITEMS=': 10, AVE: 10: 3)
  END {AVERAGE} ;
```

HEAD

30.8 → 90.4 → 60.8 → 4.8 → 16.2 → 38.0

N = 6
SUM = 241.0/6

NULL

Insertions and Deletions

The algorithm described in the AVERAGE procedure illustrates how to traverse all the nodes in a linked list. The primary usefulness of this structure, however, is in minimizing the processing time for data insertion into and deletion from the list. These operations are carried out without disturbing the data because they require rearranging only pointers. Suppose, for example, we have an alphabetically arranged linked list that appears as shown in Figure 2-3.

If we now wish to add a node containing PRIM to the list, then all we need to do is to store PRIM in an available memory location outside of the list, such as the one pointed to by P in Figure 2-4. We then reset the pointer link of the node containing OLP to point to the node containing PRIM, and the pointer link of the node containing PRIM to point to the node containing SINGH. This logically maintains the alphabetical order of the data in the nodes without physically moving any of the existing nodes.

In order to implement the procedure for inserting a node in an already existing singly linked list, it is necessary to have a procedure that supplies an unused node from the pool of available unused memory. We call this procedure GETNODE. Similarly when a node in the linked list is no longer needed we should be able to return it to the pool of available nodes. RETURNNODE is a procedure that does this.

In some languages, such as Pascal, procedures equivalent to GETNODE and RETURNNODE are provided. The reader was introduced to Pascal's heap manager and dynamic memory allocation scheme in Chapter 1. We shall first show how GETNODE and RETURNNODE can be implemented in languages where such provisions are not made. Having done that, we shall then use Pascal's built-in NEW and DISPOSE functions as functional equivalents of GETNODE and RETURNNODE for further work in this book. The reader is already familiar with the procedure NEW. The Pascal procedure DISPOSE will be introduced at the appropriate point.

The available pool of nodes can be stored as a separate linked list with its own head pointer AVAIL. Because the order of nodes is not important in this available space list, all insertions and deletions can occur at its head.

FIGURE 2-3   Alphabetically ordered linked list with 4 nodes.

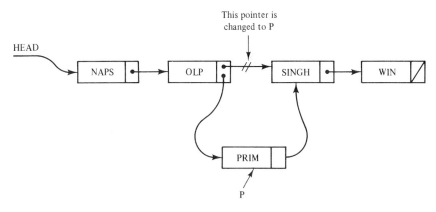

FIGURE 2-4   Insertion of the node PRIM into the linked list in Figure 2-3.

```
{Global declarations }

CONST
  N = 1000;
  NULL = 0;

TYPE
  SPACEREC =
    RECORD
      DATA: ARRAY [1..20] OF CHAR;
      LINK: INTEGER
    END;

VAR
  SPACE: ARRAY [1..N] OF SPACEREC;

PROCEDURE INITIALIZE(VAR AVAIL: INTEGER);
  {Initialize an available space to be used by procedures
  GETNODE and RETURNNODE. The head of the list is location 1.}
  This value is returned in location AVAIL.
  Thereafter location I is linked to location I+1.}

  VAR
    I: INTEGER;

  BEGIN
    FOR I := 1 TO N - 1 DO
      SPACE[I].LINK := I + 1;
    SPACE[N].LINK := NULL;
    AVAIL := 1
  END {INITIALIZE} ;
```

	AVAIL = 1
	LINK
1	2
2	3
3	4
	.
	.
N−2	N−1
N−1	N
N	NULL

```
{Global declarations}

CONST
  N = 1000;
  NULL = 0;

TYPE
  SPACEREC =
    RECORD
      DATA: ARRAY [1..20] OF CHAR;
      LINK: INTEGER
    END {RECORD} ;

VAR
  SPACE: ARRAY [1..N] OF SPACEREC;

PROCEDURE GETNODE(VAR AVAIL, P: INTEGER);
  {Returns pointer P to node taken from unused space}
  {AVAIL points to the headnode on unused space list}
  {AVAIL=NULL means no space is available}

  BEGIN
    IF AVAIL = NULL THEN
      WRITELN('NO SPACE AVAILABLE')
    ELSE
      BEGIN
      P := AVAIL;
      AVAIL := SPACE[AVAIL].LINK
      END
  END { GETNODE } ;
```

AVAIL

This pointer altered

P

Similarly the procedure RETURNNODE can be implemented as

```
{Global declarations}

CONST
  N = 1000;

TYPE
  SPACEREC =
    RECORD

      DATA: ARRAY [1..20] OF CHAR;
      LINK: INTEGER
    END {RECORD} ;

VAR
  SPACE: ARRAY [1..N] OF SPACEREC;

PROCEDURE RETURNNODE(VAR AVAIL, P: INTEGER);
            {Returns a node, pointed to by P, to the available
             space}

  BEGIN
    SPACE[P].LINK := AVAIL;
    AVAIL := P
  END {RETURNNODE} ;
```

Finally, the procedure INSERTNODE inserts a node, pointed to by P, into a linked list pointed to by HEAD immediately after the node pointed to by PREV.

```
{Global declarations}

CONST
  N = 1000;
  NULL = 0;

TYPE
  SPACEREC =
    RECORD
      DATA: ARRAY [1..20] OF CHAR;
      LINK: INTEGER
    END {RECORD} ;

VAR
  SPACE: ARRAY [1..N] OF SPACEREC;

PROCEDURE INSERTNODE(VAR HEAD, P, PREV: INTEGER);
         {Insert,into a linked list headed by HEAD,a node
            pointed to by P just after the node pointed to by
            PREV}
         {Assume P has been obtained by GETNODE and filled with
            data}
  BEGIN
    IF PREV = NULL THEN {Insert at front}
      BEGIN
      SPACE[P].LINK := HEAD;
      HEAD := P
      END
    ELSE
      BEGIN
      SPACE[P].LINK := SPACE[PREV].LINK;
      SPACE[PREV].LINK := P
      END {IF}
  END {INSERTNODE} ;
```

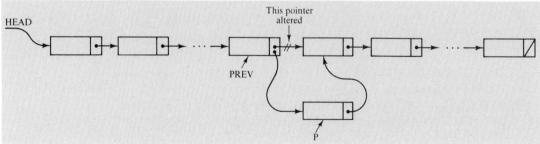

You should also note that the conditional test in INSERTNODE to determine whether the insertion is occuring at the front of the list can be eliminated if a special PREFIRST, or **dummy header,** node is maintained. This technique will be discussed in more detail later in this chapter; it then will be followed as a convention throughout the remainder of the text.

When you want to delete an existing node from the list, you can simply alter the pointers to reflect this change. *Again, no movement of data occurs.* For example, given the list in Figure 2-4, the diagram of Figure 2-6 outlines what must be done if we wish to delete the node containing OLP.

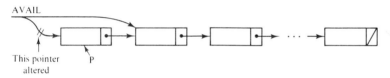

FIGURE 2-5 (a)   Action taken by procedure GETNODE.

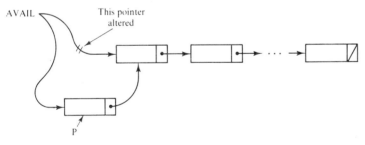

FIGURE 2-5 (b)   Action taken by procedure RETURNNODE.

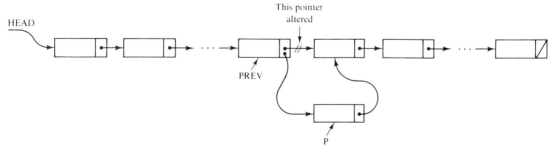

FIGURE 2-5 (c)   Action taken by procedure INSERTNODE.

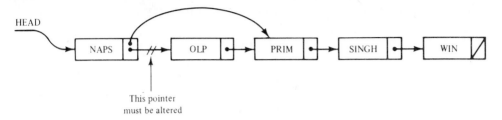

FIGURE 2-6 *Deletion of a node from the linked list in Figure 2-4.*

The procedure to delete can be implemented in a fashion similar to INSERTNODE. When a data node is deleted from the list, this node is returned to the pool of unused available nodes. In the following procedure DELETENODE, a node pointed to by P and preceded by a node pointed to by PREV is deleted and returned to the list of available nodes.

```
{Global declarations}

CONST
  N = 1000;
  NULL = 0;

TYPE
  SPACEREC =
    RECORD
      DATA: ARRAY [1..20] OF CHAR;
      LINK: INTEGER
    END {RECORD} ;

VAR
  SPACE: ARRAY [1..N] OF SPACEREC;

PROCEDURE RETURNNODE(VAR AVAIL, P: INTEGER);
  EXTERNAL;

PROCEDURE DELETENODE(VAR HEAD, P, PREV, AVAIL: INTEGER);
  {Delete node pointed to by P and preceded by}
  {a node pointed to by PREV.}
  {The condition PREV=NULL signals deletion of first node}

  BEGIN
    IF PREV = NULL THEN {Delete first node}
      HEAD := SPACE[HEAD].LINK
    ELSE
      SPACE[PREV].LINK := SPACE[P].LINK;
    RETURNNODE(AVAIL, P) {Return the deleted node}
  END {DELETENODE} ;
```

As in INSERTNODE, the special test for deletions of the first node can be eliminated by the technique of maintaining a PREFIRSTor dummy header node at the beginning of the list.

As pointed out earlier, Pascal provides built in functions NEW and DISPOSE which dynamically provide the facilities of our GETNODE and RETURNNODE procedures. If P is a declared pointer variable in a Pascal procedure then the statement

```
NEW(P)
```

provides the needed memory available to the program; and when this space is no longer needed then the statement

```
DISPOSE(P)
```

returns this space to the available memory for further use. The amount of space obtained by NEW(P) is always equal to the size of the record associated with P; that is, if P is a record such as in the following declaration

```
TYPE   RECPOINTER = ^SPACEREC;
       SPACEREC   = RECORD
                        DATA : STRING;
                        LINK : RECPOINTER
                    END;
VAR    P : RECPOINTER;
```

Then the statement NEW(P)returns a pointer P to a node such as that shown in Figure 2-7.

Thus P is simply a pointer indicating the first available node which has a DATA field and a LINK field.

The procedures INSERTNODE and DELETENODE can now be rewritten in the language of pointer variables. We shall write DELETENODE, leaving INSERTNODE as an exercise.

FIGURE 2-7 **Node made available by NEW(P).**

```
{Global declarations}

TYPE
  RECPOINTER = ^SPACEREC;
  SPACEREC =
    RECORD
      DATA: ARRAY [1..20] OF CHAR;
      LINK: RECPOINTER
    END;

VAR
  HEAD: RECPOINTER;

PROCEDURE DELETENODE(P, PREV: RECPOINTER);
 {Delete a node pointed to by P and }
 {preceded by a node pointed to by PREV}

  BEGIN
    IF PREV = NIL THEN
      HEAD := HEAD^.LINK
    ELSE
      PREV^.LINK := P^.LINK;
    DISPOSE(P)
  END {RETURNNODE} ;
```

The reserved word NIL in Pascal simply means that the pointer is NULL in the sense used earlier in the DELETENODE procedure. When a pointer variable in Pascal has the value NIL, it is not pointing to any node in memory.

From this point on, we shall not use GETNODE and RETURNNODE in this book. We shall use instead their functional equivalents, the NEW and the DISPOSE procedures. Moreover, we shall also use the Pascal up-arrow notation for dynamically allocated pointer variables.

2-4 Variations on Linked List Structures

Dummy Headers

A PREFIRST, or dummy header, node in the list before the first actual data node can often contain useful information about the structure (for example, the number of nodes). A query algorithm can then determine the status of the list by examining the contents of the PREFIRST node. This amounts to adding one more node to the list. Figure 2-8 illustrates this concept. Additions to and deletions from the list require changing this information-keeping field in the dummy header node of the list.

There is another distinct advantage of the dummy header node. If the list becomes empty and a dummy header node is not used, then the

In the world of applications ...

Operating systems typically grant their users disk storage units called **blocks.** On the magnetic disk itself, a block is a contiguous area capable of storing a fixed number of data, for example, a block in DEC's well-known RSTS timesharing system is 512 bytes. As a user enters data into a disk file, the system must grant additional blocks of storage as they are needed. In such a timesharing environment, although each block represents a physically contiguous storage area on the disk, it may not be possible for the operating system to give a user blocks that are physically next to each other. Instead, when a user needs an additional storage block, the operating system may put information into the current block about where the next block is located. In effect, a **link** is established from the current block to the next block. By the time a naive user has completed entering a 4-block file, it may well be scattered over the entire disk surface, as indicated in the diagram.

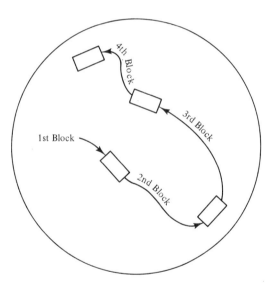

Although this may seem like an ingenious way of extending files indefinitely, one pays a price for such scattered blocks. Namely, the read/write head that seeks and puts data on the disk surface is forced to move greater distances, thereby slowing system performance. To combat such inefficiencies, shrewd users can often take advantage of options that allow them to pre-allocate the disk storage that will be required for a file. Moreover, system managers may occasionally bring down the entire system to rebuild disks, a process that entails copying all files that are presently scattered over the old disk onto a new disk in physically contiguous form.

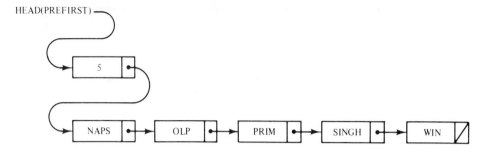

FIGURE 2-8 Linked list with dummy header containing information about the length of the list.

HEAD pointer for the list must be made NIL . But if the dummy header node is present, then the HEAD pointer never needs to be changed to NIL because it always points to this dummy header. This convention can serve to simplify the coding involved in procedures INSERTNODE and DELETENODE by removing the special handling previously required for inserts and deletes at the beginning of the list. You will write these simplified procedures as an exercise at the end of the chapter. *Because of the convenience offered by a dummy header node, we will use it for all linked lists.*

Circular Linked Lists

Although linked lists are satisfactory in many instances, the presence of a null pointer at the end of the list makes this structure most efficient only if the entire list is to be processed; the efficiency of such list processing algorithms decreases when the linked list is to be processed beginning at an arbitrary point in the list. In such situations, it would be desirable to be able to enter the list anywhere and process it efficienctly independent of the entry point. In other words, we need a linked list that has no beginning or end.

Circular linked lists are precisely such data structures. A **singly linked circular list** is a linked list in which the last node of the list points to the first node in the list. Notice that in circular list structures, there are no NIL links. Figure 2-9 depicts a singly linked circular list.

In the procedures INSERTNODE and DELETENODE we had prior knowledge about *where in the list* insertions and deletions were to be performed. In general, this information may have to be determined through a routine that searches the entire list. Because search algorithms require time proportional to half the length of the list, run time can be substantial if the list is very long. As an example, suppose we have a singly linked list in which we wish to insert a node A pointed to by POINT1 just before a node B pointed to by POINT2. We

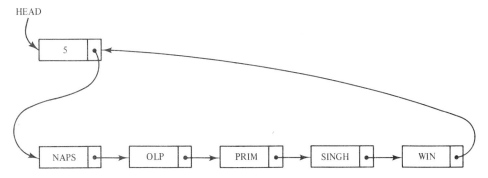

FIGURE 2-9 Singly linked circular list.

can change the linkfield of A to point B, but we do not know the address of (that is, a pointer to) the node preceding B. If we are to depend upon the current structure of the list then we must search the list for B—an inefficient procedure we wish to avoid. Figure 2-10 highlights this problem.

Doubly Linked Circular List

A satisfactory way of getting around the difficulty presented in Figure 2-10 is a **doubly linked circular list** in which each node has two pointers, a forward link and a backward link. The forward link is a pointer to the next node in the list, whereas the backward link points to the preceding node. Figure 2-11 illustrates a doubly linked circular list. This list has five nodes (plus a dummy header), each having a forward

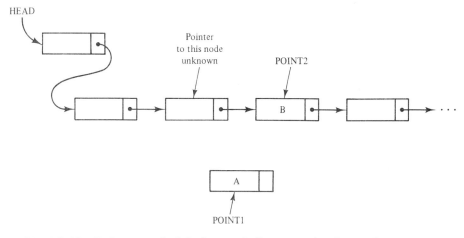

FIGURE 2-10 To insert node A before node B, we need to know the address of the node preceding B. In a singly linked structure this requires time-consuming sequential searching.

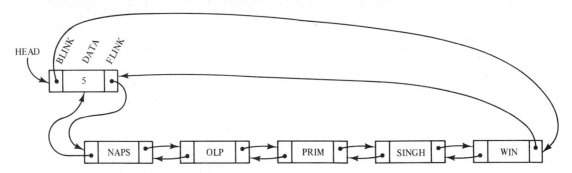

FIGURE 2-11 Doubly linked circular list.

link (FLINK) and a backward link (BLINK). FLINK points to the successor node, whereas BLINK is a pointer to the predecessor node. Because the list is circular, BLINK of the first node must point to the last node, and FLINK of the last node must point to the first node.

Inserting a node into a doubly linked list, or deleting one from it, is a much easier task because we do not have to search the list sequentially to locate a preceding node. The following procedure INSERTNODEDOUBLE inserts a node pointed to by POINT1 (already obtained via GETNODE or other means) into a doubly linked list just *before* a node pointed to by POINT2.

```
{Global declarations}

TYPE
  RECPOINTER = ^SPACEREC;
  SPACEREC =
    RECORD
      DATA: ARRAY [1..20] OF CHAR;
      FLINK: RECPOINTER;
      BLINK: RECPOINTER
    END {RECORD} ;

PROCEDURE INSERTNODEDOUBLE(VAR POINT1, POINT2: RECPOINTER);
        {Insert a node pointed to by POINT1 into a doubly linked
          list just before the node pointed to by POINT2}

  VAR
    PREV: RECPOINTER;

  BEGIN
    PREV := POINT2^.BLINK;
    POINT1^.FLINK := POINT2;
    POINT1^.BLINK := PREV;
    PREV^.FLINK := POINT1;
    POINT2^.BLINK := POINT1
  END {INSERTNODEDOUBLE} ;
```

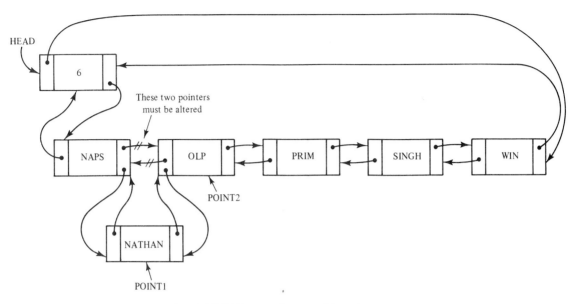

FIGURE 2-12   The INSERTNODEDOUBLE procedure avoids a time consuming sequential search by using a doubly linked circular list.

Figure 2-12 indicates the action taken by this procedure.

Note that the procedure INSERTNODEDOUBLE illustrates how streamlined insert and delete procedures become when a dummy header is used. In particular, because the empty list appears as shown in Figure 2-13, the procedure works without any awkward checking of whether the list is empty or whether the insertion is being made at the front of the list.

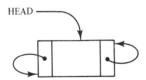

FIGURE 2-13   Empty doubly linked list. Note how a dummy header simplifies procedures in this situation.

The following procedure DELETENODEDOUBLE deletes a node pointed to by POINT1 from a doubly linked list and returns the node to the storage pool of available nodes.

```
{Global declarations}

TYPE
  RECPOINTER = ^SPACEREC;
  SPACEREC =
    RECORD
      DATA: ARRAY [1..20] OF CHAR;
      FLINK: RECPOINTER;
      BLINK: RECPOINTER
    END {RECORD} ;

PROCEDURE DELETENODEDOUBLE(VAR POINT1: RECPOINTER);
 {Delete a node pointed to by POINT1}
 {from doubly linked list}

  VAR
    SAVE: RECPOINTER;

  BEGIN
    SAVE := POINT1^.BLINK;
    SAVE^.FLINK := POINT1^.FLINK;
    SAVE := POINT1^.FLINK;
    SAVE^.BLINK := POINT1^.BLINK;
    DISPOSE(POINT1)
  END {DELETENODEDOUBLE} ;
```

Deleted node to be returned

POINT1

HEAD

POINT1

We shall end this chapter by noting that a doubly linked list is a special case of a structure known as a **multi-linked list.** Because each link field determines an order in which the nodes of a list are to be processed, we can in fact establish a different link field for every different order in which we wish to process the nodes in a list. Figure 2-14 illustrates such a multi-linked list. By following the IDLINK fields, we traverse the list in ID-NUMBER order; by following the NAMELINK fields, we traverse the list in alphabetical order by NAME.

IDHEAD

4

NAMEHEAD

3

	NAME	ID-NUMBER	NAMELINK	IDLINK
1	SINGH	8316	4	NIL
2	OLP	4212	5	5
3	NAPS	6490	2	1
4	WIN	1330	NIL	2
5	PRIM	5560	1	3

Multilink List

FIGURE 2-14 A different link field can be established for any desired order of processing nodes. NAMELINK processes the list in alphabetical order by NAME. IDLINK traverses the list by ID-NUMBER.

Program Design Considerations

The following Pascal program demonstrates the loading and then traversal of a singly linked list (with dummy header) containing employee records. The modular design of the program has been highlighted by graphical boxes, each documenting a procedure called at the appropriate time by the main program.

This program makes use of Pascal's dynamic memory allocation achieved via pointer variables. Here a record type called *empinfo* has been established in the TYPE declarations for the program. Records of type EMPINFO will contain fields:

- IDNO—Employee identification number
- INITIALS—Employee's first and middle initials
- LASTNAME—Employee's last name (up to 9 letters)
- SALARY—Employee's hourly salary
- NEXT—A pointer variable leading to the next employee on the list

```
PROGRAM LINKLIST
Responsible for
supplying number of
records parameter and
writing results
```

```
PROCEDURE READANDSTORE
Reads, stores and
arranges links
dynamically via pointer
variables
```

```
PROGRAM LINKLIST (INPUT,OUTPUT);

TYPE
  EPTR =^EMPINFO;
  EMPINFO = RECORD
        IDNO : INTEGER;
        INITIALS : ARRAY [1..2] OF CHAR;
        LASTNAME : ARRAY [1..9] OF CHAR;
        SALARY : REAL;
        NEXT : EPTR
      END;

  VAR
   HEAD,PREV,P : EPTR; { Pointer variables }
   NUMBER,J : INTEGER;

   PROCEDURE READANDSTORE(L:INTEGER);

   VAR
     I:INTEGER;
BEGIN {READANDSTORE}
   { Initialize the dummy header }
NEW(HEAD);
HEAD^.NEXT:=NIL;
PREV:=HEAD;
{ Loop to load the list }
FOR I:= 1 TO L DO
  BEGIN
   NEW(P);
   READLN(P^.IDNO);
   READLN(P^.INITIALS);
   READLN(P^.LASTNAME);
   READLN(P^.SALARY);
   PREV^.NEXT:=P;
   P^.NEXT:=NIL;
   PREV:=P
  END { FOR }
END { READANDSTORE };
```

```
BEGIN {  LINKLIST  }
WRITELN(' ENTER THE NUMBER OF RECORDS TO BE CREATED');
READLN(NUMBER);
READANDSTORE(L);
{ Next loop to print the list }
  WRITELN; WRITELN;
  WRITELN('**ECHO BACK DATA**');
  WRITELN;WRITELN;
  P:=HEAD;
  WHILE Pˆ. NEXT <> NIL DO
   BEGIN
     P:=Pˆ. NEXT;
     WRITELN(Pˆ. IDNO);
     WRITELN(Pˆ. INITIALS);
     WRITELN(Pˆ. LASTNAME);
     WRITELN(Pˆ. SALARY);
     WRITELN
   END
END.
```

SUMMARY

It is evident that the linked list structures discussed in this chapter
have endless possibilities for use in all kinds of data processing activities involving frequent insertions and deletions. The price one pays
for this efficiency in the processing of insertions and deletions is the
inability to directly access an element within the list. That is, finding
an item in a singly linked list requires searching the list sequentially,
starting at the head node. Variations on the linked list structure, such
as using a dummy header node and double linking, can serve to
streamline list processing algorithms at the expense of using slightly
more memory. As we progress, we will see that linked lists often serve
as the basis for a variety of more complex data structures.

KEY TERMS

Linked List	Dynamic Allocation
One-dimensional Array	NEW
Vector	DISPOSE
Node	Dummy Header
Logical order	Circularly Linked List
Physical Order	Doubly Linked List
Singly Linked List	Multi-linked List
Static Allocation	

EXERCISES

1. In what way is the data structure involved with the POINTER SORT in Chapter 1 *not* a linked list?
2. Modify the POINTERSORT procedure of Chapter 1 using a linked list, and then run your program.
3. Incorporate the procedure GETNODE into a complete Pascal program.
4. Write a program that deletes the last node in a linked list.
5. Initialize a one-dimensional array of size 50 with alphabetic data. Sort the array without physically disturbing the data in the array.
6. Rewrite the procedures INSERTNODE and DELETENODE using linked lists with dummy headers.
7. Write a program that employs the procedure INSERTNODEDOUBLE.
8. Write a program that employs the procedure DELETENODEDOUBLE.
9. What are some advantages of storing information about a list in a PREFIRST node?
10. Write a procedure for deleting a node from a doubly linked circular list.
11. Write a procedure for inserting a node in a singly linked circular list.
12. Write a procedure for deleting a node from a singly linked circular list.
13. What advantage does a PREFIRST node provide in a linked list?
14. What are the advantages and the disadvantages of a linked list structure over an array structure?
15. What main convenience does a doubly linked list offer as opposed to a singly linked list while searching the list?

PROGRAMMING PROBLEMS

1. The Wing-and-a-Prayer Airline Company maintains 4 scheduled flights per day which they identify by the numbers 1, 2, 3 and 4. For each of these flights, they keep an alphabetized list of passengers. The database for the entire airline could hence be viewed as 4 linked lists. Your task is to write a program that sets up and maintains this database by handling commands of the following form:

```
Command-->ADD
Flight number -->3
Passenger name-->BROWN

Command-->DELETE
From flight number-->1
Passenger name-->SMITH

Command-->LIST
Flight number-->2
(List alphabetically all passengers for the
specified flight)
```

You may assume that this program is continually online, with the passenger lists maintained in main memory at all times.

2. In order to take care of their growing business, the Fly-By-Night credit card company would like to update their customer data file. Write a program in a high level language that sets up a doubly linked list into which a record is

    1) Inserted into the list in the correct place, sorted according to the social security number of the customer;
    2) Updated if the customer record exists;
    3) Deleted if the customer no longer wishes to patronize the company.

    In the preceding data manipulation activities, the list should always remain in the sorted order by the social security number.

3. As a struggling professional football team, the Bay Area Brawlers have a highly volatile player roster. Write a program which will allow the team to maintain its roster as a linked list in alphabetical order by player last name. Other data items stored for each player are:

    - Height
    - Weight
    - Age
    - University affiliation

4. Develop a line-oriented text editor that assigns a number to each line of text and then maintains the lines in a linked list by line number order (similar to the fashion in which BASIC programs are maintained on many systems). Your program should be able to process the commands:

```
I line number 'text'
  (instruction to insert 'text' at line number)

L line1 — line2
  (instruction to list line1 through line2)

D line1 — line2
  (instruction to delete line1 through line2)
```

5. Write a program that, given a file of text, will add those words in the text that are marked by special delimiting brackets [ ] to an index, which will be printed after the text itself has been formatted and printed. Words in this index should be listed in alphabetical order with a page number reference for each page of text on which they are delimited by the special brackets. Note that this program would be part of a word processing system an author could use when developing a book with an index of terms.

6. Write a program that allows input of an arbitrary number of polynomials as coefficient and exponent pairs. Store each polynomial as a linked list of coefficient/exponent pairs ordered in descending

order by exponent. Note that the coefficient/exponent pairs need not be input in descending order; it is the responsibility of your program to put them in that order. Your program should then be able to evaluate each of the polynomials for an arbitrary argument X and be able to output each of the polynomials in the appropriate descending exponent order. Be sure that your program works for all "unusual" polynomials such as the zero polynomial, polynomials of degree one, and constant polynomials.

3

Strings and
Character Manipulation

*"Man does not live by words alone, despite the fact
that he sometimes has to eat them."*

ADLAI STEVENSON

3-1 Introductory Considerations

The manipulation of character strings plays an important role in a
wide variety of computer applications. Text editing, computer-
assisted instruction, and attempts to have computers interact with
users in natural languages are just a few examples of such applications. Some languages, like SNOBOL, COBOL, PL/1, and certain dia-
lects of BASIC, provide a great number of tools to allow their users to
manipulate character strings easily. Others, like FORTRAN and Pascal, often require their users to write these string manipulation tools
themselves in the form of procedures and functions. In this chapter,
we shall explore how the data structures used to store strings influence the ways in which the latter can be manipulated. You can then
apply such considerations to enhance programs in those languages
that are weak in their built-in string-handling capabilities. If you use
a language that provides a library of string-handling tools, this chapter
should provide you with a deeper understanding of what is happening
"under the surface" when you use such tools. This will help you to
write more efficient programs.

We will examine our string manipulation tools with respect to following typical operations:

1. **Assignment:** The copying of one string variable into another. For example, if STR1 and STR2 are two string variables, then the statement STR1 := STR2 should copy the contents of STR2 into STR1 without destroying the contents of STR2.

2. **Concatenation:** The joining together of two character strings. The concatenation of the strings "BIRD" and "DOG" is the string "BIRDDOG".

3. **Pattern Matching:** The searching of one string for an occurrence of another string. For instance, the string "BASEBALL" occurs in the string "MODERN BASEBALL HISTORY" beginning at position 8.

4. **Substring operations:** It may be desirable to examine characters I through J of a given string. For example, the substring consisting of the 4th through 7th characters in the string "TALE OF TWO CITIES" is the substring "E OF".

5. **Insertion:** In text editing applications, one frequently wishes to insert a given string in the middle of another string. The insertion of " AND" at position 5 of the string "SALT PEPPER" results in the string "SALT AND PEPPER."

6. **Deletion:** The opposite of insertion. To delete the substring occupying positions 5 through 13 of "SALT AND PEPPER" results in the string "SALTER".

We shall explore three types of structural techniques that can be used to store strings:

1. Fixed length string method
2. Workspace and index table method
3. Linked list method

In our discussion of each of these methods, we shall evaluate their performance with respect to the six string operations described above. In an abstract sense, a general goal in writing procedures to handle these fundamental string operations is to hide (as much as possible) the details related to a particular implementation within such low-level routines. In that way higher-level modules can easily be interfaced with any of the three methods. It will soon become apparent that there is no one method that is best for all six types of operations. Instead, you must choose the method that best suits a particular application, based on a thorough knowledge of their relative merits.

3-2 Fixed Length String Method

The fixed length string method has the advantage of being the easiest to program. Unfortunately, as we shall see, it can also result in a tremendous waste of memory and severely restrict the length that a string can attain. Consequently, its use is limited to those situations in which you have the luxury of large amounts of excess memory (situations that occur far less often than we would like). The general idea behind this method is that string variables are allocated to handle the maximum possible string length that is envisioned for a particular application. As strings are entered into such locations, those strings that do not attain this maximum length are left-justified and padded with blanks (or null characters) on the right. The blank padding becomes memory for which you are charged but which you cannot effectively use.

As an example, suppose that we wanted to manipulate a piece of text consisting of up to 50 lines, i.e., strings, of a maximum length of 80 characters each. In Pascal, we could then declare the following array:

```
VAR STR: ARRAY[1..50] OF PACKED ARRAY [1..80] OF CHAR;
```

Then the text

```
IF BUILDERS BUILT BUILDINGS
THE WAY THAT PROGRAMMERS WROTE
PROGRAMS, THEN THE FIRST WOODPECKER
THAT CAME ALONG WOULD
DESTROY CIVILIZATION.
```

would be stored as the 5 strings appearing in Figure 3-1.

STR[1]	IF BUILDERS BUILT BUILDINGS |.............................53 blanks_
STR[2]	THE WAY THAT PROGRAMMERS WROTE |.............50 blanks_
STR[3]	PROGRAMS, THEN THE FIRST WOODPECKER |........45 blanks_
STR[4]	THAT CAME ALONG WOULD |.............................59 blanks_
STR[5]	DESTROY CIVILIZATION. |.............................59 blanks_

FIGURE 3-1

Note that, for this choice of strings, well over half of the memory locations in STR[1] through STR[5] are being wasted. Also, although procedures for the 6 operations cited in (3.1) can be written with relative ease using the fixed-length method, other more subtle inefficiencies and limitations of this method will become apparent.

Before considering the problems of this method, you should know a generally useful function, LENGTH, which takes as arguments a fixed length string variable and the maximum number of characters that it may contain, and returns the actual length of the string in the function name: that is, the maximum possible length minus the number of padded blanks. Hence the LENGTH of STR[1] in Figure 3-1 is 27. The procedure assumes that the parameter MAXLEN is at least 1.

```
{ Global Variables }

CONST
  MAXLEN = 80;

TYPE
  STRARRAY = PACKED ARRAY [1..MAXLEN] OF CHAR;

FUNCTION LENGTH(STR: STRARRAY): INTEGER;

{ Returns the actual length of the string sent in STR as a
  parameter to the function. STR has maximum possible length
  of MAXLEN. }

{ Local Variables }

  VAR
    I: INTEGER;
    FLAG: BOOLEAN;

  BEGIN
    FLAG := TRUE;
    I := MAXLEN;
    WHILE FLAG AND (I >= 1) DO
      BEGIN
      IF STR[I] <> ' ' THEN
        BEGIN
        LENGTH := I;
        FLAG := FALSE
        END
      ELSE
        I := I - 1
      END; { WHILE }
    IF FLAG THEN
      LENGTH := 0
END;
{ End LENGTH }
```

Now consider how the fixed length method lends itself to the operation of string concatenation. The procedure given below will (apparently) concatenate the strings STR1 and STR2, producing STR3, each of the same maximum length.

```
{ Global Variables }

CONST
  MAXLEN = 80;

TYPE
  STRARRAY = PACKED ARRAY [1..MAXLEN] OF CHAR;

PROCEDURE CONCAT_FL(STR1, STR2: STRARRAY;
                    VAR STR3: STRARRAY);
{ Concatenate STR1 and STR2, producing STR3 }

{Local Variables }

VAR
  I: INTEGER;

BEGIN
  FOR I := 1 TO LENGTH(STR1) DO
    STR3[I] := STR1[I];
  FOR I := LENGTH(STR1)+1 TO LENGTH(STR2) + LENGTH(STR1) DO
    STR3[I] := STR2[I - LENGTH(STR1)];
END;
{ END CONCAT_FL }
```

One limitation of the above procedure, however, is that success may not be guaranteed if the maximum length of the resultant string is the same as that of the two operand strings. The only way to guarantee a successful operation is to specify that the resultant string must be declared longer than the two operand strings combined. Another alternative is to provide for appropriate error handling when the concatention is impossible. This is illustrated in the following version of the procedure CONCAT_FL, in which it is assumed that the maximum length of each string is the same.

```
{ Global Variables }

CONST
  MAXLEN = 80;

TYPE
  STRARRAY = PACKED ARRAY [1..MAXLEN] OF CHAR;
```

```
PROCEDURE CONCAT_FL(STR1, STR2: STRARRAY;
                       VAR STR3: STRARRAY);
  { Concatenate STR1 and STR2, producing STR3 of maximum length
    MAXLEN }

  { Local Variables }

  VAR
    I: INTEGER;

  BEGIN
    IF LENGTH(STR1) + LENGTH(STR2) > MAXLEN THEN
      ERROR_HANDLER {Call appropriate error-handling routine}
    ELSE
      BEGIN
      FOR I := 1 TO LENGTH(STR1) DO
        STR3[I] := STR1[I];
      FOR I := LENGTH(STR1)+1 TO LENGTH(STR2) + LENGTH(STR1) DO
        STR3[I] := STR2[I - LENGTH(STR1)]
      END
  END;

{ END CONCAT_FL }
```

Notice, however, that neither of these alternatives is acceptable. Forcing the resultant string to be twice as long will result in an increasing waste of memory. On the other hand, specifying certain concatenations as impossible due to the combined length of the two strings can be easily avoided in both the workspace/index table and linked list methods.

As a second example of the problems inherent in the fixed length method, consider this short procedure to handle the operation of insertion.

```
{ Global Variables }

CONST
  MAXLEN = 80;

TYPE
  STRARRAY = PACKED ARRAY [1..MAXLEN] OF CHAR;
```

```
PROCEDURE INSERT_FL(VAR MASTERSTR: STRARRAY;
                        INSTR: STRARRAY;
                        POS: INTEGER);
{ Procedure to insert INSTR in MASTERSTR, beginning at
  character position POS where MAXLEN is the maximum length of
  each string }

  { Local Variables }

  VAR
    I: INTEGER;

  BEGIN
    { First 'move over' the tail-end of MASTERSTR }

    FOR I := LENGTH(MASTERSTR) DOWNTO POS DO
      MASTERSTR[I + LENGTH(INSTR)] := MASTERSTR[I];

    { Next insert INSTR in vacated space }

    FOR I := 1 TO LENGTH(INSTR) DO
      MASTERSTR[I + POS - 1] := INSTR[I];
  END;
{ END INSERT_FL }
```

POS   LENGTH (MASTERSTRING)

Move this substring
over to make
room for INSTR

One shortcoming of the procedure INSERT_FL as it stands is the potential problem of string "overflow" similar to that which appeared in concatenation. This may be easily remedied by inserting a quick check on the string lengths involved.

```
{ Global Variables }

CONST
  MAXLEN = 80;

TYPE
  STRARRAY = PACKED ARRAY [1..MAXLEN] OF CHAR;
```

```
PROCEDURE INSERT_FL(VAR MASTERSTR: STRARRAY;
                        INSTR: STRARRAY;
                        POS: INTEGER);
{ Procedure to insert INSTR in MASTERSTR, beginning at character
  position POS where MAXLEN is the maximum length of each string }

  { Local Variables }

  VAR
    I: INTEGER;

  BEGIN
    IF LENGTH(MASTERSTR) + LENGTH(INSTR) > MAXLEN THEN
      ERROR_HANDLER {Call appropriate error-handling routine}

        { First 'move over' the tail-end of MASTERSTR }
    ELSE
      BEGIN
      FOR I := LENGTH(MASTERSTR) DOWNTO POS DO
        MASTERSTR[I + LENGTH(INSTR)] := MASTERSTR[I];

      { Next insert INSTR in vacated space }

      FOR I := 1 TO LENGTH(INSTR) DO
        MASTERSTR[I + POS - 1] := INSTR[I]
      END
  END;
{ END INSERT_FL }
```

POS   LENGTH (MASTERSTRING)

Move this substring
over to make
room for INSTR

Another more subtle problem in the INSERT procedure for fixed
length strings is the efficiency of the algorithm. For instance, to insert
the string "AND" at position 6 of the string "SALT PEPPER" we are
required actually to move 10 bytes of memory. This problem tends to
compound itself as longer strings become involved, with the result
that frequent insertions (and deletions) may degrade the performance
of a character manipulation program that employs the fixed-length
method. This problem of reducing the processing operations required
for insertions and deletions is one that *only* the linked list method can
gracefully handle.

3-3 Workspace/Index Table Method

We introduce the workspace/index table method by giving an example from a language that employs it in its string-handling package. In BASIC-PLUS, you need not declare a maximum length for a particular string variable. Instead, you are given "dynamic" storage allocation for string variables that may contain anywhere from zero to 255 characters. Before we explain in detail the implementation method used in BASIC-PLUS, you should attempt to specify what the output would be from the following BASIC-PLUS program segment (LSET is a special type of assignment operator that ensures left-justification and padding with blanks):

```
10 LET A$ = 'COFFEE'
20 LET B$ = A$
30 LSET A$ = 'TEA'
40 PRINT B$
```

If you answered that line 40 would result in the printing of the string "COFFEE", you gave the expected wrong answer. Actually, the output would be "TEA", and the reason is the manner in which BASIC-PLUS keeps track of strings. The idea behind this method is that one large memory workspace is allocated to storing all strings. Then two index tables are maintained: one that contains the address in the workspace at which each particular string starts, and one that contains the length of each string. This principle is illustrated in Figure 3-2.

Suppose now that we were to add a third string to the collection in Figure 3-2. All that we need to know is where the free portion of the workspace begins (in this case it begins at location 10). We place the

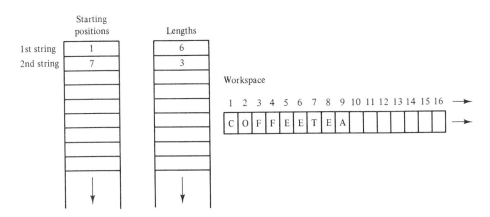

FIGURE 3-2   The BASIC-PLUS method of handling strings. All strings are stored in a large workspace, and two index tables keep track of the beginning and length of each string.

string starting at that location, add appropriate entries to our index tables, and adjust the pointer to the beginning of the free memory. This threefold process is illustrated in Figure 3-3 for the addition of the string "CREAM".

We can now explain the surprising result that occurred in our earlier BASIC-PLUS example. Consider how the assignment of one string to another would be handled in a language that kept track of strings by this method. It would not be efficient to store a second copy of the same string of characters. All that is needed is to add an entry to our index table that points to the same string of characters in the workspace. This principle as it relates to our BASIC-PLUS example is given in Figure 3-4.

Figure 3-5 illustrates what happens when we change the contents of the string variable A$ via the LSET instruction in line 30. Had we used a normal LET assignment statement, a new workspace area

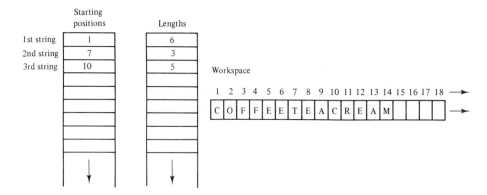

FIGURE 3-3   The string "CREAM" has been added to the BASIC-PLUS storage shown in Figure 3-2.

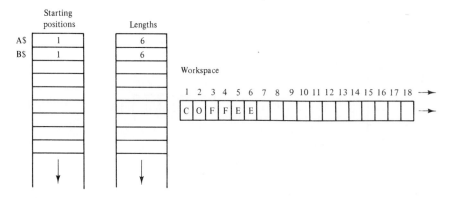

FIGURE 3-4   After LET B$ = A$, but before LSET A$ = "TEA". Instead of storing a second copy of a string, BASIC-PLUS simply adds a new entry to the indexes.

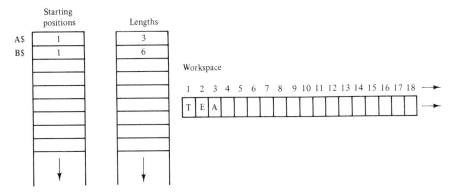

FIGURE 3-5   After LSET A$ = "TEA". LSET has changed the string A$ to "TEA" without changing the location of A$.

would have been assigned to A$. However, LSET assigns data to a string variable without changing the location of that variable in the workspace.

From Figure 3-5, it should now be immediately clear why our initial example produced such unexpected output.

Processing and Efficiency Considerations of the Workspace/Index Table Method

With regard to assignment, we have already seen that the workspace/index table method substitutes a relatively small amount of bookkeeping for the character-by-character copying used with the fixed length string method. It is also clear that strings do not waste memory as they did in the fixed length method. With the workspace/index method, memory allocation is **dynamic** in the sense that a string gets only the amount of workspace it needs at the time it needs it. The problem of what to do when a string no longer needs the memory it once occupied is one we shall take up later in the section on garbage collection.

Of the other string operations mentioned in (3.1), only concatenation and insertion present any real problem. In both cases the difficulty is that the resultant string must grow in length, and the workspace/index table method does not allow for any growing room without finding a completely new workspace area for the resultant string. That is, insertions and concatenations in which the resultant string is also an operand do not allow a string to grow in place, but rather require that the entire string be recopied to some free memory space.

To illustrate how the operation of insertion could be handled by a procedure, suppose that we wanted to give ourselves the capability of handling 100 strings taking up a total workspace area of no more than 10000 characters. To do this we would need to allocate:

1. An index table, START, of starting positions for strings 1, 2, 3, . . . , 100.
2. An index table, LEN, of lengths for strings 1, 2, 3, . . . , 100.
3. A workspace array, WORKSP, of size 10000 characters.
4. A pointer, FREESP, to the beginning of the free space in the workspace area.

Given this stage setting, let us now consider the procedure INSERT_WI, which will insert string J in string I beginning at position POS.

```
{ Global Variables }

TYPE
  SANDL = ARRAY [1..100] OF INTEGER;
  SPARRAY = PACKED ARRAY [1..10000] OF CHAR;

PROCEDURE INSERT_WI(VAR WORKSP: SPARRAY;
                    VAR FREESP: INTEGER;
                    VAR START, LEN: SANDL;
                    I, J, POS: INTEGER);
  { Insert the Jth string in the Ith string beginning at position
    POS }

  VAR
    K, OLDSTARTI, OLDLENI: INTEGER;

  BEGIN

    { Store the information on old string I }

    OLDSTARTI := START[I];
    OLDLENI := LEN[I];

    { Get new location for string I in WORKSP }

    START[I] := FREESP;
    LEN[I] := LEN[I] + LEN[J];

    { Update FREESP pointer }

    FREESP := FREESP + LEN[I];

    { Now build a new string }

    FOR K := 1 TO POS - 1 DO
      WORKSP[START[I] + K - 1] := WORKSP[OLDSTARTI + K - 1];
    FOR K := 1 TO LEN[J] DO
      WORKSP[START[I] + POS + K - 2] := WORKSP[START[J] + K -1];
    FOR K := POS + LEN[J] TO LEN[I] DO
      WORKSP[START[I] + K] := WORKSP[OLDSTARTI + K - POS];
  END;
{ END INSERT_WI }
```

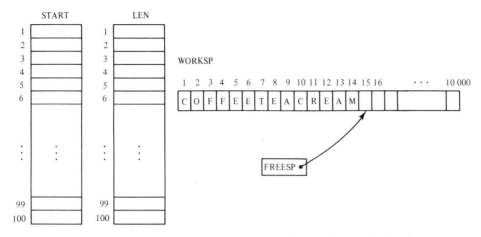

FIGURE 3-6 Design for the insert procedure using the workspace/index table method.

For example, the procedure INSERT_WI with the data from Figure 3-6—that is, when the Ith string is "COFFEE" and the Jth string "CREAM"—would alter our data structures in the fashion pictured in Figure 3-7. An analysis of the procedure INSERT_WI yields the following observations about the workspace/index table method:

1. Unlike the fixed length method, this method (generally) poses no problem with an insertion forcing a string to become too large.

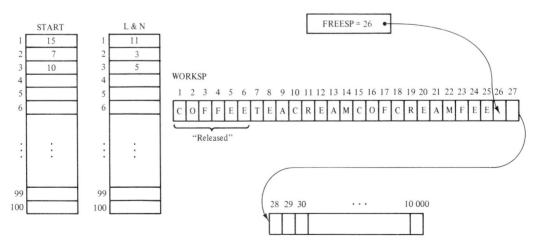

FIGURE 3-7 How INSERT_WI inserts the Jth string "CREAM" into the the Ith string "COFFEE"

2. Like that of the fixed length method, the workspace/index table insert routine requires the actual moving of bytes of memory. Hence, the latter method offers no advantage in this regard.

3. Although generally a string will not be too large for the workspace/index table method, some provision should be made (and none is in the above procedure) as to what should be done when the addition of another string forces the FREESP pointer above 10000.

4. When the FREESP pointer goes above 10000, are we necessarily out of workspace? As we have manipulated our string workspace area by adding, deleting, concatenating, and inserting strings, we have no doubt released some workspace area that was once occupied. The only problem is that our FREESP pointer is now beyond such areas. We must consider how such workspace can be reclaimed as *usable workspace.*

Garbage Collection

The problem of how to reclaim usable workspace generally can be classified as (believe it or not) a problem of **garbage collection**. A graphic illustration of the difficulty as it relates to the workspace/index table method of string handling is given in Figure 3-8. We will discuss two strategies for handling this problem. Both require declaring and maintaining two additional indexes that store information on garbage areas. These correspond to START and LEN on the beginning positions and lengths of strings. That is, as a string area is released, we will record its starting position and length in index tables GAR_START and GAR_LEN, respectively (Figure 3-9). One alternative is now to consult these two free space indexes whenever we wish to add a string. If the indexes indicate that some garbage area is large enough to accommodate the string we wish to add, then we can reclaim that space. Otherwise, we use the FREESP pointer to take space from the end of the WORKSP area.

One of the main drawbacks of this alternative is that a fair amount of extra processing must be done each time we wish to add a string. Therefore, we recommend a second alternative called **compaction**

FREESP = 73

WORKSP

Actual data	Released	Actual data	Released	Actual data	Released	Actual data	

1   12 13   24 25   38 39   49 50   58 59   65 66   72 73   10 000

FIGURE 3-8   Current status of WORKSP shows much released space that is not usable because FREE_SP points to 73.

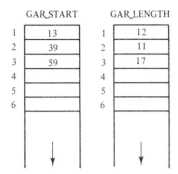

FIGURE 3-9 Garbage area Index tables for Figure 3-8.

which also makes use of the information in the GAR_START and GAR_LEN tables, although less frequently. The idea behind compaction is that only the FREE_SP pointer controls where a new string will be added; that is, new strings are added only at the end of the WORKSP area. However, when the addition of a new string would force the FREESP pointer beyond the limit of the WORKSP area, we then perform a compaction procedure that uses the information on the starting positions and lengths of garbage areas to roll down the good strings on top of them, hence freeing up area at the end of the workspace. Figure 3-10 graphically illustrates the compaction process on a small scale.

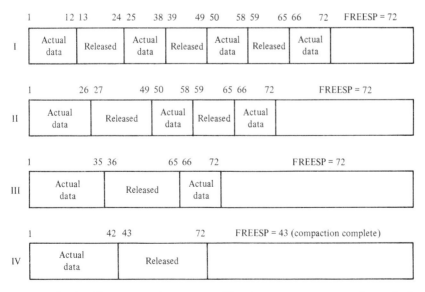

FIGURE 3-10 The compaction process. To release new space at the end of the workspace, good strings are rolled down Into garbage areas Indicated by GAR_START and GAR_LENGTH.

We will now examine a more complete version of the procedure INSERT_WI in which appropriate calls are made to procedures to perform compaction and error handling. You will write the compaction routine as an exercise at the end of the chapter.

```
{ Global Variables }

TYPE
   SANDL = ARRAY [1..100] OF INTEGER;
   SPARRAY = PACKED ARRAY [1..10000] OF CHAR;

PROCEDURE INSERT_WI(VAR WORKSP: SPARRAY;
                    VAR FREESP: INTEGER;
                    VAR START, LEN: SANDL;
                    I, J, POS: INTEGER);
```

```
{  Insert the Jth string in the Ith string beginning at position
   POS }

  VAR
    K, OLDSTARTI, OLDLENI: INTEGER;

  BEGIN
    IF FREESP + LEN[I] + LEN[J] > 10001 THEN
      COMPACT;

    { Still not enough free space? }

    IF FREESP + LEN[I] + LEN[J] > 10001 THEN
      ERROR_HANDLER
    ELSE
      BEGIN

      { Store the information on old string I }

      OLDSTARTI := START[I];
      OLDLENI := LEN[I];

      { Get new location for string I in WORKSP }
```

```
    START[I] := FREESP;
    LEN[I] := LEN[I] + LEN[J];

    { Update FREESP pointer }

    FREESP := FREESP + LEN[I];

    { Now build a new string }

    FOR K := 1 TO POS - 1 DO
      WORKSP[START[I] + K - 1] := WORKSP[OLDSTARTI + K - 1];
    FOR K := 1 TO LEN[J] DO
      WORKSP[START[I] + POS + K - 2] := WORKSP[START[J] + K - 1];
    FOR K := POS + LEN[J] TO LEN[I] DO
      WORKSP[START[I] + K] := WORKSP[OLDSTARTI + K - POS];

    { Now call to update tables for garbage areas }

    ADD_TO_GARBAGE(OLDSTARTI, OLDLENI)
    END
  END;
{ END INSERT_WI }
```

3-4   Linked List Method

Although the workspace/index table method gracefully solves the
problem of having to declare a maximum possible string length and
then wasting memory when strings are shorter than that length, it
does not adequately solve the problem of having to move a tremendous number of data when insertions and deletions occur on a large
scale. *Only* the linked list method handles *both* of these problems.
However, we shall see that it is not without its own set of
problems.

   We shall view each string as a circular doubly linked list as described in Chapter 2. Each node in the list contains a back pointer, a
forward pointer, and a data portion consisting of (for the moment) a
single character. Clearly, for each such string, we need a pointer to the
dummy header node for the list, and, for later use, we want also to
keep track of the length of each string. The following conventions will
be assumed throughout this section:

1. The array HEAD contains pointers to the dummy headers of
   all of the strings.
2. The array LEN contains the lengths of all of the strings.
3. The back pointer for each node will be referred to as BLINK,
   the forward pointer as FLINK, and the data portion as DATA.

Figure 3-11, which pictures the three strings "COFFEE", "TEA", and
"CREAM", should help to clarify these conventions.

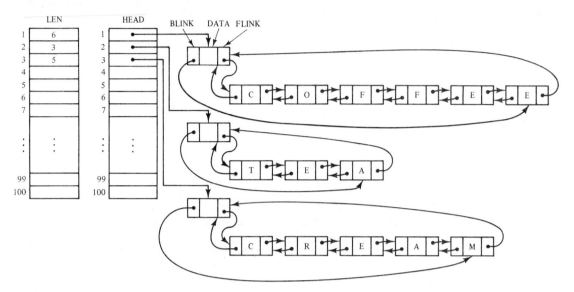

FIGURE 3-11 **The three strings "COFFEE", "TEA", and "CREAM" in a circular doubly linked list with indexes for the length and dummy header location of each string.**

The assignment of one string to another could be handled in a fashion very similar to the workspace/index table method; that is, instead of physically creating two identical strings, rather have two entries in HEAD point to the same string. Pattern matching presents no real problem and is examined in an exercise at the end of the chapter. Substring operations do present a problem and will be discussed in greater detail later. Insertion, deletion, and concatenation (which may be viewed as a special case of insertion) can be handled elegantly and efficiently using the linked list method. The following is a procedure INSERT_LL to insert the string pointed to by HEAD[J] into the string pointed to by HEAD[I] beginning at position POS.

```
{ Global Variables }

CONST
  NUMBER_STRINGS = 100;

TYPE
  STRINGPTR = ^STRINGNODE;
  STRINGNODE =
    RECORD
      BLINK: STRINGPTR;
      DATA: CHAR;
      FLINK: STRINGPTR
    END;
```

```
VAR
  HEAD: ARRAY[1..NUMBER_STRINGS] OF STRINGPTR;

PROCEDURE INSERT_LL( I, J, POS: INTEGER);
 { Insert the Jth string in the Ith string beginning at position
   POS }

  VAR
    K: INTEGER;
    FIRSTINJ, LASTINJ, P: STRINGPTR;

  BEGIN
    P := HEAD[I];
    { First find position by traversing list}
    FOR K := 1 TO POS DO
      P := P^.FLINK;

      { Now link it in }

    FIRSTINJ := HEAD[J]^.FLINK;
    LASTINJ := HEAD[J]^.BLINK;
    FIRSTINJ^.BLINK := P^.BLINK;
    LASTINJ^.FLINK := P;
    P^.BLINK^.FLINK := FIRSTINJ;
    P^.BLINK := LASTINJ;
  END;
{ END INSERT_LL }
```

This procedure closely parallels the insertion procedure for linked lists described in Chapter 2. There is one difference, however. In Chapter 2, we were only concerned with inserting one node. Here we are inserting an entire collection of nodes; we are inserting one linked list within another (Figure 3-12.) This is done with relative ease because our implementation of a doubly linked list gives us convenient pointers to both the first and last nodes in the list.

Problems with the Linked List Method

A recurrent theme in this text will be that the study of data structures to a great extent consists of acquiring knowledge about the relative advantages and disadvantages of different data storage techniques. In the string-handling application we have seen that the linked list method allows both dynamic string allocation with no practical limit on string length and extremely efficient insertion and deletion operations. However, that does not mean that the linked list method is a universal cure-all that should be used in all applications.

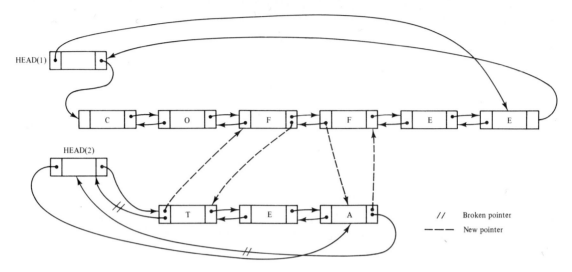

FIGURE 3-12 Two strings from Figure 3-11 after INSERT_LL(1,2,4)

Three general problem areas exist. First, the perceptive reader will already have noticed that, although the procedure INSERT_LL achieves a very efficient insertion, it renders the Jth string thereafter inaccessible *as a separate entity.* This is because the pointers within the Jth string had to be altered to chain it into the Ith string. (See Figure 3-12.)

Second, consider an application in which operating with substrings is of more importance than insertion and deletion. With both the fixed length and the workspace/index table methods, the substring consisting of the Ith through the Jth characters could be directly accessed because the characters within any given string are physically next to each other. Accessing the same substring via the linked list implementation requires beginning at the initial character in the string and traversing the entire string until the Ith character is reached. Our implementation of a string as a doubly linked list allows this process to be made somewhat more efficient. In particular, the length of the string from which we want to extract a substring could be checked to determine if the substring occurs in the front or back half. If it is in the back half, the pointer to the last character in the string could be used to begin a traversal from the rear of the list until we reach the desired substring. However, this would still require, a sequential processing of the list until the desired substring is found. Hence, for substring operations, the linked list method just does not stack up to either of the other two methods. (See Chapter 4 for a formal definition of the term *stack up.*)

A third problem arises in the efficiency of memory utilization for the linked list method as we have described it here. If the data portion of a node in the linked list contains merely one character, then the two

In the world of applications ...

All of us are familiar with coded messages in which the words and symbols are intricately combined to produce a logical text. Perhaps one of the more interesting episodes of this kind is the mystery novel *Postern of Fate* by Agatha Christie. The mystery is based on some underlined words in a book which are accidentally found and **concatenated** to yield the clue to a murder:

> "Mary Jordan did not die naturally. It was one of us. I think I know which one."

At least one software company, Prosoft, Inc. of North Hollywood, California, seems to have removed the mystery surrounding the efficient garbage collection of string space for the workspace/index method of string handling used in many microcomputer versions of BASIC. To quote their recent advertising brochure:

> When a BASIC program changes a string, it moves it to a new place in memory, and leaves a hole in the old place. Eventually, all available memory gets used up and BASIC has to push the strings together to free up some space. This takes time. Lots of time. The computer stops running for seconds or minutes, and you may even think it's crashed.

The brochure goes on to claim that, for a BASIC program using 1000 string variables, the garbage collection algorithm used by Prosoft's Trashman program outperforms the standard Radio Shack TRSDOS operating system method by a margin of 3.5 seconds to 179.6 seconds— an improvement of 98 percent; clear evidence that a better algorithm can make a real difference!

* Reprinted courtesy of the Tesler Software Corporation, Prosoft Catalog #3.

pointers associated with that node could require 4 to 8 times more memory than the data. That is, only 11 to 20 percent of memory is being utilized to store the data in which we are really interested; the rest of the memory is storing data about data.

This memory utilization problem may be somewhat alleviated by making the data portion of a node a *cluster* of characters. Suppose, for instance, we choose a cluster size of four characters. Then the same strings given in Figure 3-11 would appear as shown in Figure 3-13. Here we have used the symbol $\sim$ to represent a null character, that is, a character that is always ignored when the string is processed.

Notice that, although this technique has enabled us to devote a greater percentage of memory for storage of data, a significant complication has been added, in that our code must always account for null characters. For example, if we wish to insert the second string from Figure 3-13 in the first string beginning at position 4, the scheme pictured in Figure 3-14 emerges.

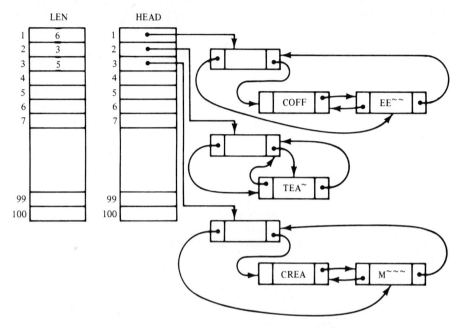

FIGURE 3-13   The strings from Figure 3-11 with a cluster size of 4

Here the node containing "COFF" had to be split into the two nodes "COF~" and "F~ ~ ~" to achieve an effective insertion. As you might expect, we have had to trade off one feature for another. To gain more effective memory utilization, we have had to make our program code more cumbersome and less efficient in its execution time.

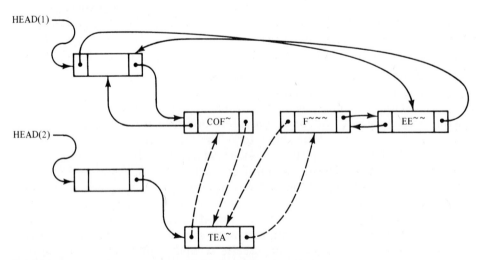

FIGURE 3-14   After insertion of the 2nd string into the 1st beginning at position 4.

Program Design Considerations

Many programs are driven by a menu in which the user is allowed to select from among various options by entering an appropriate character from the keyboard. The Pascal program given represents such a menu-driven application—a line-oriented text editor which could be viewed as an initial solution to programming problem 4 in Chapter 2. The structure of the program employs a strategy which may be generalized to a variety of menu-driven situations. The main program itself does virtually nothing but receive menu requests and then dispatch them to appropriate level routines.

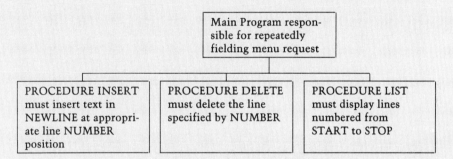

Two additional design considerations are worth noting in this program. The first of these is the elegance of the Pascal REPEAT loop CASE statement in controlling the mainline logic of the program. The user is locked into the looping structure until typing "Q". We have here used the OTHERWISE clause in the CASE statement (available in many versions of Pascal) to trap bad input easily.

The second consideration is that the modular design illustrated by this program is indicative of how a well-designed program may be quickly and easily modified to meet changing needs. The program as it currently stands uses the fixed length method for storing its strings. In problem 1 of the present chapter, you are essentially asked to modify this program to allow for a more efficient method of string storage. Such modifications may be handled almost entirely by developing a few low-level modules to be called by the modules already existing in the program. Included among the modules you need to develop are:

- A module to allow input of a string to be stored in this more efficient format
- A module to print a string stored in this more efficient format
- A module to (alphabetically) compare two strings stored in this more efficient format

Since the higher-level modules are relatively free from considerations of how the strings are stored, only minor changes will have to be made in the code at these higher levels. Hence not only is program modularity illustrated but also the concept of data abstraction. That is, the intricate details of how strings are actually to be stored are isolated in the lowest-level modules in the program structure. In higher-level modules, the emphasis is on the algorithm instead of the detailed intricacies of data storage techniques.

```pascal
PROGRAM TEXTED(INPUT, OUTPUT);

  { Line-oriented text editor }

  TYPE
    ALFA = PACKED ARRAY [1..80] OF CHAR;
    PTR =^TENTRY;
    TENTRY =
      RECORD
        LINENO: INTEGER;
        LINETEXT: ALFA;
        NEXT: PTR
      END;

  VAR
    COMMAND: CHAR;
    NUMBER, I, STOP: INTEGER;
    NEWLINE: ALFA;
    HEAD, LINK: PTR;

  PROCEDURE INSERT(NUMBER: INTEGER;
                   VAR NEWLINE: ALFA);

    { Insert NEWLINE text at specified line NUMBER }

    VAR
      PREV, P, LINK: PTR;
      DONE: BOOLEAN;

    BEGIN
      DONE := FALSE;
      PREV := HEAD;
      LINK := HEAD^.NEXT;
    WHILE (LINK <> NIL) AND NOT DONE DO
      BEGIN
      IF LINK^.LINENO = NUMBER THAN
        BEGIN
        LINK^.LINETEXT := NEWLINE;
        DONE := TRUE
        END {IF}
      ELSE IF LINK^.LINENO > NUMBER THEN
        BEGIN
        NEW(P);
        P^.LINENO := NUMBER;
        P^.LINETEXT := NEWLINE;
        P^.NEXT := LINK;
        PREV^.NEXT :=P;
        DONE := TRUE
        END {IF}
```

```
        ELSE
          BEGIN
            PREV := LINK;
            LINK := LINK^.NEXT
          END
      END {WHILE} ;
    {INSERT AT END? }
    IF NOT DONE THEN
      BEGIN
        NEW(P);
        P^.LINENO := NUMBER;
        P^.LINETEXT := NEWLINE;
        P^.NEXT := NIL;
        PREV^.NEXT := P;
      END
    END {INSERT} ;

PROCEDURE DELETE(NUMBER: INTEGER);

  { Delete specified line NUMBER }

  VAR
    PREV, LINK: PTR;
    DONE: BOOLEAN;

  BEGIN
    PREV := HEAD;
    LINK := HEAD^.NEXT;
    DONE := FALSE;
    WHILE (LINK <> NIL) AND NOT DONE DO
      BEGIN
      IF LINK^.LINENO = NUMBER THEN
        BEGIN
          PREV^.NEXT := LINK^.NEXT;
          DISPOSE(LINK);
          DONE := TRUE
        END {IF}
      ELSE
        BEGIN
          PREV := LINK;
          LINK := LINK^.NEXT
        END
      END {WHILE} ;
  END {DELETE} ;
```

```
PROCEDURE LIST(START, STOP: INTEGER);

{ List lines from START to STOP }

  VAR
    I: INTEGER;
    DONE: BOOLEAN;
    LINK: PTR;

  BEGIN
    DONE := FALSE;
    LINK := HEAD^.NEXT;
    WHILE (LINK <> NIL) AND NOT DONE DO
      BEGIN
      IF LINK^.LINENO > STOP THEN
        DONE := TRUE
      ELSE IF LINK^.LINENO >= START THEN
        BEGIN
        WRITE(LINK^.LINENO);
        WRITELN(LINK^.LINETEXT);
        LINK := LINK^.NEXT
        END {IF}
      ELSE
        LINK := LINK^.NEXT
      END {WHILE} ;
  END {LIST} ;

BEGIN

  { Begin main program processing }

  NEW(HEAD);
  HEAD^.NEXT := NIL;
  REPEAT
    WRITELN('NEXT COMMAND');
    READ(COMMAND);
    CASE COMMAND OF
      'I':
        BEGIN
        READ(NUMBER);
        READ(NEWLINE)
        INSERT(NUMBER, NEWLINE)
        END { CASE FOR 'I' } ;
      'D':
        BEGIN
        READ(NUMBER);
        DELETE(NUMBER)
        END { CASE FOR 'D'} ;
```

```
    'L';
      BEGIN
      READ(NUMBER, STOP);
      LIST(NUMBER, STOP)
      END { CASE FOR 'L' } ;
    'Q':
      BEGIN
      END; { Do nothing }
    OTHERWISE
      WRITELN('ERROR, TRY AGAIN')
    END {CASE} ;
    READLN
  UNTIL COMMAND = 'Q'
END {PROGRAM} .
```

SUMMARY

String operations are vital to all types of data processing needs. In this chapter, we have seen that a variety of data structure techniques can be used to implement strings. Each technique carries with it a set of advantages and disadvantages that must be carefully weighed when considering its use in a given application. The following table highlights the strong and weak points of each method.

Advantages and Disadvantages of the Three String Manipulation Methods.

Characteristic Method	Concatenation	Pattern Matching	Substring Operations	Insertions and Deletions	Memory Utilization	Assignment
Fixed Length	Awkward because combined lengths may overflow fixed length limit	Requires sequential searching from beginning of string	Substrings are directly accessible	Large-scale movement of characters required	Very inefficient unless all strings of uniform length	Large-scale movement of characters required
Workspace Index	Requires large-scale movement of characters, but no length limitations	Requires sequential searching from beginning of string	Substrings are directly accessible	Large-scale movement of characters required	Very efficient	May be done via pointers to avoid data movement
Linked List	May be done via pointers to avoid data movement	Requires sequential searching from beginning of string	Substrings are not directly accessible	May be done via pointers to avoid data movement	Dependent upon cluster size	May be done via pointers to avoid data movement

KEY TERMS

Assignment
Concatenation
Pattern Matching
Substring Operations
Insertion
Deletion
Fixed Length Method

Workspace/Index Table Method
Garbage Collection
Compaction
Linked List Method
String Length
Cluster

EXERCISES

1. Write a string assignment procedure for the workspace/index table method.
2. Write a string assignment procedure for the linked list method.
3. Write a string concatenation procedure for the workspace/index table method.
4. Write a string concatenation procedure for the linked list method.
5. Write a pattern matching procedure for the fixed length method.
6. Write a pattern matching procedure for the workspace/index table method.
7. Write a pattern matching procedure for the linked list method.
8. Write a procedure to handle the substring operations described in (3.1) for the fixed length method.
9. Write a procedure to handle the substring operations described in (3.1) for the workspace/index table method.
10. Write a procedure to handle the substring operations described in (3.1) for the linked list method.
11. Write a procedure to handle substring deletion for the fixed length method.
12. Write a procedure to handle substring deletion for the workspace/index table method.
13. Write a procedure to handle substring deletion for the linked list method.
14. Write the procedure COMPACT as called in the routine INSERT_WI.
15. What are the main problems associated with the linked list method for implementing strings?
16. What is the function of the index table in the workspace/index table method?

PROGRAMMING PROBLEMS

1. Modify the airline reservation system or the line-oriented text editor which you developed for programming problems 1 and 4 in Chapter 2 so that the strings involved are implemented via the workspace/index table method or the linked list method.
2. Create a separate file whose records consist of the last 32 bytes of every record in the Fly-By-Night credit card company file. Recall

from problem 2 of Chapter 1 that this portion of each record in the Fly-By-Night file only contains general text information. Using the techniques given in this chapter, write a TEXT EDITOR program, which would conveniently manipulate the new file for subsequent updating by allowing such operations as inserting a string into another string, deletion from a string, and concatenating to a string.

3. Write the roster maintenance program that you developed for the Bay Area Brawlers football team (see problems for Chapter 2) so that it allows player names and university affiliations of arbitrary length. Develop your own string handling routines for this purpose.

4. In computer-assisted instruction it is often necessary to match a user's response against the correct answer to a question. When this response is in the form of a string, it may be desirable to allow spelling that is "almost correct." Think of a computer-assisted instruction application in which string responses would be appropriate, suitably define an "almost correct" spelling, and implement the corresponding pattern matching procedure in a complete program.

4

Queues and Stacks

"The past is but the beginning of a beginning."

H. G. WELLS

4-1 Introductory Considerations

In Chapter 2 we introduced the linked list as a data structure specifically designed to handle conveniently the insertion and deletion of entries in an ordered list. In this chapter, we will discuss two special types of lists characterized by restrictions imposed on the way in which entries may be inserted and removed. One of these structures, a **queue**, is a **first-in-first-out** (sometimes referred to as **FIFO**) **list**. Insertions are limited to one end of the list, whereas deletions may occur only at the other end. Typically, these two ends of the list are called the **rear** and **front** respectively and must be maintained via FRONT and REAR pointers. The conceptual picture of a queue is that of a waiting line; for example, jobs waiting to be serviced by a computer or cars forming a long line at a busy tool booth.

The other structure that we will study is a **last-in-first-out** (sometimes referred to as **LIFO**) list, known as a **stack**. In a stack, both insertions and deletions occur at one end only. Hence a stack may be maintained with a single pointer to the **top** of the list of elements. Stacks are frequently used as a storage structure in everyday life. For instance, to maintain an orderly suitcase, the smart traveler will pack a wardrobe so that the last item packed will be the first to be worn. Perhaps the best visual example of a stack is that of the pop-up mechanism used to store trays for a cafeteria line. The terminology used to describe stack operations reinforces this analogy. Removing the top entry from the stack is **popping** the stack, whereas adding a new entry is **pushing** the stack (Figure 4-1).

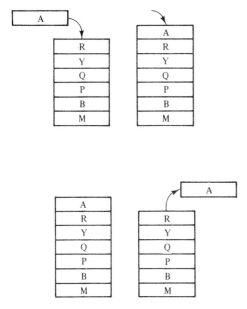

FIGURE 4-1 A stack can be thought of as the pop-up mechanism used to store cafeteria trays. Adding an item is called *pushing* onto the stack (top figure); removing one is called *popping* from the stack (bottom figure).

4-2 Queues

Let us consider computer jobs being scheduled in a batch processing environment, a nice example of a queue in use. We will suppose that all job names are six characters or less and that jobs are scheduled strictly in the order in which they arrive. Then an array and two pointers can be used to implement the scheduling queue.

```
TYPE DATASTRING = PACKED ARRAY[1..6] OF CHAR;
     QUEUEARRAY = ARRAY[1..ARRAYSIZE] OF INTEGER;

VAR  FRONT,REAR:INTEGER;
     QUEUE:QUEUEARRAY;
```

Here ARRAYSIZE would be set by a CONST declaration to the maximum number of entries which the array QUEUE may contain. We shall see that this is different from the maximum number of entries that the queue may contain at a given time in processing.

If the FRONT and REAR pointers are initially set to 1 and 0 respectively, the state of the queue before any insertions or deletions appears as shown in Figure 4-2.

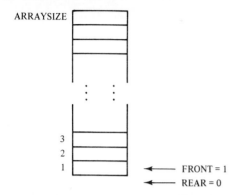

FIGURE 4-2   Queue with FRONT pointer set at 1 and REAR pointer set at 0.

Recalling that insertions may be made only at the rear of the queue, suppose that job NEWTON now arrives to be processed. The queue changes to look like Figure 4-3.

If job NEWTON is followed by PAYROL, the queue must change to look like Figure 4-4, which shows that the addition of any job contained in ITEM to the queue requires two steps:

```
REAR := REAR + 1
QUEUE[REAR] := ITEM;
```

If the system is now ready to process NEWTON, the front entry must be removed from the queue to an appropriate location designated by ITEM (Figure 4-5). Here the instructions

```
ITEM := QUEUE[FRONT];
FRONT := FRONT + 1;
```

achieve the desired effect.

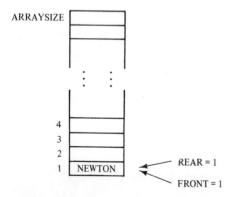

FIGURE 4-3   The job NEWTON is added to the rear of the queue.

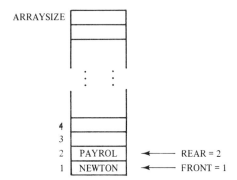

FIGURE 4-4   PAYROL is added after NEWTON.

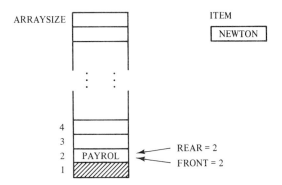

FIGURE 4-5   When the system is ready to process the next job, it removes NEWTON to the location designated by ITEM.

It should be clear from the preceding discussion that the conditions in Figure 4-6 signal the associated special situations.

These conditions allow us to develop our brief two-line sequences for adding to and removing from a queue into full-fledged procedures capable of sending back an appropriate flag should the requested operation not be successful.

Condition	Special situation
REAR < FRONT	Empty queue
FRONT = REAR	One-entry queue
REAR = ARRAYSIZE	No more entries may be added to queue

FIGURE 4-6   Special situations that can occur in the queue, and the conditions that signal them.

```
{ Global Declarations }

CONST
  ARRAYSIZE = 100;

TYPE
  DATASTRING = PACKED ARRAY [1..6] OF CHAR;
  QUEUEARRAY = ARRAY [1..ARRAYSIZE] OF DATASTRING;

PROCEDURE REMOVE(VAR FRONT: INTEGER;
                 VAR EMPTY: BOOLEAN;
                 VAR ITEM: DATASTRING;
                 REAR: INTEGER;
                 VAR QUEUE: QUEUEARRAY);
```

{ General procedure to remove FRONT entry from QUEUE and
    return it in ITEM. EMPTY flag returned as FALSE if the
    operation is successful and TRUE if the QUEUE is empty. }

```
  BEGIN
    IF REAR < FRONT THEN
      EMPTY := TRUE

    ELSE
      BEGIN
      EMPTY := FALSE;
      ITEM := QUEUE[FRONT];
      FRONT := FRONT + 1;
      END;
  END;
{ End REMOVE }
```

Empty QUEUE

REAR < FRONT
EMPTY = TRUE

REMOVE

Before REMOVE   After REMOVE

FRONT ≤ REAR

```
{ Global Declarations }

CONST
  ARRAYSIZE = 100;

TYPE
  DATASTRING = PACKED ARRAY [1..6] OF CHAR;
  QUEUEARRAY = ARRAY [1..ARRAYSIZE] OF DATASTRING;

PROCEDURE ADD(FRONT: INTEGER;
              VAR FULL: BOOLEAN;
              ITEM: DATASTRING;
              VAR REAR: INTEGER;
              VAR QUEUE: QUEUEARRAY);
```

{ General procedure to add ITEM to the REAR of QUEUE.
  FULL flag is returned as FALSE if the operation is successful
  and as TRUE if the QUEUE is full.}

```
  BEGIN
    IF REAR = ARRAYSIZE THEN
      FULL := TRUE
    ELSE
      BEGIN
      FULL := FALSE;
      REAR := REAR + 1;
      QUEUE[REAR] := ITEM;
      END;
  END;
{ End ADD }
```

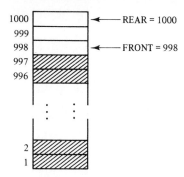

FIGURE 4-7   A full queue.

As it now stands, our implementation of a queue as a scheduling struc-ture for jobs in a batch environment functions effectively until REAR = ARRAYSIZE. Then a call to ADD returns FULL as TRUE even though only a small percentage of slots in the array may actually con-tain data items *currently* in the queue structure. In fact, given the queue pictured in Figure 4-7, we should be able to use slots 1-997 again. This is not necessarily undesirable. For example, it may be that the mode of operation in a given batch environment is to process 1000 jobs, then print a statistical report on these 1000 jobs, and finally clear the queue to start another group of 1000 jobs. In this case, the queue in Figure 4-7 is the ideal structure, because data about jobs are not lost even after they have left the queue.

However, if the goal of a computer installation were to provide continuous scheduling of batch jobs, without interruption after 1000 jobs, then the queue of Figure 4-7 would not be effective. One strategy that could be used to correct this situation is to move the active queue down the array upon reaching the condition REAR = ARRAYSIZE, as illustrated in Figure 4-8.

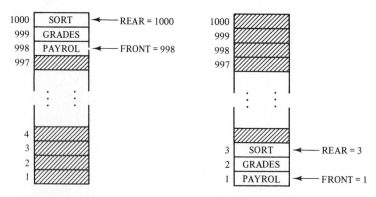

FIGURE 4-8   When REAR = ARRAYSIZE, the active queue is moved down.

Should the queue contain a large number of items, however, this strategy would not be satisfactory because it would require moving all of the individual data items. We will discuss two other strategies that allow the queue to operate in a continuous *and* efficient fashion—a **circular implementation** and a **linked list implementation.**

Circular Implementation of a Queue

This technique essentially allows the queue to **wrap around** upon reaching the end of the array. This transformation is illustrated by the addition of the item, UPDATE, to the queue in Figure 4-9.

To handle the pointer arithmetic necessary for this implementation of a queue, we must make the FRONT and REAR pointers behave in a fashion analogous to an odometer counter on a car that has exceeded its mileage capacity. A convenient way of doing this is to introduce Pascal's MOD operator where:

```
M MOD N = remainder of dividing integer M by integer N
```

(For example, 5 MOD 3 = 2 and 10 MOD 7 = 3.) It is immediately clear from Figure 4-9 that REAR < FRONT will no longer suffice as a condition to signal an empty queue. To describe this condition, consider what remains after we remove an item from a queue that has only a single item in it. There are two possible situations, as illustrated in Figure 4-10.

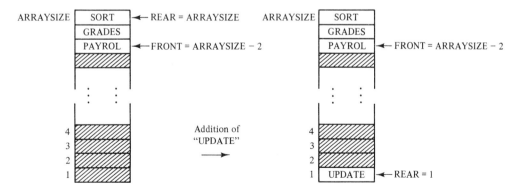

FIGURE 4-9 In this circular implementation, the queue wraps around when UPDATE is added.

Case 1: FRONT = REAR < ARRAYSIZE

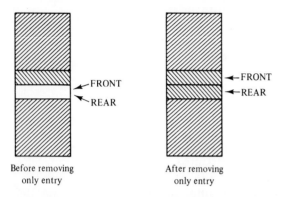

Before removing   After removing
only entry   only entry

Case 2: FRONT = REAR = ARRAYSIZE

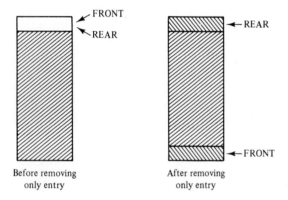

Before removing   After removing
only entry   only entry

FIGURE 4-10   Removing item from one-entry queue.

An inspection of both cases reveals that, after the lone entry has been removed, the relationship

```
(REAR MOD ARRAYSIZE) + 1 = FRONT
```

holds between the pointers. There is a problem, however, with immediately adopting this as a check for an empty queue. This same relationship between pointers also exists when the queue is full *if* we allow all slots in the array to be occupied at any one time!

This apparent contradiction can be avoided easily if one memory slot is sacrificed; that is, if we view a queue with ARRAYSIZE − 1 entries as a full queue. Then the test for fullness is met when the REAR pointer lags two behind FRONT (including consideration for wraparound). The results are summarized in Figure 4-11.

FRONT = REAR	One-entry queue
(REAR MOD ARRAYSIZE) + 1 = FRONT	Empty queue
(REAR MOD ARRAYSIZE) + 2 = FRONT	Full queue

FIGURE 4-11   Implementing a circular queue, at most ARRAYSIZE - 1 entries.

Linked List Implementation of a Queue

The linked list method allows the queue to be completely dynamic, with size restrictions imposed only by the pool of available nodes. Essentially, the queue is represented as a linked list with an additional REAR pointer to the last node in the list so that the list need not be traversed to find this node. To reduce the handling of special cases, we follow the strategy established in Chapter 2 of having a dummy header, which carries no actual data, as the first node in the list. Hence the queue containing PAYROL, GRADES, and SORT would appear as in Figure 4-12. LINK(HEAD) leads directly to the first item in the queue.

Figure 4-13 summarizes the conditional checks that signal an empty, one-entry, or full queue. Appropriate procedures for handling additions to and removals from the queue follow. Notice that, from a calling module perspective, it would make little difference whether these low-level procedures used an array or a linked list to implement the queue. That is the essence of data abstraction. That is, the details of how a data structure is actually implemented are to be hidden as deep as possible in the overall program structure.

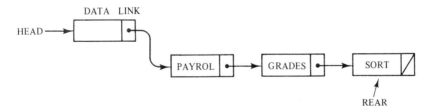

FIGURE 4-12   Linked list implementation of a queue with 3 data nodes and a dummy header.

Empty Queue ⟶ REAR = HEAD
One-Entry Queue ⟶ REAR = HEAD`.LINK
Full Queue ⟶ Handled by GETNODE or NEW
procedures of Chapter 2

FIGURE 4-13   Conditional checks for special situations in the linked list implementation.

```
{Global Declarations }

TYPE
  STRING = PACKED ARRAY [1..6] OF CHAR;
  POINTER =^QUEUENODE;
  QUEUENODE =
    RECORD
      DATA: STRING;
      LINK: POINTER;
    END;

PROCEDURE ADD(VAR REAR: POINTER;
                  FRONT: POINTER;
                  ITEM: STRING);
```

{ Add ITEM to QUEUE pointed to by REAR and FRONT.
  QUEUE is maintained via a linked list with LINK as a pointer field.

```
  VAR
    P: POINTER;

  BEGIN
    NEW(P);
    P^.DATA := ITEM;
    P^.LINK := NIL;
    REAR^.LINK := P;
    REAR := P;
  END;
{ End ADD }
```

ADD

QUEUE before ADD

P node obtained via GETNODE

Inserted

QUEUE after ADDing SORT

{ Global Declarations }

```
TYPE
  STRING = PACKED ARRAY [1..6] OF CHAR;
  POINTER =^QUEUENODE;

  QUEUENODE =
    RECORD
      DATA: STRING;
      LINK: POINTER;
    END;
```

```
PROCEDURE REMOVE(VAR REAR, FRONT: POINTER;
                 VAR ITEM: STRING;
                 VAR EMPTY: BOOLEAN);
```

{ Remove ITEM from QUEUE pointed to by REAR and FRONT.
  QUEUE is maintained via a linked list with LINK as a pointer field.

```
    VAR
      P: POINTER;

    BEGIN
      IF FRONT = REAR THEN
        EMPTY := TRUE
      ELSE
        BEGIN
        EMPTY := FALSE;
        P := FRONT^.LINK;
        ITEM := P^.DATA;
        FRONT^.LINK := P^.LINK;
        IF REAR = P THEN { Removed from one-entry queue }
          REAR := FRONT;
        DISPOSE(P);
        END;
    END;
{ End REMOVE }
```

More than one entry QUEUE before REMOVE

More than one entry QUEUE after REMOVE

Handled by
RETURNNODE

One entry QUEUE before REMOVE

One entry QUEUE after REMOVE

In the World of Applications . . .

One of the primary problems facing designers of operating systems is the allocation and scheduling of resources which must be shared by a number of users. For instance, consider a simple timesharing system which allows multiple users, each on a video terminal, and also has one shared line printer. Suppose that the currently running *process*, called process A, makes a request to use the line printer. Then, before this process completes its task on the printer, its time burst expires, and it is replaced by process B as the currently running process. If process B requests the printer while it is running, we have a clear problem. If process B is granted the printer, its output will be interspersed with that from process A, which did not complete its printing before its time burst expired. Obviously, we cannot let process B continue to run.

The solution developed by operating systems designers to honor both of these requests is to use multiple queues—one containing those processes which have cleared access to all resources they require to run, and one for processes which have requested a resource currently owned by another process. The former of these queues is often called the **ready queue** while the latter is termed the **blocked queue.** Hence the solution to the scenario described in the first paragraph involves two steps:

1. Move process A from its currently running state to the ready queue when its time burst expires (because it has all the necessary resources to start running again).
2. Move process B to the blocked queue when it requests the printer already owned by process A. Here it would remain until process A is done with the printer, at which time the front entry in the blocked queue for printer (B in this case) would be moved to the ready queue.

In practice, the addition and removal of processes to and from these queues is controlled by special flags called **semaphores** which were originally described by Dijkstra[1]. A more thorough exposition on operating system queues and semaphores appears in Deitel's *Introduction to Operating Systems*[2].

---

[1]Dijkstra, E. W. 1965. *Cooperating Sequential Processes.* Eindhoven, Netherlands: Technological University. Reprinted in Genuys, F., ed. 1968. *Programming Languages.* New York: Academic Press.

[2]Deitel, H. M. 1984. *Introduction to Operating Systems.* Rev. 1st ed. Reading, MA: Addison-Wesley.

Priority Queues

So far we have used a batch scheduling application as an example of how a queue might be used in an operating system. Typically, such batch scheduling might also give higher priorities to certain types of jobs. For instance, at a university computer center, students in introductory computer science courses may receive the highest priority for their jobs to encourage a quick turnaround. Students in upper division courses may have the next highest priority, whereas jobs related to faculty research, which require a great deal of computation, get the lowest possible priority. These types of jobs could be called A, B, and C respectively. Any A job is serviced before any B or C job, regardless of the time it enters the service queue. Similarly, any B job is serviced before any C job. A data structure capable of representing such a queue would require just one FRONT pointer but three rear pointers—one each for A, B, and C.

A queue with 8 jobs waiting to be serviced might appear as shown in Figure 4-14, which tells us that STATS, PRINT, and BANK are the A jobs awaiting service; COPY and CHECK the B jobs, and UPDATE, AVERAG, and TEST the C jobs. If a new A job PROB1 were to arrive for service, it would be inserted at the end of the A queue, between BANK and COPY. Because jobs can be serviced only by leaving the front of the queue, PROB1 would be processed before any of the B or C jobs.

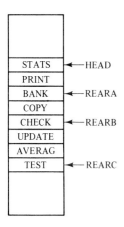

FIGURE 4-14   A priority queue with 8 jobs at 3 priority levels.

Because insertions in such a **priority queue** need not occur at the absolute rear of the queue, it is clear that an array implementation may require moving a substantial number of data when an item is inserted at the rear of one of the higher priorities. To avoid this, you can use a linked list to great advantage when implementing a priority queue. If a dummy header is included at the beginning of the list, the empty conditions for any given priority are:

```
     HEAD = REAR1 ----------> For priority 1, that is, the
                                  highest priority
     REAR1 = REAR2 ---------> For priority 2
     REAR(n-1) = REARn -----> For priority n
```

The specifics of writing procedures to add to a given priority or re-move from a priority queue are included as exercises at the end of the chapter.

4-3   Stacks

An Application in Compiler Design

Compilers for all languages allow for some sort of **subroutine call**. Of key importance to any subroutine structure is that the return from a subroutine must be to the instruction immediately following the call that originally transferred control to the subroutine. For example, in the partial coding:

```
    PROGRAM CALL DEMO;
            .
            .
            .
  ┌─ PROCEDURE SUB3;
  │         .
  │         .
  │         .
  └─ END; {SUB3}
  ┌─ PROCEDURE SUB2;
  │         .
  │         .
  │         .
  │     SUB3; {CALL SUB3}
  │     P:=P-Q;
  │         .
  │         .
  │         .
  └─ END; {SUB2}
  ┌─ PROCEDURE SUB1;
  │         .
  │         .
  │         .
  │     SUB2; {CALL SUB2}
  │     A:=A+B;
  │         .
  │         .
  │         .
  └─ END; {SUB1}
```

```
BEGIN {MAIN}
    .
    .
    .
SUB1; {CALL SUB1}
WRITELN(Q);
    .
    .
    .
END. {MAIN}
```

the order of operation would be:

1. Leave MAIN and transfer to SUB1
2. Leave SUB1 and transfer to SUB2
3. Leave SUB2 and transfer to SUB3
4. Return from SUB3 to the instruction P : = P—Q in SUB2
5. Return from SUB2 to the instruction A : = A+B in SUB1
6. Return from SUB1 to the instruction WRITELN(Q) in MAIN
7. End of MAIN

Each time a call is made, the machine must remember where to return when that procedure is completed. (For those of you who have programmed in micro assembler, the numerous PUSH operations given in this type of language are precisely implementations of a stack structure.)

A structure capable of storing the data necessary to handle calls and returns in this sequence would be a **memory stack.** In such a stack, items can enter and leave *only* at one end of the stack—the *top.* Hence the preceding partial coding would generate a stack that develops as illustrated in Figure 4-15. Each time a call to a procedure is made, a return address is placed, or *pushed,* on top of the stack. Each time a procedure is completed, the top item on the stack is *popped* to determine the memory address to which the return operation should be made. The nature of the leave-return sequence for procedures makes it crucial that the first return address accessed be the last one that was remembered by the computer. Because there is only one point, the *top,* at which data may enter or exit a stack, it is the ideal data structure to be used for this *last stored/first recalled* type of operation.

This description of the method by which a compiler actually implements procedure calls is just one illustration of the utility of stacks. We shall return in Chapter 5 to a more difficult type of procedure usage called **recursion,** and we will examine in detail the role of the stack in handling such a **recursive call.** Now, however, we will consider two ways of implementing a stack.

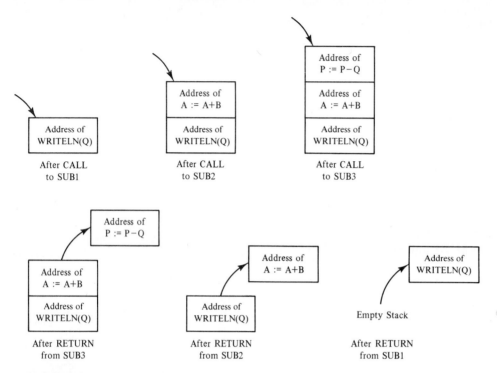

FIGURE 4-15 *Development of a memory stack generated by partial coding shown in text.*

Array Implementation of a Stack

A strategy similar to that used for an array implementation of a queue can be followed. However, because insertions and deletions occur at the same end of a stack, only one pointer will be needed, instead of the two required for a queue. We will call that pointer TOP and use Figure 4-16 to trace it through out previous subroutine example.

Thus, to push an entry in ITEM onto the stack, the two operations

```
TOP := TOP + 1;
STACK[TOP] := ITEM;
```

must occur. Popping an entry from the stack into ITEM requires:

```
ITEM := STACK[top];
TOP := TOP -1;
```

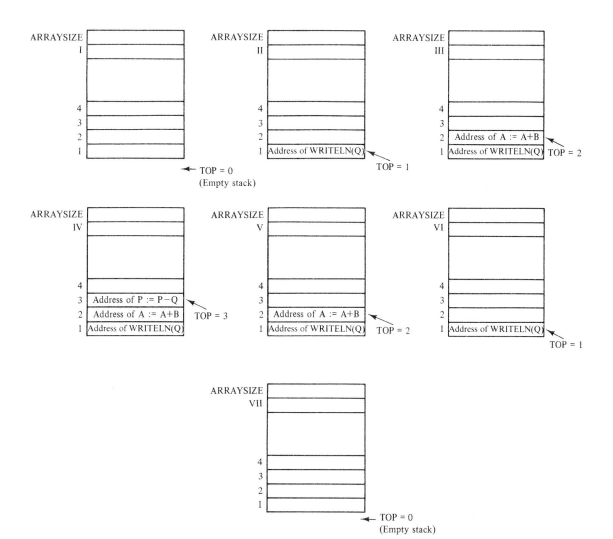

FIGURE 4-16 The development of an array implementation of a stack generated by the partial coding in the text.

Complete procedures that take into account the boundary conditions of a full and empty stack follow:

```
{ Global Declarations }

CONST
  ARRAYSIZE = 100;

TYPE
  STACKTYPE = ARRAY [1..ARRAYSIZE} OF INTEGER;
```

```
PROCEDURE PUSH(VAR ITEM, TOP: INTEGER;
               VAR STACK: STACKTYPE;
               VAR FULL: BOOLEAN);
```

{ Push ITEM onto STACK. FULL is a flag indicating whether or not there
  is room on STACK to perform this operation.   }

  { For this procedure, we are assuming the STACK contains integer data
    with room for ARRAYSIZE entries.   }

```
  BEGIN
    IF TOP = ARRAYSIZE THEN
      FULL := TRUE
    ELSE ──────────────────────────►
      BEGIN
      FULL := FALSE;
      TOP := TOP + 1
      STACK[TOP] := ITEM;
      END;
  END;
```
{ End PUSH }

{ Global Declarations }
```
CONST
  ARRAYSIZE = 100;

TYPE
 STACKTYPE = ARRAY [1..ARRAYSIZE] OF INTEGER;

PROCEDURE POP(VAR ITEM, TOP: INTEGER;
             VAR STACK: STACKTYPE;
             VAR EMPTY: BOOLEAN);
```

{ Pop top element in STACK into ITEM. EMPTY is a flag to
  indicate whether or not the operation is successful. }

```
  BEGIN
    IF TOP = 0 THEN
      EMPTY := TRUE
    ELSE ──────────────────────────►
      BEGIN
      EMPTY := FALSE;
      ITEM := STACK[TOP];
      TOP := TOP - 1;
      END;
  END;
```
{ End POP }

Linked List Implementation of a Stack

When we choose a linked list implementation, we are trading a relatively small amount of memory space needed to maintain pointers for the dynamic allocation of stack space. Following our usual convention of maintaining a dummy header node at the beginning of a linked list, a stack with the 3 entries 18, 40, 31 would appear as shown in Figure 4-17.

The condition to test for an empty stack would then be TOP = HEAD. A full stack occurs only when Pascal's NEW procedure reports that there is no available space. Full procedures to push and pop the stack now become nothing more than insertions and deletions from the beginning of a linked list. As such, they are special cases of the procedures already developed in Chapter 2, and you will write them as exercises at the end of the chapter.

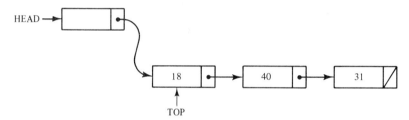

FIGURE 4-17   A linked list implementation of a stack with 3 data nodes and a dummy header.

Program Design Considerations

The Pascal program given next reads and writes a palindrome. A palindrome is a string of characters which reads the same backward and forward. For example "MOM" and "12321" are palindromes.

The design of this program uses two procedures. The procedure STACKC uses a stack to push a character read off the keyboard onto the stack. The procedure UNSTACKC pops a character off the top of the stack. Both the procedures use a pointer TOPC to point to the top of the stack which has been implemented via a linked list.

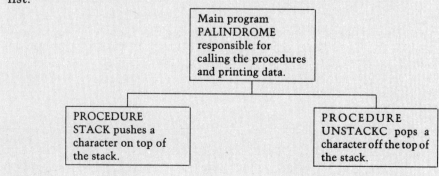

```
PROGRAM PALINDROME(INPUT,OUTPUT);
TYPE
   PTRC = ^CHSTACH;
   CHSTACK = RECORD
                CH : CHAR;
                NEXT : PTRC
             END;

VAR
   TOPC : PTRC;
      Y : CHAR;
      I : INTEGER;
      PROCEDURE STACKC(VAR X : CHAR);

      VAR
         P : PTRC;
         BEGIN
           { Call built-in procedure NEW }
           NEW(P);
           P^.CH :=X;
           P^.NEXT :=TOPC;
           TOPC :=P
         END { STACKC };
   PROCEDURE UNSTACKC(VAR X : CHAR);
   VAR
      P : PTRC;
      BEGIN
         P :=TOPC
         X :=TOPC^.CH;
         TOPC :=TOPC^.NEXT;
       { Call built-in procedure DISPOSE  }
         DISPOSE(P)
      END  { UNSTACKC };
BEGIN  { MAIN  }
      WRITELN(' Enter palindrome string ');
      WHILE NOT EOLN DO
       BEGIN
            READ(Y);
            STACKC(Y)
       END  { WHILE  };
    {  Unstack the stack  }
      WRITELN(' POPPED STACK IN REVERSE ORDER');
      WRITELN;
      WHILE TOPC <> NIL DO
       BEGIN
          UNSTACKC(Y);
          WRITE (Y);
       END
  END.
```

SUMMARY

A queue is a first-in-first-out (FIFO) data structure used in processing of data such as job scheduling in a large university computer system. There are two basic pointers, FRONT and REAR, associated with this structure. New data items to be processed are added to the rear of the queue, and the data item that is about to be processed is removed from the front of the queue. The process of cars entering and leaving a car wash is a familiar analogy.

A stack is a last-in-first-out (LIFO) data structure. There is only one pointer, TOP, associated with a stack. Implementation of subroutines and functions in many high-level languages is accomplished via stack structures. In a football game, when many players pile up on top of the ball carrier, the order in which they untangle themselves from the pile is typical of the way data items are processed in a stack.

KEY TERMS

Queue	REAR
FIFO	FRONT
LIFO	MOD
Stack	Priority queue
Pop	TOP
Push	

EXERCISES

Using any appropriate programming language:
1. Develop a calling convention and associated procedure to remove an item from a queue with n priorities.
2. Develop a calling convention and associated procedure to add an item to a queue with n priorities.
3. Develop a calling convention and associated procedure to push an item onto a stack implemented with a linked list.
4. Develop a calling convention and associated procedure to pop an item from a stack implemented with a linked list.
5. Given the discussion of circular queues presented in this chapter, determine a valid initial setting for the FRONT and REAR pointers in a circular queue.
6. Develop a calling convention and associated procedure to add an item to a circular queue.
7. Develop a calling convention and associated procedure to remove an item from a circular queue.
8. Why is a priority queue called by this name?
9. In the array implementation of a circular queue, what are the conditions to be satisfied by the pointers REAR and FRONT for a full queue, an empty queue, and a one-entry queue?

PROGRAMMING PROBLEMS

1. The Wing-and-a-Prayer Airlines Company is becoming increasingly concerned about the amount of fuel being wasted as its planes wait to land at and take off from world-famous O'Hair Airport. Write a program to simulate the operation of one day's activity at O'Hair and report on the times spent waiting to land and take off by each Wing-and-a-Prayer flight. Input data to your program should include:

   - Average number of Wing-and-a-Prayer arrivals each hour
   - Average number of other airline arrivals each hour
   - Average number of Wing-and-a-Prayer departures each hour
   - Average number of other airline departures each hour
   - Number of available runways
   - Average time runway is in use for an arrival
   - Average time runway is in use for a departure

   Your program should maintain two queues—one for arrivals waiting for a runway and one for departures waiting for a runway.

2. In order to improve their services, the Fly-By-Night credit card company decided to give incentives to their customers for prompt payment. The company decided that customers who pay their bills two weeks before the due date would receive top priority and 5% discount. Customers who pay their bills within one week of due date would receive next priority and 1% discount. Third priority would be given to customers who pay their bills on or within two days after the due date. The customers who pay their bills thereafter would be assigned the lowest priority. Write a program in a high level language to set up a priority queue to process customer records accordingly.

3. The Bay Area Brawlers professional football team has been so successful in recent weeks that team management is considering the addition of several new ticket windows at the team's stadium. However, before investing a sizable amount of money in such an improvement, they would like to simulate the operation of ticket sales with a variety of ticket window configurations. Develop a computer program which allows input of such data as number of ticket windows, average number of fans arriving each hour as game time approaches, and average length of time to process a ticket sale. Output from your program should include statistics such as the average waiting line length each hour as game time approaches and the amount of time the average fan had to wait in line before having his or her ticket request processed. Use queues to represent each of the waiting lines.

4. Develop a program to simulate the processing of batch jobs by a computer system. The scheduling of these jobs should be handled via a queue (or priority queue for more of a challenge). Examples of commands that your program should be able to process are:

```
ADD (to add entry to queue)
DELETE (to take an item out of the queue)
STATUS (to report on items currently in queue)
```

5. Develop a program to simulate the arrival of customers in a waiting line at a bank. Factors to consider in such a program would be the average time it takes to service one customer, the average number of customers that arrive in a given time period, and the number of service windows maintained by the bank. Statistics such as the length of time the average customer has to spend in the waiting line could be very helpful in the bank's future planning.

6. Develop procedures to maintain a stack in the form of a linked list. Then design a complete program to test these procedures by handling PUSH, POP, and STATUS instructions in the manner of problem 2 above.

7. Here is a problem typically encountered in text processing/formatting applications. Given a file of text, that text delimited by special bracketing symbols [and] is to be considered a footnote. Footnotes, when encountered, are not to be printed as normal text but are instead stored in a footnote queue. Then, when the special symbol # is encountered, all footnotes currently in the queue are printed and the queue should be returned to an empty state. This problem also will allow you to make good use of string storage techniques!

5

Applications of Stacks

"It is hard to think at the top."

STRINGFELLOW BARR

5-1 Introductory Considerations

Often the logic of problems for which stacks are a suitable data structure involves the necessity to **backtrack,** to return to a previous state. For instance, consider the problem of finding your way out of a maze. One approach to take would be to probe a given path in the maze as deeply as possible. Upon finding a dead end, you would need to backtrack to previously visited maze locations in order to try probing other paths. Such backtracking would require recalling these previous locations in the reverse order from which you visited them. Not many of us need to find our way out of a maze. However, the designers of compilers are faced with an analogous backtracking situation in the evaluation of arithmetic expressions. As you scan the expression A * B/C + D in left-to-right order, it is impossible to tell upon initially encountering the asterisk whether or not you should apply the indicated multiplication operation to A and the immediately following operand. Instead, you must probe further into the expression to determine whether an operation with a higher priority occurs. While you undertake this probing of the expression, you must stack previously encountered operation symbols until you are certain when they can be applied.

5-2 Parsing and Evaluation of Arithmetic Expressions Using Stacks

Compounding the backtracking problem just described, there are often many different ways of representing the same algebraic expression. For example, the assignment statements

```
Z := A * B/C + D
Z := (A * B)/C + D
Z := ((A * B)/C) + D
```

should all result in the same order of arithmetic operations even though the expressions involved are written in distinctly different form. The process of collapsing such different expressions into one unique form is called **parsing** the expression, and one frequently used method of parsing relies heavily upon stacks.

Postfix, Prefix, and Infix Notation

Usual algebraic notation is often termed **infix** notation: the arithmetic operator appears between the two operands to which it is being applied. Infix notation may require parentheses to specify a desired order of operations. For example, in the expression A/B + C, the division will occur first. If we want the addition to occur first, the expression must be parenthesized as A/(B + C).

Using **postfix*** notation, the need for parentheses is eliminated because the operator is placed directly after the two operands to which it applies. Hence, A/B + C would be written AB/C + in postfix form. This says:

1. Apply the division operator to A and B
2. To that result, add C

The infix expression A/(B + C) would be written as ABC+/ in postfix notation. Reading this postfix expression from left to right, we are told to:

1. Apply the addition operator to B and C
2. Then divide that result into A

Although relatively short expressions such as the ones in the preceding paragraphs can be converted from infix to postfix via an intuitive process, a more systematic method is required for complicated expressions. We propose the following algorithm for humans (and will soon consider a different one for computers):

---

* Also called reverse Polish notation after the nationality of its originator, the Polish logician Jan Lukasiewicz.

1. *Completely* parenthesize the infix expression to specify the order of all operations
2. Move each operator to the space held by its corresponding right parenthesis
3. Remove all parentheses

Consider this three-step method as it applies to the expression:

```
A/B^C + D*E - A*C
```

Completely parenthesizing this expression yields:

```
(((A/(B^C)) + (D*E)) - (A*C))
```

Moving each operator to its corresponding right parenthesis, we obtain:

```
(((A  (B C))  (D E))  (A C))
```

Removing all parentheses, we are left with:

```
ABC^/DE*+AC*-
```

Had we started out with:

```
A / B^C - (D*E - A*C)
```

our three-step procedure would have resulted in:

```
((A  (B C))  ((D E)  (A C)))
```

Removing the parentheses would then yield:

```
ABC-/DE*AC*--
```

In a similar way an expression can be converted into **prefix** form, in which an operator immediately precedes its two operands. The conversion algorithm for infix to prefix specifies that, after completely parenthesizing the infix expression with order of priority in mind, we move each operator to its corresponding left parenthesis. Applying the method to

```
A/B^C + D*E - A*C
```

gives us

$$((A/(B^C)) + ((D*E) - (A*C)))$$

and finally the prefix form

```
+/A^BC-*DE*AC
```

The importance of postfix and prefix notations in parsing arithmetic expressions is that these notations are completely free of parentheses. Consequently, an expression in postfix (or prefix) form is in *unique form*. In the design of compilers, this parsing of an expression into postfix form is crucial because having a unique form for an expression greatly simplifies its eventual evaluation. Thus, in handling an assignment statement, a compiler must:

1. Parse it into postfix form
2. Apply an evaluation algorithm to the postfix form

We shall limit our discussion here to postfix notation. The techniques we will cover are easily adaptable to the functionally equivalent prefix form.

Converting Infix Expressions to Postfix

First consider the problem of parsing an expression from infix to postfix form. Our three-step procedure is not easily adaptable to machine coding. Instead, we will use an algorithm that has as its essential data structures:

1. A stream of characters containing the infix expression

2. A stack OPSTACK which may contain

   ■ Arithmetic operators: '+', '−', '*', and '/'
   ■ Parentheses: '(' and ')'
   ■ A special delimiter: '#'

3. A string POSTFIX containing the final postfix expression

To eliminate details that would only clutter the main logic of the algorithm, we will assume that the string representing the infix expression contains only arithmetic operators, parentheses, the delimiting character '#', and operands that consist of a single character each. We will also omit consideration of the exponentiation operator '^', which will be covered in a later exercise. Thus, our algorithm will convert infix expressions of the form:

```
A * B + (C-D/E)#
```

into postfix notation.

The description of the algorithm is as follows:

    1. Define a function INFIXPRIORITY, which takes an operator, parenthesis, or # as its argument and returns an integer as:

Character	*	/	+	−	(	)	#
Returned value	2	2	1	1	3	0	0

    2. Define another function STACKPRIORITY, which takes the same possibilities for an argument and returns an integer as:

Character	*	/	+	−	(	)	#
Returned value	2	2	1	1	0	unde-fined	0

    3. Push # onto OPSTACK as its first entry
    4. Read the next character CH from the infix expression.
    5. Test CH and:

- If CH is an operand, append it to the POSTFIX string.
- If CH is a right parenthesis, then pop entries from stack and append them to POSTFIX until a left parenthesis is popped. Discard both left and right parentheses.
- If CH is a #, pop all entries that remain on the stack and append them to POSTFIX string.
- Otherwise, pop from the stack and append to POSTFIX string operators whose STACKPRIORITY is greater than or equal to the INFIXPRIORITY of CH. Then stack CH.

    6. Repeat steps (4) and (5) until CH is the delimiter #.

The key to the algorithm is the use of the stack to hold operators from the infix expression that appear to the left of another given operator even though that latter operator must be applied first. The defined functions INFIXPRIORITY and STACKPRIORITY are used to specify this priority of operators and the associated pushing and popping operations. The entire process is best understood by carefully tracing through an example, as shown in Figure 5-1.

The Pascal procedure for implementing the algorithm follows. Although we have chosen to represent the stack as an array, this is not crucial in the abstract sense. All that is important is a logical stack. The procedure would require only minor modifications if an alternate stack representation were used.

CH	OPSTACK	POSTFIX	Commentary
			Push #
A			Read CH
		A	Append CH to POSTFIX
*			Read CH
	* #		Stack CH
B			Read CH
		AB	Append CH to POSTFIX
+			Read CH
	+ #	AB*	Pop *, append * to POSTFIX, push CH
(			Read CH
	(+ #		Push CH
C			Read CH
		AB*C	Append CH to POSTFIX
−			Read CH
	− (+ #		Push CH
D			Read CH
		AB*CD	Append CH to POSTFIX
/			Read CH
	/ − (+ #		Push CH
E			Read CH
		AB*CDE	Append CH to POSTFIX
)			Read CH
	+ #	AB*CDE/−	Pop and append to POSTFIX until (reached
#			Read CH
		AB*CDE/−+#	Pop and append rest of stack to CH

FIGURE 5-1 Translation of the infix expression A * B + (C - D/E)# using the algorithm in the text.

```
{ Global Declarations }

CONST
  STACKSIZE = 100;

TYPE
  PSTRING = PACKED ARRAY [1..80] OF CHAR;
  STACKARRAY = PACKED ARRAY [1..STACKSIZE] OF CHAR;

PROCEDURE INTOPOST(VAR OPSTACK: STACKARRAY;
                   VAR TOP: INTEGER;
                   VAR POSTFIX: PSTRING);

  { Convert an infix expression into a POSTFIX string.
    An array implementation of OPSTACK is assumed, with PUSH and
    POP procedures as described in Chapter 4. }

  { Local Variables }

  VAR
    ITEM, CH: CHAR;
    EMPTY, FULL: BOOLEAN;

  BEGIN
    PUSH('#', OPSTACK, TOP, FULL);
    REPEAT
      READ(CH);
      IF ('A' <= CH) AND (CH <= 'Z') THEN

      { Single character operand }

        CONCATENATE(POSTFIX, CH)
      ELSE IF CH = ')' THEN
        BEGIN
        POP(ITEM, OPSTACK, TOP, EMPTY);
        WHILE ITEM <> '(' DO
          BEGIN

          CONCATENATE(POSTFIX, ITEM);
          POP(ITEM, OPSTACK, TOP, EMPTY)
          END
        END
      ELSE IF CH = '#' THEN
        BEGIN
        POP(ITEM, OPSTACK, TOP, EMPTY);
        WHILE NOT EMPTY DO
          BEGIN
          CONCATENATE(POSTFIX, ITEM);
          POP(ITEM, OPSTACK, TOP, EMPTY)
          END
        END
```

In this case, transfer CH directly to POSTFIX

In this case, pop stack until encounter matching left parenthesis

In this case, pop rest of stack to POSTFIX

```
    ELSE { Operator +, -, *, / }
      BEGIN
      POP(ITEM, OPSTACK, TOP, EMPTY);
      WHILE STACKPRIORITY(ITEM) >= INFIXPRIORITY(CH) DO
        BEGIN
        CONCATENATE(POSTFIX, ITEM);
        POP(ITEM, OPSTACK, TOP, FULL)
        END;
      PUSH(ITEM, OPSTACK, TOP, FULL);
      PUSH(CH, OPSTACK, TOP, FULL)
      END
  UNTIL CH = '#'
END;
{ End INTOPOST }
```

In this case, pop stack until encounter item of lower priority (+). Then stack incoming CH.

Evaluating Postfix Expressions

Once an expression has been parsed into postfix form, another stack plays an essential role in its final evaluation. As an example, consider the postfix expression from Figure 5-1.

```
AB*CDE/-+*
```

Let us suppose that the symbols A, B, C, D, and E had associated with them the values:

Symbol	Value
A	5
B	3
C	6
D	8
E	2

To evaluate such an expression, we repeatedly read characters from the postfix expression. If the character read is an operand, push the value associated with it onto the stack. If it is an operator, pop two values from the stack, apply the operator to them, and push the result back onto the stack. The technique is illustrated for our current example in Figure 5-2.

Assuming functions VALUE, which will return the value associated with a particular symbol, and EVAL, which will return the result of applying an operator to two values, the Pascal procedure to evaluate a postfix expression is given by:

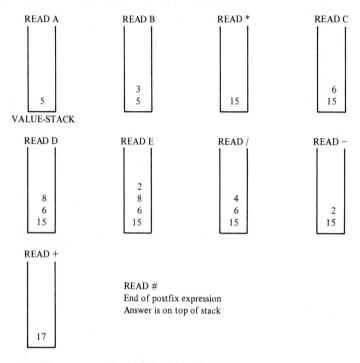

FIGURE 5-2 Evaluation of AB*CDE/-+#

```
{ GLOBAL DECLARATIONS }

CONST
  STACKSIZE = 100;

TYPE
  STACKTYPE = ARRAY [1..STACKSIZE] OF REAL;

  {---------------------------------------------------------------}

PROCEDURE EVALUATEPOSTFIX(VAR ANSWER: REAL;
                          VAR VALUESTACK: STACKTYPE;
                          VAR TOP: INTEGER);

{ Procedure to evaluate a postfix expression and return the
  result in ANSWER }

 { An array implementation of the VALUESTACK is assumed }

 { Local Variables }

  VAR
    CH: CHAR;
    V, V1, V2: REAL;
    EMPTY, FULL: BOOLEAN;
```

```
  BEGIN
    READ(CH);
    WHILE CH <> '#' DO
      BEGIN
      IF ('A' <= CH) AND (CH <= 'Z') THEN { Operand }
        BEGIN
        V := VALUE(CH);
        PUSH(V, VALUESTACK, TOP, FULL)
        END
      ELSE
        BEGIN
        POP(V2, VALUESTACK, TOP, EMPTY);
        POP(V1, VALUESTACK, TOP, EMPTY);
        V := EVAL(V1, V2, CH);
        PUSH(V, VALUESTACK, TOP, FULL)
        END;
      READ(CH)
      END;
    POP(ANSWER, VALUESTACK, TOP, EMPTY)
  END;
{ End EVALUATE POSTFIX }
```

5-3   Recursion

In section 4-3, we indicated that stacks are an essential data structure in a compiler's implementation of procedure calls. Many compilers, however, will not allow a procedure to call itself—a **recursive** call. In this section, we shall explore recursion in several ways. First, we will see that recursion can be a very powerful and compact way of describing certain complex algorithms. Hence, we will first view recursion as a technique for algorithm description. We shall then discuss how recursive algorithms may be implemented in a specific computer language. In Pascal, a relatively direct transcription of the recursively described algorithm into the computer language is possible because Pascal allows recursive calls.

We shall also discuss in detail the role of the stack in supporting such recursive calls. A thorough understanding of how recursion uses stack operations will allow us to describe a technique for non-recursive implementation of algorithms which are initially described in recursive fashion. This technique essentially requires the programmer to maintain a stack that would otherwise be maintained by system software. Why would we ever want to eliminate recursive calls in this fashion? There is a twofold answer to this question. First, it gives us a general method of implementing recursively-described algorithms in languages such as FORTRAN, COBOL, and BASIC, which do not allow recursion. Second, we shall see that by maintaining a stack ourselves instead of letting the system do it for us, we can often develop a more efficient implementation of a given recursive algorithm.

Evaluating Factorial Expressions

To introduce the notion of recursion, let us consider the problem of computing **N factorial**, denoted N!, and defined by

```
N! = N x (N-1) x (N-2) x . . . x 2 x 1
```

That is, N! is the product of the first N integers. We note that an alternate way of defining N! is by means of using (N−1)!

$$N! = \begin{cases} 1 \text{ if } N = 1 \\ N \text{ x } (N-1)! \text{ otherwise} \end{cases}$$

Such a definition is termed a **recursive** definition since it refers to the concept being defined within the definition itself. Such a recursive definition may seem to violate a principle learned early in any English composition course—avoid circularity in defining terms. However, recursion is not truly circular because it leaves us a way of eventually resolving the problem of factorial being defined in terms of factorial. In the definition above, this "recursive out" occurs in the definition of 1!

To see how recursion works, think of the preceding definition as a series of clues which eventually will allow us to unravel the mystery of how to compute N!. That is, to compute N!, the recursive definition really tells us to:

1. Remember what N is
2. Go compute (N−1)!
3. Once we've computed (N−1)!, multiply that by N to get our final answer

Of course, when we use the definition to determine how to compute (N−1)!, we find out that we must, in turn, compute (N−2)!. Computing (N−2)! will involve finding (N−3)!. This downward spiral will eventually end with 1!, allowing us to begin the actual series of multiplications that will bring us to the appropriate answer. Figure 5-3 illustrates the logic of the recursive method for computing N factorial.

In particular, if N were 4, the sequence of recursive invocations of the definition and resulting computations would be as shown in Figure 5-4.

Algorithms which are recursively defined may be easily programmed in a language such as Pascal, which allows a procedure or function to call itself. For example, the Pascal program given below calls a function FACTORIAL to compute the value of 4!. The WRITELN statements upon entry to and exit from the function are not necessary but have been included to demonstrate the precise call and return sequence triggered by the initial call of FACTORIAL(4) in the main program.

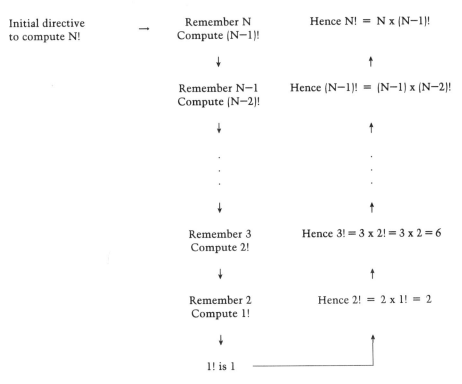

FIGURE 5-3   Recursive computation of N!

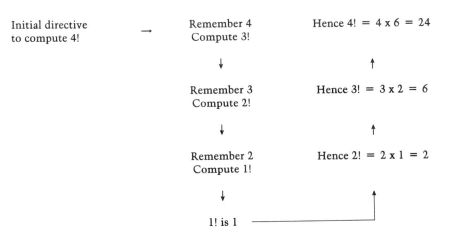

FIGURE 5-4   Recursive computation of 4!

```
PROGRAM RECURSIVEDEMO(INPUT, OUTPUT);

 { ILLUSTRATE HOW RECURSION MAY BE USED TO COMPUTE FACTORIAL }

 VAR
   M: INTEGER;

 FUNCTION FACTORIAL(N: INTEGER): INTEGER;

   BEGIN
    WRITELN('ENTERING FACTORIAL WITH N = ', N);
    IF N = 1 THEN
      FACTORIAL := 1
    ELSE
      FACTORIAL := N * { RETURN POINT 2 } FACTORIAL(N-1);
    WRITELN('LEAVING FACTORIAL WITH N = ', N)
    END; { FACTORIAL }

  BEGIN {MAIN}
    WRITE('ENTER NUMBER FOR FACTORIAL COMPUTATION-->');
    READLN(M);
    WRITELN(FACTORIAL(M)) { RETURN POINT 1 }
  END.
```

Sample run:

```
ENTER NUMBER FOR FACTORIAL COMPUTATION-->4
ENTERING FACTORIAL WITH N =          4
ENTERING FACTORIAL WITH N =          3
ENTERING FACTORIAL WITH N =          2
ENTERING FACTORIAL WITH N =          1
LEAVING FACTORIAL WITH N =          1
LEAVING FACTORIAL WITH N =          2
LEAVING FACTORIAL WITH N =          3
LEAVING FACTORIAL WITH N =          4
      24
```

The comments { RETURN POINT 1 } and { RETURN POINT 2 } have been inserted into the preceding code to allow us to see the role played by a stack as this program is run. We have already alluded to the existence of a general system stack onto which return addresses are pushed each time a function or procedure call is made. Let us now explain it more fully. Each time a procedure/function call is made, an item called a **stack frame** will be pushed onto the system stack. The data in this stack frame consist of the return address and a copy of each local variable and parameter for the procedure/function. Figure 5-5 illustrates how stack frames are pushed and popped from the system when FACTORIAL(4) is invoked. Return addresses have been indicated by referring to the appropriate comments in the Pascal code.

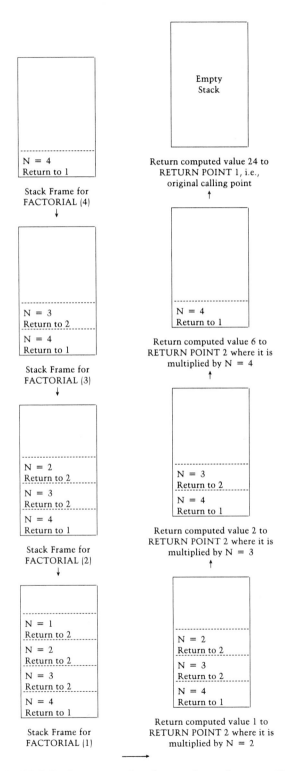

FIGURE 5-5 Sequence of pushes and pops in computing 4!

In the preceding factorial example, the type of recursion illustrated is known as *tail recursion*. In tail recursion, once an initial return operation is made, an uninterrupted series of returns are triggered. This series continues until it reaches the original calling point. Many times algorithms which use tail recursion may be implemented in a fashion which is just as easy (and does not consume system stack space) by using an ordinary loop structure. The astute reader will no doubt already have realized how to do this for our factorial example. The value of recursion, as we shall see, is that it represents a "natural" way of expressing the solution to certain types of problems. Moreover, as the problems which we solve by recursive algorithms become more complex, we shall see that tail recursion is often replaced by a more involved form of recursion which requires a much more complicated pattern of pushing and popping procedure/function frames from the system stack.

Towers of Hanoi Problem

We introduce this more complex type of recursion with a problem that, although impractical, is excellent for illustrating the technique involved. According to legend, there existed in ancient Hanoi a monastery where the monks had the painstaking task of moving a collection of N stone disks from one pillar, designated as pillar A, to another, designated as pillar C. Moreover, the relative ordering of the disks on pillar A had to be maintained as they were moved to pillar C. That is, as illustrated in Figure 5-6, the disks were to be stacked from largest to smallest, beginning from the bottom. Additionally, the monks were to observe the following rules in moving disks:

- Only one disk could be moved at a time
- No larger disk could ever be placed on a pillar on top of a smaller disk
- A third pillar B could be used as an intermediate to store one or more disks while they were being moved from their original source A to their destination C

Consider the following recursive solution to this problem.

1. If N = 1, merely move the disk from A to C.
2. If N = 2, move first disk from A to B. Then move second disk from A to C. Then move first disk from B to C.
3. If N = 3, call upon the technique already established in (2) to move the first two disks from A to B using C as an intermediate. Then move the third disk from A to C. Then use the technique in (2) to move the first two disks from B to C using A as an intermediate.

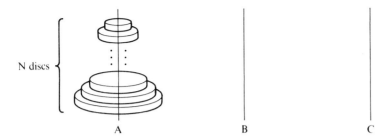

FIGURE 5-6   Towers of Hanoi problem. The monks must move N disks in order from pillar A to pillar C.

N. For general N, use the technique in the previous step to move N-1 disks from A to B using C as an intermediate. Then move one disk from A to C. Then use the technique in the previous step to move N-1 disks from B to C using A as an intermediate.

Notice that the technique described here calls upon itself but switches the order of parameters in so doing. This can be formalized in the following Pascal procedure. The labels which appear in the procedure are included for the discussion which follows.

```
PROCEDURE HANOI(N: INTEGER;
               SOURCE, INTERMEDIATE, DESTINATION: CHAR);

  LABEL
    1;

  LABEL
    2;

  BEGIN
    IF N = 1 THEN
      WRITE('MOVE DISK FROM ', SOURCE, 'TO ', DESTINATION)
    ELSE
      BEGIN
      HANOI(N - 1, SOURCE, INTERMEDIATE, DESTINATION);
```

The first recursive call transfers N − 1 discs from SOURCE to INTERMEDIATE using DESTINATION

SOURCE   INTERMEDIATE   DESTINATION

```
{ In every recursive call HANOI works with value of N less one }

1:
    WRITE('MOVE DISK FROM ', SOURCE, 'TO ', DESTINATION);
    HANOI(N - 1, INTERMEDIATE, DESTINATION, SOURCE)
    END;
2:
END;
{ End HANOI }
```

N - 1

SOURCE   INTERMEDIATE   DESTINATION

Then transfer the single disc
from SOURCE to DESTINATION

SOURCE   INTERMEDIATE   DESTINATION

The second recursive call transfers
N − 1 discs from INTERMEDIATE
to DESTINATION using SOURCE

Because we have a CALL to HANOI within the procedure HANOI, this represents a recursive CALL. Although such a procedure is easy to write in Pascal, it is somewhat more difficult to *understand thoroughly!*

The key to understanding this procedure is to be aware of what a compiler must do when the recursive call is made. The difficulty with handling recursion is that, because we call a procedure from within that procedure, eventually a return will be made to that same procedure. However, because the call also involves changing the values of the procedure's parameters, the old values of the parameters will have been destroyed upon return *unless they were preserved before the recursive call.* The best way of preserving them is to stack them with the return address. Thus, a recursive call involves stacking not only a return address but also the values of all parameters essential to the current state of the procedure. To illustrate, we will trace through the actions taken when a call of the form

```
HANOI (3, 'A', 'C', 'B')
```

is initiated. The values in the return address stack are the statement labels in our HANOI procedure.

1. N is not 1, so the condition in the IF statement is false.
2. HANOI (N-1, SOURCE, INTERMEDIATE, DESTINATION) is encountered with A, B, and C as first, second, and third arguments. Because this represents a recursive call, some stacking must be done:

1	3	A	C	B

Return   N   Source   Destination   Intermediate
Address   Parameters

Stack Frame(s)

3. Re-enter HANOI. Notice that as we enter this time, the procedure's view of the parameters is N = 2, SOURCE = A, DESTINATION = B , and INTERMEDIATE = C. Because N is not 1, the condition in the IF statement is false.
4. HANOI (N-1, SOURCE, INTERMEDIATE, DESTINATION) is encountered. Because this is a recursive call, stacking occurs:

1	2	A	B	C
1	3	A	C	B

Return   N   Source   Destination   Intermediate
Address   Parameters

Stack Frame(s)

5. We re-enter HANOI with N = 1, SOURCE = A, DESTINATION = C, and INTERMEDIATE = B. Because N = 1, the condition in the IF statement is true.

6. Hence

```
MOVE DISK FROM A TO C
```

is printed and a RETURN triggers a popping of a return address (1) and four parameters (N = 2, SOURCE = A, DESTINATION = B, and INTERMEDIATE = C).

1	3	A	C	B
Return Address	N	Source	Destination	Intermediate
		Parameters		

Stack Frame(s)

7. Because the return address popped was 1:

    MOVE DISK FROM A TO B

    is printed out and

    HANOI (N-1,INTERMEDIATE,DESTINATION,SOURCE)

    is encountered with N = 2, SOURCE = A , DESTINATION = B , and INTERMEDIATE = C.
8. The call pushes a return address and four parameters onto the stacks.

2	2	A	B	C
1	3	A	C	B
Return Address	N	Source	Destination	Intermediate
		Parameters		

Stack Frame(s)

9. We re-enter HANOI, this time with N = 1, SOURCE = C, DESTINATION = B, INTERMEDIATE = A
10. Because N = 1, the IF statement generates the output:

    MOVE DISK FROM C TO B

    and a RETURN.

11. The RETURN pops values from both stacks and we return to statement 2 with N = 2, SOURCE = A, DESTINATION = B, INTERMEDIATE = C.
12. But statement 2 triggers a RETURN itself, so both stacks are popped again and we return to statement 1 with N = 3, SOURCE = A, DESTINATION = C, INTERMEDIATE = B and both stacks temporarily empty.

13. Statement 1 triggers the output

MOVE DISK FROM A TO C

and we are immediately at another call:

HANOI (N-1, INTERMEDIATE, DESTINATION, SOURCE)

Hence the temporary empty status of the stacks is changed to

2	3	A	C	B
Return Address	N	Source	Destination	Intermediate
			Parameters	

Stack Frame(s)

14. We re-enter HANOI with N = 2, SOURCE = B, DESTINA-TION = C, INTERMEDIATE = A. Because N is not 1, another CALL is executed and more values are stacked:

1	2	B	C	A
2	3	A	C	B
Return Address	N	Source	Destination	Intermediate
			Parameters	

Stack Frame(s)

15. Re-enter HANOI with N = 1, SOURCE = B, DESTINA-TION = A, INTERMEDIATE = C. Because N = 1, we print:

MOVE DISK FROM B TO A

and RETURN.

16. The return prompts the popping of both stacks. The return address popped is statement 1 with parameters N = 2, SOURCE = B, DESTINATION = C, INTERMEDIATE = A. Statement 1 causes output

MOVE DISK FROM B TO C

with the stack frames left at

2	3	A	C	B
Return Address	N	Source	Destination	Intermediate
			Parameters	

Stack Frame(s)

17. The output from statement 1 is followed by

HANOI (N-1, INTERMEDIATE, DESTINATION, SOURCE)

so pushed onto the stack frames are:

2	2	B	C	A
2	3	A	C	B
Return Address	N	Source	Destination	Intermediate
			Parameters	

Stack Frame(s)

18. Re-enter (for the last time) HANOI with $N = 1$, SOURCE = A, DESTINATION = C, INTERMEDIATE = B. Because $N = 1$, output:

MOVE DISK FROM A TO C

and RETURN.

19. But now the RETURN pops return address 2 from the stack, so return to statement 2 with $N = 2$, SOURCE = B, DESTINATION = C, INTERMEDIATE = A

2	3	A	C	B
Return Address	N	Source	Destination	Intermediate
			Parameters	

Stack Frame(s)

20. Statement 2 is another RETURN, so pop the stacks again. Return address popped is 2, the same RETURN statement. But this time the RETURN will transfer control back to the original calling and WE ARE DONE!

Long-winded as this narrative is, it is *essential* that you understand it. Recursive procedures are crucial to many of the algorithms used in data structures, and you can acquire the necessary familiarity with recursion only by convincing yourself that it really works. If you have some doubts or are not sure you understand, we recommend that you trace through the HANOI procedure with N = 4 (be prepared to go through lots of paper!).

The key to writing recursive procedures is *always to leave a way out.* Suppose, for instance, that the IF statement were to be left out of our previous HANOI procedure. This would trigger an endless sequence of procedure calls never interrupted by a RETURN operation. The outcome is predictable—the program soon runs out of stack space. Such erroneous recursive calls are typically met with a "stack overflow" error message in languages which allow recursion.

Efficiency Considerations

We are still faced with a dilemma if we have an elegant recursive algorithm but a language in which system stack space is at a great premium or in which recursion is not supported at all. We will conclude this chapter by describing a systematic technique for implementing recursive algorithms in such situations. Essentially the technique involves:

- Substituting appropriate branching instructions for procedural call and return operations
- Using stack(s) to store return addresses and preserve necessary parameters prior to a recursive call
- Using assignment statements to simulate the passage of arguments that a procedural call would generate

To illustrate the method, we will use a non-recursive version of the HANOI algorithm in Pascal. We will assume the existence of 3 stacks—ISTACK, CSTACK, LSTACK—composed of integer, character, and label data respectively. Label data in this example turn out to be integer in type and hence could actually be pushed onto the integer data stack ISTACK. However, two separate stacks are used to emphasize the distinction between integers which are pure data and those representing return addresses. Each stack is further assumed to have its own top pointer—ITOP, CTOP and LTOP respectively.

```
{ Global Declarations }

CONST
  ARRAYSIZE = 100;

VAR { Stack space is maintained globally. }
  ISTACK, LSTACK: ARRAY [1..ARRAYSIZE] OF INTEGER;
  CSTACK: PACKED ARRAY [1..ARRAYSIZE] OF CHAR;
  ITOP, CTOP, LTOP, L: INTEGER;
  EMPTY, FULL: BOOLEAN;

  {--------------------------------------------------------------------}

PROCEDURE NONRECURSIVEHANOI(N: INTEGER;
                           SOURCE, INTERMEDIATE, DESTINATION: CHAR);

  LABEL

    1, { Corresponds to LABEL 1 in earlier recursive version }
    2, { Corresponds to LABEL 2 in earlier recursive version }
    3, { Corresponds to ENTRY point for simulated recursive call }
    10; { End of procedure, return to higher level calling procedure }

  VAR
    TEMP: CHAR;

  BEGIN
  3: { Entry }
    IF N = 1 THEN
      BEGIN
      WRITE('MOVE DISK FROM ', SOURCE, 'TO', DESTINATION);

      { Now simulate a RETURN operation }

      POP(N, ISTACK, ITOP, EMPTY);
      POP(INTERMEDIATE, CSTACK, CTOP, EMPTY);
      POP(DESTINATION, CSTACK, CTOP, EMPTY);
      POP(SOURCE, CSTACK, CTOP, EMPTY);
      POP(L, LSTACK, LTOP, EMPTY);
      IF EMPTY THEN
        GOTO 10 { RETURN to higher level calling procedure }
      ELSE { Branch to appropriate return address }
        CASE L OF
          1:
            GOTO 1;
          2:
            GOTO 2;
        END;
      END;
```

```
{ Simulate 1st recursive call from previous version.
  Stack parameters. }

    PUSH(N, ISTACK, ITOP, FULL);
    PUSH(SOURCE, CSTACK, CTOP, FULL);
    PUSH(DESTINATION, CSTACK, CTOP, FULL);
    PUSH(INTERMEDIATE, CSTACK, CTOP, FULL);

    { Arrange parameter passing }

    N := N - 1;
    TEMP := INTERMEDIATE;
    INTERMEDIATE := DESTINATION;
    DESTINATION := TEMP;

    { Stack return address }

    PUSH(1, LSTACK, LTOP, FULL);

    { Actual CALL replaced by GOTO }

    GOTO 3;

1:
    WRITE('MOVE DISK FROM ', SOURCE, 'TO', DESTINATION);

{ Next simulate 2nd recursive call in previous HANOI.
  Stack parameters.}

    PUSH(N, ISTACK, ITOP, FULL);
    PUSH(SOURCE, CSTACK, CTOP, FULL);
    PUSH(DESTINATION, CSTACK, CTOP, FULL);
    PUSH(INTERMEDIATE, CSTACK, CTOP, FULL);

    { Simulate parameter passing for 2nd call }

    N := N - 1;
    TEMP := INTERMEDIATE;
    INTERMEDIATE := SOURCE;
    SOURCE := TEMP;

    { Stack return address }

    PUSH(2, LSTACK, LTOP, FULL);

    { Actual CALL replaced by GOTO }

    GOTO 3;
```

```
{ The remaining lines simulate the RETURN operation appearing in line
  2: of the previous recursive HANOI.
  First pop parameters from the stack}

2:
    POP(N, ISTACK, ITOP, EMPTY);
    POP(INTERMEDIATE, CSTACK, CTOP, EMPTY);
    POP(DESTINATION, CSTACK, CTOP, EMPTY);
    POP(SOURCE, CSTACK, CTOP, EMPTY);
    POP(L, LSTACK, LTOP, EMPTY);
    IF EMPTY THEN
       GOTO 10 { RETURN to higher level calling procedure }
    ELSE { Branch to appropriate return address }

       CASE L OF
         1:
            GOTO 1;
         2:
            GOTO 2;
         END;
    10:
    END;
{ End NONRECURSIVEHANOI }
```

N
INTERMEDIATE
DESTINATION
SOURCE
Return Address

The first 4 POPs restore previous parameter values from the stack

The 5th POP then determines the return address

When you compare this to the previous recursive HANOI procedure, you should note that each recursive call is replaced by a considerable number of statements. CALLs are replaced by a series of push operations, assignment statements, and finally a GOTO. RETURNs are replaced by a reverse series of pop operations and then, conditionally, either a GOTO or a true RETURN to the original calling procedure. This increase in the number of statements should not be interpreted as meaning that the non-recursive version of the program is less efficient; we are merely doing what the system would otherwise do for us. Frequently, a judicious choice of the data items to be stacked can make the non-recursive version of the algorithm more efficient in both stack space and run time. Hence, there is an argument for removing recursion even in those languages that allow it. In the exercises at the end of the chapter you will be asked to identify push operations in the preceding algorithm which could be removed in order to minimize stack space used.

Unfortunately, such non-recursive versions of recursive algorithms cannot conveniently be coded in a *structured* style. This is because a RETURN following a recursive CALL may lead to any one of several possible locations in the procedure, depending upon the return address popped from the stack. In our non-recursive HANOI procedure we have used a CASE statement which dispatches control to the appropriate point via a GOTO statement in which the destination is a label popped from the stack.

In the world of applications ...

In the *Pascal User Manual and Report*, Niklaus Wirth and Kathleen Jensen made famous a diagrammatic way of representing Pascal syntax. For instance, a syntax diagram which defines a Pascal *statement* is presented below. One interesting feature to note about this diagram is that the term *statement* is used eight times in the defining *statement*. The diagrams of Wirth and Jensen are recursive in nature, and they point out the fact that the syntax of most computer languages can be recursively defined. This is of tremendous importance in the writing of compilers, many of which rely heavily upon recursion to analyze source programs. In fact, one well-known technique of compiler writing is called *recursive descent* compiling. If you intend to study compilers, you had better understand the intricacies of recursion.

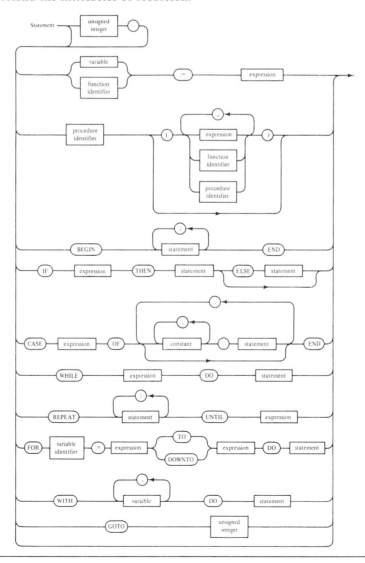

Recursion, Stacks, and Backtracking Problems

One classic type of problem ideally suited to recursion is that of **backtracking**. At the beginning of this chapter, we gave an illustration of backtracking logic as it is used when you try to find a path out of a maze. You must explore numerous paths before you find the right one. Upon exploring a given path and determining that it can lead only to a dead end, you must retrace the points on the path in reverse order, backtrack until you reach a point at which you can try a new path. This concept of trial-and-error backtracking is illustrated in Figure 5-7. The retracing in reverse order of points that have been visited previously is done using a stack. The stack can be explicitly maintained by the programmer or implicitly maintained by recursion.

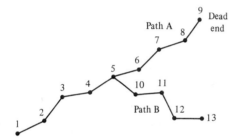

FIGURE 5-7   The backtracking problem as illustrated by maze solution. Upon reaching a dead end for path A, you must retrace steps 9 → 8 → 7 → 6 → 5 before you can try new path B.

The Eight Queens Problem

A backtracking problem that has long intrigued chess fanatics is the *Eight Queens* problem, which requires determining the various ways in which eight queens could be configured on a chess board so that none of them could capture any other queen. (The rules of chess allow a queen to move an arbitrary number of squares in a horizontal, vertical, or diagonal fashion.) Figure 5-8 illustrates one such configuration.

Applying backtracking logic to this problem, we could attempt to find a "path" to a configuration by successively trying to place a queen in each column of a chessboard until we reach a dead end: a column in which the placement of queens in prior columns makes it impossible to place the queen being moved. This situation is pictured in Figure 5-9. When we reach this dead end, we must backtrack one column (to column 5 in the case of Figure 5-6), and attempt to find a new placement for the queen in the previous column. If placement in the previous column is impossible, we must backtrack yet another column to

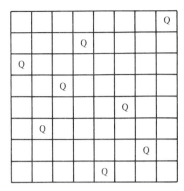

FIGURE 5-8   One successful eight queens configuration; no queen has access to any other.

attempt the new placement. This backtracking through previous columns continues until we finally are able to reposition a queen. At that point, we can begin a new path by again attempting to position queens on a column-by-column basis until another dead end is reached or until a fully successful configuration is developed.

The key to a program that finds all possible eight queens configurations is a procedure that attempts to place a queen in a given square and, if successful, recursively calls itself to attempt the placement of

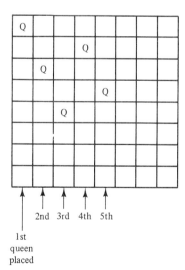

FIGURE 5-9   Dead end in queen placement. Given previous 5 placements, queen cannot be placed in 6th column. Must backtrack and attempt to re-position in column 5. If that fails, backtrack to column 4, and so on.

another queen in the next column. Such a procedure in skeleton form follows:

```
PROCEDURE PLACEQUEEN(I,J)
  {If possible, place queen in row I and column J of
   chessboard and then 'recurse' to place queen in next
   column.}

IF (no immediate danger at position I,J) THEN
   IF J = 8 THEN
      Tally configuration
   ELSE
      BEGIN
         Mark position I,J as occupied;
         FOR K:=1 to 8 DO
            PLACEQUEEN(K,J+1)
      END
 END; {PLACEQUEEN}
```

Note that this procedure has been intentionally left unfinished. Still to be resolved are such issues as:

- The initial call(s) to PLACEQUEEN.
- How to represent the chessboard.
- How to check whether placing a queen at position I,J puts it in immediate danger. That is, how to determine whether there is currently another queen sharing the same row, column, or a diagonal.

The resolution of these issues is left for your enjoyment in the Programming Problems at the end of the chapter.

In the next chapter, we will begin a careful study of data structures known as trees. We will see to an even greater degree the power and elegance of recursive algorithms; without recursion, an analysis of trees would be virtually impossible.

Program Design Considerations

Designing modular programs in Pascal inevitably gives rise to questions as to whether certain data locations should be declared as global or local variables. The general guiding principle in this regard is to make a variable global only if it *needs* to be global. In this way you minimize the chance of one module's inadvertently destroying a value crucial to another module. Questions of localizing variables become particularly important to consider when recursive calls are made to a procedure. The added complication here is that, each time a recursive call is made, another copy of a variable local to a procedure will be made in the stack space allotted for that procedure. However, global variables are only allocated space once—outside of the special stack area dedicated to procedure calls. As an example of the subtle effect this can have, consider a recursive version of the program given in the *Program Design Considerations* for Chapter 4, that is, a program which uses a stack to store incoming characters and then print them out in reverse order, enabling us to check whether the input string is a palindrome. The only essential difference between the program given below and that given in Chapter 4 is that here we use the system stack implicitly given to us by the ability to make recursive calls in Pascal. The program will work perfectly. An input of

    MADAM

will result in output of

    MADAM

while input of

    COMPUTER

will result in output of

    RETUPMOC

```
PROGRAM PALINDROME(INPUT, OUTPUT);

  { PRINT OUT A STRING IN REVERSE ORDER TO CHECK IF PALINDROME }

  PRODEDURE REVERSE;

    { KEEP RECURSIVELY STACKING CHARACTERS UNTIL END OF STRING }
    { THEN PRINT IT OUT IN REVERSE BY UNSTACKING }

  VAR
     C: CHAR;

   BEGIN
     READ(C);
     IF NOT EOLN THEN
       REVERSE;
     WRITE(C)
   END; { REVERSE }

BEGIN
  REVERSE
END.
```

We now present another version of this program altered ever so slightly from the version above. In fact, the only change made in this new version is to make the declaration

```
VAR C:CHAR;
```

global instead of local to the procedure REVERSE.

```
PROGRAM PALINDROME(INPUT, OUTPUT);

 { PRINT OUT A STRING IN REVERSE TO CHECK IF PALINDROME }

 VAR
   C: CHAR; { NOTE C NOW GLOBAL }

 PROCEDURE REVERSE;

  { KEEP RECURSIVELY STACKING CHARACTERS UNTIL END OF STRING }
  { THEN PRINT IT OUT IN REVERSE BY UNSTACKING }

  BEGIN
    READ(C);
    IF NOT EOLN THEN
      REVERSE;
    WRITE(C)
  END; { REVERSE }

BEGIN
  REVERSE
END.
```

A run of this new program fails miserably. Input of

```
MADAM
```

will result in output of

```
MMMMM
```

Why does this happen? The answer is evident from what we have said about the system stack's being implicitly available when recursive calls are made. In the first version of this program, five separate copies of the local variable C are pushed onto the system stack, to be printed out upon finally reaching the end of the input string. In the second version, there is only one copy of the global variable C. Consequently, its contents upon finally returning from the series of recursive calls are simply the last character input.

The power of recursion lies in its ability to create a separate copy of all local variables (and value parameters) at each level of the recursive calling sequence. Be sure to keep this in mind when designing recursive procedures.

SUMMARY

Parsing of expressions, and hence the use of a stack structure, is an essential part of compiler design. When an expression is parsed into a postfix or prefix form, it is rendered into an essentially unique form free from parentheses.

Additionally, as the N-factorial and Tower of Hanoi algorithms show, recursive procedures use stacks extensively and can be cumbersome to code. Modern languages such as Pascal have implemented recursion to save the programmer the trouble of this stack-oriented coding. Older languages such as BASIC and FORTRAN do not allow recursive subroutine calls. Regardless of whether or not one is working in a language which allows recursion, the details of how a stack is used in recursive calls should be thoroughly understood.

Recursion is a powerful technique and will be used heavily in the next chapter about tree structures.

KEY TERMS

Parsing	Infix Priority	N Factorial
Infix	Stack Priority	Towers of Hanoi
Postfix	Stack	Backtracking Problem
Prefix	Recursion	

EXERCISES

1. What is a stack structure?
2. What are the infix, postfix, and prefix forms of the expression:
   A + B *(C− D)/(P− R) ?
3. What are the stack priorities of (,), *, /, +, −, and # ?
4. What are the infix priorities of (,), *, /, +, −, and # ?
5. Stand between two parallel mirrors and see how recursion works for you.
6. Can any of the push operations in the NONRECURSIVEHANOI procedure be eliminated in the interest of minimizing stack space?

PROGRAMMING PROBLEMS

1. In the problems for Chapters 2 and 3, you developed a passenger list processing system for the various flights of the Wing-and-a-Prayer Airlines Company. Wing-and-a-Prayer management would now like you to extend this system so that it processes logical combinations of flight numbers. For example, the command

        LIST 1 OR 2

   should list all passengers whose name appears on the flight 1 list or the flight 2 list. Your program should also accept the logical operators AND and NOT and allow parenthesized logical expressions obeying the standard logical hierarchy

        NOT
        AND
        OR

2. A tax form may be thought of as a sequence of items, each of which is either a number or defined by an arbitrary mathematical formula involving other items in the sequence. To assist them in their tax-planning strategy, top management at the Fly-by-Night credit card company desire a program which would allow them to *interactively* enter numbers or formulas associated with given lines of a tax form. Once all such lines have been defined, users of the program may re-define the number or formula associated with a particular line, and all other lines dependent on that one should be appropriately updated. Note that, since formulas may be entered interactively, your program will have to use a stack to evaluate them. You will in effect have written a small scale *spreadsheet* program.

3. There are five other teams in the same league as the Bay Area Brawlers. Over a given five-week period, the Brawlers must play each of the other teams once. Using recursion, write a program to determine the number of ways in which such a schedule could be accomplished. For an added challenge, introduce more realistic scheduling parameters into this problem.

4. Implement in a high level language the algorithm to parse an infix expression into postfix form.

5. Implement in a high level language the algorithm to evaluate an expression given in postfix form.

6. Using your results from Programming Problems (2) and (3) write a program that will call for input of an infix expression and output the proper evaluation of that expression.

7. Add to your program from Programming Problem (4) the ability to parse expressions that contain the exponentiation operator ^.

8. Write a program that will parse infix expressions into prefix form.

9. Using stacks, write a program that will call for input of an integer N and will output all permutations of the first N integers.

10. Write a program to call for input of a decimal number and convert it to its binary equivalent using the method described in the following flowchart.

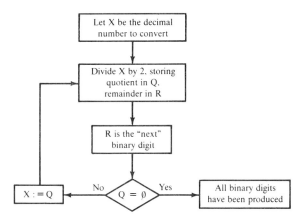

Note that this method produces the binary digits for the given number in reverse order. One strategy for printing out the digits in the correct order would be to store them in an array as they are produced and then print out the array. However, this strategy would have the drawbacks of allocating unnecessary storage for an array and then limiting the size of the binary number to the size of the array. Your program is *not* to employ this strategy. Rather call for input of the decimal number in your main program and then immediately transfer control to a procedure that in turn is called recursively, stacking the binary digits as they are produced. Once division by 2 yields 0, the succession of "returns" can be used to print out the digits one by one as they are popped from this stack.

11. Write a recursive program that will call for input of an integer N and output the value N factorial.

12. The Nth Fibonacci number is defined by

1 if N is 1
1 if N is 2
The sum of the previous two Fibonacci numbers
  otherwise

Write a recursive procedure to compute the Nth Fibonacci number.

13. Euclid devised a clever algorithm for computing the greatest common divisor of two integers. According to Euclid's algorithm,

$$GCD(M,N) = \begin{cases} GCD(N,M) \text{ if } N > M \\ M \text{ if } N = 0 \\ GCD(N, M \text{ MOD } N) \text{ if } N > 0 \end{cases}$$

Write a recursive procedure to compute greatest common divisors via Euclid's method.

14. Write a program that will accept commands of the following form:

    1. INPUT variable name
    2. variable name = infix expression involving variable names and $+, -, *, /$
    3. PRINT variable name
    4. GO

These commands are to be stored in an array of strings until the GO command is entered. Once GO is entered, your program should execute the previously stored commands. "Execute" here means:

    1. For an INPUT command: Send a question mark to the terminal and allow the user to enter a real number which is then stored in "variable name."
    2. For an assignment statement: Parse the expression into postfix form and then evaluate it, storing the result in the "variable name" on the left of the equality sign.
    3. For a PRINT instruction: Write to the terminal the numerical contents of the specified "variable name."

To make things relatively easy you may assume a syntax that:

    1. Allows "variable names" consisting of one upper case alphabetical character
    2. Allows only one "variable name" following INPUT or PRINT
    3. Allows one blank space after the keywords INPUT and PRINT and no blank spaces anywhere else

For an additional challenge, enable your program to handle successfully the exponentiation operator ^ within assignment statement expressions. The following example should illustrate the need for care in handling this exponentiation operator.

$$3^{2^3} = 3^8, \text{ not } 9^3$$

15. Write a program to analyze football team scores by computing the point spread for any team A playing any team B. Your program should compute the point spreads for:

Level I analysis:	Team A played team B in past
Level II analysis:	Average point spreads for situations such as:
	A played C—point spread 3
	C played B—point spread 7
	Total point spread 10
Level III analysis:	Average point spreads for situations such as:
	A played C—point spread 3
	C played D—point spread −14 (C lost)
	D played B—point spread 7
	Total point spread −4

Level IV analysis: Average point spreads for situations such as:
A played C—point spread 3
C played D—point spread −14
D played E—point spread 21
E played B—point spread 4
Total point spread 14

All level II point spreads are then averaged for a final level II point
spread figure. Point spreads are similarly averaged for levels III
and IV. Items that potentially need to be stacked in this program
include:

- Accumulated point spread at current position
- Number of scores reflected in the accumulated point spread
  at current position
- Current position, that is, team A playing team B
- Path to the current position, that is, teams played to get to
  the current position

16. Write a program to complete the Eight Queens problem.

6

Tree Structures

"I don't have to look up my family tree because I
know that I'm the sap."

FRED ALLEN (1894—1956)

6-1   Introductory Considerations

Most people are aware of the genealogical trees that allow a family of
individuals to trace their ancestry. In this sense a genealogical tree is
simply a way of expressing a hierarchical relationship between parents, children, brothers, sisters, cousins, aunts, uncles, and so on. The
crucial relationship in such a genealogical tree is that between parent
and child. Such a parent-child relationship is an excellent example of
a **hierarchical** relationship in which there exists a well-defined order of
precedence between the two items being related. In computer science,
a **tree** is a data structure that represents hierarchical relationships between individual data items.

To introduce some of the terminology of tree structures, we will
consider the record of a student at a typical university. In addition to
the usual statistical background information such as social security
number, name, and address, a typical student record contains listings
for a number of courses, exams and final grades in each course, overall
grade point average, and other data relating to the student's performance at the college. Figure 6-1 is an example of a tree structure representing such a student record. As in genealogical trees, at the highest

142

level (0) of a tree is its **root** (also called the **root node**). Here STUDENT is the root node. The nodes NAME, ADDRESS, SSN, COURSE, and GPA, which are directly connected to the root node, are the **child nodes** of the **parent node** STUDENT. The child nodes of a given parent constitute a set of **siblings.** Thus NAME, ADDRESS, SSN, COURSE, and GPA are siblings. In the hierarchy represented by a tree, the child nodes of a parent are one level lower than the parent node. Thus NAME, ADDRESS, SSN, COURSE, and GPA are at level 1 in Figure 6-1.

A link between a parent and its child is called a **branch** in a tree structure. Each node in a tree except the root must descend from a parent node via a branch. Thus LAST NAME, MIDDLE NAME, and FIRST NAME in Figure 6-1 descend from the parent node NAME. The

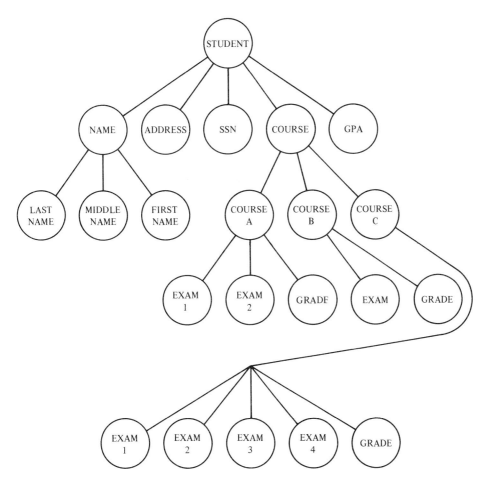

FIGURE 6-1 A tree structure representing a student record.

root of the tree is the **ancestor** of all the nodes in the tree. Each node may be the parent of any number of nodes in the tree. A node with no children is called a **leaf node.** In Figure 6-1, GPA is a leaf node. LAST NAME, MIDDLE NAME, FIRST NAME, EXAM1, and EXAM2 also are leaf nodes.

A **subtree** is a subset of a tree that is itself a tree; the tree in Figure 6-2 is a subtree of the tree in Figure 6-1. This subtree has the root node NAME. Similarly, the tree in Figure 6-3 is another subtree of the tree in Figure 6-1. Notice that the tree in Figure 6-3 is a subtree of both the tree in Figure 6-1 and the tree in Figure 6-4.

Given this intuitive background, we can now precisely define a tree in recursive fashion as a set of nodes that:

- Is either empty, or
- Has a designated node called the *root* from which descend zero or more subtrees. Each subtree itself satisfies the definition of a tree.

It is important to emphasize the recursive fashion in which a tree is defined (a strong hint that most tree-processing algorithms will also be recursive).

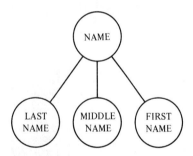

FIGURE 6-2   A subtree of the tree shown in Figure 6-1.

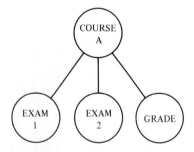

FIGURE 6-3   Another subtree of the tree shown in Figure 6-1, also a subtree of the tree shown in Figure 6-4.

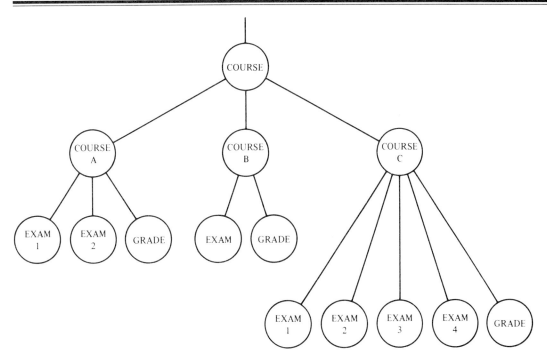

FIGURE 6-4 Another subtree of the tree shown in Figure 6-1.

6-2 Binary Trees

One of the most important of all tree structures is the **binary tree.** In a binary tree, each node has *no more than two child nodes*, each of which may be a leaf node. In other words, in a binary tree each node has two subtrees (null or non-null) known as the left subtree and the right subtree. Figure 6-5 is an example of a binary tree. Notice that both children of "−" are leaf nodes, whereas only the left child of "*" is a leaf node. The left subtree of the root "+" appears in Figure 6-6.

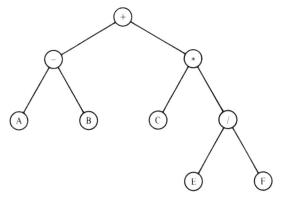

FIGURE 6-5 A binary tree. Each node has no more than 2 child nodes.

As another example, the right subtree of the right subtree of '+' is given by Figure 6-7.

From this example it should be apparent that if we sever the branch linking a child node to a parent node, the child node becomes the root of a subtree. This is consistent with the recursive definition of a tree given in (6-1). For example, breaking the branch between the child node "*" and the parent node "+" in Figure 6-5 gives us the subtree of Figure 6-8, which is a tree structure whose root is '*'. We also emphasize that binary trees are not symmetric structures: interchanging the right and left subtrees in any of the preceding figures yields a new and different tree.

Tree structures arise quite naturally in both computer science and data processing applications. File index schemes and hierarchical database management systems, such as the Information Management System (IMS) available from IBM, typically make use of tree structures. We will say more about such file-oriented applications of trees in the final two chapters. Here we will consider the computer science application of using binary trees to represent algebraic expressions. The hierarchy of algebraic operators involved in mathematical expressions can be graphically represented by the hierarchical nature of a tree structure.

The tree in Figure 6-5, when viewed in the proper way, represents the arithmetic expression shown in Figure 6-9. This expression was obtained by **traversing** the tree in Figure 6-5 in a certain manner.

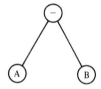

FIGURE 6-6   Left subtree of the root "+" in Figure 6-5.

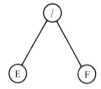

FIGURE 6-7   The right subtree of the right subtree of "+" in Figure 6-5.

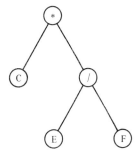

FIGURE 6-8 Subtree created when the branch between the child node "*" and the parent node "+" in Figure 6-5 is severed.

Contemporary compilers make use of tree structures in obtaining forms of an arithmetic expression for efficient evaluation. As discussed in Chapter 5, there are basically three forms of an arithmetic expression—infix, prefix, and postfix. You should recall that the forms of the expression in Figure 6-9 are:

(A − B) + C * (E / F)	infix
+−AB*C/EF	prefix
AB−CEF/*+	postfix

All three of these forms are immediately available to us if we know exactly how the corresponding tree should be traversed. Traversing a tree means processing it in such a way that each node is visited only once. The **inorder traversal** of the binary tree for an arithmetic expression gives us the expression in the infix form—the readily recognizable form of Figure 6-9. The **preorder traversal** of the same tree leads us to the prefix form of the expression, whereas the **postorder traversal** of the tree yields the postfix form of the expression.

6-3   Implementation of Binary Trees

Given the abstract requirement that a (binary) tree must represent a hierarchical relationship between a parent node and (at most two) child nodes, there are two common methods used for actually representing this conceptual structure. One which does not require the overhead of maintaining pointers is called a **linear representation;** the other, known as a **linked representation,** uses pointers.

(A − B) + C * (E / F)

FIGURE 6-9 Expression represented by the tree in Figure 6-5.

Linear Representation of a Binary Tree

The linear representation method of implementing a binary tree uses a one-dimensional array of size $(2^{(d+1)} - 1)$ where d is the **depth** of the tree, that is, the maximum level of any node in the tree. In the tree of Figure 6-5, the root "+" is at the level 0, the nodes "−" and "*" are at level 1, and so on. The deepest level in this tree is the level of "E" and "F," level 3. Therefore, $d = 3$ and this tree will require an array of size $2^{(3+1)} - 1 = 15$.

Once the size of the array has been determined, the following method is used to represent the tree:

1. Store the root in the 1st location of the array.
2. If a node is in location n of the array, store its left child at location $2n$, and its right child at location $(2n + 1)$.

With the aid of this scheme, the tree of Figure 6-5 is stored in the array IMPBIN of size 15 shown in Figure 6-10. Locations IMPBIN[8] through IMPBIN[13] are not used.

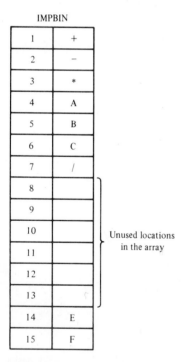

IMPBIN	
1	+
2	−
3	*
4	A
5	B
6	C
7	/
8	
9	
10	
11	
12	
13	
14	E
15	F

Unused locations in the array

FIGURE 6-10   Using the array size $2^{(d+1)} - 1$ and the storage method described in the text, the tree in Figure 6-5 is stored in this linear representation of an array.

The main advantages of this method lie in its simplicity and the fact that, given a child node, its parent node can be determined immediately. If a child node is at location N in the array, then its parent node is at location $N/2$ (integer division). Another merit of this method is that it can be implemented easily in older languages such as BASIC and FORTRAN in which only static memory allocation is directly available.

Efficiency Considerations for Binary Tree Implementations. In spite of its simplicity and ease of implementation, the linear representation method has all the overhead that comes with physically ordering items. Insertion or deletion of a node causes considerable data movement up and down the array, using an excessive amount of processing time; because insertions and deletions are major data processing activities, algorithms must be developed to maximize their processing efficiency. Also, there usually are wasted memory locations (such as locations 8 through 13 in our example) due to partially filled trees.

Linked Representation of a Binary Tree

Because each node in a binary tree may have two child nodes, a node in a linked representation has two pointer fields, one for each child, and one or more data fields containing specific information about the node itself. When a node has no children, the corresponding pointer fields are NIL.

Figure 6-11 is a linked representation of the binary tree of Figure 6-5. The LLINK and RLINK fields are pointers to (that is, memory addresses of) the left child and the right child of a node. Notice that an operand in the tree of an arithmetic expression is always a leaf node.

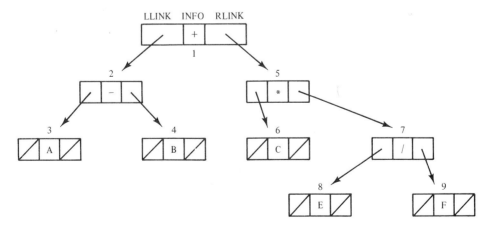

FIGURE 6-11 A linked representation of the binary tree in Figure 6-5.

Although for most purposes the linked representation of a binary tree is most efficient, it does have certain disadvantages, namely:

1. Wasted memory space in NIL pointers. The representation in Figure 6-10 has 10 NIL pointers.
2. Given a node, it is difficult to determine its parent.
3. Its implementation algorithm is more difficult in languages that do not offer dynamic storage techniques; for example, FORTRAN, BASIC, and COBOL.

Disadvantage (1) can be offset by **threading** the tree, a technique discussed in Chapter 7. Drawback (2) can be overcome by adding a parent pointer field to a node, if you can afford the luxury of using more memory. Drawback (3) is not serious, because a programmer can develop in *any* language procedures analogous to the GETNODE and RETURNNODE of Chapter 2.

For the moment, let us give a detailed description of the linked representation of the binary tree of Figure 6-11 using three parallel arrays. This is similar to the way in which we first discussed linked lists in Chapter 2. By doing this we will actually be able to trace the values of the pointers. Once the concept is thoroughly understood, we will then return to using Pascal pointer variables for the actual implementation of binary trees. For example, by using three arrays we can implement the tree of Figure 6-11 as shown in Figure 6-12, using the strategy of building the left subtree for each node before considering the right subtree. The numbers on top of the cells in Figure 6-11 represent the addresses given by the LLINK and RLINK pointer arrays.

In the linked representation, insertions and deletions involve no data movement except the rearrangement of pointers. Suppose we wish to modify the tree in Figure 6-5 to that which appears in Figure 6-13. (This change might be needed due to some recent modification in the expression represented by Figure 6-5.) The insertion of the nodes containing "−" and "P" into the tree structure can be achieved

NODE	INFO	LLINK	RLINK
1	+	2	5
2	−	3	4
3	A	NIL	NIL
4	B	NIL	NIL
5	*	6	7
6	C	NIL	NIL
7	/	8	9
8	E	NIL	NIL
9	F	NIL	NIL

FIGURE 6-12 Implementation of the binary tree in Figure 6-11 using 3 arrays.

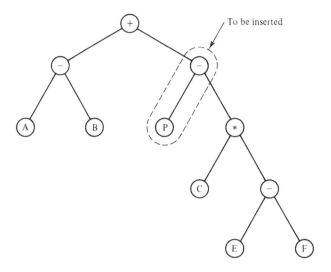

FIGURE 6-13 Desired modification of the tree in Figure 6-5.

easily by simply adding the nodes "−" and "P" in the next available spaces in the array and correspondingly adjusting the pointers. For the implementation of the tree shown in Figure 6-11, the effect of this insertion is given by Figure 6-14. The adjusted pointers and data fields have been underscored. Notice that the change in row 1 of RLINK and the additional rows 10 and 11 are all that is necessary. No data were moved.

Similarly, if we wish to shorten the tree in Figure 6-5 by deleting the nodes "*" and "C," then all we must do is rearrange the pointers to obtain the altered tree, as shown in Figure 6-15.

	INFO	LLINK	RLINK
1	+	2	10
2	−	3	4
3	A	NIL	NIL
4	B	NIL	NIL
5	*	6	7
6	C	NIL	NIL
7	/	8	9
8	E	NIL	NIL
9	F	NIL	NIL
10	−	11	5
11	P	NIL	NIL

FIGURE 6-14 Modification of Figure 6-11 by insertions of the nodes "−" and "P" into the tree shown in Figure 6-5. Underscoring indicates new or adjusted fields.

	INFO	LLINK	RLINK	Modified tree
1	+	2	7	
2	–	3	4	
3	A	NIL	NIL	
4	B	NIL	NIL	
5	*			unused space after
6	C			deletion of '*' and
				'C'
7	/	8	9	
8	E	NIL	NIL	
9	F	NIL	NIL	

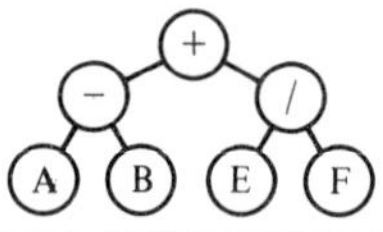

**FIGURE 6-15 Modification of tree by deletion of nodes "*" and "C".
Underscoring indicates a new or adjusted field.**

The preceding examples indicate that, as far as processing efficiency is concerned, the linked representation seems to be more efficient, particularly where frequent insertions and deletions are required. A more formal statement of the algorithm underlying such insertions and deletions will be given later in this chapter, when list maintenance using a binary tree is discussed. Now that the concept of the linked representation of a binary tree has been thoroughly explained using arrays to contain pointer values which are meaningful to the reader, we will use the following general record description using Pascal pointer variables to actually implement this structure.

```
TYPE
    POINTER = ^TREENODE;
    TREENODE = RECORD
                LLINK:POINTER;
                INFO: CHAR;
                RLINK: POINTER
                END;
```

6-4   Binary Tree Traversals

As noted earlier, traversing a tree means processing the tree so that each node is visited only once.

Preorder Traversal of a Binary Tree

Preorder traversal (which leads to prefix expressions) of a binary tree entails the following three steps:

1. Process the root node
2. Process the left subtree
3. Process the right subtree

These three **ordered steps** are recursive. Once the root of the tree is processed, we go to the root of the left subtree, and then to the root of the left subtree of the left subtree, and so on until we can go no further. Following these three steps, the preorder traversal of the tree of Figure 6-5 yields the expression

```
+-AB*C/EF
```

which is the prefix form of the expression in Figure 6-9.

The preorder traversal of an existing linked binary tree with a root node at location ROOT can be accomplished recursively using the following procedure:

```
{ Global Variables }

TYPE
  POINTER = ^TREENODE;
  TREENODE =
    RECORD
      LLINK: POINTER;
      INFO: CHAR;
      RLINK: POINTER
    END;

PROCEDURE PREORDERTRAV(ROOT: POINTER);
{ LLINK and RLINK are pointers to the left and right children
  respectively. INFO is a one-character data field.          }

  BEGIN
    IF ROOT <> NIL THEN
      BEGIN
      PROCESS(ROOT^.INFO);

        { PROCESS represents an arbitrary procedure designed to
              process a given node }

      PREORDERTRAV(ROOT^.LLINK);
      PREORDERTRAV(ROOT^.RLINK)
      END
  END;
{ End PREORDERTRAV }
```

Applying PREORDERTRAV to the tree of Figure 6-5, we obtain the prefix expression:

```
+-AB*C/EF
```

To alleviate some of the inefficiency in processing associated with recursive calls, a non-recursive procedure using a stack as described in Chapter 5 can be written to accomplish a preorder traversal. The Pascal version of a non-recursive preorder procedure is given below, with the procedures and parameters PUSH, POP, and STACK as defined in Chapter 4. In order that pointers may take on meaningful values in the tracing of this procedure, as shown in Figure 6-16, parallel arrays have been used instead of Pascal pointer variables.

```
{ Global Variables }

CONST
  NULL = MAXINT;
  TREE_NODES = 200;

VAR
  LLINK,RLINK: ARRAY [1..TREE_NODES] OF INTEGER;
  INFO: PACKED ARRAY [1..TREE_NODES] OF CHAR;

PROCEDURE PREORDER_STACK_TRAVERSAL(ROOT: INTEGER);
 { LLINK and RLINK are pointer arrays of arbitrary size.
   LLINK[ VAL ] points to the left child of the node pointed to
   by VAL. RLINK[ VAL ] points to the right child of the same
   node. }

  CONST
    MAX_STACK = 100;

  VAR
    VAL, TOP: INTEGER;
    STACK: ARRAY [1..MAX_STACK] OF INTEGER;
    EMPTY, FULL: BOOLEAN;

  BEGIN
    EMPTY := FALSE;
    VAL := ROOT;
    INITIALIZE_STACK(TOP, STACK); { Call to initialize stack }
    IF VAL = NULL THEN
      BEGIN
      WRITELN(' EMPTY TREE ');
      EMPTY := TRUE;
      END;
```

```
WHILE NOT EMPTY DO
  BEGIN
  IF VAL <> NULL THEN
    BEGIN
    PROCESS(INFO[VAL]);

    { Push pointer to the right subtree onto the stack }

    IF RLINK[VAL] <> NULL THEN
      PUSH(RLINK[VAL], TOP, STACK, FULL);

    { now process the left subtree }

    VAL := LLINK[VAL];
    END
  ELSE

    { No more movement to the left. Start popping the stack.
      If it is empty, then we are done }
    POP(VAL, TOP, STACK, EMPTY);

  END;
  END;
{ End PREORDER_STACK_TRAV }
```

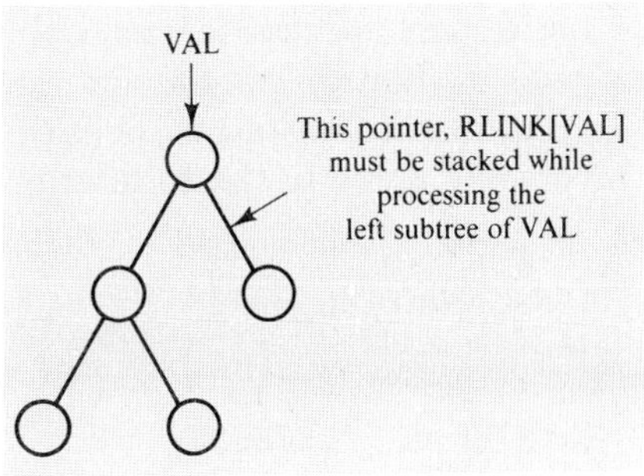

This pointer, RLINK[VAL] must be stacked while processing the left subtree of VAL

Using the PREORDER_STACK_TRAV procedure, the preorder traversal of the tree in Figure 6-5 (with its corresponding implementation from Figure 6-12) can be traced through as shown in Figure 6-16.

ITERATION	STACK (of VAL pointers)	OUTPUT
1	5	+
2	4, 5	+ −
3	4, 5	+ − A
4	5	+ − AB
5	7	+ − AB*
6	7	+ − AB*C
7	9	+ − AB*C/
8	9	+ − AB*C/E
9		+ − AB*C/EF

FIGURE 6-16 *Preorder traversal of the tree in Figure 6-5 as performed by* PREORDER_STACK_TRAV.

Inorder Traversal of a Binary Tree

The inorder traversal of a binary tree (which results in an infix expression) proceeds as outlined in the following 3 ordered steps:

1. Process the left subtree
2. Process the root node
3. Process the right subtree

It should be noted that steps (1) and (3) are recursive. By carefully following these steps for the tree of Figure 6-5, we obtain the readily recognizable infix expression

$$A-B+C*E/F$$

Unless we add parentheses, this infix expression is not algebraically equivalent to the order of operations reflected in the tree of Figure 6-5. The fact that prefix and postfix notations do not require parentheses to avoid such ambiguities make them distinctly superior to infix notation for evaluation purposes.

A more formal statement of the recursive algorithm for an inorder traversal is given in the following procedure.

```
{ Global Variables }

TYPE
  POINTER = ^TREENODE;
  TREENODE =
    RECORD
      LLINK: POINTER;
      INFO: CHAR;
      RLINK: POINTER
    END;

PROCEDURE INORDERTRAV(ROOT: POINTER);
{ LLINK and RLINK are pointer variables to the left and right
  children respectively. INFO is a one-character data field.  }

  BEGIN
    IF ROOT <> NIL THEN
      BEGIN
      INORDERTRAV(ROOT^.LLINK);
      PROCESS(ROOT^.INFO);
      INORDERTRAV(ROOT^.RLINK)
      END
  END;
{ End INORDERTRAV }
```

Again, for a potentially more efficient approach to this algorithm, we suggest the following non recursive procedure, which utilizes a stack and a parallel array to maintain pointers whose values are traced in Figure 6-17.

```
{ Global Variables }

CONST
  NULL = MAXINT;
  TREE_NODES = 200;

VAR
  LLINK,RLINK: ARRAY [1..TREE_NODES] OF INTEGER;
  INFO: PACKED ARRAY [1..TREE_NODES] OF CHAR;

PROCEDURE INORDER_STACK_TRAVERSAL(ROOT: INTEGER);
  { LLINK and RLINK are pointer arrays of arbitrary size.
    LLINK[ VAL ] points to the left child of the node pointed to
    by VAL. RLINK[ VAL ] points to the right child of the same
    node. }

  CONST
    MAX_STACK = 100;

  VAR
    VAL, TOP: INTEGER;
    STACK: ARRAY [1..MAX_STACK] OF INTEGER;
    EMPTY, FULL: BOOLEAN;

  BEGIN
    EMPTY := FALSE;
    VAL := ROOT;

    INITIALIZE_STACK(TOP, STACK); { Call to initialize stack }
    IF VAL = NULL THEN
      BEGIN
      WRITELN(' EMPTY TREE ');
      EMPTY := TRUE;
      END;
    WHILE NOT EMPTY DO
      BEGIN
      IF VAL <> NULL THEN
        BEGIN

        { Push current root pointer onto the stack }

        PUSH(VAL, TOP, STACK, FULL);

        { Now process the left subtree }

        VAL := LLINK[VAL];
        END
```

With PREORDER, we stacked RLINK[VAL] before traversing left subtree. With INORDER, stack VAL instead.

```
    ELSE
      BEGIN

        { No more movement to the left. Start popping the stack.
          If it is empty, then we are done.   }

        POP(VAL, TOP, STACK, EMPTY);
        IF NOT EMPTY THEN
          BEGIN
            PROCESS(INFO[VAL]);
            VAL := RLINK[VAL];
          END;
        END;

      END;
  END;
{ End INORDER_STACK_TRAV }
```

Applying this procedure to the tree of Figure 6-5, implemented with
the linked representation given in Figure 6-12, results in the successive iterations shown in Figure 6-17.

ITERATION	STACK (of VAL pointers)	OUTPUT
1	1	
2	2 1	
3	3 2 1	
4	2 1	A
5	1	A−
6	4 1	A−
7	1	A−B
8	5	A−B+
9	6 5	A−B+
10	5	A−B+C
11	7	A−B+C*
12	8 7	A−B+C*
13	7	A−B+C*E
14	9	A−B+C*E/
15		A−B+C*E/F

**FIGURE 6-17   Inorder traversal of the tree in Figure 6-5 as performed by
INORDERTRAV.**

Postorder Traversal of a Binary Tree

Postorder traversal of a binary tree (which results in a postfix expression) entails these three ordered steps:

1. Process the left subtree
2. Process the right subtree
3. Process the root node

The postorder traversal can be implemented recursively by the procedure POSTORDERTRAV:

```
{ Global Variables }

TYPE
  POINTER = ^TREENODE;
  TREENODE =
    RECORD
      LLINK: POINTER;
      INFO: CHAR;
      RLINK: POINTER
    END;

PROCEDURE POSTORDERTRAV(ROOT: POINTER);
{ LLINK and RLINK are pointer variables to the left and right
  children respectively. INFO is a one-character data field.}

  BEGIN
    IF ROOT <> NIL THEN
      BEGIN
        POSTORDERTRAV(ROOT^.LLINK);
        POSTORDERTRAV(ROOT^.RLINK);
        PROCESS(ROOT^.INFO)
      END
  END;
{ End POSTORDERTRAV }
```

Applying this procedure to the tree of Figure 6-5, we obtain the postfix expression

```
AB—CEF/*+
```

You can replace the POSTORDERTRAV procedure with a nonrecursive algorithm using a stack in a fashion similar to what we have already done for preorder and inorder traversals; you will write this as an exercise at the end of the chapter.

6-5 An Application of Binary Trees in Maintaining Ordered Lists

Besides being used to represent arithmetic expressions in such areas as compiler design, trees arise naturally wherever a hierarchical relationship between data items exists. In particular, consider the following example of such a relationship existing between data items in a tree:

For any given data item X in the tree, every node in the left subtree of X contains only items that are less than or equal to X with respect to a particular type of ordering. Every node in the right subtree of X contains only items that are greater than or equal to X with respect to the same ordering.

We will hereafter frequently refer to this property as the **ordering property for binary trees.** For instance, the tree in Figure 6-18 illustrates this property with respect to alphabetical ordering.

You can quickly verify that an inorder traversal of this tree (in which the processing of each node consists merely of printing its contents) leads to the alphabetized list:

```
ALLEN
DAVIS
EVENSON
FAIRCHILD
GARLOCK
GREEN
KELLER
MILLER
NATHAN
PERKINS
SMITH
TALBOT
UNDERWOOD
VERKINS
ZELLER
```

Moreover, insertion of a new string into such an ordered tree is a fairly easy process that may well require significantly fewer comparisons than insertion into a linked list. Consider, for example, the steps necessary to insert the string SALINAS into the tree in such a fashion as to maintain the ordering property. We must:

1. Compare SALINAS to MILLER. Because SALINAS is greater than MILLER, follow the right child pointer to TALBOT.
2. Compare SALINAS to TALBOT. Because SALINAS is less than TALBOT, follow the left child pointer to PERKINS.
3. SALINAS is greater than PERKINS. Hence follow the right child pointer to SMITH.

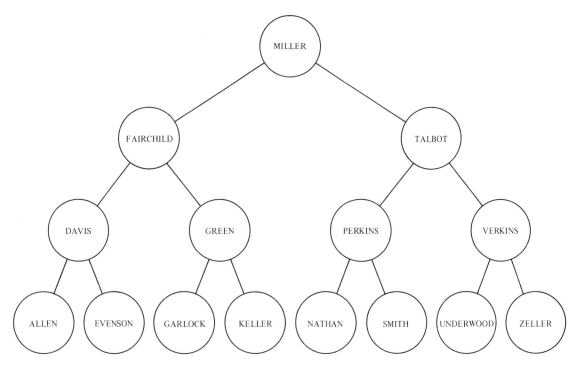

FIGURE 6-18   The ordering property for binary trees is represented with respect to alphabetical ordering.

4. SMITH is a leaf node, so SALINAS may be added as one of its children. The left child is chosen because SALINAS is less than SMITH.

The resulting tree for this sample insertion is given in Figure 6-19.

The preceding algorithm implies that insertion of new nodes will always occur at the leaf nodes of a tree. As with insertion into a linked list, no data is moved; only pointers are manipulated. However, unlike the steps required by a linked list representation, we do not have to traverse the list *sequentially* to determine where the new node belongs. Instead, using the **insertion rule:**

- If less than, go left
- Otherwise, go right

we need merely traverse one branch of the tree to determine position for a new node. Provided that the tree maintains a full shape, the number of nodes on a given branch will be at most

$$\log_2 N + 1$$

where N is the total number of nodes in the tree. By **full,** we mean that all nodes with only one child must have a leaf node as that only child.

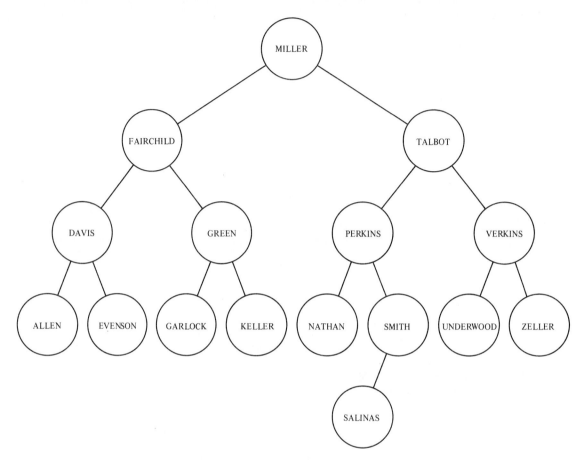

FIGURE 6-19   The tree in Figure 6-18 with the insertion SALINAS.

Hence, adding ROBERTS to the tree of Figure 6-19 by the insertion rule would destroy the fullness of the tree: the only child of SMITH no longer would be a leaf node.

Given this definition of *full*, the $\log_2 N+1$ figure for the maximum number of nodes on a branch emerges immediately upon inspection or, more formally, using a proof by mathematical induction. Our purpose here, however, is not to detail such a proof but rather to emphasize that a binary tree presents an alternative to a linked list structure for the type of processing involved in maintaining ordered lists. Moreover, it is a particularly attractive alternative when the tree is full, because substantially fewer comparisons are needed to locate where in the structure an insertion is to be made. For instance, if N is 1024, the linked list may require as many as 1024 comparisons to make an insertion. Because $\log_2 1024$ is 10, the full binary tree method will require at most 11. This difference becomes even more dramatic as N gets larger. For an ordered list with 1,000,000 entries, a linked list may require that many comparisons; the full binary tree requires a mere 21 comparisons.

In the world of applications ...

The front page headline in the January 23, 1984 issue of *Computerworld* proclaimed the **UNIX operating system** from AT&T Technologies "the operating system of the 80s". The article went on to point out that one of the reasons for the popularity of UNIX was its "hierarchical file system." In effect, the UNIX file directory system can be viewed as a large tree structure similar to that pictured below.

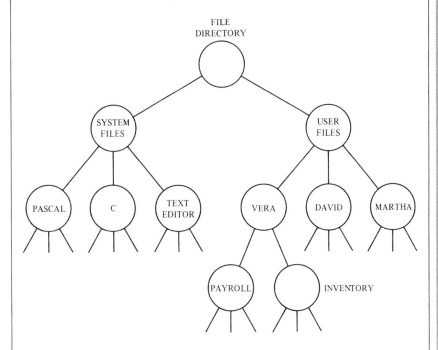

UNIX-like file directory system

Each interior node of the tree can be viewed as a directory containing various system information about those files or subdirectories that are its descendants. Hence, in the diagram, files can be broken down into system files and user files. System files consist of the Pascal library, the C library, and the text editing system. User directories are called VERA, DAVID, and MARTHA. One of the very convenient features of UNIX is that it allows the user to extend this tree structure as deep as desired. For instance, in the tree directory structure above, we see that user VERA has created subdirectories for files related to PAYROLL and INVENTORY. DAVID and MARTHA have similarly partitioned subdirectories. A UNIX command language then allows users to traverse these various subdirectories in a fashion consistent with file security. The extreme popularity of this tree-structured approach is rapidly making UNIX one of the rare operating systems that is able to migrate from one computer system to another.

Such attractiveness rarely comes without corresponding disadvantages, and this case is no exception. For instance, deleting from an ordered list maintained with a binary tree is more complex than deleting from one maintained with a linked list. Suppose we wish to remove TALBOT from the list represented by the tree in Figure 6-18. Two questions arise:

1. Can such a deletion be achieved merely by manipulating pointers?
2. If so, what does the resulting tree look like?

The answers to both of these questions are given in the algorithm in the next section.

Deletion Algorithm for Lists Maintained with Binary Tree

All that is necessary to represent an ordered list with a binary tree is that, for each node in the tree:

1. The left subtree must contain only items less than or equal to it
2. The right subtree must contain only items greater than or equal to it

With the preservation of this ordering property as the primary goal in processing a deletion, one acceptable way of restructuring the tree of Figure 6-18 after deleting TALBOT appears in Figure 6-20; essentially, SMITH moves up to replace TALBOT in the tree. The choice of SMITH to replace TALBOT is made because SMITH represents the greatest data item in the left subtree of the node containing TALBOT. As long as we choose this greatest item in the left subtree to replace the item being deleted, we guarantee preservation of the crucial ordering property that enables the tree to represent the list accurately.

Given this general motivation for choosing a node to replace the one being deleted, let us now outline a case-by-case analysis of the deletion algorithm. Throughout this analysis, we assume that we have a pointer P to the item that we wish to delete. The pointer P may be:

1. The root pointer for the entire tree, or
2. The left child pointer of the parent of the node to be deleted, or
3. The right child pointer of the parent of the node to be deleted.

Figure 6-21 highlights these three possibilities; the algorithm applies whether (1), (2), or (3) holds.

We will examine three cases of node deletion on a binary tree:

1. The node to be deleted has a left child
2. The node to be deleted has a right child but no left child
3. The node to be deleted has no children

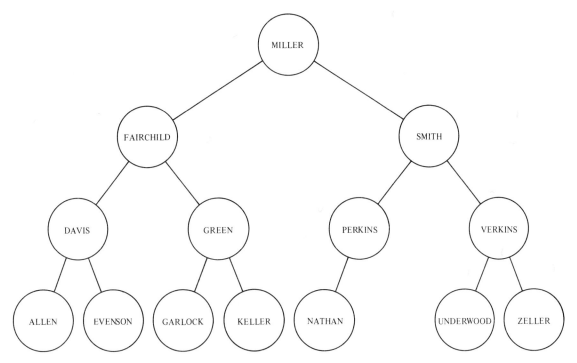

FIGURE 6-20 One way of restructuring the tree in Figure 6-18 after deleting TALBOT.

Case 1. The node pointed to by P, that is, the node to be deleted, has a left child. In Figure 6-22, node M is to be deleted, and has left child K. In this case, because we have a non-null left subtree of the node to be deleted, our previous discussion indicates that we must find the greatest node in that left subtree. If the node pointed to by P^.LLINK (node K in the figure) has no right child, then the greatest node in the left subtree of P is P^.LLINK itself. Figure 6-22 pictorially describes this situation; the dotted lines indicate new pointer values.

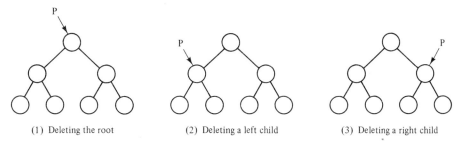

(1) Deleting the root   (2) Deleting a left child   (3) Deleting a right child

FIGURE 6-21 The three possibilities for the pointer P.

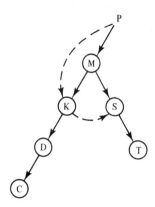

FIGURE 6-22   Case 1 with Pˆ.LLINK (node K) having no right children.

The partial coding to achieve this pointer manipulation is given by:

```
X := P;
P := Xˆ. LLINK;
Pˆ. RLINK := Xˆ. RLINK;
DISPOSE(X);
```

where LLINK and RLINK refer to the left and right child pointers described earlier in this chapter.

If the node pointed to by Pˆ.LLINK does have a right child, then to find the greatest node in the left subtree of P we must follow the right branch leading from Pˆ.LLINK as deeply as possible into the tree. Figure 6-23 gives the schematic representation, with the pointer

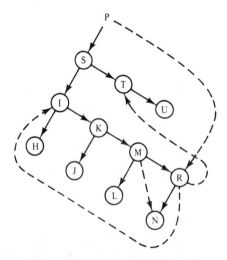

FIGURE 6-23   Case 1 with Pˆ.LLINK having a right child.
Node R is the one chosen to replace the deleted node.

changes necessary to complete the deletion. The coding necessary for this slightly more complicated version of Case 1 is:

```
X := P;
Q:=X^. LLINK^. RLINK
QPARENT := X^. LLINK;

{ Q will eventually point to node to replace P.}
{ QPARENT will point to Q's parent.}
{ The following loop forces Q as deep as possible}
{ along the right branch leaving P^. LLINK }

WHILE Q^. RLINK <> NIL DO
BEGIN
      Q := Q^. RLINK;
      QPARENT := QPARENT^. RLINK
END;

{Having found node Q to replace P, adjust}
{pointers to appropriately link it into the}
{tree.}

Q^. RLINK :=X^. RLINK;
P := Q;
QPARENT^. RLINK := Q^. LLINK;
Q^. LLINK := X^. LLINK;
DISPOSE(X);
```

Case 2. The node pointed to by P, that is, the node to be deleted, has a right child but no left child. This case is substantially easier than Case 1 and is described in Figure 6-24. The node to be deleted is merely replaced by its right child. The necessary Pascal coding is:

```
X := P;
P := X^. RLINK;
DISPOSE(X);
```

Case 3. The node pointed to by P, that is, the node to be deleted, has no children. As indicated in Figure 6-25, this is the easiest of all the cases. It can be compactly handled by the same coding used for Case 2 or, more directly, by:

```
X := P;
P := NIL;
DISPOSE(X);
```

It is important to note that, in all three cases, the deletion of a node from the tree involved only pointer manipulation and no actual data movement. Hence, in a list maintained with a binary tree, we are able to process both insertions and deletions by the same pure pointer manipulation that makes linked lists so desirable. Moreover, the binary tree approach apparently allows us to locate insertion or deletion

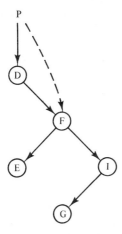

FIGURE 6-24 *Case 2: the node pointed to by P has a right but no left child.*

points much faster than a linked list representation would. However, there are aspects of the binary tree method that tarnish its performance in comparison to a linked list. In particular:

1. The binary tree method requires more memory in two respects. First, each node has two pointers instead of the one required in a singly linked list. This proliferation of pointers is particularly wasteful because many of the pointers may be NIL. Second, we presently can traverse the tree in order only by using recursive techniques. Even in a language that allows recursion, a substantial amount of overhead is needed to maintain the stack used by recursive calls.

2. The $(\log_2 N + 1)$ efficiency of the binary tree method is only an optimal, not a guaranteed, efficiency. It is contingent upon the tree's remaining full. In the worst possible case, data entering the tree structure in the wrong order can cause the tree to degenerate into a glorified linked list. (Try to identify what this worst case is.)

FIGURE 6-25 *Case 3: The node pointed to by P has no children. P must be set to NIL and the node returned.*

Hence a theme that has already emerged in previous chapters must be reiterated. There are no absolute answers to data structure questions; rather, the best you can hope for is to know the relative advantages of various structures and to apply this knowledge to particular situations. In the next chapter, we will introduce variations on tree structures that allow you to *partially* overcome the two problems cited.

Program Design Considerations

The following Pascal program will allow input of a prefix expression, such as —+AB+CD$ (with '$' as the final delimiting character,) and then build the binary tree corresponding to that expression. The program uses the three traversal procedures already given in the text, which need to be substituted at the appropriate points in the program. This has been indicated by the comment entries in the program. The modular design of the program given here highlights this activity.

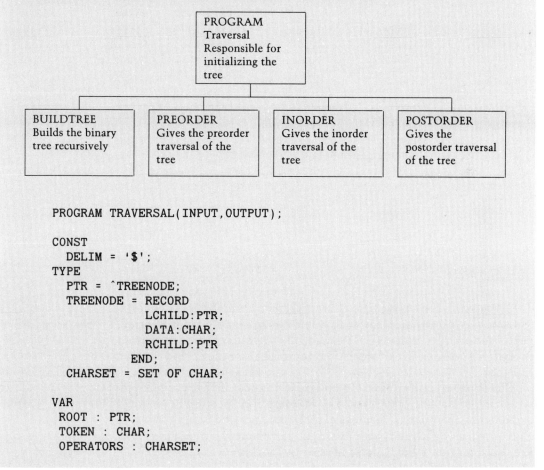

```
PROGRAM TRAVERSAL(INPUT,OUTPUT);

CONST
   DELIM = '$';
TYPE
   PTR = ^TREENODE;
   TREENODE = RECORD
                LCHILD:PTR;
                DATA:CHAR;
                RCHILD:PTR
              END;
   CHARSET = SET OF CHAR;

VAR
   ROOT : PTR;
   TOKEN : CHAR;
   OPERATORS : CHARSET;
```

```
    PROCEDURE BUILDTREE(ROOT : PTR);
    { BUILDTREE builds the appropriate binary tree }

  BEGIN
    READ(TOKEN);
    IF TOKEN IN OPERATORS
      THEN
       BEGIN
       ROOT^.DATA := TOKEN;
       {Get the new node for the left child }
       NEW(ROOT^.LCHILD);
       BUILDTREE(ROOT^..LCHILD) { Recursive call to BUILDTREE };

       { Get the new node for the right child }

       NEW(ROOT^.RCHILD)
       END
    ELSE  IF TOKEN <> DELIM THEN
      BEGIN
      ROOT^.DATA := TOKEN;
      ROOT^.LCHILD := NIL;
      ROOT^.RCHILD := NIL
      END
    END;
  {The main program calls the procedures INORDER, POSTORDER }
  { and PREORDER. Their exact equivalents are given in the
    text. }
  { These can easily be substituted here. }
```

SUMMARY

Tree structures are heavily used in representing hierarchical data relationships. A binary tree has only a left subtree and a right subtree. Postorder, inorder, and preorder traversals of a binary tree can be used in parsing expressions, statistical analyses, or sort and search routines.

There are always advantages and disadvantages for any given data structure, and a tree is by no means an exception. Despite the storage occupied by the pointers necessary to maintain a tree, search and sort algorithms using a binary tree are highly efficient in processing time. We will examine more diverse uses of trees in later chapters.

```
       BEGIN { TRAVERSAL }

         OPERATORS := ['+','-','/','*'];

         { Initialize the tree }

         NEW(ROOT);
         ROOT^.LCHILD := NIL;
         ROOT^.RCHILD := NIL;

       { Allow entry of prefix expression and build the tree }

         BUILDTREE(ROOT);

       { Now call on the three traversals }

         WRITELN;
         PREORDER(ROOT);
         WRITELN;
         INORDER(ROOT);
         WRITELN;
         POSTORDER(ROOT)
       END.
```

KEY TERMS

Tree	Right Subtree
Binary Tree	Left Child
Node	Right Child
Root	Depth of a Tree
Branch	Inorder Traversal
Child	Preorder Traversal
Left Subtree	Postorder Traversal

EXERCISES

1. Describe a full binary tree.
2. How is a linked representation of a binary tree an improvement over its linear representation?
3. How does inorder traversal of a binary tree help you to sort data?
4. Which of the three traversal schemes of a binary tree leads to the reverse-Polish notation for evaluating an arithmetic expression?

5. Draw a binary tree for the expression:

```
A * B - (C + D) * (P/Q)
```

6. Using a preorder traversal of the tree from Exercise (5) obtain the prefix form of the expression.
7. Represent STUDENTREC as a binary tree:

```
NAME = RECORD
         FIRSTNAME : ARRAY [1..10] OF CHAR;
         LASTNAME : ARRAY [1..10] OF CHAR
       END;

YEAR = RECORD
         FIRSTSEM : ARRAY [1..2] OF CHAR;
         SECONDSEM : ARRAY [1..2] OF CHAR
       END;

STUDENTREC = RECORD
         STUDENTNAME : NAME;
         YEAROFSTUDY : YEAR
       END;
```

8. Discuss the relative merits of maintaining an ordered list by a binary tree, a singly linked list, and a doubly linked list.
9. Discuss how the order in which data are entered into a binary tree representation of a list affects the fullness of the tree. Identify the best and worst possible cases.
10. Develop a complete Pascal procedure to process the insertion of a node into the binary tree representation of an ordered list.
11. Develop a complete Pascal procedure to process the deletion of a node from a binary tree representation of an ordered list. This will essentially require that you combine into one module the three cases discussed in the chapter.

PROGRAMMING PROBLEMS

1. Modify the airline reservation system you developed for the Wing-and-a-Prayer Airlines Company in Programming Problem (1) of Chapter 3 so that the alphabetized lists are maintained with binary trees instead of linked lists.
2. Write a program that sorts the records of the Fly-By-Night credit card company file in alphabetic order by the last name and then the first name of the customer. Use a binary tree and its inorder traversal to accomplish the sort.
3. Recall the roster maintenance system which you wrote for the Bay Area Brawlers in the problems for Chapters 2 and 3. The system

has been so successful that the league office would like to expand the system to include all the players in the league. Again the goal is to maintain the list of players in alphabetical order, allowing for frequent insertions and deletions as players are cut, picked up, and traded among teams. In addition to storing each player's height, weight, age and university affiliation, the record for each player should be expanded to include team affiliation, years in league, and annual salary. Because the database for the entire league is many times larger than that for just one team, maintain this list as a binary tree to increase efficiency.

4. Write a program that reads an expression in its prefix form and builds the binary tree corresponding to that expression. Then write procedures to print the infix and postfix forms of the expression using inorder and postorder traversals of this tree. Then see if you can write a program to evaluate the expression represented by the tree.

5. Write a program to implement a recursive postorder traversal for a binary tree.

6. Write a program that uses a stack to achieve a nonrecursive postorder traversal of a binary tree.

7. Using a linear representation of a binary tree, write a program to achieve inorder, preorder, and postorder traversals of the tree.

8. Re-do programming problem (1) or (2) from Chapter 2, maintaining the lists involved by using binary trees instead of linked lists.

9. Here is a problem you will encounter if you write statistical analysis software. Given an arbitrarily long list of unordered numbers with an arbitrary number of different values appearing in it, determine and print out the marginal distribution for this list of numbers. That is, count how many times each different value appears in the list and then print out each value along with its count (**frequency**). The final output should be arranged from smallest to largest value. This problem can be solved in elegant fashion using trees. An example of such output as produced by the COSAP package (Conversationally Oriented Statistical Analysis Package) package of Lawrence University appears below.

```
Command? MARGINALS JUDGE
Do you want the statistics (Yes or No) *? NO
              Outagamie County Criminal Cases 1973-74

              M A R G I N A L   F R E Q U E N C I E S
Variable  JUDGE      JUDGE BEFORE WHOM CASE BROUGHT (2)
Value label      Value        Absolute        Relative
                              Frequency       Frequency

SHAFER            1             677            80.8%
CANE              2              88            10.5%
VANSUS            3              26             3.1%
MYSE              5              47             5.6%

    838 Valid  0 Missing   838 Total Observations
```

Here the data file contained 838 occurrences of the values 1, 2, 3, and 5 representing judges.

10. Here is a problem from the area of text analysis but with logic similar to that of programming problem (7). Given a file containing some arbitrary text, determine how many times each word appears in the file. Your program should print out in alphabetical order the words that appear in the file, with their frequency counts. For an added challenge, do not assume any maximum word length; this will enable you to combine trees with the string-handling methods you learned in Chapter 3.

11. Many compilers offer the services of a cross-referencing program to aid in debugging. Such cross-referencing will list in alphabetical order all the identifiers that appear in a program and the various lines of the program that reference them. A sample of what a cross-referencer for a BASIC program might produce as output follows. (*'s in this output indicate references where the identifier may potentially be changed.) Write such a cross-referencer for your favorite language.

```
OLD SORTCL

Ready

LIST
SORTCL  11:13 AM       04-Jul-85

10 DIM A$(150)
15 INPUT 'CLASS NAME';C$
17 OPEN C$+'.LST' FOR OUTPUT AS FILE #1%
20 INPUT 'HOW MANY';N
30 FOR I+1 TO N-1
40 INPUT 'STUDENT NAME';A$(I)
50 NEXT I
60 FOR I=1 TO N-1
70 FOR J=1 TO N-I
80 X$=A$(J)
90 Y$=A$(J+1)
100 IF X$<=Y$ THEN 130
110 A$(J)=Y$
120 A$(J+1)=X$
130 NEXT J
140 NEXT I
150 PRINT/PRINT/PRINT/PRINT/PRINT
160 FOR I=1 TO N
170 PRINT #1,A$(I);TAB(20);'_/_/_/_/_/_/_/
180 NEXT I
190 END
```

```
Ready

RUN %CREF

Lawrence CREF V1.2
Input? SORTCL
Output <KB:>?
Options?
```

Cross Reference Listing of SORTCL.BAS on 04-Jul-85 at 11:14 AM

Variables

A$( )	10	*40	80	90	*110	*120	170
C$	*15	17					
I	*30	40	50	*60	70	140	*160
	170	180					
J	*70	80	90	110	120	130	
N	*20	30	60	70	160		
X$	*80	100	120				
Y$	*90	100	110				

Line Numbers

#	130	100

```
KB:SORTCL.CRF created, run time was 1.9 seconds.
There were 8 identifiers and line numbers,
and 36 references to them.
```

12. A relatively easy game to implement with a binary tree is to have the computer try to guess an animal about which the user is thinking by asking the user a series of YES/NO questions. A node in the binary tree to play this game could be viewed as

   YES/NO pointers leading to:

   1. Another question
   2. The name of the animal
   3. NIL

   If NIL, have your program surrender and then ask the user for a new question that uniquely defines the animal being thought of, and then add this new question to the growing binary tree database.

7

Variations on Tree Structures

"As the twig is bent, the tree inclines."

VIRGIL (70-19 B.C.)

7-1   Introductory Considerations

In Chapter 6, we discussed using a binary tree as an efficient alternative to a linked list. Efficiency in this context referred to speed of processing the list as opposed to storage utilization. In sections 7-2 and 7-3 we will discuss two techniques, **threading** and **height-balancing**, used to improve significantly the processing speed of a list implemented with a binary tree. Be forewarned that both of these techniques require additional data storage for each tree node; the conflict of speed versus storage efficiency emerges again. This tradeoff, along with the complexities involved in implementation, means that you should carefully weigh a decision to use either technique in a given application.

Efficiency Considerations

The primary motivation for threading a tree is to eliminate the need for recursion (or simulating recursion) in traversing a tree. The elegance of recursion in expressing an algorithm can sometimes hide the fact that it may be a very costly technique. Preserving all necessary local parameters before a recursive call requires both time and stack space. Hence, it may well be better to use an algorithm that is free from the overhead associated with recursion even if it is not as compactly stated. In threading a tree, we will use the numerous pointer locations that are normally null in a linked representation of a binary tree to store information that will lead us through a specified tree traversal in a completely nonrecursive fashion.

176

Whereas threading is used to enhance efficiency in traversing a tree, height-balancing is aimed at maximizing the speed with which insertions and searches in a tree are handled. In particular, if we restrict our attention to a tree satisfying the ordering property

- Left subtree less than
- Right subtree greater than

described in the last chapter, it is clear that nodes distributed in a tree with many short branches represent a far more efficient structure than the same collection of nodes distributed in a tree with relatively few long branches. For example, although trees A and B in Figure 7-1 contain the same data nodes, tree B requires significantly fewer comparisons for insertions and searches than tree A.

This is because tree B is *full* in the sense defined in Chapter 6. However, we have no guarantee that a full tree will develop if we merely insert nodes in any arbitrary order. Indeed, many orders of insertion result in trees that are decidedly not full. To maintain a perfectly full tree requires considerable data shifting each time a node is inserted. Height-balancing, on the other hand, allows the tree to be maintained in a form that is relatively full and yet requires only a few pointer manipulations each time a node is inserted.

7-2   Threaded Binary Trees

Consider the linked representation of a binary tree in Figure 6-11 on page 149. There are ten wasted fields taken up by NIL pointers. These could be effectively used to point to significant nodes chosen according to a traversal scheme to be used for the tree. For the inorder traversal of the binary tree in Figure 6-11, note that the node "A" comes

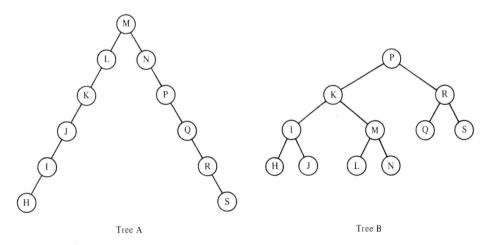

Tree A   Tree B

FIGURE 7-1   Both trees contain the same data nodes, but the many short branches of tree B require fewer comparisons for insertions and searches.

before "−" and that "B" is preceded by "−" but followed by the root node "+." With an inorder traversal, we could therefore adjust the RLINK pointer field of the node containing 'B' (presently NIL) to point to the node containing '+', and the LLINK pointer field of the node containing 'B' to point to its predecessor node '−'. The inorder traversal of this tree yields the expression

```
A-B+C*E/F
```

Notice that "B" comes after "−" but before "+." Similarly, because "E" is preceded by "*" but followed by "/", the NIL left link of the node containing "E" should, in our scheme, point to "*"; the NIL right link of "E" should point to "/."

Because we are arranging pointers to the **inorder predecessor and successor** of a leaf node, we call these pointers **inorder threads.** Following a thread pointer allows us to ascend strategically one or more appropriate levels in the tree without relying on recursion. Figure 7-2 is the transformed version of Figure 6-11 with threads indicated by dotted lines. Threads that take the place of a left child pointer indicate the inorder predecessor, whereas those taking the place of a right child pointer lead to the inorder successor.

The two threads on the left and right of Figure 7-2 are the only loose threads at this stage. To correct this situation, we shall assume that a threaded binary tree is the left subtree of a root node whose right child pointer points to itself. According to this convention, an empty threaded binary tree will appear as in Figure 7-3. This choice of

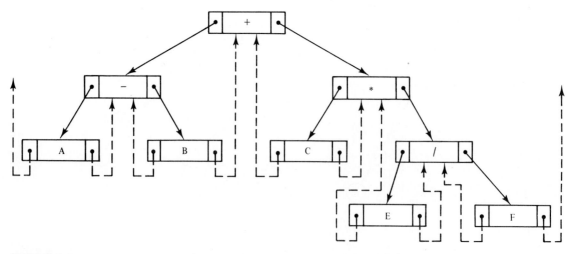

FIGURE 7-2 The threaded version of the binary tree represented in Figure 6-11.

FIGURE 7-3 *An empty threaded binary tree containing only the dummy root node.*

a dummy root node for a threaded binary tree is similar to the convention that we adopted in Chapter 2 of using a dummy header for a linked list. By initially setting the pointers as indicated in Figure 7-3, we shall see that we avoid having to treat the empty tree as a special case in our algorithms to process threaded trees.

In order to keep track of which pointers are threads, we shall include two additional boolean fields in each node. One of these fields, TLPOINT, will be used to indicate whether the left link of the node is an actual pointer or a thread. TRPOINT will be used analogously for the right link. Let P be a pointer to a node. We will follow the convention that

    P^. TLPOINT = FALSE

means that P^.LLINK is a normal pointer. Similarly

    P^. TLPOINT = TRUE

means that the left link of the node pointed to by P is a thread pointer. Similar interpretations hold for P^.TRPOINT = TRUE and P^.TRPOINT = FALSE. The purpose of this boolean information as a means of identifying various pointers is only to help facilitate algorithms for different *modes of traversing the tree.* When we incorporate the header and boolean information into the tree of Figure 6-10, it takes the form of Figure 7-4.

To achieve an inorder traversal of the tree in Figure 7-4, we must proceed from each given node to its inorder successor. The inorder successor of a node is determined by one of two methods depending upon whether or not the right child pointer to the node in question is a thread or a normal pointer. If it is a thread, then it leads us directly to the inorder successor. If it is not a thread, then we must follow the right child pointer to the node it references and, from there, follow left child pointers until we encounter a left thread. To convince yourself of this last step, consider the threaded tree that is given in Figure 7-5. In this tree, to get the inorder successor of the node containing 'M' we must first follow the right child pointer from 'M' to 'V' and then go left as deep as possible in the tree, finally arriving at the node containing

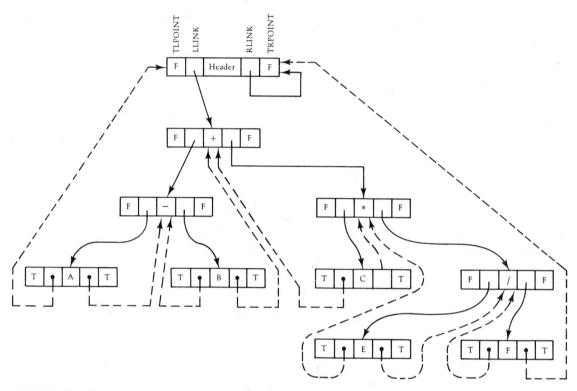

FIGURE 7-4   The threaded tree in Figure 7-2 with a header and boolean information added.

'Q'. Note also that this general strategy of "proceeding one to the right, then left as deep as possible" in combination with the initial setting of the right child pointer to the header node insures that the inorder traversal begins with the proper node.

   The following Pascal procedure more formally expresses the algorithm for a threaded inorder traversal discussed above. Note that it is achieved without any need for recursion or the use of a stack to simulate recursion.

```
{ Global Variables and Data Types }

TYPE
  POINTER = ^TREENODE;
  TREENODE =
    RECORD
      TLPOINT: BOOLEAN;
      LLINK: POINTER;
      DATA: CHAR; { Or other appropriate type }
      RLINK: POINTER;
      TRPOINT: BOOLEAN
    END;
```

```
PROCEDURE THREADEDINORDER(ROOT: POINTER);
{ Performs a threaded inorder traversal of the tree with dummy
root node pointed to by ROOT }

  { Local Variables }

  VAR
    P: POINTER;

  BEGIN
    P := ROOT;
    REPEAT
{ The following IF statement alters P to point to its
  inorder successor }

      IF P^.TRPOINT THEN
        P := P^.RLINK
      ELSE
        BEGIN
          P := P^.RLINK;
          WHILE NOT P^.TLPOINT DO
            P := P^LLINK
        END;

      { P now has been changed to point to its inorder successor }

      { Next check to see whether or not we have returned to the ROOT,
        i.e., completed the traversal }

      IF P <> ROOT THEN
        WRITELN(P^.DATA)
    UNTIL P = ROOT
  END;
{ End THREADEDINORDER }
```

We encourage the reader to trace carefully through this procedure on the tree appearing in Figure 7-5. It should also be verified that the procedure gracefully prints nothing when the ROOT pointer refers to an empty tree. A few minor modifications to the procedure will yield a new procedure

```
PROCEDURE REVERSE_THREADED_INORDER(ROOT)
```

which will employ the predecessor threads to do a reverse inorder traversal. Note that, if a given application required only forward traversing of the tree, there would be no necessity to maintain these predecessor threads. In that case, the left child pointers of the leaf nodes could remain NIL or perhaps even thread the tree for a preorder traversal. (See the exercises at the end of the chapter.)

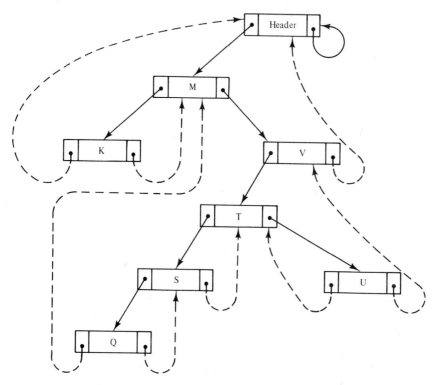

FIGURE 7-5 If the right child pointer is not a thread, you must go to the node referenced by it and then follow left child pointers until you encounter a left thread. Trace the process here to find "Q" as the inorder successor of "M".

Insertions into a Threaded Tree

A valid question at this stage is, "Where do the threads come from?" In our examples so far, they have merely been drawn as dotted line pointers in the context of an already existing tree. We stress, however, that in practice threads cannot exist unless they are continually maintained as nodes are added to the tree. In the discussion which follows we will develop a procedure to insert a node into a binary tree. In performing insertions we will preserve the ordering property cited in the last section of Chapter 6. That is, for any given node, its left subtree contains only data less than (or equal to) it while its right subtree contains only data greater than (or equal to) it. In order to insure that this property is met for the dummy root node, we stipulate that *the data portion of the dummy root node should be initialized to a value greater than any other data which will appear in the tree.*

Given this criterion, insertions require that the node to be inserted should travel down a branch of the tree following the *insertion rule:*

"Less than, go left; greater than, go right"

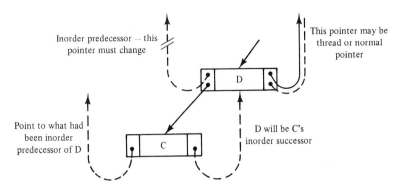

FIGURE 7-6 Insert C as left child of leaf node D.

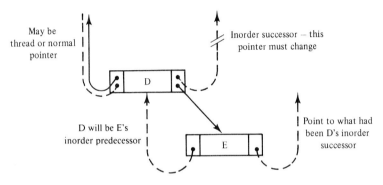

FIGURE 7-7 Insert E as right child of leaf node D.

Upon reaching a thread (that is, where a null pointer would be in an un-threaded tree), the new node is inserted appropriately as the left or right child. Figures 7-6 and 7-7 illustrate the pointer manipulations that must occur in each of these cases.

These pointer manipulations are achieved by the following procedure INSERTTHREADED. Notice that, as is essential to any efficient insertion algorithm, no actual data is moved within the tree.

```
{ Global Variables and Data Types }

TYPE
  POINTER = ^TREENODE;
  TREENODE =
    RECORD
      TLPOINT: BOOLEAN;
      LLINK: POINTER;
      DATA: CHAR; { Or other appropriate type }
      RLINK: POINTER;
      TRPOINT: BOOLEAN
    END;
```

```
PROCEDURE INSERTTHREADED(ROOT: POINTER;
                        ITEM: CHAR);
  { Procedure to insert ITEM into a threaded tree pointed to by ROOT }

  { Local Variables }

  VAR
    Q, P, PARENTQ: POINTER;
    LEFT: BOOLEAN;

  BEGIN
    NEW(P);
    P^.DATA := ITEM;
```

{ Next allow this pointer to travel down appropriate branch of the tree until an insertion spot is found. }

```
    Q := ROOT;
    PARENTQ := NIL;
    REPEAT
      IF ITEM < Q^.DATA THEN
        BEGIN
        PARENTQ := Q;
        Q := Q^.LLINK;
        LEFT := TRUE
        END
      ELSE
        BEGIN
        PARENTQ := Q;
        Q := Q^.RLINK;
        LEFT := FALSE
        END
    UNTIL (LEFT AND PARENTQ^.TLPOINT) OR (NOT LEFT AND PARENTQ^.TRPOINT);
```

UNTIL conditional controlling REPEAT

PARENTQ

Leaf node may be reached with
LEFT AND PARENTQ^.TLPOINT
OR
Leaf node may be reached with
NOT LEFT AND PARENTQ^.TRPOINT

PARENTQ

{ Now insert P as the left or right child of PARENTQ }

```
    P^.TLPOINT := TRUE;
    P^.TRPOINT := TRUE;
    IF LEFT THEN
      BEGIN
      P^.LLINK := PARENTQ^.LLINK;
      P^.RLINK := PARENTQ;
      PARENTQ^.LLINK := P;
      PARENTQ^.TLPOINT := FALSE
      END
```

```
    ELSE
      BEGIN
      P^.RLINK := PARENTQ^.RLINK;
      P^.LLINK := PARENTQ;
      PARENTQ^.RLINK := P;
      PARENTQ^.TRPOINT := FALSE
      END
  END;
{ End INSERTTHREADED }
```

Deletion of a node from a threaded tree may be handled by considering the same cases that motivated our discussion in 6-5. The only additional consideration to our previous discussion is the maintenance of the boolean thread indicators. Hence, a threaded tree is a structure with very little overhead. The only new fields required are the threads. Moreover, in practice, if space limitations are severe, they may be incorporated into a bit of the left and right child pointers (though methods for doing this will be highly system-dependent). They thus represent a true bargain. By spending very little, one regains both the time and stack space that were required for recursion.

7-3 Height-Balanced Trees

Height-balanced binary trees, on the other hand, represent an alternative which often may not be worth the additional storage space and developmental complexities introduced for the sake of increasing speed. After describing the method, we shall cite some statistics which may help in deciding whether or not to height-balance a tree in a particular application.

The technique was developed in 1962 by researchers G. M. Adelson-Velskii and Y. M. Landis. (Because of this, height-balanced trees are also referred to as **AVL trees**.) It represents an attempt to maintain trees which possess the ordering property of section 6-5 in a form which is close to fullness, thereby insuring rapid insertions and searches. One of the costs involved in doing this is that each node of the tree must store an additional item called its **balance factor**. The balance factor of a node is defined to be the difference between the height of its left subtree and the height of its right subtree. In this context the **height** of a tree is the number of nodes visited in traversing a branch which leads to a leaf node at the deepest level of the tree. An example of a tree with computed balance factors for each node is given in Figure 7-8.

A tree is said to be **height-balanced** if all of its nodes have a balance factor of 1, 0, or −1. Hence the tree appearing in Figure 7-8 is not height-balanced. Note that every tree which is full is also height-balanced. However, the converse of this statement is not true. (Convince yourself of this latter fact by constructing an example.) The AVL

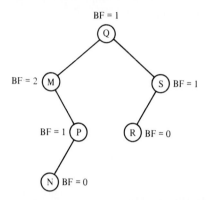

FIGURE 7-8   A tree with computed balance factors.

technique used to keep a tree in height-balance requires that, each time an insertion is made according to the insertion rule specified in 6-5, one must:

1. Let the node to be inserted travel down the appropriate branch, keeping track along the way of the deepest-level node on that branch which has a balance factor of +1 or −1. (This particular node is called the **pivot node** for reasons which will soon be apparent.) Insert the node at the appropriate point.
2. Inclusive of and below the pivot node, re-compute all balance factors along the insertion path traced in (1). It will be shown that no nodes other than these can possibly change their balance factors using the AVL method.
3. Determine whether the absolute value of the pivot node's balance factor switched from 1 to 2.
4. If there was such a switch as indicated in (3), perform a manipulation of tree pointers centered at the pivot node to bring the tree back into height balance. Since the visual effect of this pointer manipulation will be to "rotate" the subtree whose root is the pivot node, the operation is frequently referred to as an **AVL-rotation.**

We shall cover these steps in reverse order because, until one fully understands the nature of the AVL-rotation, it is not apparent why the pivot node is chosen as specified in (1).

AVL-Rotations

In the discussion which follows we assume that steps (1), (2), and (3) above have all been completed and that we have a pointer, PIVOT, to the deepest-level node whose balance factor has switched from an absolute value of 1 to 2. In practice, PIVOT may be the root pointer for the entire tree or the child pointer of a parent node inside the tree. The pointer manipulations required to rebalance the tree necessitate division into four cases distinguished by the direction of the "guilty" insertion relative to the pivot node.

Case 1.   The insertion that unbalanced the tree occurred in the left subtree of the left child of the pivot node. In this case, the situation pictured in Figure 7-9 must have occurred. Our only criterion for rebalancing the tree is the preservation of the ordering property for binary trees. Hence, if we could force a rotation (merely through changes in pointers) that made the tree pointed to by PIVOT appear as in Figure 7-10, the rebalancing would be complete. The procedure to achieve this rotation is given below.

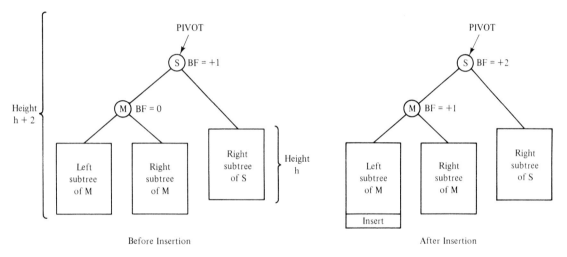

FIGURE 7-9   Case 1: The insertion occurred in the left subtree of the left child of the pivot node.

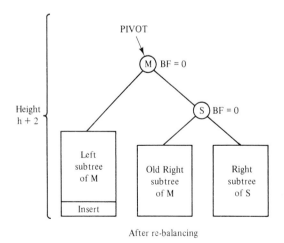

FIGURE 7-10   Case 1 after rebalancing.

```
{ Global Variables and Data Types }

TYPE
  POINTER = ^TREENODE;
  TREENODE =
    RECORD
      LLINK: POINTER;
      DATA: CHAR;
      BF: INTEGER;
      RLINK: POINTER
    END;

PROCEDURE LEFTOFLEFT(VAR PIVOT: POINTER);
  { Perform AVL rotation for Case 1 on the subtree pointed to by PIVOT }

  { Local variables }

  VAR
    P, Q: POINTER;

  BEGIN

    { Begin by altering the necessary pointers }
    P := PIVOT^.LLINK;
    Q := P^.RLINK;
    P^.RLINK := PIVOT;
    PIVOT^.LLINK := Q;
    PIVOT := P;

    { Then readjust the balance factors that have been affected }

    PIVOT^.BF := 0;
    PIVOT^.RLINK^.BF := 0
  END;
{ End LEFTOFLEFT }
```

Case 2. The insertion that unbalanced the tree occurred in the right subtree of the right child of the pivot node. In this case, the situation pictured in Figure 7-11 must have occurred. Figure 7-12 indicates the rebalancing that should occur. Again, the idea is to rotate the tree

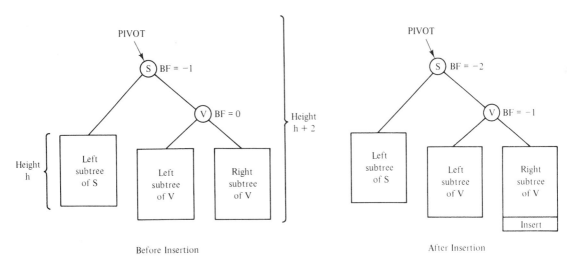

FIGURE 7-11   Case 2: The insertion occurred in the right subtree of the right child of the pivot node.

around the pivot node, except that this time the rotation must occur in the opposite direction. The procedure RIGHTOFRIGHT necessary to achieve this rotation is left as an exercise. It is essentially a mirror image of the LEFTOFLEFT procedure.

Case 3.   The insertion causing the imbalance occurred in the right subtree of the left child of the pivot node. In this case, the procedure to perform the pointer manipulations necessary to rebalance the tree will require subdivision into three subcases. The best way of describing them is via the diagrammatic form of Figures 7-13, 7-14, and 7-15 respectively.

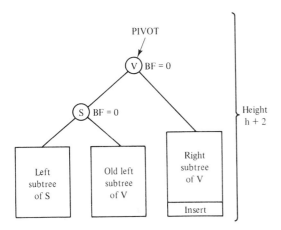

FIGURE 7-12   Case 2 after rebalancing.

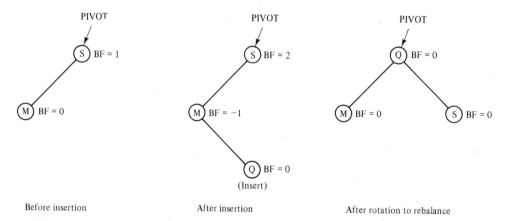

FIGURE 7-13   Case 3, subcase #1. Neither PIVOT node nor its left child have a right child. Insertion occurs as the right child or the left child of the PIVOT node.

At first glance, the need for splitting Case 3 into three subcases may not be apparent. Indeed all three subcases require nearly identical pointer changes. However, the subtle point of differentiation among the three lies in how the balance factors are re-set after the rotation has occurred. This subtlety is taken into account in the following procedure to handle Case 3.

```
{ Global Variables and Data Types }

TYPE
  POINTER = ^TREENODE;
  TREENODE =
    RECORD
      LLINK: POINTER;
      DATA: CHAR;
      BF: INTEGER;
      RLINK: POINTER
    END;

PROCEDURE RIGHTOFLEFT(VAR PIVOT: POINTER);
  { Perform AVL-rotation for Case 3 on subtree pointed to by PIVOT }

  { Local Variables }

  VAR
    X, Y: POINTER;
```

```
BEGIN
  { First adjust pointers in fashion to perform AVL rotation }
  X := PIVOT^.LLINK;
  Y := X^.RLINK;
  PIVOT^.LLINK := Y^.RLINK;
  X^.RLINK := Y^.LLINK;
  Y^.LLINK := X;
  Y^.RLINK := PIVOT;
  PIVOT := Y;

  { Then reset the balance factors according to the subcase }

  IF PIVOT^.BF = 0 THEN { Subcase #1 }
    BEGIN
    PIVOT^.LLINK^.BF := 0;
    PIVOT^.RLINK^.BF := 0
    END
  ELSE IF PIVOT^.BF = 1 THEN { Subcase #2 }
    BEGIN
    PIVOT^.BF := 0;
    PIVOT^.LLINK^.BF := 0;
    PIVOT^.RLINK^.BF := - 1
    END
  ELSE { Subcase #3 }
    BEGIN
    PIVOT^.BF := 0;
    PIVOT^.LLINK^.BF := 1;
    PIVOT^.RLINK^.BF := 0
    END
  END;
{ End RIGHTOFLEFT }
```

Case 4. The insertion which causes the imbalance in the tree is made in the left subtree of the right child of the pivot node. Case 4 is to Case 3 as Case 2 is to Case 1; it is left as an exercise to write the procedure LEFTOFRIGHT.

Why Does the AVL Height-Balancing Technique Work?

Upon first studying the AVL algorithm, it is often not apparent why the pivot node must be the *deepest* node along the path of insertion that has a balance factor of $+1$ or -1. After all, it would seem that the pictures of Figures 7-11 through 7-15 work equally well as long as

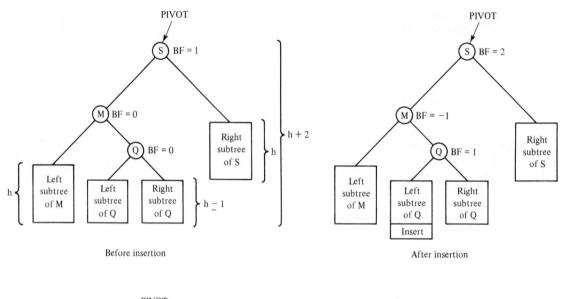

Before insertion   After insertion

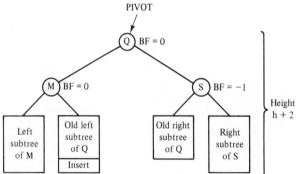

After rotation to rebalance

FIGURE 7-14 Case 3, subcase #2. Insertion is in the left subtree of the right child of the left child of the PIVOT.

PIVOT points to any node along the insertion path that has a change in the magnitude of its balance factor from 1 to 2. However, three rather subtle reasons are involved in the selection of the pivot node to be not just *any* node of balance factor of +1 or −1 along the insertion path but the *deepest* such node.

First, it is quite evident that we must choose a node whose original balance factor is +1 or −1 as the pivot node. Such nodes are the only candidates for points at which the tree can go out of height-balance. Any node with balance factor zero can at worst change to +1 or −1 after insertion, therefore not requiring any rotation at all.

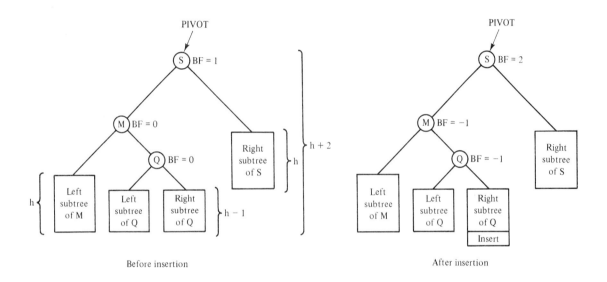

Before insertion   After insertion

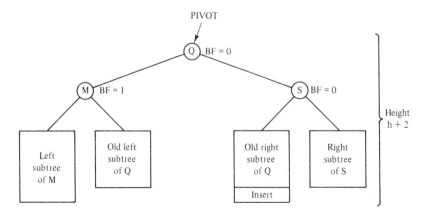

After rotation to rebalance

FIGURE 7-15 Case 3, subcase #3. Insertion occurs in the right subtree of the right child of the left child of the PIVOT.

Second, whether or not a rotation takes place, *the only balance factors in the entire tree that will be affected are those of nodes inclusive of and below the pivot node along the insertion path.* In situations where a rotation does occur, this is evident from Figures 7-11 thru 7-15. In all four cases of AVL-rotations, the overall height of the subtree pointed to by PIVOT is the same after the rotation as it was before. In situations where no rotation occurs, the balance factor of the pivot node must change from either 1 to 0 or from −1 to 0; it cannot remain what it originally was. This is because every node below it on the insertion path must have an original balance factor of zero. Consequently, there is no way that an insertion may "hide" in a fashion not affecting the balance factor of the pivot node. However, the fact that the pivot node changes to a zero balance factor in such situations again means that the rest of the tree above the pivot node is unaffected by the insertion.

Third, if we do not choose the deepest level node with balance factor equal to +1 or −1, we run the risk of having an AVL-rotation that only partially rebalances the tree. Figure 7-16 indicates how this could occur.

With this rationale in mind, we are now able to convincingly present a complete procedure to process an insertion into a height-balanced tree, re-compute all affected balance factors, and perform an AVL-rotation if necessary.

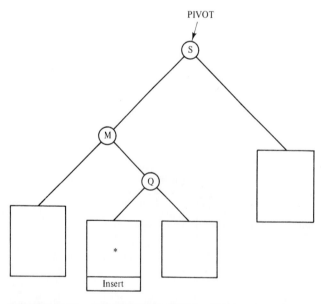

FIGURE 7-16   Case 3 incorrectly handled by not choosing proper pivot. AVL-rotation only partially rebalances the tree.

```
{ Global Variables and Data Types }

TYPE
  POINTER = ^TREENODE;
  TREENODE =
    RECORD
      LLINK: POINTER;
      DATA: CHAR;
      BF: INTEGER;
      RLINK: POINTER
    END;

PROCEDURE AVLINSERT(VAR ROOT: POINTER;
                    ITEM: CHAR);

{ Procedure to insert ITEM into the height-balanced tree pointed to by
 ROOT }

 { Local variables }

  VAR
    P, PIV, PIVPARENT, INP, INPARENT, Q: POINTER;

  BEGIN

    { First obtain tree node for ITEM via Pascal's procedure NEW(X) }

    NEW(P);
    P^.DATA := ITEM;
    P^.LLINK := NIL;
    P^.RLINK := NIL;
    P^.BF := 0;

    { Then check for an empty tree }

    IF ROOT = NIL THEN
      ROOT := P
    ELSE
      BEGIN

{Pointer INP keeps track of insertion point, with its parent
INPARENT. Pointer PIV keeps track of pivot node, with its parent
PIVPARENT. }

        INP := ROOT;
        PIV := ROOT;
        INPARENT := NIL;
        PIVPARENT := NIL;
```

```
{ Search for insertion point and pivot node }

REPEAT
    IF INP^.BF <> 0 THEN
      BEGIN
      PIV := INP;
      PIVPARENT := INPARENT
      END;
    INPARENT := INP;
    IF ITEM < INP^.DATA THEN
      INP := INP^.LLINK
    ELSE
      INP := INP^.RLINK
UNTIL INP = NIL;
```

At conclusion of REPEAT loop

```
{ Insert the node as the left or right child of INPARENT }

IF ITEM < INPARENT^.DATA THEN
    INPARENT^.LLINK := P
ELSE
    INPARENT^.RLINK := P;
```

{ Now re-compute the balance factors between PIV and INPARENT. By definition of a pivot node, all these balance factors must change by 1 in the direction of the insertion }

```
    Q := PIV;
    REPEAT
      IF ITEM < Q^.DATA THEN
        BEGIN
        Q^.BF := Q..BF + 1;
        Q := Q^.LLINK
        END
      ELSE
        BEGIN
        Q^.BF := Q^.BF - 1;
        Q := Q^.RLINK;
        END
    UNTIL Q = NIL
```

{ Need to rotate? If not, then we can now return }

```
    IF ( - l > PIV^. BF) OR (PIV^. BF > l) THEN

{ AVL rotation is necessary. Call on the appropriate procedure, passing
  one of ROOT, PIVPARENT^. LLINK or PIVPARENT^. RLINK as the pointer to
  the pivot node. }

        IF ITEM < PIV^. DATA THEN
          IF ITEM < PIV^. LLINK^. DATA THEN
            IF PIV = ROOT THEN
              LEFTOFLEFT(ROOT)
            ELSE IF PIV = PIVPARENT^. LLINK THEN
              LEFTOFLEFT(PIVPARENT^. LLINK)
            ELSE
              LEFTOFLEFT(PIVPARENT^. RLINK)
          ELSE IF PIV = ROOT THEN
            RIGHTOFLEFT(ROOT)
          ELSE IF PIV = PIVPARENT^. LLINK THEN
            RIGHTOFLEFT(PIVPARENT^. LLINK)
          ELSE
            RIGHTOFLEFT(PIVPARENT^. RLINK)
        ELSE IF ITEM > PIV^. RLINK^. DATA THEN
          IF PIV = ROOT THEN
            RIGHTOFRIGHT(ROOT)
          ELSE IF PIV = PIVPARENT^. LLINK THEN
            RIGHTOFRIGHT(PIVPARENT^. LLINK)
          ELSE
            RIGHTOFRIGHT(PIVPARENT^. RLINK)
        ELSE IF PIV = ROOT THEN
          LEFTOFRIGHT(ROOT)
        ELSE IF PIV = PIVPARENT^. LLINK THEN
          LEFTOFRIGHT(PIVPARENT^. LLINK)
        ELSE
          LEFTOFRIGHT(PIVPARENT^. RLINK)
    END { Initial ELSE }
    END;
{ End AVLINSERT }
```

A subtle question that arises from the procedure AVLINSERT is the following. Namely, consider the segment:

```
        IF PIV = ROOT THEN
          LEFTOFLEFT(ROOT)
        ELSE IF PIV = PIVPARENT^. LLINK THEN
          LEFTOFLEFT(PIVPARENT^. LLINK)
        ELSE
          LEFTOFLEFT(PIVPARENT^. RLINK)
```

In the World of Applications . . .

In Chapter 6 we already hinted at how binary trees may be used to represent an algebraic expression. Essentially a compiler could build such a tree as it parses an incoming expression. (See Chapter 5 for a discussion of parsing.) However, applications of trees in compilers go much further than the parsing of merely algebraic expressions. Actually the entire source program which serves as input to the compiler could be viewed as one large formal expression. Because the syntax of a programming language is considerably more complex than the syntax of algebraic expressions, a general tree is required to store the representation of the entire program that is constructed by the parsing phase of the compiler. For instance, a Pascal program as simple as the following:

```
PROGRAM NOTHING(INPUT,OUTPUT);

VAR
      A,B : INTEGER;

BEGIN
READ(A,B);
IF A < B THEN
  BEGIN
  WRITE(A);
  WRITE(B)
  END
ELSE
  BEGIN
  WRITE(B);
  WRITE(A)
  END
END.
```

could possibly generate the following tree:

Why couldn't this lengthy segment from AVLINSERT be replaced by the single procedure call LEFTOFLEFT(PIV)? The answer to this question lies in the fact that the procedure LEFTOFLEFT alters the argument which is sent to it. This is why the argument to LEFTOFLEFT had to be a VAR parameter. What we wish to alter in the segment above is *not* the pointer variable PIV but rather one of the pointer variables ROOT, PIVPARENT^.LLINK or PIVPARENT^.RLINK. The simple procedure call LEFTOFLEFT(PIV) would leave the variables we really wish to change unaffected.

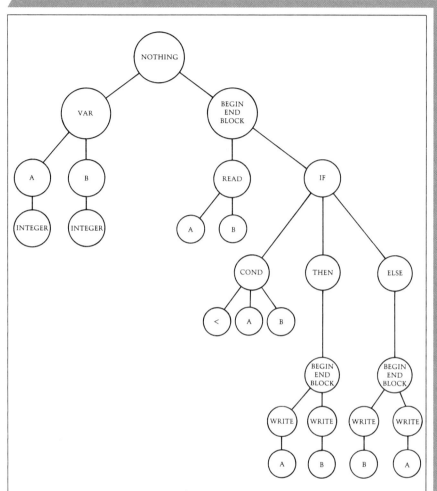

This tree representation of the incoming source program would vary slightly from compiler to compiler. Indeed, decisions about how to make such representations are often crucial in determining the efficiency of the resulting compiler. In general, trees representing the syntactical structure of a source program are called *parse trees* or *abstract syntax trees*. Once such a tree is constructed, the next phase of the compiler will then traverse it, generating object code for the native machine along the way.

Height Balancing—Is It Worth It?

This is clearly a non-trivial algorithm. Moreover, the algorithm to delete a node from a height-balanced tree is no easier and is left for an exercise. Adelson-Velskii and Landis were able to demonstrate that their method would guarantee a maximum branch length proportional to

$\log_2 N$, where N is the number of nodes in the tree.* This means that the insertion efficiency for a height-balanced tree will be, in terms of orders of magnitude, roughly equivalent to that for a full tree. Compared to the worst case efficiency of N for a non-balanced tree, it is clear that the AVL method can make a difference. Whether the difference is worth the added developmental costs is, as always, a consideration tied to a particular application.

The real problem in this regard, however, is that it is often impossible to have a realistic appraisal in the design stage of just how much height-balancing will mean to overall run-time efficiency. There is a real dilemma here. One may not be able to accurately estimate beforehand a precise need for height-balancing. Consequently, if one does employ height-balancing and it then turns out that system performance would have been adequate without it, a considerable amount of development time may have been wasted. We recommend a rather empirical approach out of this dilemma. Unless for some reason the need for height-balancing is obvious, design and write the application without height-balancing. However, leave enough storage space in the tree nodes to accommodate balance factors. (Note that you can get by with a mere two bits in this regard if storage is at a real premium and your version of Pascal allows specific bit access.) After empirically testing the performance of your application without height-balancing, make the decision whether or not to rewrite insertion and deletion routines to incorporate height-balancing.

7-4 General Trees

Our introduction to the topic of trees cited the example of genealogical trees similar to that appearing in Figure 7-17. In its most abstract sense, a tree is simply a data structure capable of representing a hierarchical relationship between a parent node and an unlimited number of child nodes. However, thus far we have been strictly enforcing a birth control rule of no more than two children per node. Seemingly, we must now relax this rule if we are to represent **general trees** such as our genealogical example.

Since, in a general tree, a node may have any number of children, the implementation of a general tree is more complex than that of a binary tree. One alternative is to use a maximum but fixed number of children for each node. This strategy, however, has the disadvantage of being very wasteful of memory space taken up by null nodes. Another equally wasteful technique is to allow variable size nodes. This plan requires providing extra memory space to store the size of the

---

*Adelson-Velskii, G. M., and Y. M. Landis. "An Algorithm for the Organization of Information," *Dokl. Acad. Nauk. SSSR* 146 (1962): 263–66.

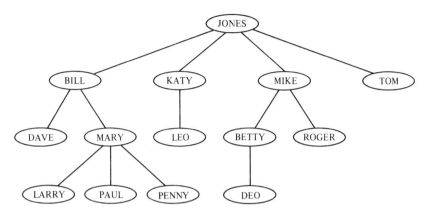

FIGURE 7-17 A genealogical tree.

node. Additionally, algorithms needed to handle a variable size node structure are much less elegant than those for tree structures with fixed size nodes. Figure 7-18 shows the tree of Figure 7-17 using variable size nodes.

Binary Tree Representation of General Trees

A more practical way of implementing a general tree is to use a binary representation. This requires that each node have only two pointer fields. The first pointer points to the leftmost child of the node, and the second pointer identifies the next sibling to the right of the node

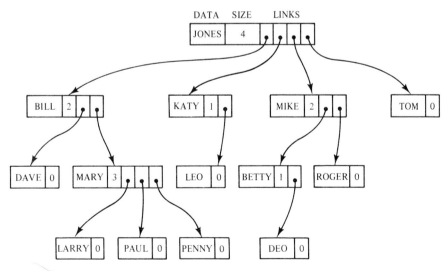

FIGURE 7-18 The genealogical tree in Figure 7-17, represented with variable size nodes.

under consideration. Since the children of a node taken in this context form an ordered set of nodes, we can regard the leftmost child of a node as FIRSTCHILD and the sibling to the right of this node as SIBLING. We will henceforth adopt this terminology for the two link fields involved with the binary tree representation of a general tree. Figure 7-19 gives the binary representation of the general genealogical tree shown in Figure 7-17.

Although we will typically give the binary tree representation of a general tree in terms of Pascal pointer variables, it is worth noting that integer arrays can still be used for pointers just as they were for linked lists in Chapter 2. Indeed, because this array perspective allows us to specify some actual values for pointers, we have portrayed the tree of Figure 7-17 as parallel arrays in Figure 7-20. You should carefully check all FIRSTCHILD and SIBLING values to convince yourself that the scheme used to fill these arrays was to store a node before any of its children, and then recursively store the leftmost child. The integer 0 has been used to represent NIL in this interpretation. The analogous representation in terms of Pascal pointer variables(and the representation we shall henceforth use) requires the following type declarations:

```
GENTREEPTR :  ^GENTREENODE;
GENTREENODE : RECORD
                DATA : {Appropriate Type};
                FIRSTCHILD : GENTREEPTR;
                SIBLING : GENTREEPTR
              END;
```

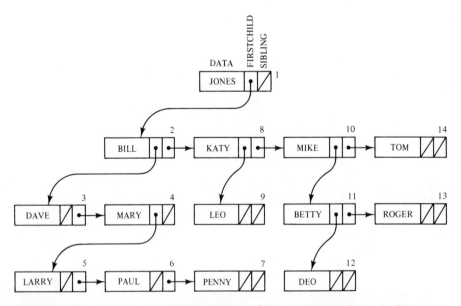

FIGURE 7-19 A binary tree representation of the genealogical tree in Figure 7-17.

LOCATION	DATA	FIRSTCHILD	NEXTCHILD
1	JONES	2	0
2	BILL	3	8
3	DAVE	0	4
4	MARY	5	0
5	LARRY	0	6
6	PAUL	0	7
7	PENNY	0	0
8	KATY	9	10
9	LEO	0	0
10	MIKE	11	14
11	BETTY	12	13
12	DEO	0	0
13	ROGER	0	0
14	TOM	0	0

FIGURE 7-20 **The tree in Figure 7-17 stored in arrays for data and pointers. "0" represents a NIL pointer.**

Traversals of a General Tree Implemented Via a Binary Tree

Since this implementation scheme for a general tree is nothing more than a special interpretation of a binary tree, all of the traversals defined for a binary tree clearly exist for the general tree. A more relevant question than the mere existence of a traversal, however, is the significance of the order in which the nodes of a general tree are visited when its corresponding binary tree is traversed. Of particular interest in this regard are the preorder and postorder traversals.

It should be verified at this point that the preorder traversal algorithm for a binary tree applied to Figure 7-19 yields the listing:

```
JONES
    BILL
        DAVE
        MARY
            LARRY
            PAUL
            PENNY
    KATY
        LEO
    MIKE
        BETTY
            DEO
        ROGER
    TOM
```

The indentation here has been added to highlight the fact that the preorder traversal will recursively:

1. Process a parent node, and then
2. Process the child nodes from left to right

Relative to the general tree pictured in Figure 7-17, we see that the effect of the preorder traversal is to fix on a node at one level of the tree and then run through all of that node's children before progressing to the next node at the same level (the sibling). There is a hint here of a generalized nested loop situation which we will soon see has some interesting applications.

The other traversal of interest in a binary tree representation of a general tree is the postorder traversal. In this regard, it should first be verified that the postorder traversal applied to Figure 7-19 yields the listing:

```
PENNY
PAUL
LARRY
MARY
DAVE
LEO
DEO
ROGER
BETTY
TOM
MIKE
KATY
BILL
JONES
```

In general, the postorder traversal works its way up from the leaf nodes of a tree, insuring that no given node is processed until all nodes in the subtree below it have been processed.

Ternary Tree Representation of a General Tree

An alternate to a binary tree representation of a general tree which uses a node containing three pointers is called a **ternary tree** representation. In such a representation, the left-to-right order of siblings along any given level of the tree is more efficiently maintained. A given node within the tree appears as in Figure 7-21. In this scheme:

1. LSIBLING is a pointer to the node immediately preceding the given node relative to the ordered list of siblings at this level.
2. RSIBLING is a pointer to the node immediately following the given node relative to the ordered list of siblings at this level.
3. CHILDREN is a pointer to the ordered list of children of a given node.

LSIBLING	DATA	CHILDREN	RSIBLING

FIGURE 7-21   A node in a ternary tree representation of a general tree. See text for explanation of terms.

Thus, a ternary tree representation of the general tree of Figure 7-17 which maintains the left-to-right order of siblings is given by Figure 7-22.

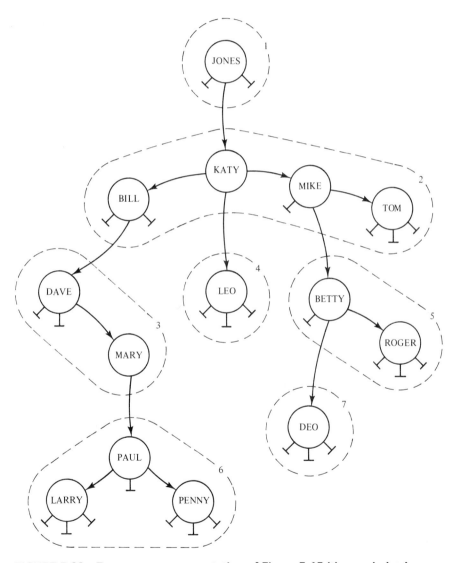

FIGURE 7-22   Ternary tree representation of Figure 7-17 (the symbol ⊥ is used to emphasize NIL pointers).

Interestingly enough, a close perusal of the ternary tree representation of Figure 7-22 will show that it is composed of strategically located binary trees (highlighted by dotted lines). For instance, an inorder traversal of the binary tree encircled by the dotted line numbered 2 yields the listing

```
BILL
KATY
MIKE
TOM
```

This is precisely the alphabetical order of the siblings that are the children of JONES in Figure 7-17! Similarly, an inorder traversal of the binary tree encircled by the dotted line numbered 6 yields the alphabetical order of the children of MARY in Figure 7-17. Thus, the LSIBLING and RSIBLING pointers are tied to the ordering of children relative to an inorder traversal of an appropriate binary subtree of the entire structure. The CHILDREN pointer, on the other hand, is actually the root pointer to a binary tree which, in turn, represents an ordered list of children at the next deeper level.

The implications of the ternary tree representation in the area of database management are significant. At first glance, it would seem that the only difference is that we are charged for one extra pointer per node. However, consider for a moment the following application, which is typical of the type of problem encountered in database management. A university has a list of departments, which it wishes to maintain in alphabetical order. Each department has a list of professors, which is to be kept in alphabetical order within that department. Each professor teaches a list of courses; this course list is to be kept in order by course number. Finally each course has a list of students enrolled, also to be kept in alphabetical order. Figure 7-23 illustrates such a database for a university with enrollments kept small enough to fit conveniently on one page.

Now consider the maintenance that is likely to be necessary for this tree-structured database. Insertions and deletions will frequently occur at the class section and student enrollment level. Depending upon the tenure density at this institution, this type of processing will not occur as often at the higher levels of the tree. Insertions and deletions in a large database necessarily lead to considerations of efficiency. If this tree is implemented via the binary tree representation of a general tree, each class list, each list of courses taught, and each list of departmental faculty becomes essentially a linked list. As such, each list's insertion and search efficiency is proportional to the number of members in the list. However, with the ternary tree representation of this general tree, each sublist within the data is implemented with the binary tree method described in 6-5. Hence, insertion and deletion efficiency could well be proportional to the $\log_2 N$ figure we have cited

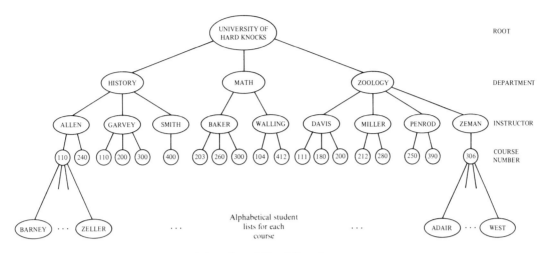

FIGURE 7-23 Database for the University of Hard Knocks.

previously. To insure maximum efficiency, each binary tree sublist could be threaded and/or height-balanced. Clearly, for such a list-oriented database, the third pointer of the ternary tree representation seems a relatively small price to pay for the added efficiency achieved.

In regard to traversing a general tree represented by the ternary tree method, we can duplicate the order of nodes visited by the preorder and postorder traversals of a binary tree representation. However, although the order can be duplicated, the method is slightly different. Suppose, for instance, that we wish to achieve the equivalent of a preorder traversal with a ternary representation. We must insure that, immediately after processing a given node, we process *in order* all the children of that node. But to process in order all the children of a node, we need merely call on an inorder traversal procedure with the root pointer being the CHILDREN pointer of a given node. That is, we essentially duplicate the effect of a preorder traversal for a binary representation by recursively calling on an inorder traversal for the tree of children! The procedure may be written quite elegantly in Pascal.

```
{ Global Variables }

TYPE
  POINTER = ^TERNARYNODE;
  TERNARYNODE =
    RECORD
      LSIBLING: POINTER;
      CHILDREN: POINTER;
      RSIBLING: POINTER;
      DATA: CHAR { or other appropriate type }
    END;
```

```
PROCEDURE TERNARYPREORDER(ROOT: POINTER);
{ Achieve preorder traversal of a general tree represented via
  ternary tree representation }

  BEGIN
    IF ROOT <> NIL THEN
     BEGIN
      TERNARYPREORDER(ROOT^. LSIBLING);

    { Then apply an appropriate process to the root node }

      PROCESS(ROOT);

    { Then visit the children }

      TERNARYPREORDER(ROOT^. CHILDREN);

    { Finally continue on at sibling level }

      TERNARYPREORDER(ROOT^. RSIBLING);
     END
  END;
{ End TERNARYPREORDER }
```

First visit ROOT's left siblings

Finally visit ROOT's right siblings

ROOT

LSIBLING

RSIBLING

CHILDREN

Second visit ROOT's children

Program Design Considerations

The section "In the World of Applications. . ." for Chapter 6 describes a way (patterned after the UNIX operating system) in which trees may be used to represent the general file directory structure of a computer system. For instance, the diagram below depicts a situation in which the root node SUPER has "super" privileges to access all accounts/files below it in the tree structure. Below SUPER exist two general divisions of files—system files (/SYSTEM) and user files (/USER). System files are divided into accounts for the editor (/EDITOR), Pascal language (/PASCAL), and C language (/C). User files are subdivided into accounts for SMITH, JONES, and HORTON. Individual files within each of these accounts are then listed at the next level of the tree structure.

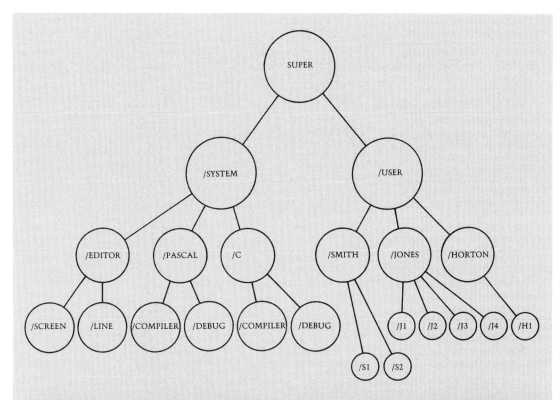

The following program partially illustrates how such a tree-structured directory could be maintained. A ternary tree representation of the general tree directory may be entered by the user, as indicated in the sample run. The procedure LOADTREE is responsible for this data entry phase of the program. The procedure TERNARYPREORDER then traverses the tree, using the global variable LEVEL to control a simple graphic representation of the tree. The relationship between these modules of the program is highlighted in the modular structure chart which follows.

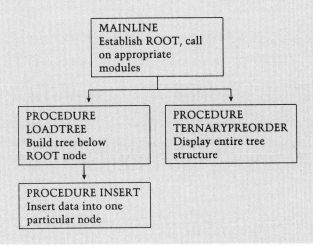

The program, along with a sample run, appears below. Programming Problem 7 of this chapter suggests ways in which this directory system could be extended, building upon the program which already exists.

```
PROGRAM TESTTREE(INPUT, OUTPUT);

{ ILLUSTRATE TREE-STRUCTURED DIRECTORY PROCESSING }

TYPE
  STRING = PACKED ARRAY [1..20] OF CHAR;
  TREEPTR = ^TREENODE;
  TREENODE =
    RECORD
      LSIBLING: TREEPTR;
      DATA: STRING;
      CHILDREN: TREEPTR;
      RSIBLING: TREEPTR
    END;

VAR
  NAME: STRING;
  ROOT: TREEPTR;
  LEVEL: INTEGER;

PROCEDURE INSERT(VAR NAME: STRING;
                 VAR ROOT: TREEPTR);

  {INSERTS ACCOUNT NAME INTO BINARY TREE POINTED TO BY ROOT VIA
   INSERTION RULE OF CHAPTER 6}

  VAR
    P, Q: TREEPTR;

  BEGIN
    P := ROOT;
    NEW(Q);
    Q^.LSIBLING := NIL;
    Q^.RSIBLING := NIL;
    Q^.DATA := NAME;
    Q^.CHILDREN := NIL;
    IF P = NIL { THE EMPTY TREE } THEN
      ROOT := Q
    ELSE { WALK DOWN TREE FINDING INSERTION POINT }
```

```
      BEGIN
      WHILE P<> NIL DO
         BEGIN
         IF (NAME < P^.DATA) AND (P^.LSIBLING = NIL) THEN
            BEGIN
            P^.LSIBLING := Q;
            P := NIL
            END
         ELSE IF (NAME > P^.DATA) AND (P^.RSIBLING = NIL) THEN
            BEGIN
            P^.RSIBLING :=Q;
            P := NIL
            END
         ELSE IF NAME < P^.DATA THEN
            P := P^.LSIBLING
         ELSE
            P := P^.RSIBLING
         END
      END
   END;
{END INSERT}

PROCEDURE LOADTREE(ROOT: TREEPTR);

   {GETS ACCOUNT NAMES AND CALLS ON INSERT TO
    BUILD TREE}

   VAR
    NAME: STRING:

   BEGIN
     IF ROOT <> NIL THEN
       BEGIN
       LOADTREE(ROOT^.LSIBLING);
       WRITE('ENTER CHILDREN FOR ', ROOT^.DATA, '--->');
       REPEAT
         READLN(NAME);
         IF NAME[1] < > '*' {USE * TO SIGNAL END OF CHILDREN} THEN
            INSERT(NAME, ROOT^.CHILDREN)
       UNTIL NAME[1] = '*';
       LOADTREE(ROOT^.CHILDREN);
       LOADTREE(ROOT^.RSIBLING)
       END
   END;
{END LOADTREE}
```

```
PROCEDURE TERNARYPREORDER(ROOT: TREEPTR);

 {TERNARY PREORDER WITH LEVEL USED FOR INDENTATION EFFECT}

   VAR
    I: INTEGER;

   BEGIN
     IF ROOT <> NIL THEN
       BEGIN
       TERNARYPREORDER(ROOT^ . LSIBLING);
       FOR I := 1 TO (LEVEL + 1) DO
           WRITE('      ');
       WRITELN(ROOT^ . DATA);
       LEVEL := LEVEL + 1;
       TERNARYPREORDER(ROOT^ . CHILDREN);
       LEVEL := LEVEL - 1;
       TERNARYPREORDER(ROOT^ . RSIBLING);
       END
   END;
{END TERNARYPREORDER}

BEGIN

  {INITIALIZE TREE}

  ROOT :=NIL;
  WRITE('ROOT ACCOUNT NAME-->');
  READLN(NAME);
  INSERT(NAME, ROOT);

   {THEN LOAD CHILDREN INTO TREE}

  LOADTREE(ROOT);
  WRITELN('***********************************');
  LEVEL := 0;
  TERNARYPREORDER(ROOT)
END.
```

Sample Run:

```
ROOT ACCOUNT NAME-->SUPER
ENTER CHILDREN FOR SUPER          --->/SYSTEM
/USER
*
ENTER CHLDREN FOR /SYSTEM         --->/EDITOR
/PASCAL
/C
*
ENTER CHILDREN FOR /C             --->/COMPILER
/DEBUGGER
*
ENTER CHILDREN FOR /COMPILER      --->*
ENTER CHILDREN FOR /DEBUGGER      --->*
ENTER CHILDREN FOR /EDITOR        --->/SCREEN
/LINE
*
ENTER CHILDREN FOR /LINE          --->*
ENTER CHILDREN FOR /SCREEN        --->*
ENTER CHILDREN FOR /PASCAL        --->/COMPILER
/DEBUGGER
*
ENTER CHILDREN FOR /COMPILER      --->*
ENTER CHILDREN FOR /DEBUGGER      --->*
ENTER CHILDREN FOR /USER          --->/SMITH
/JONES
/HORTON
*
ENTER CHILDREN FOR /HORTON        --->/H1
*
ENTER CHILDREN FOR /H1            --->*
ENTER CHILDREN FOR /JONES         --->/J1
/J2
/J3
/J4
*
ENTER CHILDREN FOR /J1            --->*
ENTER CHILDREN FOR /J2            --->*
ENTER CHILDREN FOR /J3            --->*
ENTER CHILDREN FOR /J4            --->*
ENTER CHILDREN FOR /SMITH         --->/S1
/S2
*
ENTER CHILDREN FOR /S1            --->*
ENTER CHLDREN FOR /S2             --->*
```

```
SUPER
     /SYSTEM
            /C
                  /COMPILER
                  /DEBUGGER
            /EDITOR
                  /LINE
                  /SCREEN
            /PASCAL
                  /COMPILER
                  /DEBUGGER
     /USER
            /HORTON
                  /H1
            /JONES
                  /J1
                  /J2
                  /J3
                  /J4
            /SMITH
                  /S1
                  /S2
```

SUMMARY

In the course of Chapters 6 and 7, trees have shown themselves as one of the most potent of all data structures. They combine the insertion/deletion capabilities of a linked list with a $\log_2 N$ efficiency (as opposed to N for a linked list.) Moreover, threading and height-balancing offer enhancements which may be chosen to tailor the efficiency of tree processing to a particular application. Already in these chapters, we have seen examples of trees in the parsing of algebraic expressions and in database management. The programming problems will further serve to highlight the use of trees in databases, statistical analysis packages, and artificial intelligence (game playing.) Moreover, we have just begun to see the power of trees. Applications of trees will emerge again in Chapter 11 when we talk about the use of indices in file searching.

KEY TERMS

Inorder predecessor   AVL-rotation
Inorder successor   General tree
Threaded tree   Binary tree representation of general tree
Dummy root node   Ternary tree representation of general tree
Height-balanced tree   Tree-structured database

EXERCISES

1. What, in an abstract sense, does a tree structure represent?
2. Redraw the threads in Figure 7-4 to indicate preorder traversals of the tree.
3. If the inorder predecessor pointers appearing in Figure 7-4 were not maintained, that is, if NIL pointers were stored in their place, it would still be possible to complete a threaded inorder traversal. Indeed we would only lose the ability to complete a threaded reverse inorder traversal. How would the procedure THREADED-INORDER of Section 7-2 need to be modified if no predecessor threads were maintained?
4. Write a Pascal procedure for the preorder traversal diagram suggested in exercise (2).
5. Explain why it is not possible to thred a tree for a postorder traversal.
6. Why is the inorder traversal of a general tree not appropriate?
7. Modify the Pascal procedure TERNARYPREORDER to obtain the postorder traversal of a general tree.
8. Write a Pascal procedure which uses the predecessor pointers in a threaded binary tree to generate a reverse inorder traversal.
9. Write a Pascal procedure to delete a node from a threaded binary tree.
10. Write a Pascal procedure to delete a node from a height-balanced tree.
11. Convince yourself that a height-balanced tree is not necessarily full by drawing an example which is height-balanced but not full.
12. Complete the Pascal procedures RIGHTOFRIGHT and LEFTOFRIGHT for insertion of a node into a height-balanced tree.
13. Consider the following alphabetical binary tree. Draw the tree after the data item "A" has been inserted and the tree has been height-balanced.

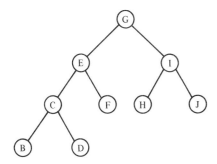

14. Repeat exercise 12 for the insertion of "D" and the corresponding height-balancing of the following tree.

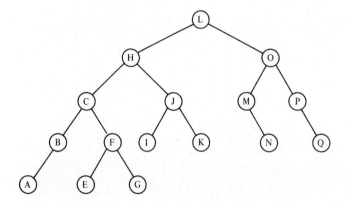

PROGRAMMING PROBLEMS

1. The Wing-and-a-Prayer Airlines Company of programming problem (1) in Chapter 2 is expanding their record-keeping database. This database may now be pictured hierarchically as:

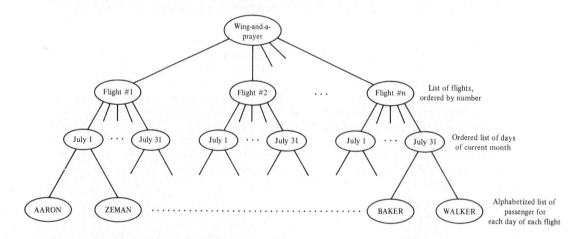

Write a program to maintain this database. Your program should process requests to add, delete, or list:

- Specified flight number
- Specified day of the month (for a given flight number)
- Specified passenger or all passengers (for a given flight number and day of the month)

2. Write a program which implements a height-balanced and threaded binary tree to maintain in sorted order the records of the Fly-By-Night credit card company file. That is, as a record is read,

it is inserted into its proper place according to the sorted linear list (by social security number) as given by the inorder traversal of the corresponding threaded binary tree.

3. To improve performance, thread and/or height-balance the tree which you developed in the problems for Chapter 6 to maintain player lists for the Bay Area Brawlers' football league.

4. Many statistical analysis packages support a "cross-tabulation" command designed to explore the relationship between statistical variables. A cross-tabulation between two variables produces a two-dimensional table containing a frequency count for each possible ordered pair of values of the two variables. However, these statistical packages typically allow this type of analysis to proceed even further than merely exploring two variables. For instance, in a legal system database, we might be interested in cross-tabulating a defendant's age with the judge before which he/she stood trial. We may then wish to cross-tabulate this result with the sex of the defendant. The output produced by the COSAP statistical package of Lawrence University for this type of request is given following this problem. Of interest in this output is the fact that the value of the control variable (SEX in this case) is held fixed at 1 while the cross-tabulation table for the two primary variables (AGEBRACK and JUDGE) is printed. Then the next largest value for SEX is fixed and another AGEBRACK by JUDGE table is produced. This could continue for larger values of SEX (provided we were capable of using more than two sexes). Note that this type of output is not limited to just one control variable. There may be an arbitrary number of control variables and tables to cycle through. Moreover the variables have an arbitrary number of observations and are all in arbitrary order. Yet for each variable the list of possible values is always printed out in smallest to largest order! The general tree structure that emerges for handling cross-tabulations is:

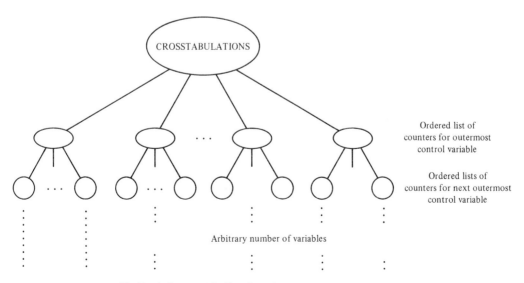

Ordered list of counters for outermost control variable

Ordered lists of counters for next outermost control variable

Arbitrary number of variables

Final level of tree contains lists of counters for the innermost variable

Write a program to handle the task of producing statistical cross-tabulations. Pattern its output after the sample which follows.

```
Command?  CROSSTABS
Enter variables for CROSSTABULATION?  AGEBRACK/JUDGE/SEX

Enter Options?
          4 categories for JUDGE
          8 categories for AGEBRACK
          2 categories for SEX
CROSSTABS will print  2   8  by  4 tables
Proceed (Yes or No) *?  YES
```

CRIMINAL HISTORY DATABANK

C R O S S T A B U L A T I O N

AGEBRACK by JUDGE by SEX

AGEBRACK REGROUPED AGE (4R) OF PERSON CHGD
JUDGE   JUDGE BEFORE WHOM CASE BROUGHT (2)

Controlling for ...
SEX   SEX OF PERSON CHARGED (3)   Value =   1 MALE

		JUDGE SHAFER	CANE	VANSUS	MYSE	Row
	Count	1	2	3	5	Total
AGEBRACK		---	----	---	---	
<18	1	1	0	0	0	1
18-20	2 :	157	11	1	19	188
21-24	3 :	103	8	4	16	131
25-29	4 :	58	14	3	6	81
30-39	5 :	58	4	2	1	65
40-49	6 :	40	5	1	1	47
50-71	7 :	27	1	0	1	29
DKNA	9 :	117	37	7	2	163
Column Total		561	80	18	46	705

```
AGEBRACK   REGROUPED AGE (4R) OF PERSON CHGD
JUDGE      JUDGE BEFORE WHOM CASE BROUGHT (2)

Controlling for ...
SEX        SEX OF PERSON CHARGED (3)       Value =    2 FEMALE
```

Count		JUDGE SHAFER 1	CANE 2	VANSUS 3	MYSE 5	Row Total
AGEBRACK		---	----	---	----	
<18	1	0	0	1	0	1
18-20	2 :	29	0	6	0	35
21-24	3 :	18	1	0	1	20
25-29	4 :	14	0	1	0	15
30-39	5 :	21	1	0	0	22
40-49	6 :	7	0	0	0	7
50-71	7 :	5	1	0	0	6
DKNA	9 :	22	5	0	0	27
Column Total		116	8	8	1	133

```
Command?  EXIT
```

5. Trees find significant applications in the area of artificial intelligence and game playing. Consider, for instance, the game of FIFTEEN. In this game, two players take turns selecting digits between 1 and 9 with the goal of selecting a combination of digits that adds up to fifteen. Once a digit is chosen, it may not be chosen again by either player. Rather than immediately considering a tree for the game of FIFTEEN, let us first consider a tree for the trivial game of SEVEN with digits chosen in the range 1 to 6. A tree which partially represents the states that may be reached in this game is given on page 220.

   In this tree, circular nodes represent the states that may be reached by the player who moves first (the computer), and square nodes represent the states that may be reached by the player who moves second (a human opponent). The +1, 0, or −1 attached to each node represent weighting factors designed to help the computer choose the most advantageous move at any given stage of the game. The rule used to compute these weighting factors is:

- If the node is a leaf node, its weight is determined by some static weighting function. In this case, the static weighting function used was to assign +1 to a leaf node representing a computer win, 0 to a leaf node representing a draw, and −1 to a leaf node representing a human win.
- If the node is a node in which the computer will move next (that is, a state occupied by the human opponent), then the weighting factor of the node is the maximum of the weighting factors of its children.
- If the node is a node in which the human opponent will move next, then the weighting factor of the node is the minimum of the weighting factors of its children.

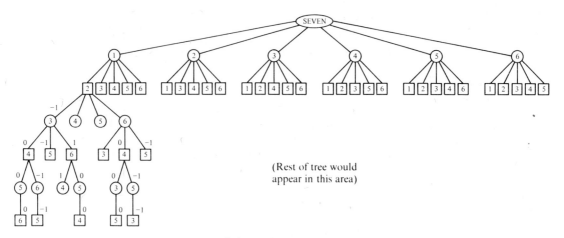

(Rest of tree would appear in this area)

Some of the nodes appearing in tree
for game of SEVEN using 1–6

In its turn, the computer should always choose to move to the node having the maximum possible weighting factor. The rationale behind this technique, called the **minimax** technique, is that the computer will move in such a way as to always maximize its chances of winning. The human opponent, if he is playing intelligently, will always move to a node having a minimum weighting factor. Thus in the partial game tree above the computer would choose to select 4 if the human had been naive enough to select the 6 node with weighting factor +1.

Write a program to build a weighted game tree for the game of FIFTEEN and then have the computer play against a human opponent. Note that this game is really the game of tic-tac-toe if one considers the matrix given below.

4	9	2
3	5	7
8	1	6

All winning tic-tac-toe paths add up to 15

Give some consideration as to time and memory utilization efficiency of your algorithm. Many games simply cannot be completely represented via a binary tree. Consequently, a partial game tree is built in which the leaf nodes may not actually be the final move made in the game. In such situations, the static weighting function applied to the leaf nodes in the game tree requires a bit more insight to develop.

6. Write a program to print out the nodes of a tree level by level, that is, all level 0 nodes, followed by all level 1 nodes, followed by all level 2 nodes, etc. As a hint in getting started, note that this program will afford an excellent opportunity to practice using a queue in addition to a tree.

7. Extend/modify the tree-structured directory system described in the "Program Design Considerations" at the end of the chapter by:

   ▪ Developing a routine which will call for input of a given tree node and then list all account/file names which are descendent from it, that is, list those directory nodes to which it would have access.
   ▪ Developing a routine to delete a given account/file name from the directory.
   ▪ Using a binary tree representation of the general tree in the program.
   ▪ Experimenting with different ways of graphically outputing the tree.

8

Multidimensional Arrays and Sparse Matrices

"But as soon as we wish to grasp this being, it slips
between our fingers, and we find ourselves faced
with a pattern of duality, with a game of reflections."

JEAN-PAUL SARTRE (1905—1980)

8-1   Introductory Considerations

In preceding chapters we have frequently used singly-dimensioned arrays. In fact, they have been used as the data structure from which other more sophisticated data structures such as linked lists, stacks, queues, and trees have been built. However, in the next chapter on graphs and networks, it will become necessary to consider arrays of dimension higher than one. Of particular importance will be the **two-dimensional array** or matrix, in which the position of a data element must be specified by giving two coordinates, typically called row and column coordinates. For instance, in Pascal, the declaration

```
VAR GRID: ARRAY[1..6,1..5] OF INTEGER;
```

specifies the data structure with a sample assignment of values pictured in Figure 8-1.

When in procedural statements we specify the entry

```
GRID[5,4]
```

we are referring to the entry in the 5th row and 4th column of GRID (as marked by an asterisk in Figure 8-1).

222

	Column				
	1	2	3	4	5
1	10	18	42	6	14
2	13	19	8	1	44
3	63	80	12	90	51
4	16	13	9	8	4
5	12	11	12	14*	83
6	1	4	18	99	90

Row

FIGURE 8-1   Structure established by the array GRID.

8-2   Implementing a Multidimensional Array

Within main memory, storage locations are not arranged in the grid-like pattern of Figure 8-1. Instead, they are arranged in linear sequence beginning with location 1, and then 2, 3, . . . Because of this, there must be manipulations "behind the scenes" when a program requests the entry in the 5th row and 4th column of a two-dimensional array. Essentially, the coordinates of 5th row and 4th column must be transformed into an address in this linear sequence of memory locations. The nature of the transformation is dependent upon how the designers of the compiler have chosen to arrange the application programmer's mental image of rows and columns within the linear sequence of memory locations. Suppose that our compiler has chosen to store the 30 entries in the two-dimensional array GRID as indicated in Figure 8-2.

According to this arrangement, the first row would take up the first five locations in the list allocated for the array, the second row the second five locations, and so on. The entry in the 5th row and 4th column would in fact be located in the 24th position within the list. In this array the Ith row and Jth column must be transformed into the

```
(5 * (I-1) + J)th
```

position in the list. In even more general terms, if NCOL is the number of columns in the array, then the entry in the Ith row and Jth column is given as the

```
(NCOL * (I-1) + J)th
```

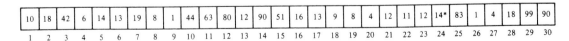

FIGURE 8-2   Linear storage of data from Figure 8-1.

entry in the linear list corresponding to the two-dimensional array. Most high-level computer languages implement two- (and higher-) dimensional arrays in such a **row major** fashion and do so in a way which is largely transparent to the applications programmer. However, all programmers should be aware that multidimensional arrays are inherently less efficient than one-dimensional arrays because of the computations required by the transformation from row/column to linear address each time an entry of the array is accessed. Such a transformation is often called a **mapping function.**

Those readers who have programmed in FORTRAN will recall that, when initializing a two-dimensional array via a DATA statement, the entries for the array must be listed by column, that is, first column, second column, etc. This is because FORTRAN is one of the few high-level languages which chooses to store a multidimensional array in **column major** order, as indicated in Figure 8-3.

To access the entry in the *I*th row and *J*th column of a two-dimensional array stored in column major order, the transformation

```
NROW * (J-1) + I
```

is required, where NROW represents the number of rows in the array. The fact that this transformation requires the number of rows but not the number of columns also explains why many FORTRAN compilers insist that a subroutine be informed of the number of rows in an array passed down from a calling program but not the number of columns.

Our discussion of sparse matrices in 8-2 will necessitate our understanding at a deeper level how compilers implement multidimensional arrays in general and two-dimensional arrays in particular. *We will assume for the remainder of this chapter that all two-dimensional arrays are to be implemented in row major order.*

When a source program makes reference to a simple variable, for instance, COUNT, that variable name must be looked up (by methods to be described in Chapter 11) in a **symbol table** created by the compiler. (See Figure 8-4.) Once the variable name COUNT is found in the symbol table, its memory address is then known. This strategy works perfectly if COUNT is merely an ordinary variable using one memory location. However, suppose the reference being made is to the two-dimensional array entry GRID[3,2]. Now, a look-up of GRID in the

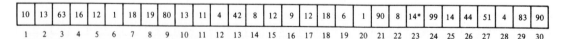

FIGURE 8-3 Matrix from Figure 8-1 in column major form.

Identifier	Associated Memory Address
⋮	
COUNT	017646
⋮	
GRID	017422
⋮	

FIGURE 8-4   Symbol table for Identifiers in a program.

symbol table of Figure 8-4 still yields a memory address, as with the simple variable COUNT. But the memory address does not *directly* lead us to where the data in GRID is stored. Rather it leads us to what is commonly called the **dope vector** for the array. This dope vector contains information which will help us to interpret the array's actual data once it is located. In particular, this dope vector information must include:

1. The **rank** of the array, that is, the number of dimensions of the array.
2. The number of entries in the first dimension, second dimension, third dimension, etc. For a two-dimensional array, this amounts to the number of rows and columns.
3. The total number of entries in the array.
4. The beginning address of the linear sequence of memory locations actually containing the array's data. A given data item's offset from this beginning address essentially determines its coordinate position in the multidimensional structure. (This last informational item is unnecessary if the array's data is always stored immediately after the dope vector.)

Additional variations, such as subscripts with arbitrary lower limits instead of 1, would result in the need for more dope vector information. To keep our discussion as simple as possible, we shall avoid this complication.

For example, if the data in the two-dimensional array GRID described earlier in this section actually began at memory address 17442, then the dope vector corresponding to GRID would appear as in Figure 8-5. Note in particular that the dope vector contains information crucial to performing the transformation from row/column to linear address that enables the applications programmer to think in terms of row and column while the computer is actually working in terms of a linear sequence.

RANK	2
NROW	6
NCOL	5
TOTENTRIES	30
BEG-ADD	Address of initial data location

FIGURE 8-5 Dope vector for the two-dimensional array GRID.

We remark here that everything we have said about two-dimensional arrays in particular can quite easily be generalized to arrays of dimension greater than two. For instance, the declaration

```
VAR MGRIDS: ARRAY[1..2,1..3,1..4] OF INTEGER;
```

generates an image of two 3-row by 4-column tables as illustrated for the sample assignment of values pictured in Figure 8-6. Hence MGRIDS[2,2,3] would refer to the value 18 stored in the second row and third column of the second occurrence in Figure 8-6. To store this data in a linear sequence of memory locations would necessitate adopting one of two reasonable conventions:

1. Grouping together all the data associated with a given value of the leftmost subscript, that is, **left subscript major form,** or
2. Grouping together all the data associated with a given value of the rightmost subscript, that is, **right subscript major form.**

For example, the left subscript major form of the data in Figure 8-6 would appear in a linear list as pictured in Figure 8-7. We leave as exercises the problems of translating a given set of three-dimensional coordinates to the appropriate position in the linear list and representing this same data in right subscript major form.

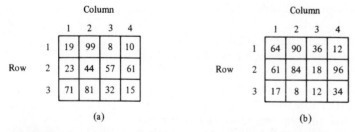

**FIGURE 8-6   (a) First occurrence of two-dimensional table in MGRIDS.
(b) Second occurrence of two-dimensional table in MGRIDS.**

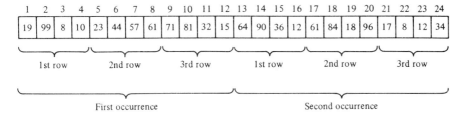

FIGURE 8-7   Left subscript major form for the data of Figure 8-6.

It should be clear to the reader that the total number of entries in a multidimensional array could quite easily exceed main memory limitations. For instance, an array to store the coefficients for a 50 x 50 system of equations requires 2500 memory locations. In the next chapter we shall see that a two-dimensional array necessary to contain data about a transportation network involving 200 cities would require 40000 memory locations. Yet, in actual applications, it quite often turns out that a very high percentage of these memory locations are filled with zeroes. Such an array with a low percentage of non-zero entries is said to be *sparse,* and the data structure problem of a sparse array is to develop techniques which accurately represent the data it contains without wasting the memory required to store an exceedingly large number of zeroes. In the remaining two sections of this chapter, we shall discuss two techniques for handling the sparse matrix problem—the generalized dope vector method and the linked list method.

8-3   Sparse Matrices and Generalized Dope Vector Implementation

Our previous discussion about dope vectors has focused upon what the compiler does beneath the surface for the applications programmer. Now, however, the sparse matrix problem will force us to look at a variation on dope vectors in which the data structure we are using is not built into the language. Hence it must be maintained explicitly by the programmer using the tools available in the chosen language.

The **generalized dope vector method** for implementing sparse matrices is particularly effective for **band** matrices, that is, matrices in which the non-zero entries tend to cluster around the diagonal running from the upper left corner to the lower right. Fortunately, in many applications, this is precisely what happens, thereby making the generalized dope vector method highly usable in the "real world". For such matrices, we are able to specify for each row the column numbers of the first and last non-zero entries. We will add this information to a dope vector for such a band matrix, enabling us to physically store in memory only those entries between the first non-zero entry and the last non-zero entry in each row. For instance, suppose that we have a 5 x 14 band matrix called SPARSE as pictured in Figure 8-8. Then the linear sequence of data corresponding to the non-zero bands in this matrix could be stored as indicated in Figure 8-9. Notice that those zero values embedded within the band must be stored. Consequently, if the band of the matrix becomes wider, this method will tend to lose its effectiveness.

To compensate for the leading and trailing zeroes which are not stored, we must add some information to the dope vector for the array SPARSE. Such a generalized dope vector for the array pictured in Figure 8-8 is given in Figure 8-10. In this figure, although FIRSTNONZERO[I] and LASTNONZERO[I] are pictured as neighboring locations, they would in practice be the Ith locations in two parallel arrays, FIRSTNONZERO and LASTNONZERO.

Now the value for the Jth entry in the Ith row of SPARSE is obtained by:

1. Checking to see if J is less than FIRSTNONZERO[I] or greater than LASTNONZERO[I]. If it is, then the value of SPARSE[I,J] is zero.
2. Otherwise SPARSE[I,J] is the Nth entry in the sequential list of data stored for the array, where N is calculated via:

$$N = \sum_{K=1}^{I-1}(LASTNONZERO[K]-FIRSTNONZERO[K]+1) + (J-FIRSTNONZERO[I]+1)$$

To avoid frequently recomputing the summation term in the expression above each time an array entry is accessed, we recommend storing the sum corresponding to the Ith row as part of the dope vector for the array. Following this convention, the dope vector for the sample matrix SPARSE with which we have been working would appear as in Figure 8-11.

	1	2	3	4	5	6	7	8	9	10	11	12	13	14
1	0	83	19	40	0	0	0	0	0	0	0	0	0	0
2	0	0	0	91	0	42	12	0	0	0	0	0	0	0
3	0	0	0	0	0	18	4	0	0	0	0	0	0	0
4	0	0	0	0	0	0	0	0	71	64	0	13	0	0
5	0	0	0	0	0	0	0	0	0	0	0	0	21	40

FIGURE 8-8 Example of band matrix.

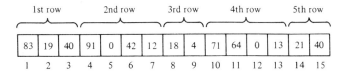

FIGURE 8-9 **Linear representation of non-zero bands in Figure 8-8.**

Hence the computation of N in the situation described earlier becomes

```
N := SUM[I] + (J - FIRSTNONZERO[I] +1)
```

The NROW additional storage locations required to store these sums represent a small price to pay in order to avoid continually recomputing a sum of potentially many terms each time an array entry is accessed. We leave for the exercises the question of whether the data stored in LASTNONZERO is now even necessary at all.

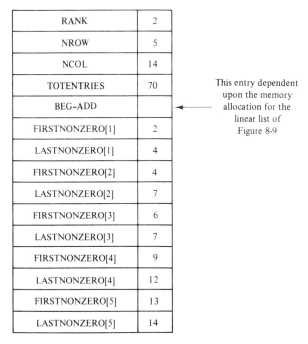

RANK	2
NROW	5
NCOL	14
TOTENTRIES	70
BEG-ADD	
FIRSTNONZERO[1]	2
LASTNONZERO[1]	4
FIRSTNONZERO[2]	4
LASTNONZERO[2]	7
FIRSTNONZERO[3]	6
LASTNONZERO[3]	7
FIRSTNONZERO[4]	9
LASTNONZERO[4]	12
FIRSTNONZERO[5]	13
LASTNONZERO[5]	14

This entry dependent upon the memory allocation for the linear list of Figure 8-9

FIGURE 8-10 **Generalized dope vector for matrix of Figure 8-8.**

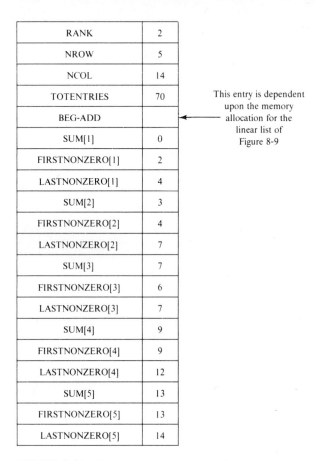

RANK	2
NROW	5
NCOL	14
TOTENTRIES	70
BEG-ADD	
SUM[1]	0
FIRSTNONZERO[1]	2
LASTNONZERO[1]	4
SUM[2]	3
FIRSTNONZERO[2]	4
LASTNONZERO[2]	7
SUM[3]	7
FIRSTNONZERO[3]	6
LASTNONZERO[3]	7
SUM[4]	9
FIRSTNONZERO[4]	9
LASTNONZERO[4]	12
SUM[5]	13
FIRSTNONZERO[5]	13
LASTNONZERO[5]	14

This entry is dependent upon the memory allocation for the linear list of Figure 8-9

FIGURE 8-11   Dope vector augmented with sums to avoid recalculation.

The development of procedures to assign data to and retrieve data from a specified location in a sparse matrix presents an excellent illustration of the advantages of modular programming. Such procedures may be written in a fashion which makes them virtually transparent to their calling program; that is, the calling program sees little difference between working with an actual two-dimensional array and a generalized dope vector representation of such an array.

The notion of hiding the actual implementation of a data structure from a calling module is called **data abstraction**. In particular, the retrieval of values from the the Ith row and Jth column of SPARSE would require no adjustment in the calling program other than the realization that the statement

```
V := SPARSE(I,J);
```

is now a call to a function procedure instead of a direct access to an entry in an actual two-dimensional array. The function procedure SPARSE is given below.

```
{ Global declarations }

  { LIST represents the global linear sequence of storage }
  { locations where the sparse array's non-zero bands are }
  { are stored. }
  { Dope vector entries are assumed global and named as }
  { indicated in Figure 8-11.}

CONST
  N = 100; { Or any other appropriate size }
  N1 = 300;

TYPE
  ARR = ARRAY [1..N] OF INTEGER;

VAR
  FIRSTNONZERO, LASTNONZERO, SUM: ARR;
  RANK, NROW, NCOL, TOTENTRIES: INTEGER;
  LIST: ARRAY [1..N1] OF INTEGER;

FUNCTION SPARSE(I, J: INTEGER): INTEGER;

  VAR
    K: INTEGER;

  BEGIN

    IF J < FIRSTNONZERO[I] OR J > LASTNONZERO[I] THEN
      SPARSE := 0
    ELSE
      BEGIN
      K := SUM[I] + (J - FIRSTNONZERO[I] + 1);
      SPARSE := LIST[K]
      END {IF}
  END { SPARSE } ;
```

The assignment of values to the Ith row and Jth column of SPARSE is a situation for which the generalized dope vector procedure cannot be written in a completely transparent manner. This is because a function cannot appear on the left of the $:=$ operator in an assignment statement. Hence the assignment statement functionally equivalent to

```
SPARSE(I,J):=V
```

in a calling program must be changed to

```
PUT(V,I,J);
```

where the procedure PUT is given below.

```
{ Global declarations }

    { LIST represents the global linear sequence of storage }
    { locations where the sparse array's non-zero bands are }
    { are stored. }
    { Dope vector entries are assumed global and named as }
    { indicated in Figure 8-11.}

CONST
  N = 100; { Or any other appropriate size }
  N1 = 300;

TYPE
  ARR = ARRAY [1..N] OF INTEGER;

VAR
  FIRSTNONZERO, LASTNONZERO, SUM: ARR;
  RANK, NROW, NCOL, TOTENTRIES: INTEGER;
  LIST: ARRAY [1..N1] OF INTEGER;
```

```
PROCEDURE PUT(I, J, V: INTEGER);

  BEGIN
    IF V <> 0 AND (J < FIRSTNONZERO[I] OR J > LASTNONZERO[I]) THEN
        { Assign non-zero values that will increase band width }
      EXPAND(I, J)
```

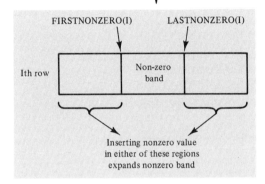

```
    ELSE IF V = 0 AND (FIRSTNONZERO[I] = J OR J = LASTNONZERO[I]) THEN
              {Assign zero that may decrease band width }
      CONTRACT(I, J);
```

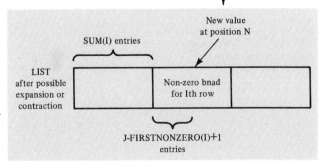

```
    { Now the appropriate expansion or contraction has been taken
        care of....}
    IF (FIRSTNONZERO[I] <= J AND J <= LASTNONZERO[I]) THEN
      LIST[SUM[I] + (J - FIRSTNONZERO[I] + 1)] := V
  END { PUT } ;
```

The call to EXPAND is intended to update the values stored in SUM, FIRSTNONZERO, and LASTNONZERO when the insertion of a non-zero entry will increase the size of the band in the Ith row. The procedure EXPAND will also have to insert an appropriate sequence of zeroes in LIST, shifting a designated portion of LIST to the right to do so.

The call to CONTRACT in PUT will appropriately check whether the insertion of a zero within the present non-zero band necessitates a contraction of that band. If this is the case, SUM, FIRSTNONZERO, and LASTNONZERO will be appropriately updated and a corresponding sequence of entries removed from LIST. Notice that expansions or contractions of LIST within the procedures EXPAND and CONTRACT are situations which we hope do not occur too often, since the processing involved will significantly decrease the run-time efficiency of the algorithm. The writing of these two procedures has been left for the exercises.

Efficiency Considerations for the Dope Vector Method

Before beginning our discussion of the linked list method of implementing a sparse matrix, we should mention the notion of the **efficiency ratio** of the generalized dope vector method. This ratio is defined by the fraction

$$\frac{\text{Number of storage locations used by generalized dope vector method}}{\text{Number of storage locations used by standard row major form}}$$

Since the generalized dope vector method will require three additional dope vector entries—SUM[I], FIRSTNONZERO[I], and LASTNONZERO[I]—for each row, it is clear that we achieve a desirable efficiency ratio less than one only when the average band width for all rows in the array is four or more less than the number of columns in the matrix. For instance, in the sparse band matrix of Figure 8-8, the efficiency ratio would be:

$$\frac{\text{15 memory locations to store the 5 non-zero bands} + \text{15 "overhead" locations for SUM, FIRSTNONZERO, LASTNONZERO}}{\text{70 locations necessary for row-major form}}$$

Here, since the average band width of 3 is 11 less than the number of columns in the matrix, a desirable efficiency ratio of 3/7 is achieved.

In the world of applications...

Sparse matrices have diverse uses in almost all areas of the natural sciences. One such application is in the equilibrium conditions across an electrical network. Kirchhoff's Laws of Electrical Equilibrium state:

1. The sum of incoming currents at each node is equal to the sum of the outgoing currents.
2. Around every closed loop, the sum of voltage is 0.

Now consider the electrical network shown below.

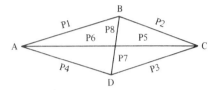

	P1	P2	P3	P4	P5	P6	P7	P8
A	-1	0	0	-1	0	1	0	0
B	1	-1	0	0	0	0	0	-1
C	0	1	-1	0	-1	0	0	0
D	0	0	1	1	0	0	1	0

The rows in the matrix represent nodes. The columns indicate directed electrical paths. −1 is used to indicate a node where a path ends, 1 to indicate a node where a path begins, and 0 to indicate that the particular path does not meet the corresponding node. If we look at node A, we notice that P1 and P4 end at A while P6 starts at A. According to Kirchhoff's first law, the sum of incoming currents along P1 and P2 must equal the outgoing current along P6. Similarly, the second law is also completely manifested by this sparse matrix.

An important and interesting principle about equilibrium is the Principle of Le Chatelier, from the French chemist Henri Louis Le Chatelier (1850–1936). The principle may be expressed in the following way: If the conditions of a system initially at equilibrium are changed, the system will shift in such a way as to restore the original conditions. Sparse matrices are used in the analysis of this principle in all areas of science. Kirchhoff's Laws are just one such example.

8-4 Linked List Implementation of a Sparse Matrix

This method is completely dynamic and, instead of a dope vector, requires an array of pointers, each leading to a linked list storing the non-zero data in a given row of the sparse matrix. Each node in one of these linked lists would need to contain not only an entry from the matrix but also an indication of which column within that particular row is occupied by the data in this node. We further stipulate that, for efficiency in processing, each linked list be arranged in ascending order of column numbers within that row. Given these conventions, the 5 x 14 matrix SPARSE of Figure 8-8 would be represented as in Figure 8-12.

Using the procedures INSERTNODE and DELETENODE already developed for linked lists in Chapter 2, a function SPARSE and a procedure PUT analogous to those for the generalized dope vector method in 8-2 are given below.

```
{Global declarations for SPARSE}

CONST
  N = 100;

TYPE
  NODEPOINTER = ^RECORDPOINTER;
  RECORDPOINTER =
    RECORD
      DATA: INTEGER;
      COL: INTEGER;
      NEXTCOL: NODEPOINTER
    END;

VAR
  HEAD: ARRAY [1..N] OF NODEPOINTER;

FUNCTION SPARSE(I, J: INTEGER): INTEGER;
{ As before this function accesses the (I,J)th entry in }
{ a sparse matrix.}

  VAR
    P: NODEPOINTER;
    EXIT: BOOLEAN;
```

```
BEGIN
  EXIT := FALSE;
  P := HEAD[I];
  WHILE (P <> NIL) AND NOT EXIT DO
    IF P^.COL < J THEN
       P := P^.NEXTCOL
    ELSE
       EXIT := TRUE;
    IF P = NIL THEN
       SPARSE := 0
    ELSE IF P^.COL > J THEN
       SPARSE := 0
    ELSE
       SPARSE := P^.DATA
END { SPARSE } ;
```

Example of P = NIL CASE, suppose J = 8

HEAD(I)

Example of P^.COL > J CASE, suppose J = 6

HEAD(I)

WHILE loop left P
pointing at
this node

{Global declarations for PUT}

Example of ELSE CASE, J = 5

HEAD(I)

WHILE loop left P
pointing at this node,
12 to be returned

```
CONST
  N = 100;

TYPE
  NODEPOINTER = ^RECORDPOINTER;
  RECORDPOINTER =
    RECORD
      DATA: INTEGER;
      COL: INTEGER;
      NEXTCOL: NODEPOINTER
    END;

VAR
  HEAD: ARRAY [1..N] OF NODEPOINTER;

PROCEDURE PUT(I, J, V: INTEGER);
{ This procedure like its predecessor PUT inserts a value in }
{ the (I,J)th position of a sparse matrix.}

  VAR
    P, Q, PREV: NODEPOINTER;
    EXIT: BOOLEAN;
```

```
BEGIN
  EXIT := FALSE;
  P := HEAD[I];
  WHILE (P <> NIL) AND NOT EXIT DO
    BEGIN
    IF P^. COL < J THEN
        P := P^. NEXTCOL
    ELSE
      EXIT := TRUE;
    PREV := P;
    P := P^. NEXTCOL
    END;
```

Example of P^. COL > J CASE, suppose J = 5

HEAD(I) → [6 | 3 | •] → [12 | 5 | •] → [2 | 7 | /]

DATA COL NEXTCOL

P

If V = 0, delete this node;
otherwise, new value
needed in data portion

```
  IF P^. COL = J AND V = 0 THEN
          { Assign 0 where non-zero entry had been. }
          { Call procedure to delete appropriate node from
            Ith linked list. }
    DELETENODE(I, PREV, Q)
  ELSE IF P^. COL = J THEN
  {Assigning non-zero where non-zero had been }
    P^. DATA := V
  ELSE IF V <> 0 THEN {Assign new non-zero entry }
    BEGIN
    NEW(Q);
    Q^. DATA := V;
    Q^. COL := J;
    INSERTNODE(I, PREV, Q)
          { Assume procedures RETURNNODE AND
            INSERTNODE of Chapter 2 as external }
    END
END { PUT } ;
```

Example of V <> 0 case, J = 6

HEAD(I) → [6 | 3 | •] → [12 | 5 | •] ⫽ → [2 | 7 |]

DATA COL NEXTCOL

New node to be
inserted here

Efficiency Considerations for the Linked List Method

Assuming that the data in a sparse matrix is of integer type, the efficiency ratio for this linked list implementation of a sparse matrix

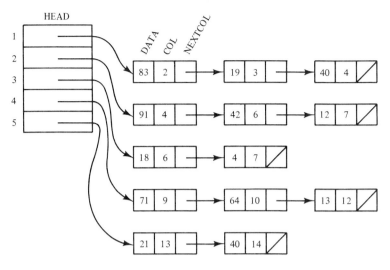

FIGURE 8-12 Linked list representation of sparse matrix from Figure 8-8.

drops below 1 only when the number of non-zero locations in the matrix is less than

$$NROW * (NCOL - 1) / 3$$

To see this, note that each non-zero matrix entry requires three integers to represent it in the linked list implementation. Moreover, each row requires an integer head pointer. Thus the total number of integers required to store N non-zero entries via the linked list method is

$$NROW + N*3$$

Since we want to force the efficiency ratio

$$\frac{NROW + N*3}{NROW * NCOL}$$

to be less than 1, we conclude that

$$NROW + N*3 < NROW * NCOL$$
$$N*3 < NROW*NCOL - NROW$$
$$N < NROW*(NCOL - 1) / 3$$

We close this chapter with a discussion of the relative merits of the linked list method vis-a-vis the generalized dope vector method.

1. It has been our experience that the linked list method is conceptually easier. Given already existing routines to insert in and delete from a linked list, it requires less detailed code.
2. Due to the procedures NEW and DISPOSE in Pascal, the linked list method is completely dynamic. All insertions and deletions are processed by altering pointers instead of moving data. The generalized dope vector method, on the other hand,

requires an initial static storage allocation for the maximum band width which is anticipated. Also, the dope vector method may require considerable data movement when the band width of a given row is altered.

3. The generalized dope vector method tends to save more storage when band matrices are involved. In particular, it requires a less sparse matrix to drop its efficiency ratio below 1.

4. The generalized dope vector method directly accesses a matrix entry via a computation instead of requiring the sequential search performed by the linked list method. This means that the dope vector method will access entries faster than the linked list method.

As with all data structure techniques, it is clear that the choice of which method to use is not black and white, but instead depends upon the particular application.

Program Design Considerations

Programming Problem (7) of this chapter asks you to develop a system to perform generalized matrix operations such as matrix addition, matrix multiplication, matrix inversion, and evaluation of determinants. A nice way of structuring this type of program would be to employ the menu-driven REPEAT loop strategy introduced in the Program Design Considerations for Chapter 3. Given this strategy, you would need to write procedures to fit into the following hierarchial scheme of control.

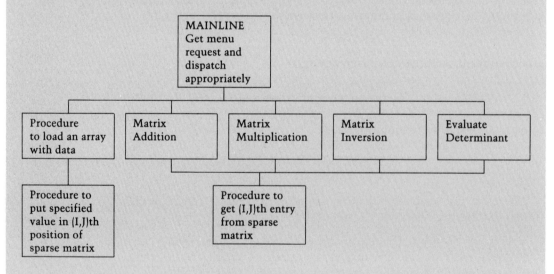

Two comments are in order concerning the type of modular structure chart which emerges in applications such as this. First, such structure charts typically assume a "fan-out-fan-in" shape as illustrated above. The narrowness at the top is due to there being a small number of modules controlling the major logic of the program. In this particular example, there is just one such module—the main program which fields menu requests and then dispatches to the appropriate matrix routine. The "fanning out" of the structure chart occurs in the middle levels where separate modules must exist for each of the numerous menu choices. The "fanning in" takes place at the lower levels of the chart where input and output routines must be written for each of the data structures involved in the program. Since these input/output routines must be called from many higher-level routines, the structure chart narrows at the bottom.

Second, the existence of basic input/output routines at the lowest level of the hierarchial structure chart for the system is an excellent illustration of how data abstraction is reflected in actual programs. By following this structural methodology, only those modules at the deepest level of a program's design need actually concern themselves with how the data structure involved is actually being implemented. In a sense, these low-level modules act as filters which keep such implementation details hidden from higher-level modules. This is as it should be, since these higher-level modules have "more important" logical decisions to make. For instance, in the design described above, only the two modules at the deepest level of the structure chart need concern themselves with whether the matrix under consideration is being implemented via direct row or column major storage, the generalized dope vector method, or the linked list method. Because of this it would be relatively easy to link different implementation techniques into the program without affecting the logic of any but these two modules.

SUMMARY

A matrix is an important mathematical tool which will be used extensively in the next chapter. As a data structure, a matrix must be implemented with space-saving economy in mind. Since many matrices used in practice are large sparse matrices, they cannot be implemented simply as two-dimensional arrays. The two techniques given in this chapter are space-saving means of implementing such a sparse matrix. There is a third technique, called **hashing subscripts,** which is treated in the programming exercises of Chapter 12.

KEY TERMS

Multidimensional array	Left subscript major
Matrix	Right subscript major
Row major	Sparse matrix
Column major	Band matrices
Mapping function	Generalized dope vector method
Dope vector	Efficiency ratio
Rank	Linked list method

EXERCISES

1. What do the terms row major and column major mean? Left subscript major? Right subscript major?
2. What is a dope vector? A generalized dope vector?
3. What is sparse about a sparse matrix?
4. Is a two-dimensional $M \times M$ array more or less efficient than a one-dimensional array of extent $M \times M$?
5. Write the data elements of the three-dimensional array pictured in Figure 8-6 in a linear list arranged via right subscript major form.
6. Write the procedures EXPAND and CONTRACT as called in the procedure PUT for the generalized dope vector implementation of a sparse matrix.
7. Develop data structures and appropriate procedures to adapt the generalized dope vector method to a sparse three-dimensional array.
8. The linked list implementation of a sparse matrix as presented in 8-4 will only allow access of an array entry by first accessing the linked list corresponding to the row of the entry and then proceeding along that row until the appropriate column is found. For applications which would frequently be accessing the data in a sparse matrix *by columns*, this would be highly inefficient. Devise data structures and develop appropriate procedures which would allow either row or column access to entries of the matrix.
9. Specifically describe how your solution to exercise 8 would affect the efficiency ratio of the sparse matrix representation.
10. Generalize the linked list method for sparse matrices so that it could be used for a sparse three-dimensional array.
11. Many languages, such as Pascal, allow subscripts for an arbitrary range of ordinal values, not necessarily always starting at 1. Specify how this would affect the techniques developed in this chapter to translate multidimensional array coordinates into linear list positions.
12. Is the LASTNONZERO data stored in the generalized dope vector still necessary once the data in SUM has been added to the vector? Justify your answer.
13. What would the mapping function be for a three-dimensional array stored in left subscript major form? Right subscript major form?
14. Compute the efficiency ratio of the generalized dope vector method for a sparse matrix that has 5 nonzero bands of width 3 each, and which would normally require a 14 by 5 matrix (14 rows and 5 columns) to store in row major form.

PROGRAMMING PROBLEMS

1. Due to factors such as type of airplanes, amount of pilot experience, and pilot geographic location, each of the pilots employed by the Wing-and-a-Prayer Airlines Company qualifies to fly on only a relatively small percentage of flights offered by this growing company. The information concerning the flights for which a given

pilot qualifies could be stored as a large boolean array. Help Wing-and-a-Prayer by developing a program that will accept as input a flight or a pilot number and then print all pilots or flights, respectively, that correspond to the input. Because a given pilot qualifies for only a small percentage of flights, a sparse matrix technique should be used to store the data.

2. The Fly-By-Night credit card company would like to maintain a statistical profile of the cities from which they draw their customers. The information contained in this profile would later be used for streamlining the business. A two-dimensional array consisting of the cities and the mileage between them would be needed for analysing traveling costs. Since this matrix would be sparse by nature, space needs to be conserved for its storage. Write a program in Pascal to store this matrix using the linked list method. Also print out this sparse matrix for verification.

3. The Bay Area Brawlers professional football team has a long and glorious history dating back to 1920. Records on the number of points scored by each of its players throughout its history may be viewed as a large two-dimensional array with:

   - Columns being indexed by year (1920-1984)
   - Rows being indexed by player name
   - The entry at a given row and column representing the number of points scored by the given player in that year.

   Since the duration of any one player's career is rarely more than 10 years, most entries in this two-dimensional array will be zero. That is, the array will be a sparse matrix. Write a program for the Brawlers that will:

   - Allow entry of a player's name and year and then report the number of points scored by that player in the specified year
   - Allow entry of a year and report the name of the player who scored the most points in that year
   - Allow entry of a player and output the total number of career points scored by that player.

4. *The Game of Life:* Invented by mathematician John H. Conway (*Scientific American*, October 1970, p. 120), this game models the growth and changes in a complex collection of living organisms. The model can be interpreted as applying to a collection of micro-organisms, an ecologically closed system of animals or plants, or an urban development.

   Start with an N X N checkerboard on which "counters" are to be placed. Each location has 8 neighbors. The counters are born, survive, or die during a "generation" according to the following rules:

   - *Survival:* Counters with two or three neighboring counters survive to the next generation.
   - *Death:* Counters with four or more neighbors die from overcrowding and are removed for the next generation. Counters with zero or one neighbors die from isolation and are removed for the next generation.

■ *Birth:* Each empty location which has exactly three counters in the eight neighboring locations is a birth location. A counter is placed in the location for the next generation.

For example, on a 6 x 6 space the pattern on the left would look like the one on the right in the next generation:

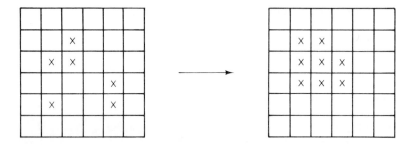

Certain patterns are stable:

Other patterns repeat a sequence:

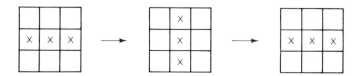

After initializing the first generation, print it out. Then calculate the next generation in another array and print. Repeat for a specified number of generations. Your output should be an "X" for live cells and a blank otherwise.

Since two $N \times N$ matrices are actually required to implement the Game of Life as described above, it is clear that memory limitations could easily become a problem for large N. Choosing one of the sparse matrix methods described in this chapter, design a program in a high-level language to implement the Game of Life.

5. Develop a procedure that will translate (X,Y) Cartesian coordinates into the row and column subscripts of a two-dimensional array. Using this and one of the two sparse matrix strategies discussed in this chapter, implement in Pascal a graphics program that will plot the graph of a specified equation by plotting points on the graph of the equation in a suitably dimensioned sparse matrix.

6. If you are familiar with linear algebra, implement the Gaussian elimination procedure to solve an N X N system of equations using one of the sparse matrix techniques discussed in this chapter.

7. For each of the two sparse matrix presentations developed in this chapter, devise a system to perform typical matrix operations such as matrix addition, matrix multiplication, matrix inversion, and evaluation of determinants. See the program design considerations for this chapter to get yourself started on this problem.

9

Graphs and Networks

"I'd rather wake up in the middle of nowhere than in any city on earth."

STEVE MCQUEEN

9-1 Introductory Considerations

In chapters 6 and 7, the reader was introduced to trees as a structure which could be used to describe a certain type of relationship between data items. The tree structure is a special kind of **graph** in which the relationship between parent and child is hierarchical. A general graph, on the other hand, represents a less restricted relationship between data items. A common example of a graph is a collection of cities and the roads between them. In such a graph, two cities are related if there is a route between them. Such a relationship is not hierarchical because the routes between cities may exist in both directions. Graphs are frequently applied in such diverse areas as artificial intelligence, cybernetics, chemical structures of crystals, transportation networks, electrical circuitry, and the analysis of programming languages. In this chapter, we shall focus on the concept of graphs in general and then look at some specific applications in communications, transportation, and the scheduling of projects.

A graph is formally defined as a set of objects called **nodes** and **edges.** A node is a data element of the graph, and an edge is a path between two nodes. An **undirected graph** such as in Figure 9-1 is a graph such that an edge between two nodes is not directionally oriented. Thus, in an undirected graph, if AG (that is, from A to G) is an edge, so is GA.

A **directed graph** or **digraph** is a graph in which an edge between two nodes is directionally oriented. In the directed graph of Figure 9-2, AB is an edge but BA is not an edge. Thus, there are **directed edges**

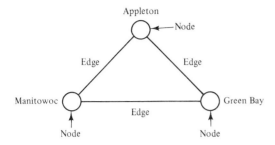

FIGURE 9-1   Undirected graph.

from A to B, B to C, C to D, and D to E. A directed edge is also called an **arc.** The digraph of Figure 9-2 can be looked upon as expressing the alphabetical order relationship between the letters. We shall denote an arc from node x to node y by $x \rightarrow y$. In order to use graphs effectively, we need to know which nodes are directly connected by an edge, and also those nodes which are indirectly connected by a set of edges. For example, in Figure 9-2, A is directly connected to B, and B is indirectly connected to E via the arcs $B \rightarrow C$, $C \rightarrow D$, and $D \rightarrow E$. In a digraph, therefore, we say that there is a **directed path** connection from node I to node J if and only if there is a sequence of nodes $I = I_1, I_2, \ldots, I_n = J$ such that I_{i-1} is connected to I_i via an arc. In Figure 9-2, there is no path from node E to node A, although there is a path from node A to E. A digraph is said to be **strongly connected** if, for any two nodes I and J in the graph, there is a directed path from I to J. A digraph is said to be **weakly connected** if, for any two nodes I and J, there is a directed path from I to J or J to I. The digraph in Figure 9-2 is weakly connected. However, it is not strongly connected, since, for the nodes C and E, there is a directed path from C to E but none from E to C. The digraph shown in Figure 9-3 is strongly connected. Clearly, any digraph which is strongly connected is also weakly connected.

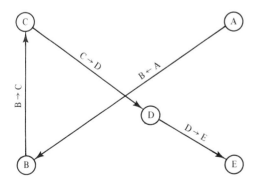

FIGURE 9-2   Directed graph.

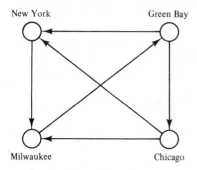

FIGURE 9-3 *Strongly connected digraph.*

By the **outdegree** of a node in a digraph we mean the number of arcs exiting from the node; the **indegree** of a node is the number of arcs entering the node. In Figure 9-3, the indegree of NEW YORK is 2 and its outdegree is 1. The indegree and the outdegree of CHICAGO are 1 and 2 respectively. The indegree and the outdegree of a node in a digraph indicate its relative importance in data processing activity involved with the graph. A node whose outdegree is 0 largely acts as a depository of information and hence is called a **sink node.** A node whose indegree is 0 is called a **source node.** The fundamental input-to-output operation, which is common to all data processing activity and is shown in Figure 9-4, illustrates this concept.

By a **cycle** in a directed graph, we mean a directed path of length at least 1 which originates and terminates at the same node in the graph. In Figure 9-3, New York → Milwaukee → Green Bay → New York is a cycle of length 3.

The concepts discussed in the preceding three paragraphs also hold for an undirected graph wherever they apply. Thus, a path between two nodes is a sequence of edges, directly or indirectly connecting the two nodes. There is a path between any two nodes in Figure 9-1. Since the concept of indegree and outdegree cannot apply to a node in an undirected graph, we then define the **degree** of a node to be the number of edges connected directly to the node. In Figure 9-1, the degree of each node is 2.

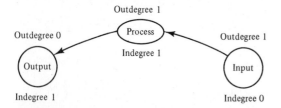

FIGURE 9-4 *Indegrees and outdegrees of nodes.*

9-2 Implementation of Graphs— The Adjacency Matrix

The physical structure of a graph (undirected or directed) can be conveniently represented by a matrix called the **adjacency matrix** or **incidence matrix** for the graph. A graph containing n nodes can be represented by a matrix containing n rows and n columns. The matrix is formed by placing a 1 in the ith row and jth column (that is, the (i,j) th entry) of the matrix if there is an edge between node i and node j of the graph. Consider the graph in Figure 9-5. Its adjacency matrix, as given in Figure 9-6, clearly shows whether or not there is an edge between any two nodes. For example, the presence of 1 in the 4th row and 3rd column means there is an edge between node L and C; 0 in the 1st row and 5th column, by the same token, signifies the absence of an edge between the nodes A and R.

We stress that matrices are only a convenient way of thinking about the memory representation of a graph. You will *not* necessarily use a two-dimensional array to store a graph in memory. Clearly a graph with a substantial number of nodes could consume an inordinately large amount of memory if a two-dimensional array were actually used in its implementation. Fortunately, most graphs are sparse matrices. Consequently, any of the space-saving techniques discussed in Chapter 8 may actually be used in the implementation of the adjacency matrix for a graph. For the rest of this chapter, we will continue to speak in terms of the adjacency matrix M for a graph and use the notation

$$M[I,J] <> 0 \text{ or } M[I,J] = 0$$

to refer to the presence or absence respectively of an edge between nodes I and J in the graph. $M[I,J]$ in such a reference could actually

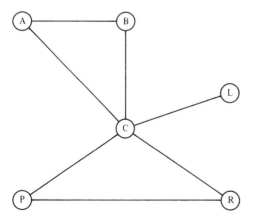

FIGURE 9-5 Undirected graph for the adjacency matrix in Figure 9-6.

	A	B	L	C	R	P
A	0	1	0	1	0	0
B	1	0	0	1	0	0
L	0	0	0	1	0	0
C	1	1	1	0	1	1
R	0	0	0	1	0	1
P	0	0	0	1	1	0

FIGURE 9-6   Adjacency (incidence) matrix for graph of Figure 9-5.

refer to a two-dimensional array or to a function call which retrieves a value from some sparse matrix representation. The details of the actual representation are not a concern of this chapter. Instead, in this chapter we will concentrate upon the algorithms which manipulate a graph, regardless of its representation. Here again, the notion of *data abstraction* has emerged. To the greatest degree possible, data structure algorithms should be independent of a particular type of representation.

For an undirected graph such as that appearing in Figure 9-5, the incidence matrix must have its *i*th row and *i*th column identical. Such a matrix is called a **symmetric matrix**. The adjacency matrix of a digraph in most cases is not symmetric due to the directional nature of the arc from one node to another. Figure 9-7 shows the adjacency matrix of the digraph in Figure 9-2.

For further manipulation of a graph and its adjacency matrix, we need to introduce the concept of the **length** of a path. The length of a path between nodes *I* and *K* is defined to be the number of nodes on the path from *I* to *K* minus one (that is, the number of edges). For example, in the graph of Figure 9-5, there are more than two paths between A and R. If we choose the path ABCR, then the length of this path is 3; but if we choose the path ACR, then its length is 2. In many practical applications of graphs, it is important to know whether there

	A	B	C	D	E
A	0	1	0	0	0
B	0	0	1	0	0
C	0	0	0	1	0
D	0	0	0	0	1
E	0	0	0	0	0

FIGURE 9-7   Adjacency (incidence) matrix for digraph of Figure 9-2.

is a path between nodes I and K and, if so, what the length of this path is.

To answer these questions we shall use the adjacency matrix of the graph. In particular, we will need to use the algebraic notion of matrix multiplication. Briefly, the product of two square matrices A x B of the same order is another square matrix C such that the (i,j)th entry in C is the sum of the products of the corresponding entries from row i in A and column j in C.

Suppose we wish to multiply

$$A = \begin{bmatrix} 2 & 3 & 4 \\ 1 & 6 & 7 \\ 2 & 1 & 3 \end{bmatrix} = \begin{bmatrix} a_{11} & a_{12} & a_{13} \\ a_{21} & a_{22} & a_{23} \\ a_{31} & a_{32} & a_{33} \end{bmatrix}$$

and

$$B = \begin{bmatrix} 1 & 2 & 3 \\ 3 & 2 & 4 \\ 5 & 6 & 7 \end{bmatrix} = \begin{bmatrix} b_{11} & b_{12} & b_{13} \\ b_{21} & b_{22} & b_{23} \\ b_{31} & b_{32} & b_{33} \end{bmatrix}$$

then

$$A \; X \; B \; = \; C$$

where the matrix C also has 3 rows and 3 columns

$$C = \begin{bmatrix} c_{11} & c_{12} & c_{13} \\ c_{21} & c_{22} & c_{23} \\ c_{31} & c_{32} & c_{33} \end{bmatrix}$$

$$c_{11} = a_{11} \times b_{11} + a_{12} \times b_{21} + a_{13} \times b_{31}$$

Similarly

$$c_{ij} = a_{i1} \times b_{1j} + a_{i2} \times b_{2j} + a_{i3} \times b_{3j}$$
$$\text{for } i = 1, 2, 3 \quad \text{and} \quad j = 1, 2, 3$$

Following this strategy we obtain

$$C = \begin{bmatrix} 31 & 34 & 46 \\ 54 & 56 & 76 \\ 20 & 24 & 31 \end{bmatrix}$$

Note that in matrix multiplication $A \times B$ is not always the same as $B \times A$. You should convince yourself of this fact by doing Exercise (6). The writing of a procedure to perform such multiplication is also left as an exercise; we shall assume its existence in future algorithm discussions.

In the World of Applications. . .

The Traveling Salesman Problem

A well-known problem of classical graph theory, which is easy to state but difficult to solve, is the traveling salesman problem. The problem essentially relates to minimizing the round trip cost of visiting once and only once every city on the business route of the salesman. This problem was first proposed by the Irish mathematician Sir William Rowan Hamilton (1805–1865).

The problem can be looked upon as a network such as in Figure 9-22. The cities to be visited are the vertices in the network, and the weighted edges are the distances between the cities. The minimum spanning tree algorithm discussed in the text is not the solution to this problem, but it can be adapted to yield the solution in the following way:

1. Set the total cost of traveling to 0.
2. Select a home node (home city of the salesman), and designate it as X.
3. Find an *unused* node which minimizes the sum of the edgeweight connecting it to X plus the remaining round trip distance. Add this edgeweight to the total cost.
4. Designate the node found in step (3) as the new home node; that is, as node X.
5. Repeat steps (3) and (4) until all nodes are visited and the salesman is back at home; that is, until X is the home node chosen in step (2).

Although the algorithm described above solves the traveling salesman's problem, it is slow because of the extensive computation involved in step 3. When the number of cities on the salesman's tour is large (even as large as 20), the solution is annoyingly slow, but nothing better is known.

Prototypes of this classical algorithm find frequent application in the design of computer operating systems. For instance, suppose we have a collection of processes all waiting to access a popular disk file. (See "In the World of Applications . . ." for Chapter 4.) The operating system designer is concerned with scheduling these processes in a fashion which minimizes the total disk access time. By viewing each process P_i as a network node, and the edgeweight connecting node P_i to node P_j as the disk access time required if process P_j immediately follows process P_i in the scheduling, the solution to this operating system problem is essentially the traveling salesman problem. A complicating factor is that the slowness of the algorithm cited above may make it impractical to incorporate into an interactive operating system.

Who says being on the road and making a buck is easy?

If M is the adjacency matrix of a graph, then non-zero entries in it represent those nodes which are joined together by a path of length 1. The matrix M^2 (that is, $M \times M$) identifies those nodes which are joined by paths of length 2. The presence of a nonzero number in the (i,j)th entry of M^2 means that the ith node and jth node have a path between them of length 2. In general an integer r present in the (i,j)th entry of the matrix M^n tells us that the ith and jth nodes in the original graph have r paths between them of length n. Consider the digraph of Figure 9-8 and its adjacency matrix in Figure 9-9. The presence of 1 in the 1st row and 2nd column of M^2 means that A and B are connected by 1 path of length 2. Similarly 3 in M^3 signifies the existence of 3 directed paths of length 3 from A to C. The 2 in the 3rd row and 2nd column in M^3 means C and B are connected by 2 paths of length 3.

At first glance, the fact that the (i,j)th entry of M^n tells us precisely the number of paths of length n between the two corresponding nodes may seem to be an extremely fortunate coincidence. However, the claim can be mathematically proven. For those familiar with mathematical induction, we present here a partial inductive argument intended to illustrate that there is a basis for the claim.

Suppose we know that the claim is valid for $n - 1$, that is, the (i,j)th entry of M^{n-1} is indeed the number of paths of length $n - 1$ between nodes i and j. We must use this knowledge to show that the claim is valid for n. The validity of the claim for $n - 1$ means that the entries $a_{i1}, a_{i2}, \ldots, a_{in}$ along the ith row of M^{n-1} in Figure 9-10 are precisely the number of paths of length $n - 1$ from node i to node 1, node i to node 2, $\ldots$, node i to node n.

The jth column of M contains 1's and 0's. A 1 in the kth row of column j indicates an edge connecting node k to node j. If there are a_{ik} paths of length $n - 1$ from node i to node k, then each one of these will generate a path of length n from node i to node j provided there is an edge connecting node k to node j. If there is no such edge, then no paths are generated. In terms of the coefficients used in Figure 9-10, each of the a_{ik} paths will become a path to node j if and only if m_{kj} is

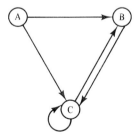

FIGURE 9-8 Digraph with number of paths computed using matrix multiplication in Figure 9-9.

$$
M = \begin{array}{c} \\ A \\ B \\ C \end{array}
\begin{array}{ccc}
A & B & C \\
\left[\begin{array}{ccc}
0 & 1 & 1 \\
0 & 0 & 1 \\
0 & 1 & 1
\end{array}\right]
\end{array}
$$

$$
M^2 = \begin{array}{c} \\ A \\ B \\ C \end{array}
\begin{array}{ccc}
A & B & C \\
\left[\begin{array}{ccc}
0 & 1 & 2 \\
0 & 1 & 1 \\
0 & 1 & 2
\end{array}\right]
\end{array}
$$

$$
M^3 = \begin{array}{c} \\ A \\ B \\ C \end{array}
\begin{array}{ccc}
A & B & C \\
\left[\begin{array}{ccc}
0 & 2 & 3 \\
0 & 1 & 2 \\
0 & 2 & 3
\end{array}\right]
\end{array}
$$

FIGURE 9-9   Adjacency matrix for Figure 9-8.

1, making the product $a_{ik} m_{kj} = a_{ik}$. Otherwise it will be 0. This means that there are

$$
\sum_{k=1}^{n} a_{ik} m_{kj}
$$

paths of length n from node i to node j. But this sum is precisely the (i,j)th coefficient in the matrix M^n.

In addition to this matrix multiplication property, you may easily verify that, for an undirected graph, the row sum of the ith row in its adjacency matrix gives the degree of the ith node. The row sum of ith row and column sum of jth column in the adjacency matrix of a directed graph give the outdegree of the ith node and the indegree of the jth node respectively.

In many applications, it is of interest to determine whether there is a path (or a directed path in a digraph) between any two nodes in a graph. The adjacency matrix also contains information which may be used to answer this question. From the foregoing discussion you may

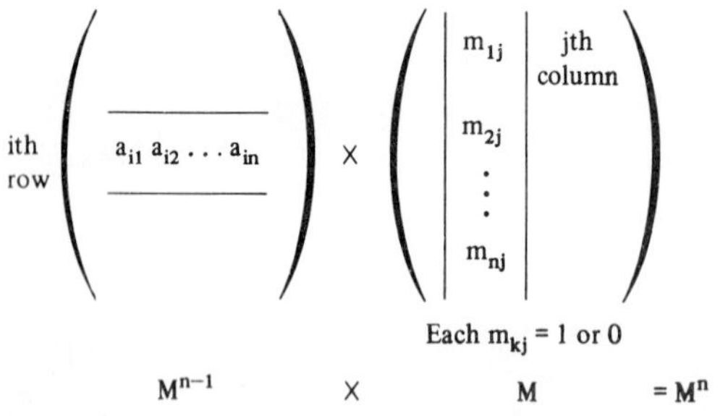

FIGURE 9-10   Matrix multiplication of M^{n-1} by M.

already have guessed part of the answer. Put simply there is a path of length n between the ith and jth nodes if and only if the (i,j)th entry of the matrix M^n is non-zero. Now the question arises: how many times do we multiply the adjacency matrix M with itself (that is, what should n be?) to answer whether or not there exists a path between any two nodes?

Consider the simple digraph of Figure 9-11, whose adjacency matrix M is given in Figure 9-12. Since $M^3, M^4, M^5, \ldots$ are simply repetitions of M and M^2, all paths of length more than 2 are mere duplications of paths of length 1 or 2. This shows that if there is any path at all from A to B (or B to A) there must be one of length 2 or less between them. Looking at M, we notice that there is indeed a path of length 1 from A to B and from B to A, although M^2 shows no path of length 2 from A to B.

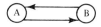

FIGURE 9-11 **Simple digraph corresponding to the adjacency matrix in Figure 9-12.**

When the graph contains more than two nodes, the situation is completely analogous. Suppose a graph contains r nodes. Then there is a path between the ith and jth nodes if and only if the (i,j)th entry in at least one of the matrices $M, M^2, \ldots, M^r$ is not zero. Therefore we need not bother computing any higher powers of M. The following Pascal procedure determines the existence of a path between any two nodes of a graph containing N nodes using this property of its adjacency matrix M. If a path between the designated nodes exists, the procedure returns PATHEXISTS with the value TRUE; otherwise FALSE is returned in PATHEXISTS.

```
{ Global declarations }

CONST
  N = 100;

TYPE
  ARR = ARRAY [1..N, 1..N] OF INTEGER;

PROCEDURE FINDPATH(VAR M: ARR;
                   I, J: INTEGER;
                   VAR PATHEXISTS: BOOLEAN);

  VAR
    KPOWER: ARR;
    K: INTEGER;
```

```
BEGIN
      {Determine whether there is a path between nodes I and J
         in the graph represented by the N by N adjacency matrix
         M}

   PATHEXISTS := FALSE;
   {Check first for the easiest possible case}
   IF M[I, J] <> 0 THEN
      PATHEXISTS := TRUE
   ELSE
      BEGIN
      K := 2;
      WHILE (K < N + 1) AND NOT PATHEXISTS DO
         BEGIN
         POWER(M, K, KPOWER);
               {This call is to return in KPOWER the matrix M raised
                  to the power K}
         IF KPOWER(I, J) <> 0 THEN
            PATHEXISTS := TRUE
         ELSE
            K := K + 1
         END { WHILE }
      END { ELSE }

END { FINDPATH } ;
```

Diagraph with adjacency matrix

POWER (M, 2, KPOWER)
returns

$$\text{KPOWER} = \begin{matrix} & 1 & 2 & 3 \\ 1 & \begin{bmatrix} 0 & 0 & 1 \\ 0 & 0 & 0 \\ 0 & 0 & 0 \end{bmatrix} \\ 2 & & \\ 3 & & \end{matrix}$$

One path
from
1 to 3 of
length 2

No path from 3 to 1

$$M = \begin{matrix} & A & B \\ A & \begin{bmatrix} 0 & 1 \\ 1 & 0 \end{bmatrix} \\ B & \end{matrix}$$

$$M^2 = \begin{matrix} & A & B \\ A & \begin{bmatrix} 1 & 0 \\ 0 & 1 \end{bmatrix} \\ B & \end{matrix}$$

$$M^3 = \begin{matrix} & A & B \\ A & \begin{bmatrix} 0 & 1 \\ 1 & 0 \end{bmatrix} \\ B & \end{matrix}$$

$$M^4 = \begin{matrix} & A & B \\ A & \begin{bmatrix} 1 & 0 \\ 0 & 1 \end{bmatrix} \\ B & \end{matrix}$$

FIGURE 9-12 Adjacency matrix for digraph of Figure 9-11.

Our procedure FINDPATH uses another procedure POWER which simply finds successive powers M, M × M, M × M × M, etc. of a square matrix M. The procedure POWER has been left as an exercise. When implementing FINDPATH and POWER, the program can be designed to take advantage of the previously computed powers of the matrix.

9-3 Graph Traversal

In many practical applications of graphs, there is frequently a need to systematically visit all the nodes on a graph. One such application occurs in a political campaign when the organizers of the campaign are interested in having their candidate visit all important political centers. The presence or absence of direct transportation routes (that is, edges) between such centers will determine the possible ways in which all the centers could be visited. At the moment our only concern is the development of an algorithm which insures that all nodes are visited. Later in the chapter we shall investigate how to determine the most economical way of doing this.

Depth-First Search

The main logic of the **depth-first search** algorithm is analogous to the preorder traversal of a tree. It is accomplished recursively as follows:

1. Choose any node in the graph. Designate it as the *search node* and mark it as *visited*.
2. Using the adjacency matrix of the graph, find a node adjacent to the search node (that is, connected by an arc from the search node) which has not yet been visited. Designate this as the new search node (but remember the previous one) and mark it as visited.
3. Repeat (2) using the new search node. If no nodes satisfying (2) can be found, return to the previous search node and continue from there.
4. When a return to the previous search node in (3) is impossible, the search from the originally chosen search node is complete.
5. If the graph still contains unvisited nodes, choose any node that has not been visited and repeat steps (1) through (4).

The algorithm above is called a depth-first search because the search continues progressively deeper in a recursive manner.

To illustrate this procedure more clearly we consider the directed graph in Figure 9-13. (Although our examples will illustrate the depth-first search for a directed graph, note that the algorithm also applies to

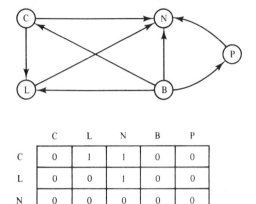

	C	L	N	B	P
C	0	1	1	0	0
L	0	0	1	0	0
N	0	0	0	0	0
B	1	1	1	0	1
P	0	0	1	0	0

FIGURE 9-13   Directed graph used to illustrate depth-first search and its associated adjacency matrix.

undirected graphs.) Suppose we have a procedure called SEARCH which is invoked to begin a depth-first search from a given node on the graph. The steps followed by the algorithm are listed below.

1. We begin by marking C visited and invoke SEARCH (C).
2. Since both N and L are adjacent to C according to the adjacency matrix of the graph, but L is encountered first on a left-to-right scan of the row for C, the search goes to L. We invoke SEARCH (L) and L is marked as visited.
3. Since N is the only node adjacent to L, the search now goes to N, SEARCH (N) is invoked, and N is marked as visited.
4. Since there is no node adjacent to N, we say that N has *exhausted* the search, the search goes back to its predecessor, that is, to L.
5. But all nodes adjacent to L have also been visited, so the search returns to C.
6. Now N is the next node adjacent to C. However, N has already been visited, so the search from C is now completed.
7. All nodes except P and B have been visited. We choose B next and mark it as visited. Since P is the only unvisited node adjacent to B, the search proceeds to P and we invoke SEARCH (P). N being the only node adjacent to P, the search goes to N which has already been visited. The search then backtracks to B, at which point the total search is complete.

Figure 9-14 highlights the steps of this algorithm. Before giving a formal statement of the algorithm in Pascal, let us first consider some

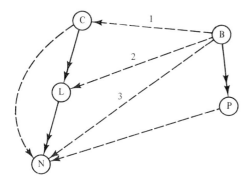

FIGURE 9-14 Depth-first search applied to Figure 9-13.

definitions and applications which arise when it is applied to directed graphs. In Figure 9-14 and Figure 9-16 there are three types of arcs. Double arrow arcs, known as **tree arcs,** indicate natural descent from one adjacent node to its next adjacent node in the depth-first search. All other arcs are dotted and are called **cross arcs.** Notice that the depth-first search decomposes the graph into a set of trees defined by tree arcs, with cross arcs connecting various nodes on different trees within this set. The set of these trees is called the **depth-first spanning forest** for the graph.

Single arrow arcs represent **backward arcs.** During an incomplete depth-first search from a node, if a previously visited node becomes adjacent to the current node being visited, it indicates the presence of a backward arc. Backward arcs indicate that there are cycles in the digraph. There are no backward arcs in Figure 9-14, consistent with there being no cycles in the graph in Figure 9-13. A graph with no cycles in it is also called an **acyclic graph.** (Note that an undirected graph cannot be acyclic. Why?)

As another example, consider the graph in Figure 9-15. Beginning the depth-first search with A and choosing C as adjacent to A before B, we arrive at the spanning forest shown in Figure 9-16. A second spanning forest is shown in Figure 9-17 in which we applied the depth-first search algorithm beginning at node B. The node D was

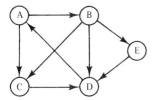

FIGURE 9-15 Directed graph with cycle ACD.

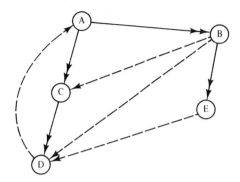

FIGURE 9-16   Depth-first search and spanning forest derived from graph in Figure 9-15.

chosen adjacent to B before E. Notice that a different spanning forest is obtained each time the search is initiated at a different node. In both spanning forests, there are back arcs; thus the graph in figure 9-15 contains cycles. We now have a simple test to determine whether or not a particular graph contains cycles. If a spanning forest of the graph has no back arcs, the graph contains no cycles.

Acyclic graphs are particularly useful in arranging various modules in order of priority in a large project. Suppose that a large job consists of modules A, B, C, and D. Suppose you must finish A first and C last, and you must do B before you start C and D. An acyclic graph such as that shown in Figure 9-18 in conjunction with its adjacency matrix in Figure 9-19, establishes an ordering for the various modules

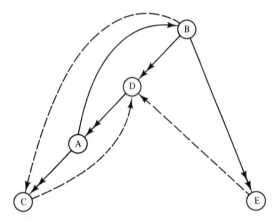

FIGURE 9-17   Spanning forest arising from different depth-first search of graph in Figure 9-15.

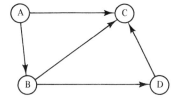

FIGURE 9-18   Digraph ordering nodes in sample project.

of the project. Scanning the rows of the matrix from *left to right* essentially declares B adjacent to A before C. This linear ordering is expressed:

> Between any two modules X and Y, choose X to precede Y if there is an arc from X to Y.

According to the digraph in Figure 9-18, the project should be performed in the order A, B, D, and C. The depth-first search can be used effectively to arrive at this ordering provided that the adjacency matrix representation of the graph *forces* the choice of B adjacent to A before C, and D adjacent to B before C. That is, we must have the adjacency matrix in **topological order,** as it appears in Figure 9-19, if the depth-first search is to indicate the order in which modules are to be scheduled for completion of the project. In Section 9-6, we will define topological order more precisely, and consider this question: Given an *arbitrary* adjacency matrix for a digraph corresponding to the ordering of modules in a project, is there an algorithm which can be invoked to reconstruct the adjacency matrix in topological order?

Given the importance of the depth-first search, it is appropriate at this time to present it formally in a procedure. The recursive procedure SEARCHFROM below is used to visit each node and then progress deeper (if possible) along a given tree in the spanning forest of the graph.

	A	B	D	C
A	0	1	0	1
B	0	0	1	1
D	0	0	0	1
C	0	0	0	0

FIGURE 9-19   Adjacency matrix for digraph in Figure 9-18.

```
{ Global declarations }

CONST
  N = 100;

VAR
  M: ARRAY [1..N, 1..N] OF INTEGER;
  VISITED: ARRAY [1..N] OF BOOLEAN;

PROCEDURE DFSEARCH;
 {Depth-first search of a graph with N nodes}

  VAR
    I: INTEGER;

  PROCEDURE SEARCHFROM(K: INTEGER);

    VAR
      J: INTEGER;

    BEGIN
      VISITED[K] := TRUE;
      FOR J := 1 TO N DO
        IF NOT VISITED[J] AND (M[K, J] <> 0) THEN
          SEARCHFROM(J) { Recursive call}
    END {SEARCHFROM} ;

  BEGIN
    FOR I := 1 TO N DO
      VISITED[I] := FALSE;
    {Begin searching for unvisited nodes }
    FOR I := 1 TO N DO
      IF NOT VISITED[I] THEN
        SEARCHFROM(I)
  END { DFSEARCH } ;
```

Initially
VISITED(I) = FALSE
For all I

Begin
SEARCH-FROM(I)
and proceed
down recursively

Breadth-First Search

Another widely used scheme for graph traversal is the **breadth-first search.** Although it can be used for both directed and undirected graphs, we shall describe it in relation to undirected graphs. Essentially the breadth-first search begins at a given node and then proceeds to all the nodes which are directly connected to this node. The following steps are involved in the algorithm:

1. Begin with any node, and mark it as *visited.*
2. Proceed to the next node having an edge connection to the node in step (1). Mark it as visited.
3. Come back to the node in step (1), descend along an edge toward an unvisited node, and mark the new node as visited.
4. Repeat step (2) until all nodes adjacent to the node in step (1) have been marked as visited.
5. Repeat steps (1)–(4) starting from the node visited in (2), then starting from the nodes visited in step (3) in the order visited. Keep this up as long as possible before starting a new scan.

Notice that the algorithm amounts to choosing a tree in the graph, visiting the root, then visiting all nodes at level 1, level 2, and so on. A queue is a convenient structure to keep track of nodes that are visited during a breadth-first search. As a given node is visited, it is entered into the queue of nodes which are waiting to have their children visited. Once we complete visiting all the children of a given node, we remove the node currently at the front of the queue and subsequently visit its children.

As in the case of a depth-first search, this algorithm also results in a spanning forest for the graph. This spanning forest is called the **breadth-first spanning forest.** Figure 9-21 gives a breadth-first spanning forest for the graph in Figure 9-20, assuming that we begin the traversal at P. You will write the implementation of a breadth-first search as an exercise at the end of the chapter.

The term breadth-first search comes from the fact that the graph is being searched *broadly* by exploring all the nodes adjacent to a node, that is, by visiting all nodes on a given level of the chosen tree. In relational data base applications, data items are related by graphs. Since a

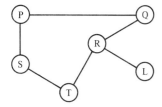

FIGURE 9-20   Undirected graph yielding Figure 9-21.

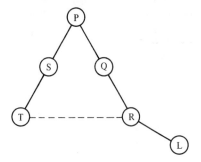

FIGURE 9-21   Breadth-first spanning forest from Figure 9-20.

graph represents a *many-to-many* relationship between nodes, as opposed to trees in which a *one-to-many* hierarchical relationship exists, graphs are first decomposed into a set of trees (a spanning forest) before they are actually stored. Data base management systems use this concept extensively, as we will see in Chapter 12.

9-4   Networks

In many natural applications of graphs, it is not only the edges between nodes that play an important role, but also the **weights** of these edges. For example, an airline may be interested not only in the existence of an air route between two cities but the shortest such air route. The distance between the two cities is then the weight of the edge connecting the two cities. A graph with weighted edges, such as the one in Figure 9-22, is called a **network**. An immediate question that arises in regard to this type of network is:

What is the shortest path between any two given nodes of a network?

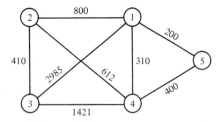

FIGURE 9-22   A network with weighted edges representing the distances between nodes.

Before answering this question, we shall consider a more general problem which is usually involved in communication networks. Given a network, devise a way to connect all the nodes in the network so that the total edge weight is minimized. In a telephone communication network, a more vital question than being able to link any two cities in the most economical fashion is that of being able to link *all* cities in the network for the least possible cost. To solve this latter problem, we shall devise an algorithm which converts the network into a tree structure called the **minimum spanning tree** of the network.

Minimum Spanning Tree

The minimum spanning tree algorithm results in a tree which contains branches chosen from the edges in the original network. Given an original network in which there is a path between any two nodes, the edges for the minimum spanning tree are chosen in such a way that two properties result:

1. Every node in the network must be included in the spanning tree.
2. The total edge weight of the spanning tree is the minimum possible that will allow the existence of a path between any two nodes in the tree.

A generalized pseudocode algorithm to do this may be stated as follows:

```
INCLUDE any node to begin with
REPEAT
    FOR all nodes not yet INCLUDED
        INCLUDE the node having an edge of minimal weight
            connecting it to an already INCLUDED node
        ADD this node and edge to the tree
    ENDFOR
UNTIL all nodes INCLUDED
```

Here the keywords INCLUDE and ADD imply in some sense the marking of nodes and edges as they are chosen for the minimal spanning tree.

Before getting into the details of a specific Pascal implementation of this algorithm, let us trace it for a small network to see why it works. Consider the network of Figure 9-22 with adjacency matrix as shown in Figure 9-23. Since the algorithm allows us to begin with any node, let us INCLUDE node 1. We then enter the REPEAT loop of the algorithm, first searching for a node having an edge of minimum weight connecting it to node 1. Clearly, this is node 5, so node 5 is INCLUDED and the edge connecting 1 to 5 is ADDED to the tree. Next

	1	2	3	4	5
1	0	800	2985	310	200
2	800	0	410	612	0
3	2985	410	0	1421	0
4	310	612	1421	0	400
5	200	0	0	400	0

FIGURE 9-23   Adjacency matrix for network of Figure 9-22.

time through the REPEAT loop, we search for a node not yet IN-CLUDED (that is, node 2, 3, or 4) having an edge of minimal weight connecting it to an already INCLUDED node (that is, node 1 or 5). A visual scan of the network will verify that the edge of weight 310 connecting node 4 to node 1 is the appropriate choice this time through the loop. Hence node 4 is INCLUDED and this edge is ADDED to the tree. We leave it to the reader to verify that the edge connecting node 2 to node 4 and then the edge connecting node 3 to node 2 would be ADDED to complete construction of the minimal spanning tree. The result is shown in Figure 9-24.

It is obvious that, if the original network has a path between any two nodes, the minimum spanning tree constructed by the above method will also have a path between any two nodes. It is perhaps not as obvious that the method will necessarily produce a tree of the minimal possible edge weight allowing the existence of a path between any two nodes. An intuitive rationale as to why this indeed *must* be is given by the following argument. Consider any other method for choosing nodes and edges for the minimal spanning tree. Since our method allows us to start with any node, we could easily identify the choice at which our method and the proposed other method deviate. Let us group the nodes and edges for which the two methods dictate the same choice as indicated in Figure 9-25. The edge leaving the circled edges in Figure 9-25 identifies the choice at which the proposed method and our method would deviate. That is, this edge cannot be an

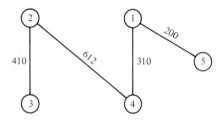

FIGURE 9-24   Minimal spanning tree derived from Figures 9-22 and 9-23.

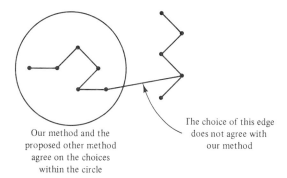

The choice of this edge does not agree with our method

Our method and the proposed other method agree on the choices within the circle

FIGURE 9-25 *Comparison of two methods for constructing a minimum spanning tree.*

edge of minimal weight connecting a node outside the circle to one within the circle. There must be an edge of lesser weight connecting a node outside the circle to one within the circle. Such an edge is indicated by a dotted line in Figure 9-26.

It should now be obvious that Figure 9-26 has given us a spanning tree of smaller overall edge weight than the one of Figure 9-25. Hence we have informally shown that any other proposed method of selecting nodes and edges *cannot* result in a minimal overall edge weight! Our prescribed method can always improve upon any method which would dictate a different choice.

Having justified the minimum spanning tree algorithm on an intuitive basis, let us now give a formal statement of it in Pascal. In particular, the following procedure MINSPAN assumes:

■ The existence of a global adjacency matrix M for the network in question. In practice, M may be an actual two-dimensional array or a function call which returns a value from some sparse matrix representation scheme.

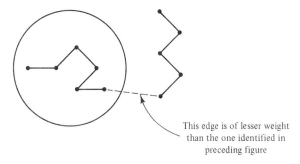

This edge is of lesser weight than the one identified in preceding figure

FIGURE 9-26 *The edge denoted by the arrow is of lesser weight than the one identified in Figure 9-25.*

- A one-dimensional boolean array INCLUDED which is indexed by the nodes in the network
- A procedure FINDMIN(I,J) which returns in I and J the nodes determining an edge of minimal weight connecting a node J, with INCLUDED[J] = FALSE, to a node I, with INCLUDED[I] = TRUE.
- A procedure ADDTOTREE(I,J) which may be called when we wish to add the edge connecting nodes I and J to the minimal spanning tree.
- A boolean-valued function ALL(INCLUDED) which returns TRUE only when all locations in the boolean array INCLUDED are true.

The actual writing of the procedures listed above has been left for the exercises. The main procedure MINSPAN follows.

```
{Global declarations }

CONST N=40;

TYPE NETWORKARRAY = ARRAY[1..N, 1..N] OF INTEGER;
        { Without sparse matrix representation, a maximum
          of 40 nodes may be accommodated. }
        INCLUSIONARRAY = ARRAY [1..N] OF BOOLEAN;

VAR
      M:NETWORKARRAY;

PROCEDURE MINSPAN;
      VAR INCLUDED: INCLUSIONARRAY;
          I,J,K: INTEGER;
      BEGIN
        FOR K:=1 TO N DO INCLUDED[K]:=FALSE;

        INCLUDED[1]:=TRUE;
        REPEAT
            FINDMIN(I,J);
            INCLUDED[J]:=TRUE;
            ADDTOTREE(I,J)
        UNTIL ALL(INCLUDED)
      END; { MINSPAN }
```

The 1st time through the REPEAT loop FINDMIN would return 1 and 3, then 2 and 3, finally 2 and 4

9-5   The Shortest Path Algorithm

If we look at the minimal spanning tree of the graph in Figure 9-22, we find that this tree gives no indication of the shortest path between two nodes. Rather, in the minimum spanning tree, only the overall edge weight is minimized. For instance, the minimum spanning tree pictured in Figure 9-24 does not include the shortest path between nodes 4 and 5, the direct edge of weight 400 which connects these two nodes.

In this section we consider a network such as one shown in Figure 9-27, and give an algorithm which finds the shortest path between any two given nodes of the network. The network of Figure 9-27 could be thought of as showing airline routes between cities. An airline would be interested in finding the most economical route between any two given cities in the network. The numbers listed on the edges would, in this case, represent distances between cities. Thus, the airline wishes to find the shortest path that can be flown from node 5 in order to reach node 2.

To solve this problem, we first set up the adjacency matrix in a fashion analogous to what we did in constructing Figure 9-23. Suppose we want to find the shortest path from node 1 to node 3. From Figure 9-27, we note that this path should be $1 \rightarrow 2 \rightarrow 3$, yielding a total weight of $800 + 410 = 1210$. The algorithm to find such a path was first discovered by E. W. Dijkstra.*

Given a collection of nodes 1, 2,..., N, Dijkstra's algorithm requires three arrays in addition to the network's adjacency matrix M (or a suitable sparse matrix representation of M). These three arrays are identified as:

```
VAR DISTANCE, PATH: ARRAY[1..N] OF INTEGER;
          INCLUDED: ARRAY[1..N] OF BOOLEAN;
```

Identifying one node as the SOURCE, the algorithm proceeds to find the shortest distance from SOURCE to all other nodes in the network. At the conclusion of the algorithm, the shortest distance from SOURCE to node J is stored in DISTANCE[J] while PATH[J] contains the immediate predecessor of node J on the path determining this shortest distance. While the algorithm is in progress, DISTANCE[J] and PATH[J] are being continually updated until INCLUDED[J] is switched from FALSE to TRUE. Once this switch occurs, it is definitely known that DISTANCE[J] contains the *shortest* distance from SOURCE to J. The algorithm progresses until all nodes have been so included. Hence it actually gives us the shortest distance from SOURCE to every other node in the network.

Given the SOURCE node, the algorithm may be divided into two phases—an *initialization* phase followed by an *iteration* phase in which nodes are included one by one in the set of nodes for which the shortest distance from SOURCE is definitely known.

---

*Dijkstra, E. W. 1954. A note on two problems in connections with graphs. *Numeriche Mathematik* 1:269–272.

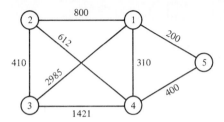

FIGURE 9-27 **Network with edge weights representing distances.**

During the initialization phase, we must:

1. Initialize INCLUDED[SOURCE] to TRUE and INCLUDED[J] to FALSE for all other J.
2. Initialize the DISTANCE array via the rule

$$\text{DISTANCE[J]} = \begin{cases} 0 \text{ if J} = \text{SOURCE} \\ \text{M[SOURCE,J] if M[SOURCE,J]} <> 0 \\ \infty \text{ if J is not connected to SOURCE by a} \\ \quad \text{direct edge (that is, if} \\ \quad \text{M[SOURCE,J]} = 0 \end{cases}$$

3. Initialize the PATH array via the rule:

$$\text{PATH[J]} = \begin{cases} \text{SOURCE if M[SOURCE,J]} <> 0 \\ \text{undefined otherwise} \end{cases}$$

Given this initialization, the iteration phase may be expressed in a generalized pseudocode form as follows:

```
REPEAT
    FIND the node J which has the minimal DISTANCE
            among those nodes not yet INCLUDED.
    MARK J as now INCLUDED
    FOR each R not yet INCLUDED
        IF R is connected by an edge to J THEN
            IF DISTANCE[J]+M[R,J]<DISTANCE[R] THEN

                DISTANCE[R]:=DISTANCE[J]+M[R,J]
                PATH[R]:=J

            ENDIF
        ENDIF
    ENDFOR
UNTIL ALL nodes are INCLUDED
```

The crucial part of the algorithm occurs within the innermost IF of the FOR loop above. Figure 9-28 provides a pictorial representation of the logic involved here. In Figure 9-28, the circled nodes represent those

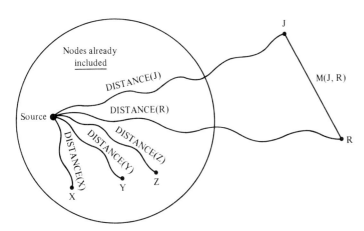

FIGURE 9-28   REPEAT loop logic in shortest path (Dijkstra's) algorithm.

nodes already INCLUDED prior to a given iteration of the REPEAT loop. The node J in Figure 9-28 represents the node found in the first step of the REPEAT loop, while R represents another arbitrary node which has not yet been INCLUDED. The lines emanating from SOURCE in Figure 9-28 represent the paths corresponding to the current entries in the DISTANCE array. For nodes within the circle—that is, those already INCLUDED—these paths are guaranteed to be the shortest-distance paths. If J is the node having the minimal entry in DISTANCE among those not yet INCLUDED, we will add J to the circle of INCLUDED nodes and then check to see if J's connections to other nodes in the network which are not yet INCLUDED may result in a newly found shorter path to such nodes. Referring to Figure 9-28 again, the sum of two sides of a triangle DISTANCE[J] + M[J,R] may in fact be shorter than the third side, DISTANCE[R]. This geometric contradiction is possible because we are not dealing with true straight-sided triangles but rather with "triangles" whose sides may be very complicated paths through a network.

It is also apparent from Figure 9-28 why Dijkstra's algorithm works. As the node J in this figure is found to have the minimal DISTANCE entry from among all those nodes not yet INCLUDED, we may now INCLUDE it among the nodes whose minimal distance from the source is absolutely known. Why? Because the very fashion in which we update the DISTANCE and PATH arrays guarantees that nodes which will be INCLUDED in the future could never alter DISTANCE[J] and PATH[J]. DISTANCE[J] is already minimal among DISTANCE[X] for X which have not yet been INCLUDED!

To be sure you understand Dijkstra's complicated algorithm before you examine a formal version of it, trace it through on the network of Figure 9-27 with SOURCE = 1. Initially, we would have

```
DISTANCE[2]  = 800        PATH[2]  = 1
DISTANCE[3]  = 2985       PATH[3]  = 1
DISTANCE[4]  = 310        PATH[4]  = 1
DISTANCE[5]  = 200        PATH[5]  = 1
```

in accordance with steps 2 and 3 of the initialization phase. According to iteration phase of the algorithm, we would then, in order:

1. INCLUDE node 5; no changes in DISTANCE and PATH needed.

```
DISTANCE[2]  = 800        PATH[2] = 1
DISTANCE[3]  = 2985       PATH[3] = 1
DISTANCE[4]  = 310        PATH[4] = 1
DISTANCE[5]  = 200        PATH[5] = 1
```

2. INCLUDE node 4; update DISTANCE and PATH to:

```
DISTANCE[2]  = 800        PATH[2] = 1
DISTANCE[3]  = 1731       PATH[3] = 4
DISTANCE[4]  = 310        PATH[4] = 1
DISTANCE[5]  = 200        PATH[5] = 1
```

(Note that it is shorter to go from node 1 to node 4 to node 3 than to follow the edge directly connecting node 1 to node 3.)

3. INCLUDE node 2; update DISTANCE and PATH to:

```
DISTANCE[2] = 800         PATH[2] = 1
DISTANCE[3] = 1210        PATH[3] = 2
DISTANCE[4] = 310         PATH[4] = 1
DISTANCE[5] = 200         PATH[5] = 1
```

(Now we find that traveling from node 1 to node 2 to node 3 is even better than the path determined in 2!)

4. Finally node 3 is INCLUDED with (obviously) no changes made in DISTANCE or PATH.

The shortest path from node 1 to node 3 may be obtained in reverse order from the contents of array PATH. It is $1 \rightarrow 2 \rightarrow 3$.

The formal Pascal version is now given for Dijkstra's algorithm in the procedure SHORTPATH. SHORTPATH in turn must call on procedures and functions INITIALIZE, FINDMIN, UPDATE, and ALL. The responsibilities of these procedures are documented; you will write them as exercises at the end of the chapter.

```
{ Global declarations }

CONST
  N = 100; { Assume a network with <=100 nodes }

VAR
  M: ARRAY [1..N, 1..N] OF INTEGER;
  DISTANCE, PATH: ARRAY [1..N] OF INTEGER;

PROCEDURE SHORTPATH(SOURCE: INTEGER);
 { Determine the shortest path from SOURCE to all other nodes }
 { in the network represented by the adjacency matrix M. Shortest }
 { distances stored in the global array DISTANCE. Nodes on the }
 { shortest path stored in the global array PATH. }

  VAR
    INCLUDED: ARRAY [1..N] OF BOOLEAN;
    J, R: INTEGER;

  BEGIN
    INITIALIZE(SOURCE);
    { Initialize global arrays DISTANCE and PATH, and }
    { also initialize the local array INCLUDED }

    REPEAT
      FINDMIN(J);
      { This procedure call should return in J }
      { the node with minimum DISTANCE among those with }
      { INCLUDED entry still FALSE }
      INCLUDED[J] := TRUE;
      FOR R := 1 TO N DO
        IF NOT INCLUDED[R] THEN
          UPDATE(R, J)
          { Potentially alter DISTANCE[R] and PATH[R] }
          { based on the inclusion of J }
    UNTIL ALL(INCLUDED)
  END { SHORTPATH } ;
```

UPDATE(R, J) potentially must "cancel" this old path to R and switch it to the combination of the path from SOURCE to J followed by the direct edge from J to R.

J's DISTANCE to SOURCE is less than any other node not yet INCLUDED. FINDMIN must find J among nodes outside circle.

Efficiency Considerations for the Shortest Path Algorithm

A further modification of Dijkstra's algorithm is due to R. W. Floyd[*] and takes slightly longer computing time than Dijkstra's. Floyd's algorithm computes the minimum value path matrix between any two nodes. Dijkstra's algorithm has a run time proportional to N^2 where N is the number of nodes in the network. Floyd's algorithm first initializes a matrix P so that $P[I,J]$ is equal to $M[I,J]$ if $M[I,J] <> 0$, or to 0 if $I = J$ (that is, diagonal entry), and to ∞ otherwise. If the network contains N nodes, then N passes are made in such a way that after the Lth pass,

```
P[I,J] = MINIMUM (P[I,J], P[I,L] + P[L,J])
```

This in turn achieves the shortest path value from node I to J not passing through a node whose subscript is greater than J.

The procedure MINPATHFLOYD implements this algorithm. As an exercise you will trace this procedure for the network of figure 9-27 and compute the minimum path between node I and node J.

```
{ Global declarations }

CONST
  N = 100;

TYPE
  MATRIX = ARRAY [1..N, 1..N] OF INTEGER;

PROCEDURE MINPATHFLOYD(VAR P, PATH, M: MATRIX);

  VAR
    L, I, J: INTEGER;
    { The resultant matrix PATH contains the numerical values }
    { indicating the value of the shortest path between nodes }
    { I and J as seen in PATH[I,J] }
```

---

*Floyd, R. W. 1962. Algorithm 97: Shortest path. *Communications of the Association for Computing Machinery* 5:345.

```
BEGIN
  FOR I := 1 TO N DO
    FOR J := 1 TO N DO
      BEGIN
      P[I, J] := M[I, J];
      PATH[I, J] := 0
      END
  FOR I := 1 TO N DO
    P[I, I] := 0;
  FOR L := 1 TO N DO
    BEGIN
    FOR I := 1 TO N DO
      BEGIN
      FOR J := 1 TO N DO
        BEGIN
        IF P[I, L] + P[L, J] < P[I, J] THEN
          BEGIN
          P[I, J] := P[I, L] + P[L, J];
          PATH[I, J] := L
          END
        END
      END
    END
END { MINPATHFLOYD } ;
```

MIN-PATH-FLOYD

P obtained from the adjacency matrix
of the network by zeroing the main
diagonal entries and replacing other
zeroes by ∞.

If, for example, for the iteration
L = 2, I = 1 and J = 3, we have
P(I, L) + P(L, J) < P(I, J)
(i.e., ⊛$_1$ + ⊛$_2$ < ⊛$_3$), then ⊛$_3$ is
replaced by ⊛$_1$ + ⊛$_2$.

The matrix PATH can now be used to retrieve the shortest path as
well, which you will do as an exercise. The run-time efficiency of
Floyd's algorithm has been estimated to be $O(N^3)$ where N is the number of nodes in the network[†].

[†]Knuth, D. E. 1973. *The Art of Computer Programming.* Vol. 1: *Fundamental
Algorithms.* Menlo Park, Ca: Addison-Wesley.

9-6 Topological Ordering

The graph of Figure 9-18 as represented by its adjacency matrix in Figure 9-19 essentially states that A precedes B, B precedes D, and D precedes C. Forcing a **topological order** on the adjacency matrix in Figure 9-19 means putting it into the form of Figure 9-29. Once topologically ordered, the adjacency matrix is guaranteed to generate a depth-first search corresponding to the scheduling of modules in a project as discussed in 9-3.

An elegant human algorithm (its counterpart computer algorithm is not efficient since it takes time proportional to N^3 where N is the number of nodes) is as follows:

1. Initialize a variable L to 1.
2. Find the leftmost matrix column containing all zeros. This amounts to finding a node with no predecessors. If none exists you are done; either each node has been assigned a precedence number, or the graph contains a cycle and hence cannot be topologically ordered.
3. If found, assign it the numerical ordering L. This is the Lth node, with precedence number L.
4. Increment L by 1.
5. Delete the found column and its corresponding row; that is, if the rth column contains all zeros, simply delete the rth row and rth column.
6. Repeat steps (2)–(5) until all the nodes have been assigned their precedence numbers.

This algorithm is carried out pictorially in Figures 9-30 through 9-32. Rewriting the matrix again according to precedence numbers of rows, we get the matrix as shown in Figure 9-29. Notice that all the entries below the main diagonal of this matrix are zeros. Such a matrix is also known as an **upper triangular** matrix.

The procedure TOPOLOGICALORDER given next makes use of two procedures—DELETE and BUILD—which are left as exercises. The procedure DELETE simply deletes the row and column corresponding to an assigned node and returns a reduced matrix of order less than the one passed to it. The procedure TOPOLOGICALORDER assumes that the graph has at least 2 nodes. The procedure BUILD

	A	B	D	C
A	0	1	0	1
B	0	0	1	1
D	0	0	0	1
C	0	0	0	0

FIGURE 9-29 Topologically ordered adjacency matrix.

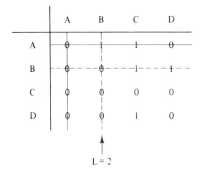

FIGURE 9-30   The precedence number of node A is 1. Thus row A should be the first row.

	A	B	C	D
A	0	1	1	0
B	0	0	1	1
C	0	0	0	0
D	0	0	1	0

L = 2

FIGURE 9-31   The precedence number of node B is 2. Thus row B should be the second row.

then builds the new matrix K which is in upper triangular form. The procedure TOPOLOGICALORDER assumes that the nodes in the corresponding digraph are designated numerically as $1, 2, \ldots, N$.

```
{ Global declarations }

CONST
  N = 100; {There are N nodes in the graph }

TYPE
  MATRIX = ARRAY [1..N, 1..N] OF INTEGER;

PROCEDURE TOPOLOGICALORDER(VAR M, K: MATRIX);
    { M is the adjacency matrix of an acyclic graph. K is an exact }
    { copy of M to begin with.}

  VAR
    S, P, I, J, L: INTEGER;
    TRACK: ARRAY [1..N] OF INTEGER;
    FLAG: BOOLEAN;
```

```
BEGIN
  FOR P := 1 TO N DO
    TRACK[P] := 0;
  L := 0;
  S := N;
  REPEAT { Keeps track of nodes }
    L := L + 1;
    { S is the size of current matrix }
    FOR J := 1 TO S DO { J controls columns }
      BEGIN
      FLAG := TRUE;
      I := 1; { I controls rows }
      WHILE (M[I, J] = 0 AND FLAG) DO
        BEGIN
        I := I + 1;
        IF I > S THEN
          BEGIN
          FLAG := FALSE;
          I := N
          END { IF}
        END { WHILE}
      END { FOR } ;
    { FALSE FLAG at the end of the WHILE }
    { loop indicates a column of all zeros has been found }
    IF NOT FLAG THEN
      BEGIN
      DELETE(M, J, S);
      TRACK[J] := L
      END { The procedure DELETE reduces rank of the matrix M by 1 }
      { by deleting the row and column of zeroed column. }
      { The current size of the matrix is S X S }
  UNTIL L = N;

  FLAG := TRUE;
  FOR I := 1 TO N DO
    BEGIN
    IF TRACK[I] = 0 THEN
      FLAG := FALSE {indicating that graph is cyclic}
    END;
  IF FLAG THEN
    BUILD(K, TRACK, N)
    { The procedure BUILD builds the new matrix }
    { K which is upper triangular }
END {TOPOLOGICALORDER } ;
```

INDICATES END OF COLUMN

AVOIDS SUBSCRIPT OUT OF RANGE IN WHILE

TRACK(1) = 1
TRACK(2) = 2
TRACK(3) = 4
TRACK(4) = 3

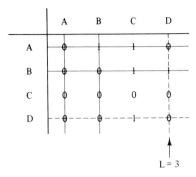

FIGURE 9-32 *The precedence number of node D is 3. Thus row D should be the third row.*

As noted earlier this procedure is not efficient and can be modified. One possible area for modification is the WHILE loop which simply looks for a column with all zeros. This has been left as an exercise.

Program Design Considerations

The following program MINSPAND implements the minimum spanning tree discussed in the text. The main program calls only the procedure MINSPAN; but the procedure MINSPAN depends upon the procedures ADDTOTREE, FINDMIN, and the function ALL. The functions of all these procedures have been explained in the corresponding comment entries. The modular design and the program follow:

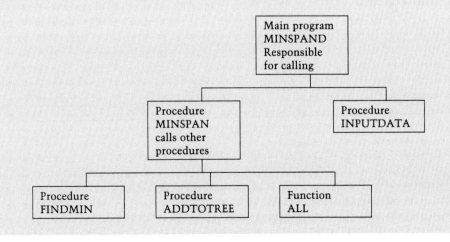

```
PROGRAM MINSPAND(INPUT, OUTPUT);

  CONST NODES = 40;

  TYPE

    NETWORKARRAY = ARRAY [1..NODES, 1..NODES] OF INTEGER;
      { Without the sparse matrix representation, a maximum
        of 40 nodes may be accommodated. }
    INCLUSIONARRAY = ARRAY [1..NODES] OF BOOLEAN;

  VAR
    N: INTEGER;
    M: NETWORKARRAY;

  PROCEDURE FINDMIN(VAR I, J: INTEGER);
    EXTERNAL;
              { FINDMIN is an external array to find the minimum
                entry in the Ith row }

  PROCEDURE ADDTOTREE(I, J: INTEGER);
    EXTERNAL;
              { ADDTOTREE is an external procedure to add a node
                to the tree }

  FUNCTION ALL(INCLUDED: INCLUSIONARRAY): BOOLEAN;
    EXTERNAL;
              { The external function ALL determines when all
                the nodes from the network have been added
                to the tree. }

  PROCEDURE INPUTDATA;
    EXTERNAL;

  PROCEDURE MINSPAN; { This is the main procedure to find the minimum
                spanning tree }

    VAR
      INCLUDED: INCLUSIONARRAY;
      I, J, K: INTEGER;
```

SUMMARY

Graphs and networks represent general relationships between data base objects called nodes. Traversal of graphs solves many important data processing problems. There are basically two types of

```
    BEGIN
      FOR K := 1 TO N DO
        INCLUDED[K] := FALSE;
      INCLUDED[1] := TRUE;
      REPEAT
        FINDMIN(I, J);
        INCLUDED[I] := TRUE;
        INCLUDED[J] := TRUE;
        ADDTOTREE(I, J)
      UNTIL ALL(INCLUDED)
    END { OF MINSPAN } ;

  BEGIN {MAIN}
    INPUTDATA;
    MINSPAN
  END.
```

traversals—depth-first search and breadth-first search. Modern data base implementations decompose graphs into their spanning forests. A depth-first search can be used to schedule the modules of a large project efficiently.

Networks are essentially graphs with weighted edges. These are used in design analysis to minimize cost. Minimum spanning trees and shortest-path algorithms are extensively used in fields such as electrical circuit analysis, communication networks, and transportation systems.

KEY TERMS

Graph
Edge
Digraph
Arc
Path
Strongly connected
Weakly connected
Indegree
Outdegree
Source node
Sink node
Cycle
Adjacency matrix
Incidence matrix

Symmetric matrix
Depth-first search
Tree arc
Cross arc
Back arc
Acyclic graph
Spanning forest
Topological order
Breadth-first search
Network
Weight
Minimum spanning tree
Shortest path

EXERCISES

1. What kind of graph represents a hierarchical relationship?
2. What is the outdegree of a sink node?
3. What is the indegree of a source node?
4. Draw a graph that has cycles in it.
5. Can an undirected graph be acyclic?
6. What is an adjacency matrix of a graph?
7. When you multiply two square matrices A and B of the same order, is $A \times B = B \times A$?
8. What is a spanning tree?
9. Define the term *spanning forest* as it is associated with a digraph.
10. Does the minimum spanning tree of a network give any indication of the shortest path between nodes?
11. What are the indegree and outdegree of each node in the following figure?

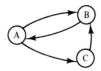

12. Write the adjacency matrix of the following graph.

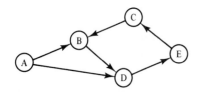

13. Write a program which stores the adjacency matrix of the digraph in exercise (11) and finds the sum of each row. What is the significance of such sums?
14. Consider the digraph

    Use its adjacency matrix to find how many paths of length 3 exist from A to B.

15. Incorporate FINDPATH in a complete program. Test your program on an arbitrary graph containing at least 5 nodes.
16. Implement procedure POWER (M,N,KPOWER,K) which computes all multiples of a square matrix M for values of K from 1 to N.
17. Write the procedure FINDMIN which is called by procedure MINSPAN as discussed in this chapter.
18. Write the procedure ADDTOTREE which is called by procedure MINSPAN as discussed in this chapter.
19. Trace Floyd's algorithm as applied to the network of Figure 9-27 and obtain the matrix PATH.
20. Write a procedure that retrieves the shortest path between any two nodes of a network from the associated matrix PATH of procedure MINPATHFLOYD.
21. Modify SEARCHFROM so it can be used in the breadth-first search for the graph given below.

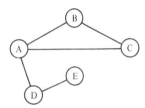

22. Compute A × B and B × A where B and A are the square matrices used in section 9-2 of this chapter.
23. If you have mathematical experience in proofs by induction, attempt to prove the validity of:

    1. The minimal spanning tree algorithm
    2. The shortest path algorithm.

24. Remember that the adjacency matrix for a substantial graph or network will usually have to be implemented by the generalized dope vector or linked list representation of a sparse matrix. For each of the algorithms presented in this chapter, discuss how the choice of a sparse matrix representation would affect run-time efficiency of the algorithm.
25. Write the procedures/functions INITIALIZE, FINDMIN, UPDATE, and ALL that are called by the procedure SHORTESTPATH, which implements Dijkstra's algorithm.

PROGRAMMING PROBLEMS

1. The network on the next page indicates air routes supported by Wing-and-a-Prayer Airlines. Design a program that will:

    1. Compute the shortest path between any two nodes.
    2. Compute the shortest paths from one given node to all other nodes.

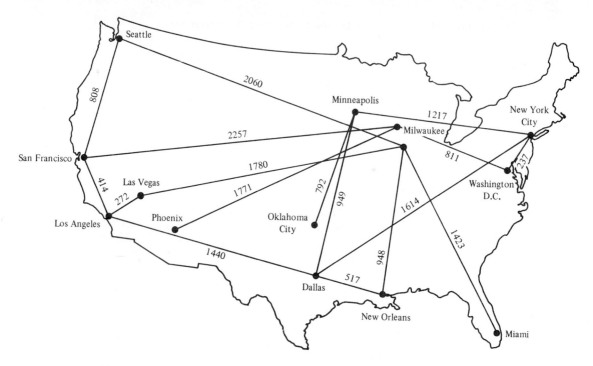

2. The Fly-By-Night company would like to have an approximate
   cost estimate for sending a group of representatives to those cities
   where their clients are. For this the company needs to know the
   minimum cost of travelling to these cities in the most efficient
   manner. Write a program in a high-level language which prints and
   stores the adjacency matrix of a network having all the cities and
   the mileage between them. Then print and store the minimum
   spanning tree of this network, from which the conclusions about
   the minimum cost of travelling should be drawn.
3. The Bay Area Brawlers professional football team is considering
   building a new stadium. The entire process of building the stadium has been broken down into a series of subtasks as specified
   in the diagram below:

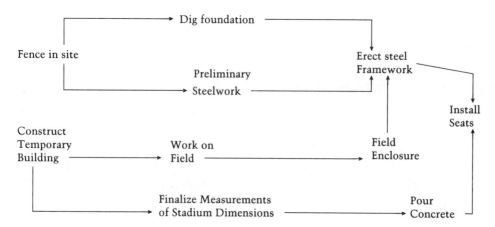

One subtask preceding another in this graph means that the first
subtask must be completed before the second can be started. Write
a program which will topologically order the subtasks in the preceding graph. Note that this ordering represents a possible ordering in which the subtasks could be performed by the workers.

4. Consider the network

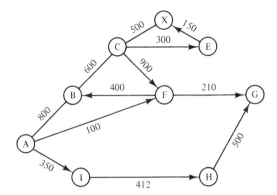

Run a complete program that gives the minimum spanning tree of
this network.

5. Write a program that traverses the network from Problem (4)
using a breadth-first search. Then do the same for a depth-first
search. A graph (or network) is said to be **connected** provided any
two nodes are connected by some path. How might your depth-
first or breadth-first procedure be used to test whether or not a
network is connected?

10
Sorting

*"The people whose seats are farthest from the aisle
invariably arrive last."*

AXIOM OF ORDERING

10-1   Introductory Considerations

There is practically no data processing activity which would not require the data to be in some order. **Ordering** or **sorting** data in an "increasing" or "decreasing" fashion according to some linear relationship between data items is of such a fundamental importance that the subject mandates a careful analysis. Sorting algorithms are designed with the following objectives:

1. Minimize exchanges or wholesale movement of data. When data items are large and the number of data items is excessive, swapping of data items would take an inordinate amount of processing time.
2. Move data from secondary storage to main memory in large blocks, since the larger the data block to be moved, the more efficient is the corresponding algorithm. This is a key part of **external sorting.**
3. If possible, retain all the data in main memory. In this case, random access into an array can be effectively used. This is a key part of **internal sorting.**

Some Thoughts of "Sorts"

There are basically three main considerations which should affect a programmer's decision to choose from a variety of sorting methods:

1. Programming time
2. Execution time of the program
3. Memory or auxilliary space needed for the program environment.

The programmer should first evaluate carefully the need for sorting data. It is pointless to write a complex program to sort a short file. If the number of records in the file is no more than 100, and each record no longer than 80 bytes, any sorting procedure probably would be adequate. However, when both the file size and the record size are large, it is necessary to minimize processing time by choosing an efficient sorting routine. Quite often, advance knowledge about the structure of the file and the data in it can help you to make a proper choice. However, if no such advance knowledge about the data is available, then you need to assume the worst-case scenario for the job. Unfortunately, there is no such thing as the "best" sorting method fitting all applications.

The efficiency of a sorting method is measured by the amount of time taken in actual execution of the algorithm. When the file is large, choice of a proper sorting method resulting in the least possible run time is crucial. One sorting method may use different run times on different machines, and consequently you must consider machine environment in making this choice. The various sort algorithms considered in this chapter have been compared for their relative efficiencies as n, the number of items to be sorted, becomes larger; efficiency is usually proportional to some function of n. This function is denoted by $f(n)$; we use the notation $O(f(n))$ to mean *proportional to $f(n)$*. As we shall see later in this chapter, the efficiency of a sort routine generally falls between $O(n \log_2 n)$ and $O(n^2)$, the latter being the worst case.

Sometimes, in an effort to improve the efficiency of a sort, more complex code introduces more variables, and hence the space needs of the program increase. The overhead placed on the software to fetch and execute instructions in a large program may create a "Catch-22" situation. However, if the machine environment allows for ample memory capacity and increasing program complexity increases the program's run-time efficiency considerably, then it is worth the tradeoff.

Be careful to maintain a proper balance between program efficiency and readability. Making a subroutine call from inside of a FOR, WHILE, or REPEAT loop, although structured and readable, places an unusual demand on the software and slows the execution. If the subroutine involved is not very long, substitution of its code within these loops may be a better program strategy—especially if the run-time needs to be shortened.

10-2 Some Common Internal Sorts

The Bubble Sort and its Efficiency

The **bubble sort** derives its name from the fact that the smallest data item "bubbles up" to the top of the array. It was discussed briefly in Chapter 1. The algorithm begins by comparing the top item of the array with the next, and swapping them if necessary. After $n-1$ comparisons, the largest among a total of n items descends to the bottom of the array, to the nth location. The process is reapplied to the $n-1$ items in the array. For n data items, the method requires $n(n-1)/2$ comparisons, and on the average, almost one-half as many swaps. (A formal derivation of the efficiency of the bubble sort may be found in Appendix B.) The bubble sort, therefore, is very inefficient in large sorting jobs. A modified version of the bubble sort has been given in Chapter 1 as the POINTERSORT procedure. Recall that this modified version used the bubble sort algorithm to rearrange an array of pointers without actually moving any data. The idea of the POINTERSORT could be incorporated into any of the sorting algorithms we are about to describe.

The Insertion Sort

The main idea behind the insertion sort is to insert in the ith pass the ith element in A[1], A[2], ..., A[i] in its rightful place. The following steps essentially define the insertion sort as applied to sorting into ascending order an array ALPHA containing N elements.

1. Set J = 2, where J is an integer.
2. Check if ALPHA [J] < ALPHA [J − 1]. If so, interchange them; set J = J − 1 and repeat step (2) until J = 1;
3. Set J = 3, 4, 5, ..., N and keep on executing step (2).

The following Pascal code describes the insertion sort for sorting the array ALPHA in ascending order:

```
{Global declarations }

CONST
  N1 = 15;
  M1 = 100;

TYPE
  STRINGSTUFF = ARRAY [1..N1] OF CHAR;
  ALPHASTUFF = ARRAY [1..M1] OF STRINGSTUFF;
```

```
PROCEDURE INSERTION(VAR ALPHA: ALPHASTUFF;
                        N: INTEGER);
{ N is the current size of the array ALPHA }

  VAR
    I, J: INTEGER;
    S: STRINGSTUFF;
    FLAG: BOOLEAN;

  BEGIN
    IF (N >= 2) THEN
      BEGIN
      { This is the nontrivial case }
      FOR I := 2 TO N DO
        BEGIN
        FLAG := TRUE;
        J := I;
        WHILE (J >= 2) AND FLAG DO
          IF ALPHA[J] < ALPHA[J - 1] THEN
            BEGIN
            S := ALPHA[J];
            ALPHA[J] := ALPHA[J - 1];
            ALPHA[J - 1] := S;
            J := J-1
            END
          ELSE
            FLAG := FALSE
        END { FOR }
      END { INITIAL IF }
  END {PROCEDURE INSERTION } ;
```

Insertion sort

Figure 10-1 indicates the sorting achieved by the algorithm for each value of I. In each row the data items are in sorted order relative

ALPHA		I = 2		I = 3		I = 4		I = 5		I = 6
PAM	.	PAM	.	DAVE	.	ARON	.	ARON	.	ARON
SINGH	:	SINGH*	:	PAM	:	DAVE	:	DAVE	:	BEV
DAVE	:	DAVE	:	SINGH*	:	PAM	:	PAM	:	DAVE
ARON	:	ARON	:	ARON	:	SINGH*	:	SINGH	:	PAM
TOM	:	TOM	:	TOM	:	TOM	:	TOM*	:	SINGH
BEV	:	BEV	:	BEV	:	BEV	:	BEV	:	TOM*

FIGURE 10-1   Insertion sort algorithm applied to ALPHA.

to each other above the item with the asterisk; below this item the data are not affected.

The Efficiency of the Insertion Sort.   Although the insertion sort is almost always better than the bubble sort, the time element in both methods is approximately the same—that is, $O(n^2)$, where n is the number of data elements in the array. The number of interchanges needed in both the methods is on the average $(n^2)/4$, and in worst cases about $(n^2)/2$. Where the data are partially ordered, the insertion sort will normally take less time than the bubble sort. The insertion sort is highly efficient if the array is already in almost sorted order.

The Selection Sort

The main idea behind the **selection sort** is to find the smallest entry among ALPHA [J], ALPHA [J+1], . . . , ALPHA [N], and then interchange it with ALPHA[J]. This proces is then repeated for each value of J. The following Pascal code gives this algorithm:

```
{Global declarations }

CONST
  N1 = 100;

TYPE
  SUB = 1..N1;
  ARRAYOFINTEGER = ARRAY [SUB] OF INTEGER;

PROCEDURE SELECTION(VAR ALPHA: ARRAYOFINTEGER;
                    N: INTEGER);
  { N is the current size of the array ALPHA }

  VAR
    I, J, S, K: INTEGER;
```

```
BEGIN
  FOR J := 1 TO N - 1 DO
  { This loop generates the block ALPHA[J],...,ALPHA[N] }
    BEGIN
    K := J;
    { K carries the smallest element in the decreasing block }
    S := ALPHA[J];
    FOR I := J + 1 TO N DO
      { This loop places the smallest in ALPHA[K] }
      BEGIN
      IF ALPHA[I] < S THEN
        BEGIN
        S := ALPHA[I];
        K := I
        END
      END {FOR} ;
    S := ALPHA[J];
    ALPHA[J] := ALPHA[K];
    ALPHA[K] := S
    END
END {END SELECTION } ;
```

Selection sort

In the ith pass select
lowest in
A(i), A(i+1), ..., A(n)
and swap it with
A(i)

| | | | A(i) | A(i+1) | ... | ... | | A(n) |

The Efficiency of the Selection Sort. A look at the last line of the outer loop of the procedure indicates that the selection sort always will be more efficient than the bubble sort or the insertion sort, because there are no more than $N - 1$ actual interchanges. Thus, if excessive swapping is a problem, the selection sort should be chosen over the insertion sort or the bubble sort. Figure 10-2 outlines each iteration of the FOR loop of the procedure SELECTION as applied to the array ALPHA. Notice how the selection sort causes an item to leap over a whole section of the array to reach its proper place. Also notice that each column in Figure 10-2 is in the required sorted order beginning with the first and above the last item with an asterisk; that is, for each J the portion of the array ALPHA[1], ALPHA[2], ALPHA[3],..., ALPHA[J] is in the appropriate sorted order. In spite of the superiority

ALPHA	J = 1	J = 2	J = 3	J = 4	J = 5
PAM	ARON*	ARON*	ARON*	ARON*	ARON*
SINGH	SINGH	BEV*	BEV*	BEV*	BEV*
DAVE	DAVE	DAVE*	DAVE*	DAVE	DAVE
ARON	PAM	PAM	PAM*	PAM*	PAM*
TOM	TOM	TOM	TOM	TOM	SINGH*
BEV	BEV	SINGH	SINGH	SINGH	TOM*

FIGURE 10-2   The FOR loop of SELECTION applied to ALPHA.

of the selection sort over the bubble sort and the insertion sort, there is no *significant* gain in run-time; its efficiency is also $O(n^2)$ for n data items.

Do not be misled by the $O(n^2)$ efficiency of each of the preceding three sorts: the constants of proportionality in the three methods are different. Nonetheless, an $O(n^2)$ efficiency is severely limiting when n is reasonably large. It would be nice to reduce $O(n^2)$ and design algorithms whose run time is of the order of $O(n^r)$ for $r < 2$.

The Shell Sort

We commented that the insertion sort was most efficient for data already sorted. This is the basis of the **shell sort**. Instead of sorting the entire array at once, it first divides the array into smaller segments which are then separately sorted using the insertion sort. The array ALPHA originally appears as:

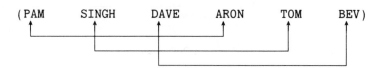

We first divide this into three segments of two elements each.

```
PAM      ARON ---->     Segment 1
SINGH    TOM ----->     Segment 2
DAVE     BEV ----->     Segment 3
```

and sort each of the segments:

```
ARON     PAM
SINGH    TOM
BEV      DAVE
```

The original array, partially sorted, now appears as:

```
( ARON      SINGH      BEV      PAM      TOM      DAVE)
```

We divide this partially sorted array as:

```
ARON     BEV     TOM  -----> Segment 1
SINGH    PAM     DAVE------> Segment 2
```

The segments are sorted and the array ALPHA takes the form

```
( ARON      DAVE      BEV      PAM      TOM      SINGH)
```

Finally this array is sorted as one segment; DAVE and BEV, and TOM and SINGH get swapped to give us the sorted array:

```
( ARON      BEV      DAVE      PAM      SINGH      TOM)
```

The key to the shell sort algorithm is that the whole array is first fragmented into K segments for some number K, where K is preferably a prime number.* If the size of the array ALPHA is N, then the segments are

```
ALPHA [1], ALPHA [K+1], ALPHA [2*K+1], ..., ALPHA [N/K+1]
ALPHA [2], ALPHA [K+2], ALPHA [2*K+2], ..., ALPHA [N/K+2]
 .
 .
 .
ALPHA [K], ALPHA [2*K], ALPHA [3*K], ...... ALPHA [N/K+K]
```

Because each segment is sorted, the whole array is partially sorted after the first pass. For the next pass, the value of K is reduced, which increases the size of each segment—hence reducing the number of segments. The next value of K is also chosen so that it is relatively prime to its previous value. The process is repeated until $K = 1$, at which point the array is sorted. The insertion sort is applied to each segment, so each successive segment is partially sorted. Consequently, the later applications of the insertion sort became very efficient, dramatically increasing the overall efficiency of the shell sort.

*Knuth, D. E. 1973. *The Art of Computer Programming*, Vol. 3, Menlo Park, CA: Addison-Wesley.

The Efficiency of the Shell Sort.   The shell sort is also called the **diminishing increment sort** because the value of K (the number of segments) continually decreases. The method is more efficient if the successive values of K are kept relatively prime to each other. (Incidentally, two integers are said to be **relatively prime** to each other if they have no common factor greater than 1.) D. E. Knuth has mathematically estimated that, with relatively prime values of K, the shell sort will execute in an average time proportional to $O(n(\log_2 n)^2)$.* However, the sort will work for any values of K as long as the last value of K is 1. When the values of K are not relatively prime, then the efficiency of the shell sort is of the order $O(n^r)$, where $1 < r < 2$. The particular value of r makes the sort less efficient than $O(n(\log_2 n)^2)$ for large values of n.

The shell sort is most efficient on arrays that are already nearly sorted. In fact, the first chosen value of K is large to ensure that the whole array is fragmented into small individual arrays, for which the insertion sort is highly effective. Each subsequent sort causes the entire array to be more nearly sorted, so that the efficiency of the insertion sort as applied to larger partially sorted arrays is increased. Trace through a few examples to convince yourself that the partially ordered status of the array for one value of K is not affected by subsequent partial sorts for a different value of K.

It is not clearly known with what value of K the shell sort should start, but Knuth suggests a sequence of values as 1, 3, 7, 15, . . . for reverse values of K; that is, the (J + 1)th value is two times the Jth value plus 1. There are other possible values of K suggested by Knuth, but generally the initial guess at the first value of K is all that you need. The initial guess will depend on the size of the array, and, to some extent, on the type of data being sorted.

The Pascal procedure SHELLSORT given next sorts an array ALPHA of size N.

```
{Global declarations}

CONST N1 =100;

TYPE
 SORTARRAY=ARRAY [1..N1] OF INTEGER;
 VAR ALPHA: SORTARRAY;

PROCEDURE SHELLSORT (VAR A:SORTARRAY; N: INTEGER);
{ N is the current size of the array A }

VAR
  I, J, K, S: INTEGER;
```

*Knuth, D. E., Op. Cit.

```
BEGIN
  I := N DIV 2;
  WHILE I > 0 DO
    BEGIN
    J := I;
    REPEAT ────────────────────────────►
      J := J + 1;
      K := J - I;
      WHILE K > 0 DO
        BEGIN
        IF ALPHA[K] > ALPHA[K + I] THEN
          BEGIN
          S := ALPHA[K];
          ALPHA[K] := ALPHA[K + I];
          ALPHA[K + I] := S;
          K := K - I
          END
        ELSE
          K := 0
        END
    UNTIL J = N;
    I := I DIV 2
    END
END { SHELLSORT } ;
```

(PAM SINGH DAVE ARON TOM BEV)

We first divide this into 3 segments of 2 elements each.

PAM   ARON — Segment 1
SINGH TOM —— Segment 2
DAVE   BEV —— Segment 3

and sort each of the segments:

ARON   PAM
SINGH TOM
BEV   DAVE

The Quick Sort

Even though the shell sort provides a significant advantage in run time over its $O(n^2)$ predecessors, its average efficiency of $O(n(\log_2 n)^2)$ may still not be good enough for large arrays. The next group of methods, including the quick sort, have an average execution time of $O(n(\log_2 n))$, which is seemingly the best that can be achieved.* Compared to $O(n(\log_2 n)^2)$ or $O(n^r)$ for $1 < r < 2$, an $O(n(\log_2 n))$ sort is often a good choice as the main vehicle for large sorting jobs.

The purpose of the quick sort is to move a data item in the correct direction just enough for it to reach its final place in the array. The method, therefore, reduces unnecessary swaps, and moves an item a great distance in one move. A pivotal item is chosen and then moves are made so that data items on one side of the pivot are smaller than the pivot, whereas those on the other side are larger. The pivot item is now in its correct position. The procedure is then applied recursively to the two parts of the array on either side of the pivot until the whole array is sorted. We shall illustrate the mechanics of this method by applying it to an array of numbers. Suppose the array A initially appears as:

(15   20   5   8   95   12   80   17   9   55)

*Knuth. Op. Cit.

Figure 10-3 shows a quick sort applied to this array. The following steps are involved:

1. Remove the 1st data item 15, mark its position and scan the array from right to left, comparing data item values with 15. When you find the 1st smaller value, remove it from its current position and put in position A[1]. This is shown in line 2 of Figure 10-3.

2. Scan line 2 from left to right beginning with position A[2], comparing data item values with 15. When you find the first value greater than 15 extract it and store in the position marked by parentheses in line 2. This is shown in line 3 in Figure 10-3.

3. Begin the right to left scan of line 3 with position A[8] looking for a value smaller than 15. When you find it, extract it and store it in the position marked by the parentheses in line 3 of Figure 10-3.

4. Begin scanning line 4 from left to right at position A[3], find a value greater than 15, remove it, mark its position, and store it inside the parentheses in line 4. This is shown in line 5 of Figure 10-3.

5. Now, when you scan line 5 from right to left beginning at position A[7], you find no value smaller than 15 before you come to a parenthesized position, position A[5].This is the location to put the first data item, 15, as shown in line 6 of Figure 10-3. At this stage 15 is in its correct place relative to the final sorted array.

Notice that all values to the left of 15 are less than 15, and all values to the right of 15 are greater than 15. The method will still work if two values are the same. The process can now be applied recursively to the two segments of the array on the left and right of 15.

The Pascal procedure QUICKSORT given here uses a stack to avoid the overhead associated with recursion. The recursive version of this procedure follows afterwards.

A(1)	A(2)	A(3)	A(4)	A(5)	A(6)	A(7)	A(8)	A(9)	A(10)
15*	20	5	8	95	12	80	17	9	55
9	20	5	8	95	12	80	17	( )	55
9	( )	5	8	95	12	80	17	20	55
9	12	5	8	95	( )	80	17	20	55
9	12	5	8	( )	95	80	17	20	55
9	12	5	8	15	95	80	17	20	55

FIGURE 10-3   Quick sort of an array.

```
{ Global declarations }

CONST
  N = 100;

TYPE
  ARR = ARRAY [1..N] OF INTEGER;

VAR
  STACK: ARR;
  { STACK is a general purpose stack manipulated by
    the procedures POP and PUSH discussed in Chapter 4 }

PROCEDURE QUICKSORT(VAR A: ARR;
                        M: INTEGER);
 { M is the current logical size of the array A }

 VAR L, R, I, J, K, REF : INTEGER;

  BEGIN
    PUSH(STACK, 0, 0); { Initial contents of STACK }
    L := 1;
    R := M;
    REPEAT
      I := L;
      J := R;
      REF := A[L];
      WHILE I < J DO
        BEGIN {Begin right to left scan }
        WHILE (REF < A[J]) AND (I < J) DO
          J := J - 1;
        IF J <> I THEN
          BEGIN
          A[I] := A[J];
          I := I + 1
          END;
```

Quick sort

REF = 12

Right-to-left scan until
smaller value found here

| 12 | 8 | 7 | 6 | 14 | 20 | 30 | 5 | 19 | 13 | 15 | J = 8 |
| 1 | 2 | 3 | 4 | 5 | 6 | 7 | 8 | 9 | 10 | 11 | |

```
        { Begin left to right scan }
        WHILE (REF > A[I]) AND (I < J) DO
          I := I + 1;
        IF J <> I THEN
          BEGIN
          A[J] := A[I];
          J := J - 1
          END
        END {WHILE I<J} ;
    { I and J met somewhere between L and R }
    A[J] := REF;
    { Have I and J met at the right boundary,i.e., R?}
    IF J = R THEN
      R := R - 1
    { Have I and J met at the L boundary?}
    ELSE IF I = L THEN
      L := L + 1
    {I and J have not met at the left or right boundary.}
    { Which segment is bigger? }
            { Handling a smaller segment first will minimize
              the size of the stack needed in the
              program. }
    ELSE IF (I - L) < (R - J) THEN
      BEGIN
      K := J + 1;
      PUSH(STACK, K, R);
      R := I - 1
      END
    ELSE
      BEGIN
      K := I - 1;
      PUSH(STACK, L, K);
      L := J + 1
      END;
    IF R <= L THEN
      POP(STACK, L, R)
  UNTIL (R = 0) AND (L = 0)
  {i.e., until stack empty}
END {QUICKSORT} ;
```

REF = 12   Left-to-right scan until larger value found here

| 12 | 8 | 7 | 6 | 14 | 20 | 30 | 5 | 19 | 13 | 15 | I = 5
| 1 | 2 | 3 | 4 | 5 | 6 | 7 | 8 | 9 | 10 | 11 |

Right-to-left scan for smaller value

| 5 | 8 | 7 | 6 | 14 | 20 | 30 | 5 | 19 | 13 | 14 | A[I] = A[J]
| 1 | 2 | 3 | 4 | 5 | 6 | 7 | 8 | 9 | 10 | 11 |

Meeting crossover point between I and J

| 5 | 8 | 7 | 6 | 12 | 20 | 30 | 14 | 19 | 13 | 15 | J = I = 5
A[I] = REF
| 1 | 2 | 3 | 4 | 5 | 6 | 7 | 8 | 9 | 10 | 11 |

Algorithm repeated for this segment   This segment pushed onto stack

The Efficiency of the Quick Sort. As mentioned earlier, the *average* run-time efficiency of the quick sort is $O(n(\log_2 n))$, which is the best that has been achieved for a large array of size n. In the worst case situation, when the array is already sorted, the efficiency of the quick sort may drop down to $O(n^2)$ due to the continuous right to left scan all the way to the last left boundary.*

You may wonder how large a stack is needed to sort an array of size n. (Remember that this stack is implicitly created even when you use a language that permits recursion.) Knuth has mathematically estimated that the size of the stack cannot exceed $(1 + \log_2((1/3)(n+1))$.†

Quick Sort (Recursive Version)

The recursive version of the quick sort given next uses the recursion structure available in Pascal. Notice that the code is not only shorter but also structurally more elegant.

```
{ Global declarations }

CONST
  N = 100;

TYPE
  ARR = ARRAY [1..N] OF INTEGER;

PROCEDURE QUICKSORTRECURSIVE(VAR A: ARR;
                            L, R: INTEGER);
 { N is the physical size of the array A }
 { L marks the left boundary of the current array A }
 { R marks the right boundary of the current array A }
VAR
   I, J:INTEGER;
```

---

*Knuth. Op. Cit.
†Knuth. Op. Cit.

```
BEGIN

  I := L;
  J := R;
  REF := A[L];
  WHILE I < J DO
    BEGIN {Begin right to left scan }
    WHILE (REF < A[J]) AND (I < J) DO
      J := J - 1;
    IF J <> I THEN
      BEGIN
      A[I] := A[J];
      I := I + 1
      END;
    { Begin left to right scan }
    WHILE (REF > A[I]) AND (I < J) DO
      I := I + 1;
    IF J <> I THEN
      BEGIN
      A[J] := A[I];
      J := J - 1
      END
    END {WHILE I<J} ;
  { I and J met somewhere between L and R }
  A[J] := REF;
  IF L < J THEN
    QUICKSORT(A, L, J - 1);
  IF R > I THEN
    QUICKSORT(A, I + 1, R)

END {QUICKSORTRECURSIVE} ;
```

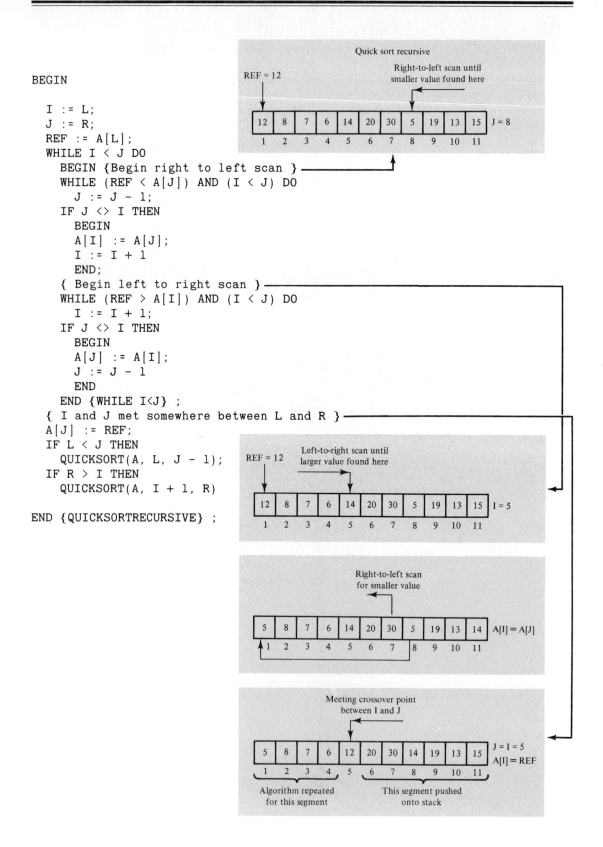

Quick sort recursive

REF = 12

Right-to-left scan until smaller value found here

| 12 | 8 | 7 | 6 | 14 | 20 | 30 | 5 | 19 | 13 | 15 | J = 8
| 1 | 2 | 3 | 4 | 5 | 6 | 7 | 8 | 9 | 10 | 11 |

REF = 12

Left-to-right scan until larger value found here

| 12 | 8 | 7 | 6 | 14 | 20 | 30 | 5 | 19 | 13 | 15 | I = 5
| 1 | 2 | 3 | 4 | 5 | 6 | 7 | 8 | 9 | 10 | 11 |

Right-to-left scan for smaller value

| 5 | 8 | 7 | 6 | 14 | 20 | 30 | 5 | 19 | 13 | 14 | A[I] = A[J]
| 1 | 2 | 3 | 4 | 5 | 6 | 7 | 8 | 9 | 10 | 11 |

Meeting crossover point between I and J

| 5 | 8 | 7 | 6 | 12 | 20 | 30 | 14 | 19 | 13 | 15 | J = I = 5
| 1 | 2 | 3 | 4 | 5 | 6 | 7 | 8 | 9 | 10 | 11 | A[I] = REF

Algorithm repeated for this segment

This segment pushed onto stack

In The World of Applications . . .

Sorting lists of data can be so consumptive of resources that it can bring large computer systems to their knees. Consequently, there is big money in writing more versatile and faster generalized sorting software. Syncsort, Inc., is one of the world's leaders in producing this type of software. In *Computerworld* of January 23, 1984, Syncsort took a full page advertisement to proclaim:

> We knew that the new hardware and software systems would create opportunities for the evolution of advanced sort pro-grams. Speed would still be essential. But productivity would continue to skyrocket in importance. So that's why we bred Syncsort 2.5.

> You can expect savings in critical resources up to those shown (in the table below). And that can add up to a big increase in total systems throughput.

SyncSort OS 2.5
Performance Improvements
EXCPs: 35%
TCB CPU Time: 15%
SRB CPU Time: 25%
(Courtesy of Computerworld)

Want to put yourself in demand? Just learn how to write more efficient user-friendly sorting programs. It sure has worked for Syncsort!

The Heap Sort

The heap sort is a sorting algorithm which is roughly equivalent to the quick sort; its average efficiency is $O(n(\log_2 n))$ for an array of size n. The method, originally described by Floyd, has two phases.[†] In the first phase, the array containing the n data items is viewed as equivalent to a binary tree that is full at all levels except for its rightmost elements (Chapter 6). As an example, suppose we wish to sort the array:

11	1	5	7	6	12	17	8	4	10	2

The first phase tree appears as shown in Figure 10-4. The goal of phase 1 is now to sort the data elements along each path from leaf node level

---

†Floyd, R. W. 1964. Algorithm 245: tree sort 3. *Communications of the Association for Computing Machinery* 7:701.

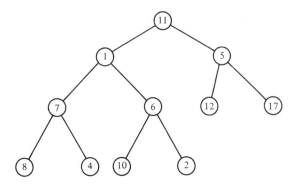

FIGURE 10-4 **Binary tree representation of the array.**

to the root node. If we wish to sort in ascending order, then the numbers along any path from leaf node to root (except the root) should be in increasing order.A full binary tree with the property that a parent is always greater than or equal to either of its children is called a **heap**. To achieve this, we take the following steps:

1. Process the node which is the parent of the rightmost node on the lowest level. If its value is less than the value of its largest child, swap these values, otherwise do nothing.
2. Move left on the same level. Compare the value of the parent node with the values of the children. If the parent is smaller than the largest child, swap them.
3. When the left end of this level is reached, move up a level, and, beginning with the rightmost parent node, repeat step (2). Continue swapping the original parent with the larger of its children until it is larger than its children. In effect, the original parent is being walked down the tree in a fashion which insures that numbers will be in increasing order along the path.
4. Repeat step (3) until level 1 nodes have been processed. Remember that the root is at the level 0.

Figure 10-5 shows these steps applied to Figure 10-4.

Phase 2 of the heap sort finds the node with the largest value in the tree and cuts it from the tree. This is then repeated to find the second largest value, which is also removed from the tree. The process continues until only two nodes are left in the tree, which are exchanged if necessary. The precise steps for phase 2 are as follows:

1. Compare the root with its children, swapping it with the largest child if this child is larger than the root.
2. If a swap occurred in step (1), then continue swapping the value which was originally in the root position until it is larger than its children. In effect, this original root value is now being walked down a path in the tree to ensure that all paths

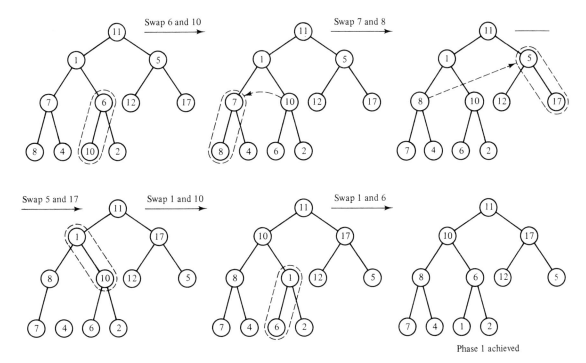

FIGURE 10-5 Phase 1 of heap sort applied to the binary tree in Figure 10-4.

retain values arranged in ascending order from leaf node to root node.

3. Swap the root node with the bottom rightmost child, and sever this new bottom rightmost child from the tree. This is the largest value.

4. Repeat steps (1) through (3) until only two elements are left.

Phase 2 of the heap sort begun in Figure 10-5 is shown for the three highest values in Figure 10-6. Both phase 1 and phase 2 use the same strategy of walking a parent down a path of the tree via a series of swaps with its children. The Pascal HEAPSORT given below calls another procedure WALKDOWN, which accomplishes this series of steps.

```
{ Global declarations }

CONST
  N1 = 100;

TYPE
  ARR = ARRAY [1..N1] OF INTEGER;

VAR
  L, P, Y: INTEGER;
```

```
PROCEDURE WALKDOWN(VAR A: ARR;
                   J, N: INTEGER);

  VAR
    REF, I, K: INTEGER;
    {This procedure exchanges parent with child}
    {and repeats this process all the way to leaf nodes.}
    {J is index of original parent and N is size of array.}

  BEGIN { PROCEDURE WALKDOWN}
    I := J;
    REF := A[I];
    {A[I] moves along an appropriate path }
    { in the tree. }
    K := 2 * I;
    REPEAT
      IF K < N THEN
        BEGIN
        IF A[K + 1] > A[K] THEN
          K := K + 1
        END {IF} ;
      IF A[K] > REF THEN
        BEGIN
        A[I] := A[K];
        I := K;
        K := 2 * I;
        A[I] := REF
        END {IF}
      ELSE
        BEGIN
        I := K;
        K := 2 * I
        END;
      REF := A[I]
    UNTIL (K >= N)
  END {WALKDOWN} ;

PROCEDURE HEAPSORT(VAR A: ARR;
                   N: INTEGER);
 {Beginning of PHASE 1 }
 {PHASE 1 arranges the tree in a heap }
```

Reference
REF = A[I]
A[I] = A[K]

A[K] larger of

IF * is larger than REF then * goes up

```
BEGIN
  P := 1;
  Y := N DIV 2 + 1;
  WHILE Y > 2 DO
    BEGIN
    Y := Y - 1;
    WALKDOWN(A, Y, N)
    END {WHILE} ;
  { Note that N div 2 gives the location of the parent }
  { of the rightmost leaf node in the tree. }

  {Beginning of PHASE 2}
  Y := N + 1;
  WHILE Y > 2 DO
    BEGIN
    Y := Y - 1;
    WALKDOWN(A, P, Y);
    { Now flip the root with bottom right leaf node }
    L := A[P];
    A[P] := A[Y];
    A[Y] := L
    END {WHILE}
END {HEAPSORT} ;
```

Parent at location N/2

Child at location N or N+1, N even

The Efficiency of the Heap Sort. As mentioned earlier, when n is large, the run-time efficiency of this sort both for average and worst cases has been calculated to be $O(n \log_2 n)$.

In general the heap sort does not perform better than the quick sort. Only when the array is nearly sorted to begin with does the heap sort algorithm gain an advantage. In such a case, the quick sort deteriorates to its worst performance of $O(n^2)$.

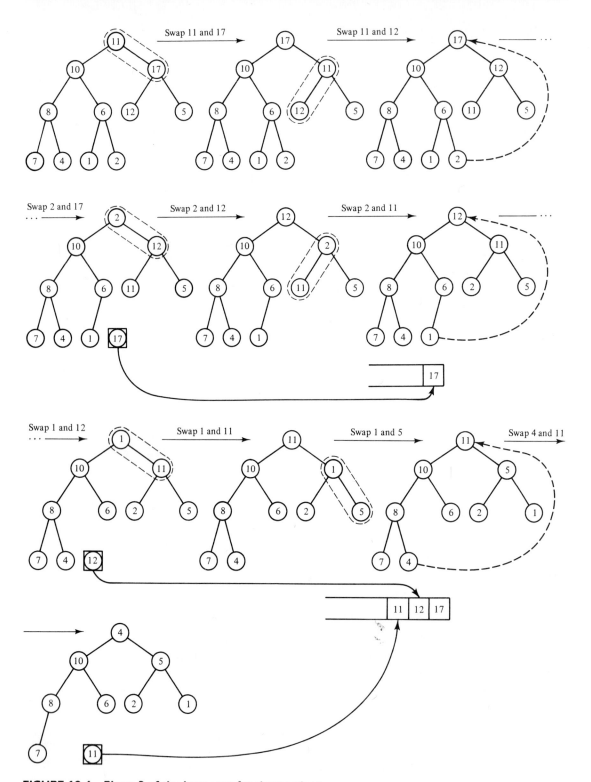

FIGURE 10-6   Phase 2 of the heap sort for three values.

10-3   External Sorting or File Sorting

The sorting algorithms discussed so far apply to arrays which reside in memory. Quite often voluminous files such as a master file for all the employees in a large corporation must exist on external storage devices because of their size. These on-line storage devices, such as tapes and disks, carry with them specific software and hardware considerations relating to access of stored data.

Only portions of large files can be brought into main memory and sorted. That portion of a file that can reside in main memory is a **segment.** The sorted segment can be sent back to the external storage medium and the next segment brought in. Finally, the partially sorted segments must be merged into a completely sorted file.

Because of the nature of secondary storage devices, bringing a segment of data items into main memory takes longer than does processing it. For instance, it takes time to position the read-write head over the appropriate track of a disk, and more time for the disk to rotate to bring the correct segment to the read-write head. An average input/output operation may take as long as 200 milliseconds. When you design sort algorithms for files on external media, you must consider this time delay.

The Merge Sort

The most common algorithm used in external sorting is the **merge sort.** A file (or subfile) is divided into 2 files, O_1 and O_2. These two files are then compared, a pair of records at a time, and merged. This is done by writing them on two new separate files M_1 and M_2. The elements which do not pair off are simply rewritten into the new files. The records in M_1 and M_2 are now **blocked** with two records in each segment. The two blocks (that is, 4 records), one from M_1 and one from M_2, are merged and written onto the original files O_1 and O_2. The length of the segments in each of O_1 and O_2 is now increased to 4, the merge process applied again and the new files are now M_1 and M_2. The process is continued until one of the two files is empty.

After r such passes, O_1 and O_2 consist of segments each of which is 2^r records in length. If $2^r > = n$, then one of the files is empty while the other contains the entire original file which is now sorted. Each merge operation requires reading and writing of two files, both of which are on the average about $n/2$ records long. Thus the total number of blocks read or written in a merge operation is approximately $2n/c$, where c is the number of records in a segment. The number of segments accessed for the whole operation is $O((n\log_2 n)/c)$ which amounts to $O(\log_2 n)$ passes through the entire original file. This is a considerable improvement over $O(n)$ passes needed in the preceding algorithms.

In order to clarify these concepts, suppose we have an external file containing the data:

[2,6,3,1,4,31,23,8,11,19,21,37,14,57,28,45,30,9,35,12,13,18,5, 89,77]

We divide it into two original files as:

O_1: [2,6,3,1,4,31,23,8,11,19,21,37]
O_2: [14,57,28,45,30,9,35,12,13,18,5,89,77]

After the first pass of segments of length 1, we have:

M_1: [(2,14),(3,28),(4,30),(23,35),(11,13),(5,21)]
M_2: [(6,57),(1,45),(9,31),(8,12),(18,19),(37,89),77]

After the second pass of segments of length 2:

O_1: [(2,6,14,57),(4,9,30,31),(11,13,18,19)]
O_2: [(1,3,28,45),(8,12,23,35),(5,21,37,89),77]

After the third pass of segments of length 4:

M_1: [(1,2,3,6,14,28,45,57),(5,11,13,18,19,21,37,89)]
M_2: [(4,8,9,12,23,30,31,35),77]

After the fourth pass of segments of length 8:

O_1: [(1,2,3,4,6,8,9,12,14,23,28,30,31,35,45,57)]
O_2: [5,11,13,18,19,21,37,77,89]

After the fifth pass of blocks of length 16

M_1: [1,2,3,4,5,6,8,9,11,12,13,14,18,19,21,23,28,30,31,35,37, 45,57,77,89]
M_2: is empty

When one of the files (M_1 or M_2) is empty, the merge sort is done.

The algorithm was described beginning with segments of length 1. Substantially larger length segments can be stored in main memory, so the efficiency of the algorithm can be enhanced by taking conveniently larger segments. For example, if an external file has 100,000 records, and a segment of 1000 such records can be stored in main memory, then the entire file can be sorted in 7 passes since 2^7 x 1000 is greater than 100,000. The segments in each pass can be ordered by a suitable sorting method such as quick sort.

The merge sort procedure usually deals with external file media and therefore is system dependent. Hence we have not provided a Pascal procedure for it. A specific language implementation of it is considered in the programming problems.

The **polyphase merge sort** is a merge sort with multiple channels. If there is a channel for each of r disk units, then r files $O_1, O_2, \ldots O_r$ each of block length p, can be merged into $M_1, M_2, \ldots, M_r$ files of blocks of rp length.

Program Design Considerations

Certain versions of Pascal allow one procedure to pass **conformant arrays** as parameters. The main program SHELL below implements the shell sort discussed in the text, and passes a conformant array as an argument to the procedure SHELLSORT. When the main program calls the procedure SHELLSORT it supplies the array as an argument *without* the subscript bounds of the array which are automatically and implicitly supplied. The concept of conformant arrays provides a degree of data abstraction in the sense that the procedure is written independently of the array size. Ada is one programming language in which a procedure to sort an array can be written without consideration as to even the data type, which is a higher degree of data abstraction. The modular design of the program follows:

```
+----------------------------+
| Main program SHELL         |
| responsible for            |
| passing conformant         |
| array as a parameter       |
| to the procedure           |
| SHELLSORT                  |
+----------------------------+
              |
+----------------------------+
| PROCEDURE                  |
| SHELLSORT sorts            |
| the array of extent        |
| LOWER..UPPER               |
+----------------------------+
```

```
PROGRAM SHELL(INPUT, OUTPUT);

  CONST
    HUND = 100;

  TYPE
    SORTARRAY = ARRAY [1..HUND] OF INTEGER;

  VAR
    ALPHA: SORTARRAY;
    P, Q, R: INTEGER;

  PROCEDURE SHELLSORT(VAR A: ARRAY [LOWER..UPPER: INTEGER] OF INTEGER;
                      N: INTEGER);

    VAR
      I, S, J, K: INTEGER;
```

```
      BEGIN
        { Divide the array by a prime number - 2 will do. }
        { This yields N/2 segments to be sorted. }
        I := N DIV 2;
        WHILE I > 0 DO { Sort the Ith segment }
          BEGIN
          J := I;
          REPEAT { Compare (J+1)th and (J-I)th }
            J := J + 1;
            K := J - I;
            WHILE K > 0 DO { Swap if necessary }
              BEGIN
              IF A[K] > A[K + I] THEN
                BEGIN
                S := A[K];
                A[K] := A[K + I];
                A[K + I] := S;
                K := K - I
                END
              ELSE
                K := 0
              END
          UNTIL J = N;
          I := I DIV 2
          END
      END; { THIS THE END OF THE PROCEDURE SHELLSORT }

  BEGIN { THE MAIN PROGRAM }
    WRITELN('   THIS PROCEDURE WILL SORT UP TO 100 INTEGERS');
    WRITELN;
    WRITELN(' ENTER HOW MANY (<=100) YOU WANT SORTED');
    READLN(P);
    WRITELN(' NOW ENTER YOUR DATA ONE NUMBER PER LINE');
    FOR Q := 1 TO P DO
      READLN(ALPHA[Q]);
    WRITELN(' SORTED DATA FOLLOWS ');
    SHELLSORT(ALPHA, P);
    FOR Q := 1 TO P DO
      BEGIN
      WRITELN;
      WRITELN(ALPHA[Q])
      END;
  END.
```

SUMMARY

Efficient and reliable data processing depends upon sorted data. The internal and external sorting methods each have their relative efficiencies in different applications. It appears that the quick sort, heap sort, and merge sort can handle arrays of heterogeneous data fairly efficiently. The shell sort is more efficient than the bubble sort, selection sort, and insertion sort. Sorting of larger files that cannot fit in main memory is best accomplished by external sorting techniques such as the merge sort.

Comparison Summary Table of Sorting Methods

Sorting Method	Chapter	Run-Time Proportional to*	Comments
Bubble	1	n^2	Good for small n ($n \leq 100$)
Selection	11	n^2	Good for partially sorted data and small n
Insertion	11	n^2	Good for almost sorted data
Shell	11	$n^{1.5}$	Good for moderate size data
		(For appropriate increments may approach $n(\log_2 n)^2$)	
Binary tree	6	$n \log_2 n$	Excellent for random homogeneous data
Quick	11	$n \log_2 n$	Excellent
Heap	11	$n \log_2 n$	Excellent
Merge	11	$\log_2 n$	Good for external file sorting.
		(passes through original file with $n \log_2 n$ total comparisons	

*n is the number of data items to be sorted.

KEY TERMS

External sorting
Internal sorting
Execution time
Bubble sort
Insertion sort
Selection sort
Shell sort
Diminishing increment sort
Quick sort
Heap sort
Binary sort
Merge sort
Polyphase sort

EXERCISES

1. Why is there a need for sorting?
2. Is it necessary to employ a fancy, most efficient sort routine if the number of data items is no more than 100, and each data item is no more than 80 bytes?
3. Why is the insertion sort called by that name?
4. Why is the bubble sort called by that name?
5. Why is the heap sort called by that name?

6. What is a heap?
7. Why is the shell sort called by that name?
8. Is a heap sort always better than a quick sort?
9. When is a bubble sort better than a quick sort?
10. Why is the insertion sort most efficient when the original data are in almost sorted order?
11. Write a procedure SHELLSORT in which the diminishing increments are not relatively prime.
12. Why does the shell sort work for any sequence of diminishing increments as long as the last one is 1?
13. What advantage do the relatively prime values of the increments have over other values in a shell sort?
14. Under what circumstances would you not use a quick sort?
15. What is the worst case and average case efficiency of the heap sort?
16. In Chapter 1, POINTERSORT uses an index of pointers to sort data logically without rearranging it. Identify the sort algorithm that was behind the Pascal POINTERSORT procedure. Adapt the pointer sort procedure to each of the other algorithms presented in this chapter.
17. A sorting method is said to be *stable* if two data items of matching value are guaranteed *not* to be rearranged with respect to each other as the algorithm progresses. For example, in the four element array

$$60 \quad 42_1 \quad 80 \quad 42_2$$

a stable sorting method would guarantee a final ordering

$$42_1 \quad 42_2 \quad 60 \quad 80$$

Classify each of the sorting algorithms studied in this chapter as to their stability. (To see why stability may be important, consider Programming Problem (8).)

PROGRAMMING PROBLEMS

1. Given a sequential file containing an unordered list of passengers and their flight numbers for the Wing-and-a-Prayer Airlines Company, produce a listing arranged in flight-number order. Passengers on the same flight should be ordered by last name. The easy version of this program assumes that all information will fit in the memory, allowing the use of an internal sort. For an added challenge, write the program using an external sort algorithm.
2. Use a merge sort to sort the records of the Fly-By-Night file by the social security numbers of the customer records. Also sort this file using the segmented sort by respectively the last name, the first name of the customers, and then the middle initial. Store the two files on disk separately for later use.
3. The Bay Area Brawlers professional football team has stored the records of all the players who have played on the team during the history of the team. One player's record consists of:

Name
Total points scored
Number of touchdowns
Number of field goals
Number of safeties
Number of extra points

Write a program which will list players in order from the most prolific scorer in the team's history down to the least prolific. Those players who have scored the same number of points should then be arranged in alphabetical order.

4. Take 1000 randomly generated integers. Now apply a bubble sort, a shell sort, a quick sort and a heap sort. Observe and compare their execution time.

5. Put some hypothetical data on an external file and apply a merge sort to them.

6. Write a Pascal program to complete the following steps:

Artificially create a file F of 1000 randomly chosen names. Read into a separate file F1 all those names from F whose last names begin with A thru G. Sort this file with heap sort and store this sorted file into another file LARGE. Now read into F1 all those names from F whose names begin with H thru N, sort it and append it to the end of LARGE. Repeat this process until all names from F are exhausted. The file LARGE will be the sorted version of the original file F. Observe the execution time of your program.

7. Write a merge sort in Pascal and apply it to the file in Programming Problem (4). Compare its execution time to that obtained with the first program you wrote.

8. Consider a list of records, each containing four fields:

Name
Month of birth
Day of birth
Year of birth

Write a program to sort this list in oldest to youngest order. People with the same birthdate should be arranged alphabetically. One strategy you could employ would be to concatenate strategically the four fields into one, and then just sort that one field. Another strategy would be to sort the list four times, each time by a different field. (Think carefully about which field to sort on first.) Which of the strategies would require that you choose a stable sorting algorithm?

11

Search Strategies

"You always find something the last place you look."

AXIOM OF SEARCHING

11-1   Introductory Considerations

The problem of searching may be likened to a situation that we have all faced in manual record-keeping systems. In such systems, records are typically kept in a metal filing cabinet. Each individual record is kept in a manila folder. The various papers within a folder constitute the **data** associated with that record, while the tab on the folder has written on it the **key** by which we identify the record. When we want to pull the folder associated with a particular key, there are several intuitive methods that may be used to find it. If we have been sloppy and stuffed the folders into the filing cabinet in arbitrary order, we are forced to flip through the folders one by one, comparing the key on each tab to the **target** we are trying to find. In the absence of any **file organization,** such a **sequential** search is the best that can be done. If we have been more careful in initially organizing the file (that is, by alphabetically ordering the keys), it is clear that more effective search methods may be used. However, these more effective methods require not only a more sophisticated file organization but also the ability to **directly access** records in the file, that is, select a record by its relative position in the file without having to sift through all the records preceding it.

At this point, we shall establish the conventions we will follow for all of the computer-based search procedures to be developed in this chapter. The procedures will assume a global array of records:

```
{ Global Declarations }

    CONST  RECORDSPACE = 100;
           STRSIZE = 30;

    TYPE   DATARRAY = PACKED ARRAY [1..STRSIZE] OF CHAR;
           INFOREC = RECORD
                           KEY:INTEGER;
                           DATA:DATARRAY {or other appropriate data
                                               type}
                     END;
    VAR INFO = ARRAY [1..RECORDSPACE] OF INFOREC;
```

The KEY field here contains the key values for all the data we wish to search; that is, it corresponds to what is found on the tabs of our manila filing folders. The parallel field DATA contains, for each key value, the data corresponding to it. That is, the DATA field corresponds to the contents of a manila folder. This concept is highlighted in the parallel fields pictured in Figure 11-1.

Our algorithms will be written using keys which are of integer data type. As appropriate, remarks will be made concerning modifications that would be necessary if the keys were of a different data type, such as character. The parallel fields of Figure 11-1 should be thought of as potentially existing either in main memory or on a permanent storage medium such as a magnetic disk. Hence, although we have formally declared INFO as an array in Pascal, this declaration should not be taken too literally. We are merely implying that INFO is to be regarded as a directly accessible list of records. Since standard Pascal offers no means for directly accessing records in a file, we will continue to write our search algorithms in terms of arrays. However, we

Relative position	KEY	DATA
1	414	JONES
2	437	GARLAND
3	442	SMITH
4	450	ROSEN
⋮	⋮	⋮
	806	RITTER
	913	GARLOCK
NUMBERREC	917	SIMMS

FIGURE 11-1 General format of data for search algorithm.

emphasize that the logic of these algorithms applies to both arrays and files. Moreover, whether the search logic is being applied to an array or a file is often an important distinction since the efficiency of an algorithm may be influenced by the type of storage medium to which it is being applied. Wherever this distinction is important, it will always be noted and discussed. We have also provided in Appendix A a convenient guide to the non-standard direct access file statements which exist in many versions of Pascal. This should help facilitate translation of our algorithms, expressed in terms of arrays, into appropriate file-searching algorithms. As an example of such translation, the last programming problem in this chapter provides an illustration of direct access file processing using Oregon Software's Pascal-2 compiler. Other compilers offer similar capabilities, though perhaps implemented via different commands.

Our calls to a search procedure will take the form:

```
{Global Declarations}

CONST RECORDSPACE=100;
      STRSIZE=30;

TYPE  DATARRAY=PACKED ARRAY [1..STRSIZE] OF CHAR;
      INFOREC = RECORD
                      KEY:INTEGER;
                      DATA:DATARRAY {or other appropriate data
                                           type}
                END;

VAR INFO=ARRAY [1..RECORDSPACE] OF INFOREC;

PROCEDURE SEARCHNAME(TARGET:INTEGER; VAR ITEM: DATARRAY; VAR
                     FOUND:BOOLEAN);
    {Search the KEY fields in global array INFO for key value
     matching TARGET.}

    {Return DATA associated with TARGET key in ITEM.}

    {FOUND returned as TRUE if search successful, FALSE
     otherwise.}
```

In those procedures where it is necessary to detect the end of the keys being searched, we will assume the existence of a variable ENDFLAG which has been assigned to the final position in the KEY list prior to entering the procedure. In those procedures where it is necessary to know the number of records being searched, we will assume that a global variable NUMBERREC has been similarly initialized outside the search procedure.

11-2 Quantity-dependent Search Techniques

Sequential Search

The first class of search techniques we shall consider all have efficiencies dependent only upon the pure numeric quantity of records in the list to be searched. Easiest and least efficient among these techniques is the **sequential search**. This is the technique that must be used when records are stored without any consideration given to order, or when the storage medium involved lacks any type of direct access facility (for instance, magnetic tape). The logic of the procedure SEQUENTIALSEARCH is extremely straightforward; it begins with the first available record and repeatedly proceeds to the next record until we find the key we are seeking or can conclude that it will not be found.

```
{ Global Declarations }

CONST
  RECORDSPACE = 100;
  STRSIZE = 30;
  ENDFLAG = MAXINT;

TYPE
  DATARRAY = PACKED ARRAY [1..STRSIZE] OF CHAR;
  INFOREC =
    RECORD
      KEY: INTEGER;
      DATA: DATARRAY { or other appropriate type}
    END;

VAR
  NUMBERREC: INTEGER; { Number of records currently in file }
  INFO: ARRAY [1..RECORDSPACE] OF INFOREC;

PROCEDURE SEQUENTIALSEARCH(TARGET: INTEGER;
                          VAR ITEM: DATARRAY;
                          VAR FOUND: BOOLEAN);

  {Local variables }

  VAR
    I: INTEGER;
```

```
BEGIN
  { Begin the procedure by assuming failure }
  { Recall ENDFLAG is the sentinel found in final KEY position }

  FOUND := FALSE;
  I := 1;
  REPEAT
    IF INFO[I].KEY = TARGET THEN
      BEGIN
      FOUND := TRUE;
      ITEM := INFO[I].DATA;
      END
    ELSE
      I := I + 1
  UNTIL (INFO[I].KEY = ENDFLAG) OR FOUND
END { End SEQUENTIALSEARCH };
```

Efficiency Considerations for the Sequential Search.   The efficiency of
the sequential search is clearly very poor. On the average, it will
require

NUMBERREC/2

accesses to the list to find a key. In the worst case, the TARGET being
sought is not in the list of keys and each record must be accessed. This
worst-case efficiency can be improved somewhat if the list is ordered
(left as an exercise). However, no improvements can change the fact
that the efficiency of the sequential search is basically proportional to
the number of records in the list. Hence, users searching an external
file of 50,000 records for which the average retrieval time for each record is 5 milliseconds may expect to wait over two minutes for responses to their requests. Obviously, that sort of performance will not
result in happy users; something better is needed!

Binary Search

By paying what may initially seem like a small price, we can dramatically increase the efficiency of our search effort using a simple technique called the **binary search**. The price we must pay is threefold:

1. The list of keys must be maintained in physical order.
2. The number of keys in the list (NUMBERREC) must be
   maintained.
3. There must be direct access by relative position for the keys in
   the list.

Suppose for instance that the list appearing in Figure 11-2 has the
direct access facility cited in (3) above and that we wish to locate the

	KEY
1	1119
2	1203
3	1212
4	1519
5	1604
6	1649
7	1821
8	2312
9	2409
10	3612

NUMBERREC = 10
TARGET = 1649

FIGURE 11-2 Physically ordered direct access KEY list for binary search.

data associated with TARGET key 1649. The strategy of the binary search is to begin the search in the middle of the list. In the case of Figure 11-2, this would mean beginning the search with the key found at position 5. Since the TARGET we are seeking in Figure 11-2 is greater than the key found at position 5, we are able to conclude that the key we want will be found among positions 6 through 10 if it is to be found at all. We will split those positions that remain viable candidates for finding the TARGET by accessing position

$$(6 + 10)/2 = 8$$

Since the key at position 8 is greater than TARGET, we are able to conclude that the key being sought will be found in positions 6 or 7 if it is to be found at all. Notice that, after only two accesses into the list, our list of remaining viable candidates for a match has shrunk to 2. (Compare this figure to a sequential search after two accesses into the same list.) We now split the distance between positions 6 and 7, arriving (by integer arithmetic) at position 6. Here we find the key being sought after a mere three probes into the list.

Crucial to the entire binary search algorithm are two pointers, LOW and HIGH, to the bottom and top respectively of the current list of viable candidates. Should these pointers ever cross, that is, if HIGH were to become less than LOW, we would conclude that the TARGET does not appear in the list. The entire algorithm is formalized in the Pascal procedure which follows.

```
{ Global Declarations }

CONST
  RECORDSPACE = 100;
  STRSIZE = 30;

TYPE
  DATARRAY = PACKED ARRAY [1..STRSIZE] OF CHAR;
  INFOREC =
    RECORD
      KEY: INTEGER;
      DATA: DATARRAY { or other appropriate type}
    END;

VAR
  NUMBERREC: INTEGER; { Number of records currently in file }
  INFO: ARRAY [1..RECORDSPACE] OF INFOREC;

PROCEDURE BINARYSEARCH(TARGET: INTEGER;
                       VAR ITEM: DATARRAY;
                       VAR FOUND: BOOLEAN);

 {Local variables }

  VAR
    HIGH, LOW, MID: INTEGER;

  BEGIN
    { Begin the procedure by assuming failure }

    FOUND := FALSE;
    LOW := 1;
    HIGH := NUMBERREC;
    REPEAT
      MID := (LOW + HIGH) DIV 2;
      IF TARGET < INFO[MID].KEY THEN
        HIGH := MID - 1
      ELSE IF TARGET > INFO[MID].KEY THEN
        LOW := MID + 1
      ELSE { Success! }
        BEGIN
        ITEM := INFO[MID].DATA;
        FOUND := TRUE;
        END
    UNTIL FOUND OR (HIGH < LOW)
  END;
{ End BINARYSEARCH }
```

	KEY	
1	102	Initial LOW
2	183	
.	219	
.	264	
MID	351	If TARGET < 351, then HIGH must be reset to point at 264
	499	
.	506	
.	530	
NUMBERREC	642	Initial HIGH

	KEY	
1	102	Initial LOW
2	183	
.	219	
.	264	
MID	351	If TARGET > 351, then LOW must be reset to point at 499
	499	
.	506	
	530	
NUMBERREC	642	Initial HIGH

Efficiency Considerations for the Binary Search. The effectiveness of the binary search algorithm lies in its continual halving of the list to be searched. When applied to the list of keys in Figure 11-2, the method in the worst case would require 4 accesses. For an ordered list of 50,000 keys, the worst case efficiency is a mere 16 accesses. (In case you do not believe this dramatic increase in efficiency as the list gets larger, try plugging 50,000 into a hand-held calculator and count how many times you must halve the displayed number to reduce it to 1.) The same file that would have necessitated an average wait of two minutes using a sequential search will result in a virtually instantaneous response for the user when the binary search strategy is used. In more precise algebraic terms, the halving method yields a worst case search efficiency of

$$(\log_2 \text{NUMBERREC}) + 1$$

A formal derivation of the efficiency may be found in Appendix B.

This efficiency may at times be even further enhanced by choosing a technique other than halving to split the remainder of the list into two parts. One such candidate for a different splitting function is to use an interpolative guess as to the most probable position of the key in the list. This is the type of logic used by most humans when searching a phone book for a given name. However, interpolative splitting strategies are dependent upon the distribution of the keys in the list. Because of the significant effectiveness of the halving strategy, interpolative techniques rarely improve efficiency enough to be worth the added complications involved in their implementation. Moreover, the wrong set of data can actually cause interpolative techniques to become significantly slower than the guaranteed efficiency of halving.

The drawback of the binary search lies not in any consideration of its processing speed but rather in a re-examination of the price that must be paid for being able to use it. What appears on the surface to be a relatively small price is in fact quite steep. We must, for instance, maintain a count of the number of records in the search list. For a **volatile** list, that is, one undergoing frequent insertions and deletions, this consideration can be a nuisance. But mere nuisances can be endured; what makes the binary search impractical for a volatile list of any size is the requirement that the list be kept in *physical* order. Our discussion of linked lists in Chapter 2 pointed out the enormous amount of data movement involved in such physical ordering. Unfortunately, the linked list structure, while eliminating the data movement problem, cannot be adapted to the binary search technique because of the direct access requirement. We are seemingly faced with an inescapable quandary!

Binary Tree Search

However, you should know by this point in your study of data structures that ingenuity can always overcome inescapable quandaries. Actually the answer to our dilemma has already been presented in Chapters 6 and 7. The order in which the keys of Figure 11-2 would be accessed for a given TARGET can clearly be represented by the full binary tree appearing in Figure 11-3. In other words, if we are willing to add left and right child pointers to our data records, we can store the list to be searched as a binary tree and duplicate the high efficiency of the binary search *provided* the tree remains full. Notice that as insertions and deletions destroy the fullness of the tree, this search efficiency can deteriorate. However, the height-balancing technique described in Chapter 7 will control the processing of insertions and deletions in such a fashion that a given search path in the resulting binary tree will never be more than 45% longer than it would be in an optimal full tree. For a proof of this fact, the reader is referred to Knuth.* Hence, the binary tree emerges as the best of both worlds—combining the excellent search efficiency of the binary method with the ability to quickly process insertions and deletions. For this reason, the tree and various derivatives of it will be seen again in Section 11-4 of this chapter when we discuss the concept of an index.

11-3 Density-dependent Search Techniques

In an ideal data processing world, all identifying keys such as product codes, Social Security numbers, etc., would start at 1 and follow in sequence thereafter. Then, in any given list, we would merely store the key and its associated data at the position which matched the key. The search efficiency for any key in such a list would be 1 access to the list, and all data processors could live happily ever after! Unfortunately, in the real world, users (not being concerned with the happiness of data processing personnel) desire keys that consist of more meaningful characters, such as, names, addresses, region codes, etc. For instance, it may be that in a given inventory control application, product codes are numbered in sequence beginning with 10000 instead of 1. A moment's reflection should indicate that this is still a highly desirable situation since, given a key, we need merely locate the key at position

```
KEYVALUE - 9999
```

in the list, and we still have a search efficiency of 1. What we have done here is to define what is known as a **key-to-address transformation,** or **hashing function.** The idea behind a hashing function is that

---

*Knuth, Donald. 1973. *The Art of Computer Programming.* Vol. 3. *Searching and Sorting.* Menlo Park, CA: Addison-Wesley.

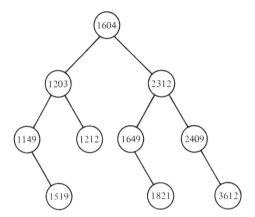

FIGURE 11-3 Paths in the binary tree correspond to the order in which keys are accessed in a binary search.

it acts upon a given key in such a way as to return the relative position in the list where we expect to find the key.

Most hashing functions are not as straightforward as the preceding one and present some additional complications which we can quickly illustrate. Let us at this point introduce the hashing function

```
HASH(KEYVALUE) = (KEYVALUE MOD 4) + 1
```

Then the set of keys 3, 5, 8, and 10 will be scattered as illustrated in Figure 11-4. However, if we happen to have 3,4,8, and 10 as keys instead of 3,5,8 and 10, a problem arises. Namely, 4 and 8 **hash** to the same position. They are said to be **synonyms,** and the result is termed a **collision.** This situation is shown in Figure 11-5. Clearly, one of the goals of the hashing functions we develop should be to reduce the number of collisions to the greatest degree possible.

The Construction of Hashing Functions

The business of developing hashing functions can be quite intriguing. The essential idea is to build a mathematical black box which will take

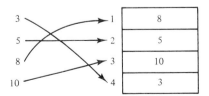

FIGURE 11-4 Keys 3, 5, 8, and 10 loaded using the hashing function (KEYVALUE MOD 4) + 1.

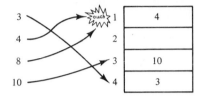

FIGURE 11-5 *If keys 3, 4, 8, and 10 are loaded by the hashing function (KEYVALUE MOD 4) + 1, the result is a collision at position 1.*

a key value as input and issue as output the position in the list where that key value should be located. The position emitted should have as low as possible a probability of colliding with the position that would be produced for a different key. In addition, the black box we create must insure that a given key will always produce the same position as output. The reader who has used a random number generator in past programming projects should begin to note a similarity between some of the properties possessed by a good hashing function and a good random number generator. Indeed, list access via a hashing function is sometimes called **randomized storage,** and the first type of hashing function we discuss below makes direct use of a random number generator.

Method 1: Use of a Random Number Generator. Many high-level languages provide their users with a random number generator which takes an argument to control how the random numbers generated by it are produced. We use as an example here DEC's FORTRAN, which supplies as a random number generator

    RAN(I,J)

When calling this function, I and J act as **seeds** which are used to produce a real random value between 0 and 1. I and J are then altered by the random number generator to insure (with a high degree of probability) that a different random number will be produced the next time the function is called. In traditional applications of such a random number generator, a user will derive the initial seeds by a method which has only a small likelihood of producing the same random sequence twice. For instance, many operating systems supply the time, day, month, and year, which could be converted into appropriate initial seeds. However, in a hashing application, values of the keys can be supplied as seeds. The random number between 0 and 1 which is correspondingly produced can then be appropriately multiplied, truncated, and shifted to produce a hash value within the desired range of positions. If you are working in a language that does not offer a supplied random number generator, they are not difficult to write. We offer one written in Oregon Software's Pascal-2 in the Program Design Considerations section at the end of this chapter. Teague* and Maurer & Williams[†] both offer readable discussions on other methods of random number generation.

Method 2: Folding. In situations where the key to be positioned is not a pure integer, some preliminary work may be required to translate it into a usable form. Take, for instance, the case of a Social Security number such as

387-58-1505

which, viewed as one number, would cause overflow on many machines. By a method known as **shift folding**, this Social Security number would be viewed as three separate numbers to be added

```
    387
     58
+ 1505
```

producing the result 1950. This result could either be regarded as the hash position itself or, more likely, as a pure integer which now could be further acted upon by Method 1 or 4 to produce a final hash position in the desired range. Another often-used folding technique is called **boundary folding.** The idea behind boundary folding is that, at the boundaries between the numbers making up the key under consideration, every other number is reversed before being added in to the accumulated total. Applying this method to our previous Social Security number example, we would have

```
    387
     85   (this number reversed)
+ 1505
```

yielding a result of 1977. Clearly, the two methods do not differ by much, and a choice between them must often be made on the basis of some experimentation as to which will produce more scattered results for a given application.

Regardless of whether shift or boundary folding is used, one of the great advantages of the folding method is its ability to transform non-integer keys into an integer suitable for further hashing action. For keys such as names which contain alphabetic characters, the type of folding illustrated above may be done by translating the characters into their ASCII (or other appropriate) codes.

*Teague, Robert. 1972. *Computing Problems for FORTRAN Solution.* San Francisco: Canfield.

[†]Maurer, H. A., and Williams, M. R. 1972. *A Collection of Programming Problems and Techniques.* Englewood Cliffs, NJ: Prentice-Hall.

Method 3: Digit or Character Extraction. In certain situations, a given key value may contain specific characters which are likely to bias any hash value arising from the key. The idea in extraction is to remove such digits or characters before using the result as a final hash value or passing it on to be further transformed by another method. For instance, a company may choose to identify the various products it manufactures by using a nine-character code which always contains either an A or B in the first position and either a 1 or 0 in the fourth position. The rest of the characters in the code tend to occur in a more unpredictable fashion. Character extraction would involve the removal of the first and fourth characters, leaving a seven-character result to pass on to further processing.

Method 4: Division Remainder Technique. All hashing presupposes a given range of positions which can be valid outputs of the hash function. In the remainder of this section, we shall assume the existence of a global constant RECORDSPACE which represents the upper limit of our hashing function. That is, the function should produce values between 1 and RECORDSPACE. (Note that RECORDSPACE is not necessarily the same as the dynamic count NUMBERREC.) It should then be evident that

```
HASH(KEYVALUE) = (KEYVALUE MOD RECORDSPACE) + 1
```

is a valid hashing function for integer KEYVALUE. To begin examining criteria for choosing an appropriate RECORDSPACE, let us load

ARRAY	KEY
1	0
2	91
3	92
4	0
5	0
6	50
7	0
8	0
9	0
10	0
11	0
12	41
13	12
14	58
15	0

FIGURE 11-6 Array with RECORDSPACE 15 loaded with keys 41, 58, 12, 92, 50, and 91 using a hashing function.

the keys 41, 58, 12, 92, 50, and 91 into a list with RECORDSPACE 15. Figure 11-6 shows the results. In this figure, zeroes are used to denote an empty position. However, if we keep RECORDSPACE the same and try to load the keys 10, 20, 30, 40, 50, 60, and 70, Figure 11-7 shows a result with many collisions. Hence, with this choice of RECORDSPACE, a different set of keys causes disastrous results even though the list seemingly has plenty of room available. On the other hand, if we choose RECORDSPACE to be 11, we have a list with considerably less room but no collisions. Figure 11-8 indicates the hashing positions when the same set of keys is acted upon by 11 instead of 15. Although the above examples are far from conclusive, they suggest that choosing a prime number for RECORDSPACE may produce a more desirable hashing function. In fact, this is true, and Radke has shown that primes of the form $4k + 3$ for some integer k tend to be particularly effective.*

Despite such results, no hashing function can rule out the possibility of collisions; it can only make them less likely. The reader should quickly be able to imagine a key value which will produce a collision for the hashing function used in determining the list of Figure 11-8. Notice that the more full the list becomes, the easier it becomes to produce a collision. Hence, when using hashing as a search strategy, one must be willing to waste some positions in the list; otherwise search efficiency will drastically deteriorate. How much space

ARRAY	KEY			
1	30	60		(collision)
2	0			
3	0			
4	0			
5	0			
6	20	50		(collision)
7	0			
8	0			
9	0			
10	0			
11	10	40	70	(collision)
12	0			
13	0			
14	0			
15	0			

FIGURE 11-7 **The same array as in Figure 11-6, when loaded with a different set of keys, shows several collisions.**

---

*Radke, C. E. 1970. The use of quadratic residue research. *Communications of the Association for Computing Machinery* 13:103–105.

ARRAY	KEY
1	0
2	0
3	0
4	0
5	70
6	60
7	50
8	40
9	30
10	20
11	10

FIGURE 11-8   An array with RECORDSPACE 11 and the same set of keys as Figure 11-6; no collisions result.

to waste is an interesting question that we will soon discuss. Another conclusion that emerges from the previous discussion is that, since *no* hashing function can eliminate collisions, we must be prepared to handle them when they occur.

Collision Processing

The essential problem in collision processing is to develop an algorithm that will position a key in a list when the position dictated by the hashing function itself is already occupied. Ideally, this algorithm should minimize the possibility of future collisions; that is, the problem key should be located at a position that is not likely to be the hashed position of a future key.

However, the very nature of hashing makes this latter criterion difficult to meet with any degree of certainty, since a good hashing function does not allow prediction of where future keys are likely to be placed. We will discuss five methods of collision processing—**linear, quadratic, rehashing, linked,** and **buckets.** In all of the methods, it will be necessary to detect when a given list position is not occupied. To signify this we use a sentinel key value of zero (identified in our Pascal procedures by the global constant EMPTY) to distinguish unoccupied positions. As the methods are being discussed, the reader should give some thought to the question of how deletions could be processed from a list accessed via one of these hashing methods. In particular, will the zero flag suffice to denote both the *never occupied* and *previously occupied but now vacant* conditions? This question is explored in the exercises at the end of the chapter.

Linear Collision Processing.   The **linear method** of resolving collisions is the simplest to implement (and therefore by Murphy's Law the least efficient). It requires that, when a collision occurs, we proceed down the list in sequential order until a vacant position is found. The key causing the collision is then placed at this first vacant position. If we come to the physical end of our list in the attempt to place the problem key, we merely wrap around to the top of the list and continue looking for a vacant position. For instance, suppose we use a hashing function of

```
HASH(KEYVALUE) = (KEYVALUE MOD RECORDSPACE) + 1
```

with RECORDSPACE equal to 7, and attempt to insert the keys 18, 31, 67, 36, 19, and 34. The sequence of lists in Figure 11-9 shows the results of these insertions. The Pascal algorithm to seek a TARGET loaded by the linear method is given below.

```
{ Global Declarations }

CONST
  RECORDSPACE = 100;
  STRSIZE = 30;
  EMPTY = 0; { Empty in key field flags empty records }

TYPE
  DATARRAY = PACKED ARRAY [1..STRSIZE] OF CHAR;
  INFOREC =
    RECORD
      KEY: INTEGER;
      DATA: DATARRAY { or other appropriate type}
    END;

VAR
  INFO: ARRAY [1..RECORDSPACE] OF INFOREC;

PROCEDURE LINEARHASH(TARGET: INTEGER;
                     VAR ITEM: DATARRAY;
                     VAR FOUND: BOOLEAN);

 {Local variables }

  VAR
    I, J: INTEGER;
    WRAPAROUND: BOOLEAN;
```

```
BEGIN
  FOUND := FALSE; { Assume failure }
  WRAPAROUND := FALSE; { Toggled to TRUE when the entire list is
                          traversed }
  I := HASH(TARGET); { Call on the hashing function }
  J := I;
  WHILE (INFO[J].KEY <> EMPTY) AND NOT (WRAPAROUND OR FOUND) DO
    IF TARGET = INFO[J].KEY THEN
      BEGIN
      ITEM := INFO[J].DATA;
      FOUND := TRUE
      END
    ELSE
      BEGIN
      J := (J MOD RECORDSPACE) + 1; { MOD to insure wraparound }
      IF J = I THEN
         WRAPAROUND := TRUE
      END
  { End WHILE }
END;
{ End LINEARHASH }
```

1	419
	⋮
RECORDSPACE–2	511
RECORDSPACE–1	312
RECORDSPACE	705

TARGET = 419

HASH(419) = RECORDSPACE–2

Repeated applications of ELSE clause insure eventual wraparound to 1st slot

Several remarks are in order concerning this procedure. First, note that the procedure as it stands would not handle list processing in which deletions were required. In such a situation, an additional flagging value would be needed to indicate a list position that had once been occupied and was now vacant because of a deletion. Second, we

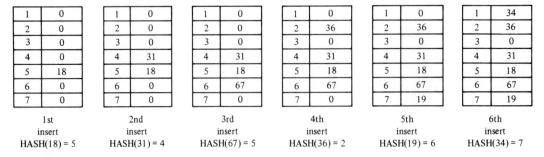

1	0
2	0
3	0
4	0
5	18
6	0
7	0

1st insert HASH(18) = 5

1	0
2	0
3	0
4	31
5	18
6	0
7	0

2nd insert HASH(31) = 4

1	0
2	0
3	0
4	31
5	18
6	67
7	0

3rd insert HASH(67) = 5

1	0
2	36
3	0
4	31
5	18
6	67
7	0

4th insert HASH(36) = 2

1	0
2	36
3	0
4	31
5	18
6	67
7	19

5th insert HASH(19) = 6

1	34
2	36
3	0
4	31
5	18
6	67
7	19

6th insert HASH(34) = 7

FIGURE 11-9 When a collision occurs at the third insert, it is processed by the linear method. 67 is thus loaded into position 6.

note that the linear method is not without its flaws. In particular, it is prone to a problem known as **clustering**. Clustering occurs when a hashing function is biased toward the placement of keys into a given region within the storage space. When the linear method is used to resolve collisions, this clustering problem is compounded. This is because the linear method locates keys which collide with an already existing key relatively close to the initial collision point. Hence, linear hashing is more likely than the other methods we will discuss to result in the clustering type of situation pictured in Figure 11-10.

Efficiency Considerations for Linear Hashing.   A final point to note about the linear hashing method is its search efficiency. Knuth* has shown that the average number of list accesses for a successful search using the linear method is

$$(1/2) * (1 + 1/(1 - D))$$

where

$$D = NUMBERREC/RECORDSPACE$$

An interesting fact about this search efficiency is that it is dependent *not* solely upon the number of records in the list but rather upon the

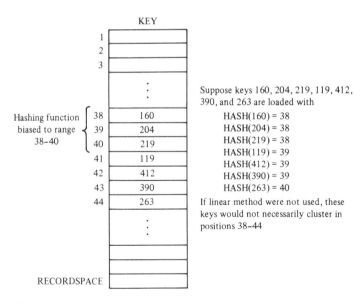

FIGURE 11-10   Clustering due to biased hashing function and linear processing.

*Knuth. Op. cit.

density ratio of the number of records currently in the list divided by the total record space available. In other words, no matter how many records there are, a highly efficient result can be obtained if one is willing to waste enough vacant records. This is what is meant by a **density-dependent** search technique. In the case of searching for a key which cannot be found, Knuth's results indicate that the average search efficiency will be

$$(1/2) * (1 + 1/(1 - D)^2)$$

Figure 11-11 illustrates the effectiveness of linear collision resolution by showing the computed efficiencies for a few strategic values of D.

Quadratic and Rehashing Methods of Collision Processing.   Both the **quadratic** and **rehashing** methods attempt to correct the problem of clustering which occurs with the linear method. They force the problem-causing key to immediately move a considerable distance from the initial collision. By the rehashing method, an entire sequence of hashing functions may be applied to a given key. If a collision results from the first hashing function, a second is applied, then a third, and so on, until the key can be successfully placed.

The quadratic method has the advantage of not requiring numerous hashing functions for its implementation. Suppose that a key value initially hashes to position K and a collision results. Then, on its first attempt to resolve the collision, the quadratic algorithm attempts to place the key at position

$$K + 1^2$$

Then if a second attempt is necessary to resolve the collision, position

$$K + 2^3$$

is probed. In general, the Rth attempt to resolve the collision probes position

$$K + R^2$$

D	Efficiency for Successful Search	Efficiency for Unsuccessful Search
0.10	1.06	1.18
0.50	1.50	2.50
0.75	2.50	8.50
0.90	5.50	50.50

FIGURE 11-11   Efficiency for linear collision processing.

(with wraparound taken into account). Figure 11-12 highlights this scattering pattern. The reader should verify at this point that, if the hashing function

```
HASH(KEYVALUE) = (KEYVALUE MOD RECORDSPACE) + 1
```

is used with RECORDSPACE equal to 7, the keys 17, 73, 32, and 80 will be located in positions 4, 5, 6, and 1 respectively.

Efficiency Considerations for the Quadratic and Rehashing Methods. Knuth's results* demonstrate the effectiveness of the rehashing and quadratic methods vis-a-vis the linear method. Average search efficiencies improve to

$$-(1/D) * \log_e (1 - D)$$

for the successful case and

$$1 / (1 - D)$$

for an unsuccessful search. The numbers presented in Figure 11-13 should be compared to those for the linear method given in Figure 11-1.

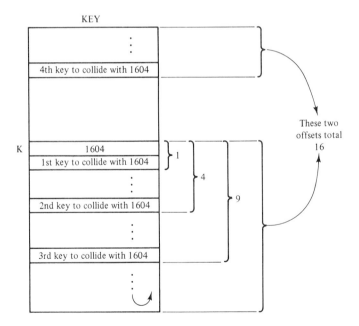

FIGURE 11-12 Quadratic collision processing.

---

*Knuth, Op. cit.

D	Efficiency for Successful Search	Efficiency for Unsuccessful Search
0.10	1.05	1.11
0.50	1.39	2.00
0.75	1.84	4.00
0.90	2.56	10.00

FIGURE 11-13   Efficiency for quadratic collision processing.

The astute reader should have surmised that the increased efficiency of the quadratic method brings with it some drawbacks that must be reckoned with. First, the computation of a position to be probed when a collision occurs is somewhat more obscure than it was with the linear method. We leave it for you to verify that the position for the Rth probe after an initial unsuccessful hash to position K is given by

$$(K + R^2 - 1) \text{ MOD RECORDSPACE} + 1$$

A more significant problem, however, is that the quadratic method seemingly offers no guarantee that we will try every position in the list before concluding that a given key cannot be inserted. With the linear method, as the list became relatively dense with keys and insertions were attempted, the only way that the insertion could fail is for every position in the list to be occupied. The linear nature of the search, although inefficient, insured that every position would be checked. However, with the quadratic method applied to the RECORDSPACE of Figure 11-14, you can confirm that an initial hash to position 4 will only lead to future probing of positions 4, 5, and 8.

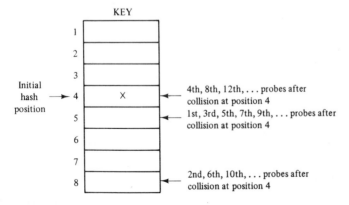

FIGURE 11-14   Quadratic probing will never check positions 1, 2, 3, 6, 7 after initial hash to 4.

A satisfactory answer to the question of what portion of a list will be probed by the quadratic algorithm was fortunately provided by Radke for values of RECORDSPACE that are a prime number of the form $4k + 3$ for some integer k.* He showed that, with such a choice of RECORDSPACE, *every* position in the list can eventually be probed by the quadratic method.

Linked Method of Collision Processing. The logic of this method completely eliminates the possibility that one collision could beget another. It requires a storage area divided horizontally into two regions—**a prime hash area** and an **overflow area**. Each record requires a LINK field in addition to the KEY and DATA fields. The global constant RECORDSPACE is applicable to the prime hash area only. This storage concept is illustrated in Figure 11-15.

Initially, the hashing function translates keys into the prime hashing area. If a collision occurs, the key is inserted into a linked list with its initial node in the prime area and all following nodes in the overflow area (no dummy header is used). Figure 11-16 shows how this method would load the keys 22, 31, 67, 36, 29, and 60 for a RECORDSPACE equal to 7 and hashing function

    HASH(KEYVALUE) = (KEYVALUE MOD RECORDSPACE) + 1

The Pascal procedure to implement the linked method of collision processing follows. We have made the LINK fields integer pointers to

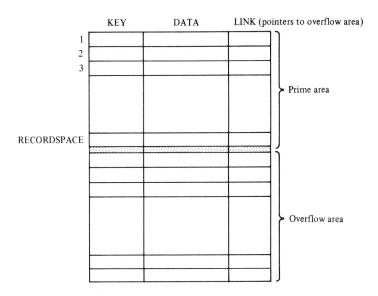

FIGURE 11-15 *Storage allocation for linked collision processing.*

---

*Radke, Op. cit.

	KEY	LINK
1	0	NULL
2	22	8
3	0	NULL
4	31	NULL
5	67	10
6	0	NULL
7	0	NULL
8	36	9
9	29	NULL
10	60	NULL
11	0	NULL
12	0	NULL
13	0	NULL
14	0	NULL
15	0	NULL
16	0	NULL
17	0	NULL

FIGURE 11-16   Loading keys 22, 31, 67, 36, 29, and 60 with KEYVALUE MOD 7+1 and linked collision processing.

other array locations instead of Pascal dynamic memory pointers to facilitate using the algorithm with a direct access file. As written, the procedure assumes that all key locations in the prime area have had their corresponding KEY and LINK fields initialized to zero (identified by the constant EMPTY for KEY fields and NULL for LINK fields). The assumption is also made that no keys will be deleted.

```
{ Global Declarations }

CONST
  RECORDSPACE = 100; { Record space in prime area }

  PRIMEPLUSOVERFLOW = 140; {Actual array size }
  STRSIZE = 30;
  EMPTY = 0; { Used in key field to flag empty record }
  NULL = 0; { Used to signal end of linked list }

TYPE
  DATARRAY = PACKED ARRAY [1..STRSIZE] OF CHAR;
  INFOREC =
    RECORD
      KEY: INTEGER;
      DATA: DATARRAY; { Or other appropriate type}
      LINK: INTEGER
    END;

VAR
  INFO: ARRAY [1..PRIMEPLUSOVERFLOW] OF INFOREC;
```

```
PROCEDURE LINKEDHASH(TARGET: INTEGER;
                     VAR ITEM: DATARRAY;
                     VAR FOUND: BOOLEAN);

{Local variables }

  VAR
    I: INTEGER;

  BEGIN
    FOUND := FALSE; { Assume failure }
    I := HASH(TARGET); { Call on the hashing function }
    REPEAT
      IF TARGET = INFO[I].KEY THEN
        BEGIN
        ITEM := INFO[I].DATA;
        FOUND := TRUE
        END
      ELSE
        I := INFO[I].LINK
    UNTIL FOUND OR (I = NULL)
  END;
{ End LINEARHASH }
```

Figure: KEY / LINK table, Primary hash area, with TARGET = 419, showing 511 → 312 → 705 → 419. "ELSE clause leads out of primary hash area" and "Statement I := INFO[I].LINK progresses along chain"

Efficiency Considerations for Linked Hashing. Knuth's efficiency results for the linked hashing method depend on a density factor (D) which is computed using the RECORDSPACE in the prime hashing area only. Hence, unlike the other hashing methods we have discussed, the linked method allows a density factor greater than 1. Given this variation, average search efficiencies for the successful and unsuccessful cases are

$$1 + D/2 \text{ and } D$$

respectively. Figure 11-17 shows computations of this search efficiency for selected values of D, and should be compared to the corresponding results for the linear and quadratic methods, which were presented in Figures 11-11 and 11-13 respectively.

D	Efficiency for Successful Search	Efficiency for Unsuccessful Search
2	2	2
5	3.5	5
10	6	10
20	11	20

FIGURE 11-17 **Search efficiencies for the linked method.**

Bucket Hashing. In the **bucket hashing** strategy of collision processing, the hashing function transforms a given key to a physically contiguous region of locations within the list to be searched. This contiguous region is called a **bucket.** Thus, instead of hashing to the Ith location, a key would hash to the Ith bucket of locations. The number of locations contained in this bucket would depend upon the bucket size. (We assume that all buckets in a given list are of the same size.) Figure 11-18 illustrates this concept for a list with 7 buckets and a bucket size of 3.

Once having hashed to a bucket, the TARGET must then be compared in sequential order to all of the keys in that bucket. On the surface, it would seem as if this strategy could do no better than duplicate

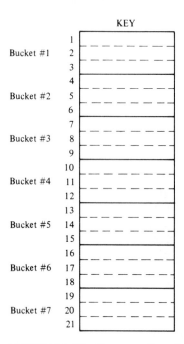

FIGURE 11-18 **Storage allocation for bucket hashing.**

the efficiency of the linked hash method discussed earlier. Indeed, since after the initial hash is made, a sequential search is conducted in both cases, the average number of list accesses for a successful or unsuccessful search cannot be improved by using buckets. Moreover, provisions for linking to some sort of overflow area must still be made in case a series of collisions consumed all of the space in a given bucket.

What then could be a possible advantage of using buckets? If the list to be searched resides entirely in main memory, there is no advantage. However, if the list resides in a disk file, the bucket method will allow us to take advantage of some of the physical characteristics of the storage medium itself. To see this, let us assume a one-surface disk divided into concentric *tracks* and pie-shaped *sectors* as indicated in Figure 11-19.

There are two ways in which the bucket hashing strategy may take advantage of the organization of the data on the disk. First, when records in a contiguous direct-access file are stored on a disk, they are generally located in relative record number order along one track, then along an adjacent track, and so on. The movement of the read-write head between tracks is generally the cause of the most significant delays in obtaining data from a disk. The further the movement,

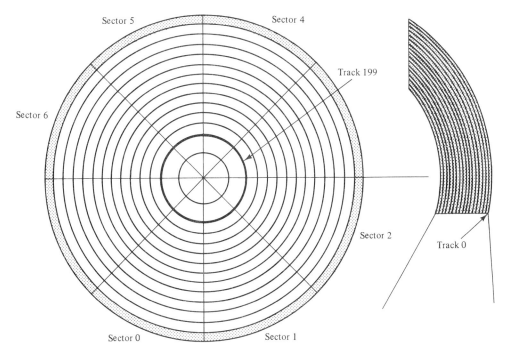

FIGURE 11-19 A one-surface disk divided into concentric tracks and pie-shaped sectors.

the greater the delay will be. Hence, if our knowledge of the machine in question allows us to make a bucket coincide with a track on the disk, then hashing to the beginning of a bucket and proceeding from there using a sequential search within the bucket (that is, the track) will greatly reduce head movement. A linked hashing strategy, on the other hand, could cause the read-write head to be moving a great deal between tracks on the disk, thereby slowing program execution. This consideration is an excellent example of how one must examine more than just the number of list accesses when measuring the efficiency of a program involving disk files.

A second advantage in using the bucket hashing algorithm when disk files are being searched is related to the way in which records are transferred between the disk and main memory. Frequently, programming languages create the illusion that each record accessed requires a separate disk access. However, records are frequently **blocked**, that is, positioned in contiguous regions on a track of the disk, so that a fixed number are brought into main memory when a record in that block is requested. This means that, if the record requested happens to be part of the block presently in main memory, a program statement which requests a record may not even require a disk access but only a different mask applied to the block already in main memory. With main memory manipulations being orders of magnitude faster than the rate of data transfer to and from a disk, this means that positioning our buckets to coincide with a disk block will necessitate only one disk access each time an entire bucket is sequentially searched. Here again, the more scattered nature of a purely linked hashing algorithm would not allow this disk-oriented efficiency consideration to be taken into account.

11-4 Indexed Search Techniques

This section is especially applicable in searching direct access secondary storage devices. One should read the last two paragraphs of the preceding section until they are thoroughly understood before proceeding with this section. The idea behind the use of an **index** is analogous to the way in which we routinely use an address book to find a person whom we are seeking. That is, if we are looking for a person, we do not knock on the doors of numerous houses until we find the one where that person lives. Instead, we apply a search strategy to an address book. There we use the name of the person as a key to find a pointer, that is, an address, which swiftly leads us to where the person can be found. Only one actual "house access" must be made, although our search strategy may require numerous accesses into the address book index.

In computer systems, records (or more precisely blocks) could play the role of houses in the search scenario described above. Data records on disk are (when compared to main memory) terribly slow and awkward creatures to access. One of the reasons for this is that there is often so *much* data that must be moved from disk to main memory every time a record is accessed. The DATA array which we originally presented in Figure 11-1 may in many situations have thousands of bytes of data associated with each of its positions. Because of this, it can often be advantageous to revise the general picture of Figure 11-1 so that our list of keys is no longer parallel to the actual data they are logically associated with but rather is parallel to a list of pointers which will lead us to the actual data. This revised picture is presented in Figure 11-20.

The general strategy of an indexed search is to use the key to efficiently search the index, find the relative record position of the associated data, and from there make *only one* access into the actual data. Because the parallel lists of keys and relative record positions require much less storage than the data itself, frequently the entire index can be loaded and permanently held in main memory, necessitating only one disk access for each record being sought. For larger indices, it still remains true that large blocks of keys and associated pointers may be manipulated in main memory, thereby still greatly enhancing search efficiency.

Indexed Sequential Search Technique

The **indexed sequential search technique** is also commonly recognized by the acronym ISAM, which stands for Indexed Sequential Access Method. Essentially it involves carefully weighing the disk-dependent factors of blocking and track size to build a partial index.

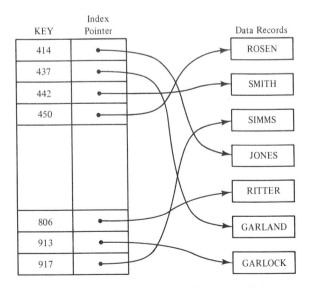

FIGURE 11-20 Rearrangement of the parallel array in Figure 11-1 to provide a general context for an indexed search.

The partial index, unlike some other index structures we will study, does not reduce to 1 the number of probes which must be made into the actual data. To continue the analogy between searching for data and searching for a person, the indexed sequential strategy is somewhat like an address book which would lead us to the street on which a person lives but leave us to check each of the houses on that street. The ISAM method correspondingly leads us to an appropriate region (often a track or a **cylinder** containing multiple tracks within a disk pack) and then leaves us to search sequentially within that region.

As an example, let us suppose that we can conveniently fit the partial index, or **directory,** pictured in Figure 11-21 into main memory and that the organization of our disk file allows six records per track. The partial index, or directory, of Figure 11-21 is formed by choosing the highest key value in each six-record track along with a pointer indicating where that track begins. Here our pointers are simply relative record numbers; in practice they could well be a more disk-dependent locator. The strategy to conduct an indexed sequential search is to:

1. Search the main memory directory for a key which is greater than or equal to the TARGET
2. Then follow the corresponding pointer out to the disk and there search sequentially until we find a match (success) or the key that the directory maintains as the high key within that particular region (failure)

For the data given in Figure 11-21, this technique would mean that the 36-record file would require no more than six main memory index accesses plus six disk accesses, all of which are located in the same track.

For larger files, it may be advantageous to have more than one level of these directory structures. Consider, for instance, the two-level directory structure for a file with 216 records as given in Figure 11-22. Here we might suppose that storage restrictions allow the entire primary directory to be kept in main memory, the secondary directory to be brought in as a single block of a disk file, and the actual data records to be stored six per track. The primary directory divides the file into regions of 36 records each. The key in the primary directory represents the highest-valued key in a given 36-record region, but the pointer leads us into the subdirectory instead of the actual file. So, we search the primary directory for a key greater than or equal to the target we are seeking. Once this is done, we follow the primary directory pointer into the secondary directory. Beginning at the position indicated by the primary directory's pointer, we again search for a key greater than or equal to the TARGET. Notice that the subdirectory has necessitated one disk access in our hypothetical situation. For this price, the 36-record region determined by the primary directory is subdivided into 6-record regions, each of which will lie entirely on one track by the time we get out to the disk file. Following the subdirectory's pointer to the actual file, we end up with a relatively short sequential search on the actual storage medium.

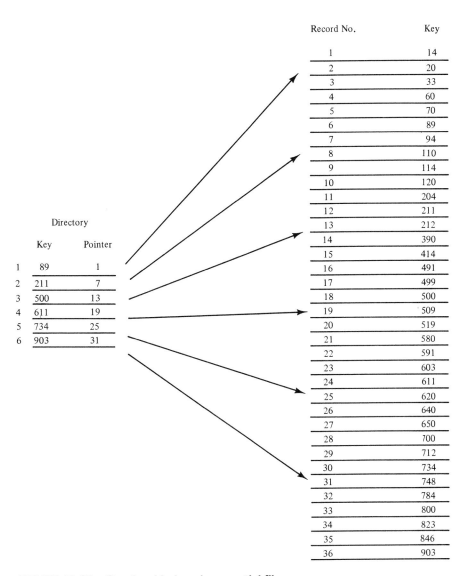

FIGURE 11-21 One-level indexed sequential file.

It should be clear from this discussion that the search efficiency of the indexed sequential technique depends on a variety of factors. Included among them are:

1. To what degree the directory structures are able to subdivide the actual file
2. To what degree the directory structures are able to reside in main memory
3. The relationship of data records to physical characteristics of the disk such as blocking factors, track size, cylinder size, etc.

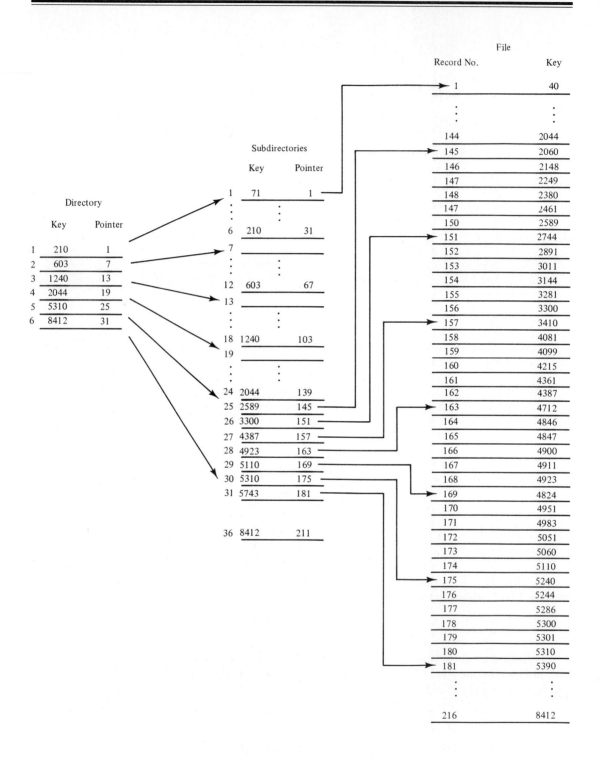

FIGURE 11-22 Two-level directory structure.

A mathematical verification of the optimal choice for index size is presented in Appendix B.

It should also be clear that the indexed sequential method may not be ideal for a highly volatile file. This is because, as implicitly indicated in Figures 11-21 and 11-22, the actual data records must be physically stored in increasing (or decreasing) key order. The requirement for physical ordering is obviously not conducive to frequent insertions and deletions. In practice, the solution to this problem is that each file subregion which is ultimately the subject of a sequential search is equipped with a pointer to an overflow area. Insertions are located in this overflow area and linked to the main sequential search area. As the overflow area builds up, the search efficiency tends to deteriorate. In some applications, this deterioration can be so severe that data processing personnel have been known to refer to the ISAM technique as the Intrinsically Slow Access Method. The way to avoid deterioration is to periodically *reorganize* the file into a new file with no overflow. However, such reorganization cannot be done dynamically. It requires going through the file in key sequential order and copying it into a new one. Along the way, the indices must be re-built, of course. These types of maintenance problems involved with the ISAM structure have led to the development of several more dynamic indexing schemes.

Binary Tree Indexing

The concept of a binary tree search has already been covered in depth in Section 11-2 and in Chapters 6 and 7. The only twist added when the binary tree is an index is that each node of the tree contains a key and a pointer to the record associated with that key in some larger data aggregate. The advantages of using a binary tree as an index structure include:

1. A search efficiency proportional to $\log_2 \text{NUMBERREC}$, provided the tree is height-balanced
2. The ability to traverse the list indexed by the tree in key order
3. Dynamic insertion and deletion capabilities

These qualities make the binary tree the ideal index structure for situations in which the entire tree can fit in main memory. However, if the data collection is so large that the tree index must itself be stored on disk, the efficiency of the structure is less than optimal. This is because each node of the index may lie in a disk block separate from the other nodes and hence require a separate disk access. Using the example of 50,000 keys presented in section 11-2, a search of a binary tree index could require *minimally* 16 disk accesses. To solve this problem, we would like to cluster those nodes along a given search path into one, or at least relatively few, disk blocks. The B-tree index structure is a variation on the tree index which accomplishes this goal.

B-tree Indexing

We begin this discussion of B-trees by reminding the reader that one index entry requires nothing more than a key and a pointer. Moreover, we have been assuming that both the key and the pointer are integers, and we will continue to operate under this assumption during our discussion of B-trees. We emphasize this point here because, in a B-tree, a given tree node will in fact contain many such key-pointer pairs. This is because a given B-tree node will in fact coincide with one disk block. The idea behind a B-tree is that we will somehow group key-pointer pairs which are related in the search algorithm into a few strategic B-tree nodes, that is, disk blocks. At this point, we make the following formal definition. The definition will then be clarified via some examples. A **B-tree of order n** is a structure with the following properties:

1. Every node in the B-tree has sufficient room to store $n-1$ key-pointer pairs.
2. Additionally, every node has room for n pointers to other nodes in the B-tree (as distinguished from the pointers within key-pointer pairs, which point to the position of a key in the file).
3. Every nonterminal node except for the root must have at least $n/2$ non-null pointers to other nodes in the B-tree.
4. All terminal nodes are on the same level.
5. If a node has $m+1$ non-null pointers to other B-tree nodes, then it must contain m key-pointer pairs for the index itself

Stipulation (5) above says that we can think of a B-tree node as a list

$$P_0, KP_1, P_1, KP_2, P_2, KP_3, \ldots, P_{m-1}, KP_m, P_m$$

where P_i represents the ith pointer to another B-tree node and KP_i represents the ith key-pointer pair. Note that a B-tree node will always contain one more pointer to another B-tree node than it does key-pointer pairs. With this picture in mind, we can present the sixth and final stipulation.

6. For each B-tree node, we require that the key value in key-pointer pair KP_{i-1} is less then the key value in key-pointer pair KP_i, that all key pointer pairs in the node pointed to by P_{i-1} contain keys which are less than the key in KP_i, and that all key-pointer pairs in the node pointed to by P_i contain key values which are greater than the key in KP_i.

A B-tree of order 6 index structure for the thirty-six record file of Figure 11-21 appears in Figure 11-23. The reader should carefully verify that all six defining properties are satisfied. We remark as an aside here that the choice of order 6 for Figure 11-23 was made only for the purposes of making the figure fit on a page of text. In practice, the order chosen would be the maximum number of B-tree pointers and

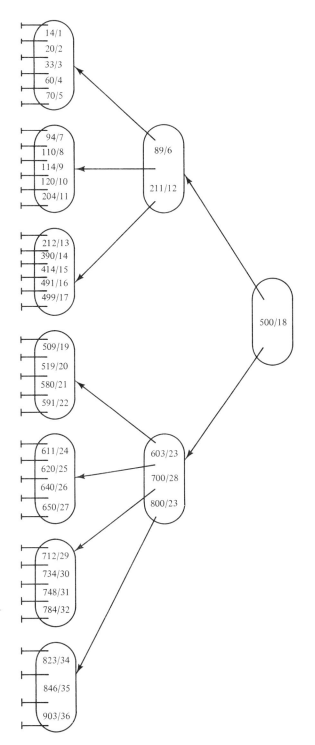

FIGURE 11-23   B-tree index of order 6 for file in Figure 11-21. A/B denotes key-pointer pair. ⊥ denotes null pointer.

key-pointer pairs that we could fit into one disk block. That is, the choice should be made to force a disk block to coincide with a B-tree node.

Efficiency Considerations for B-Tree Indexing. Let us now consider what is involved in searching a B-tree for a given key. Within the current node (starting at the root), we must search sequentially through the key values in the node until we come to a match, a key value which is greater than the one being sought, or the end of the key values in that particular node. If a match is not made within a particular B-tree node, we have a pointer to follow to an appropriate follow-up node. Again, you should verify this algorithm for several of the keys appearing at various levels of Figure 11-23. The sequential search on keys within a given node may at first seem unappealing. However, the key fact to remember here is that each B-tree node is a disk block which is loaded entirely into main memory. Hence, it may be possible to search sequentially on hundreds of keys within a node in the time it would take to load one new node from disk. Our main concern is to minimize disk accesses, and here we have achieved a worst case search for our thirty-six entry file in three disk accesses.

What in general is the search efficiency for a B-tree index? It should be clear from the nature of the structure that the number of disk accesses for any particular key will simply be the number of levels in the tree. So the efficiency question really amounts to knowing the maximum number of levels that the six defining criteria would allow for a B-tree containing NUMBERREC key-pointer pairs. That is, this number would be the worst case search efficiency. To determine this number, we use the minimum number of nodes that must be present on any given level. Let L be the smallest integer greater than or equal to $N/2$ where N is the order of the B-tree in question. Then:

> Level 1 contains at least 1 node.
> Level 2 contains at least 2 nodes.
> Level 3 contains at least $2*L$ nodes.
> Level 4 contains at least $2*L^2$ nodes.
> . .
> . .
> Level m contains at least $2*L^{(m-2)}$ nodes.

An argument due to Knuth* uses this progression to show that the maximum number of levels (and thus the worst case search efficiency) for NUMBERREC key-pointer pairs is

$$1 + \log_N((\text{NUMBERREC}+1)/2)$$

---

*Knuth. Op. cit.

In the World of Applications . . .

Suppose you are driving a car with Wisconsin license plates and are stopped for speeding in Illinois. You may notice a brief delay before the officer begins to approach your car. However, according to Daniel and Joan Slotnick in *Computers: Their Structure, Use, and Influence*, the delay will be no longer than 20 seconds.* In that 20 seconds, the following will have occurred. The officer will have radioed your license plate number to Illinois headquarters. From there, it is relayed to the Wisconsin Department of Transportation, where it must be located in the computer file of information on all Wisconsin license plates. If it happens that you are driving a stolen vehicle, the license plate number may be communicated to the National Crime Information Center in Washington, D.C. to obtain further information about the missing car in that agency's massive databank. This information is then routed back to Illinois headquarters and finally to the officer on the scene.

"Armed" with this information, the officer now knows whether (s)he should expect trouble when approaching your vehicle. You on the other hand, being guilty of nothing but speeding, have not been kept waiting an annoyingly long time—thanks to the efficiency of some computer searching algorithms!

———————

*Slotnick, D., and Slotnick, J. 1979. Computers: Their Structure, Use, and Influence, Englewood Cliffs, N.J.: Prentice-Hall, p. 239.

As an example, the index for a file of 50,000 records which would require on the order of 16 disk accesses using a binary tree structure could be searched with 3 disk accesses using a B-tree of order 250. The reader should note here that, given typical block sizes for files, the choice of order 250 for this example is not at all unrealistic.

Unlike the ISAM indexing method, the B-tree index can dynamically handle insertions and deletions without a resulting deterioration in search efficiency. We will presently discuss how B-tree insertions are handled; the problem of deletions is left for an exercise. The essential idea behind a B-tree insertion is that we must first determine which bottom-level node should contain the key-pointer pair to be inserted. For instance, suppose that we wanted to insert the key 742 into the B-tree of Figure 11-23. By allowing this key to walk down the B-tree from the root to the bottom level, we could quickly determine that this key belongs in the node presently containing

712/29   734/30   748/31   784/32

Since, by the definition of a B-tree of order 6, this node is not presently full, no further disk accesses would be necessary to perform the insertion. We would merely need to determine the next available record space in the actual data file (37 in this case) and then add the key-pointer pair 742/37 to this terminal node, resulting in

$$(\ 712/29 \quad 734/30 \quad 742/37 \quad 748/31 \quad 784/32 \ )$$

A slightly more difficult situation arises when we find that the key-pointer pair we wish to add should be inserted into a bottom level node that is already full. For instance, this would occur if we attempted to add the key 112 to the B-tree of Figure 11-23. We would load the actual data for this key into file position 38 (given the addition already made in the preceding paragraph) and then determine that the key-pointer pair 112/38 belongs in the bottom level node

$$(\ 94/7 \quad 110/8 \quad 114/9 \quad 120/10 \quad 204/11 \ )$$

The stipulation that any given B-tree node have minimally $6/2 = 3$ pointers to other B-tree nodes will now allow us to split this node, creating one new node with two key-pointer pairs, and one with three key-pointers; and moving one of the key-pointer pairs up to the parent of the present node. The resulting B-tree is given in Figure 11-24. Although it does not happen in this particular example, note that it would be entirely possible that the moving of a key-pointer pair up to a parent node that is already full would necessitate a split of this parent node, using the same procedure. Indeed it is possible that key-pointer pairs could be passed all the way up to the root and cause a split of the root; this is in fact how a new level of the tree would be introduced. A split of the root would force the creation of a new root which would only have one key-pointer pair and two pointers to other B-tree nodes. However, at the root level this is still a sufficient number of pointers to retain the B-tree structure. Because the insertion algorithm for a B-tree requires checking whether a given node is full and potentially moving back up to a parent node, it is convenient to allow space within a node to store:

1. A count of the number of key-pointer pairs in the node, and
2. A back pointer to the node's parent

Trie Indexing

In all of the indexing applications we have discussed so far, the keys involved have been assumed to be integer. In practice, however, we must be prepared to deal with keys of different types. Perhaps the worst case is that of keys which are variable length character strings. **Trie indexing** has developed as a means of retrieving keys in this worst case. (The term itself is derived from the four middle letters of "re*trie*ve" though usually pronounced like "try.") Let us suppose, for instance, that the strings in the following list represent a set of keys.

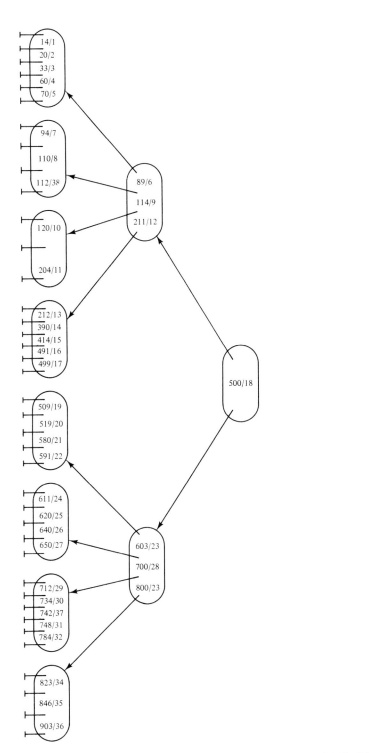

FIGURE 11-24   B-Tree of Figure 11-23 after insertion of 112/38 and 742/37.

Each string may be thought of as a last name followed by initials and a delimiting "$".

```
ADAMS BT$
COOPER CC$
COOPER PJ$
COWANS DC$
MAGUIRE WH$
MCGUIRE AL$
MEMINGER DD$
SEFTPM SD$
SPAN KD$
SPAN LA$
SPANNER DW$
ZARDA JM$
ZARDA PW$
```

An individual node in a trie structure for these keys appears in Figure 11-25. It is essentially a fixed length array of 28 pointers—one for each letter of the alphabet, one for a blank, and one for the delimiter. Each pointer within one of these nodes can lead to one of two entities—either another node within the trie or the actual data record for a given key. Hence it may be convenient to embed a flag bit in each pointer indicating the type of entity to which it is pointing. The trie structure for the preceding list of keys is given in Figure 11-26. In this figure, circular nodes are used to represent the destinations of those pointers leading to actual data records outside the trie structure itself.

The logic behind a trie structure may best be seen by tracing through an example. This search algorithm involves examining the target key on a character-by-character basis. Let us begin by considering the easy case of finding the data record for ADAMS BT$. In this case, we look at A, the first character in the key, and follow the A pointer in the root node to its destination. From what we have previously said, we know that its destination will be either another node withing the trie structure or an actual data record. If it were a node within the trie, it would be a node on the search path for all keys which begin with A. In this case, there is only one key in our list which begins with A, so the A pointer in the root node leads us directly to the actual data record for ADAMS BT$. On the other hand, the search path to find the key COOPER CC$ in the trie is somewhat longer. We follow the C pointer from the root node down a level to a node shared by all keys starting with C. From there, the O pointer is followed to a trie node shared by all keys which start with CO. The process continues

Trie Node

FIGURE 11-25 Trie node.

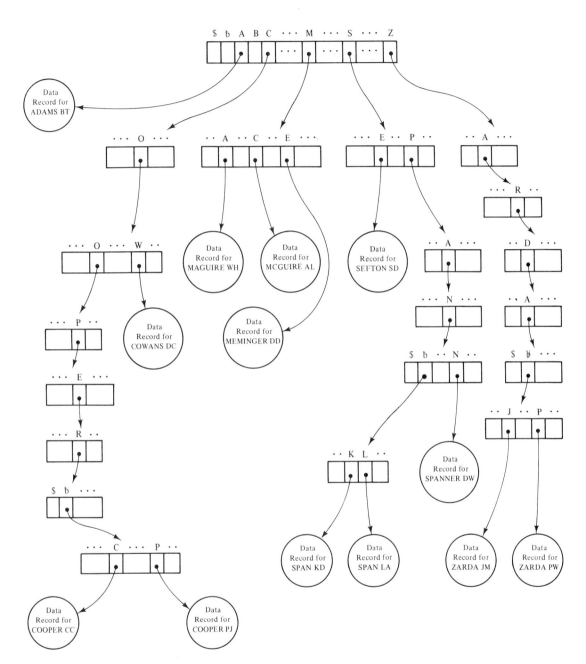

FIGURE 11-26 Trie index structure.

down level by level, following the O pointer to a trie node shared by all keys starting with COO, then the P pointer to a node for all keys starting with COOP, the E pointer to a node for all keys starting with COOPE, the R pointer to a node for all keys starting with COOPER, and the blank pointer to a node shared by all keys starting with "COO-PER ". Notice that, as each character is read in, we must continue following these pointers from trie node to trie node (instead of from trie node to actual data record) until we finally reach a point where the next character to be read will uniquely define the key. At this point, the key in question need no longer share its pointer with other keys which match it on an initial substring. Hence the pointer may now lead to an actual data record. This is what happens in our example when we read in the next C to form the uniquely defining substring COOPER C.

Efficiency Considerations for Trie Indexing. The search efficiency for the trie index is quite easily determined. The worst case occurs when a key is not uniquely defined until its last character is read in. In this case, we may have as many disk accesses as there are characters in the key before we finally locate the actual data record. The astute reader should observe, however, that there is another efficiency considera-tion to be taken into account when using the trie method, which is the amount of wasted storage in the trie nodes. In our example using a short list of keys, only a small percentage of the available pointers is ever used. In practice, however, a trie would only be used for an ex-tremely large file; such as the list represented by a phone book with names as keys. In such a situation, a much larger number of character combinations occurs and the resulting trie structure is correspond-ingly much less sparse.

A final point to consider relative to trie indexes is their ability to dynamically handle insertions and deletions. We will discuss the case for insertions and leave deletions as an exercise. Insertion may be bro-ken down into two cases. For both we must begin by reading the key to be inserted, character by character, and following the appropriate search path in the trie until:

1. We come to a trie node which has a vacant pointer in the char-acter position corresponding to the current character of the in-sertion key

OR

2. We come to an actual data record for a key different from the one which is being inserted.

The first case is illustrated by trying to insert the key COLLINS RT$ into the trie of Figure 11-26. We would follow the search path point-ers until we came to the trie node shared by all keys starting with CO. At this point, the L pointer is null. The insertion is completed by merely aiming the presently null L pointer to a data record for the key COLLINS RT$. The second case is illustrated by trying to insert the key COOPER PA$ into the trie of Figure 11-26. Here following the search path of the trie would eventually lead us to the data record for the key COOPER PJ$. The dynamic solution here is to get a new trie node, aim the P pointer presently leading to the data record for COO-PER PJ$ to this new trie node, and use the A and J pointers in the new trie node to lead us to data records for COOPER PA$ and COOPER

PJ$ respectively. Both the COLLINS RT$ and COOPER PA$ insertions are shown with the resulting trie of Figure 11-27.

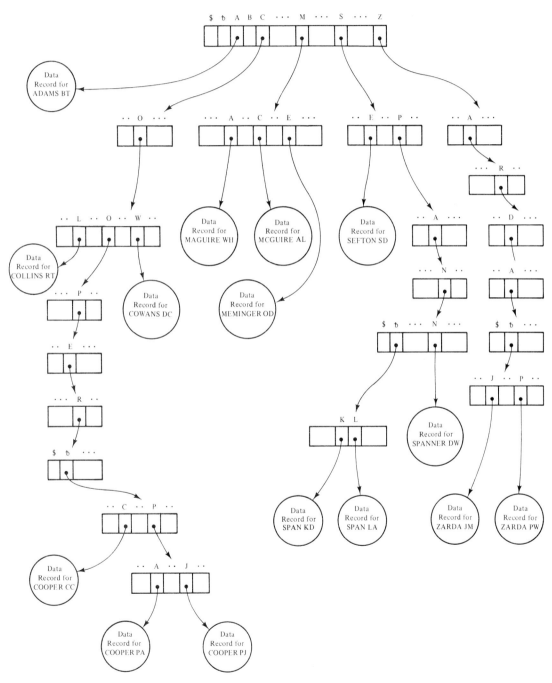

FIGURE 11-27 **Trie of Figure 11-26 after inserting COLLINS RTS and COOPER PAS.**

Program Design Considerations

The following Pascal program uses hashing to add records to a file and then search for them via the program's INSPECT menu option. The hierarchical structure of the program is given by the modular structure chart below.

Two aspects of the program need to be more fully explained since their implementation in Pascal will be system-dependent. First, the hashing function used in the program employs a random number generator which is designed to take advantage of integer overflow on a 16-bit machine. This would have to be suitably adjusted for a machine with a larger word size.

Second, the program uses the direct access file command SEEK(F,N) to bring the Nth record of the file F into the main memory buffer area for that file. Standard Pascal makes no provisions for direct access files; the SEEK statement is an extension provided in Oregon Software's Pascal-2 compiler. Appendix A gives a more complete description of direct access file commands available in various implementations of Pascal; local system reference manuals should also be consulted.

The program as it stands needs additional features to become a full-fledged file processing system. For instance, modules to change and delete records should be added. As an example of how a well-structured program may be easily modified to meet changing requirements, the final programming problem of this chapter asks you to extend the program along these lines.

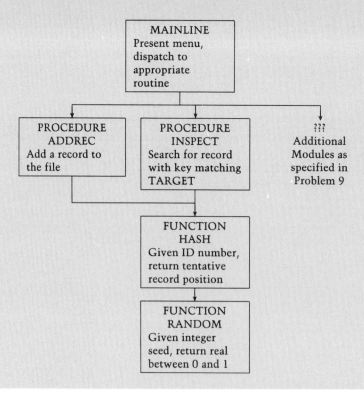

```pascal
PROGRAM HASHFILE(INPUT, OUTPUT, F);
 { Demonstrate hashing as file search technique }

  CONST
    RECORDSPACE = 200;

  TYPE
    BIGINTEGER = 0..65535;
    RECORDPOSITION = 1..RECORDSPACE;
    EMPLOYEERECORD =
      RECORD
        IDNO: BIGINTEGER;
        INITIALS: PACKED ARRAY [1..2] OF CHAR;
        LASTNAME: PACKED ARRAY [1..9] OF CHAR;
        SALARY: REAL
      END;

  VAR
    F: FILE OF EMPLOYEERECORD;
    COMMAND: CHAR;
    WORKINGCOPY: EMPLOYEERECORD;

  FUNCTION HASH(ID: BIGINTEGER): RECORDPOSITION;

    { HASHING FUNCTION - GIVEN ID, RETURN TENTATIVE RECORD POSITION }

    FUNCTION RANDOM(SEED: BIGINTEGER): REAL;

      { USE INTEGER OVERFLOW TO PRODUCE RANDOMIZED RESULTS }

      BEGIN { RANDOM }
        SEED := (SEED * 13077 + 6925) MOD 32768;
        RANDOM := SEED / 32768.0
      END { RANDOM } ;

  BEGIN
    HASH := TRUNC(RECORDSPACE * RANDOM(ID)) + 1
  END;
{ HASH }

PROCEDURE ADDREC;
 { Add record to the file. }

  VAR
    POS, ORIGPOS: RECORDPOSITION;
    EMPTYSLOT: BOOLEAN;
```

```
  BEGIN
    WRITE('Enter ID number-->');
    READLN(WORKINGCOPY.IDNO);
    WRITE('Enter initials-->');
    READLN(WORKINGCOPY.INITIALS);
    WRITE('Enter last name-->');
    READLN(WORKINGCOPY.LASTNAME);
    WRITE('Enter salary-->');
    READLN(WORKINGCOPY.SALARY);
    POS := HASH(WORKINGCOPY.IDNO);
    ORIGPOS := POS;
    EMPTYSLOT := FALSE;
    REPEAT
      SEEK(F, POS);
      IF F^.IDNO = 0 { FOUND EMPTY SLOT? } THEN
        BEGIN
        F^ := WORKINGCOPY;
        PUT(F);
        EMPTYSLOT := TRUE
        END
      ELSE
        POS := POS MOD RECORDSPACE + 1
    UNTIL (POS = ORIGPOS) OR EMPTYSLOT;
    IF EMPTYSLOT THEN
      WRITELN('Record has been added.')
    ELSE
        WRITELN('No room for record in file.')
  END;
{ ADDREC }

PROCEDURE INSPECT
  { Search for and display record }

  VAR
    POS, ORIGPOS, TARGET: RECORDPOSITION;
    FOUND: BOOLEAN;
```

```
    BEGIN
      WRITE('ID number to inspect-->');
      READLN(TARGET);
      POS := HASH(TARGET);
      ORIGPOS := POS;
      FOUND := FALSE;
      SEEK(F, POS);
      REPEAT
        WORKINGCOPY := F^;
        IF WORKINGCOPY.IDNO = TARGET { Found it? } THEN
          BEGIN
          FOUND := TRUE;
          WRITELN(WORKINGCOPY.IDNO);
          WRITELN(WORKINGCOPY.INITIALS, WORKINGCOPY.LASTNAME);
          WRITELN(WORKINGCOPY.SALARY):
          WRITELN
          END
        ELSE {ADVANCE THROUGH FILE }
          BEGIN
          POS := POS MOD RECORDSPACE + 1;
          SEEK(F, POS)
          END
      UNTIL (ORIGPOS = POS) OR FOUND OR (WORKINGCOPY.IDNO = 0);
      IF NOT FOUND THEN
        WRITELN('Record ', TARGET, 'cannot be found.')
    END;
{ INSPECT }

BEGIN { Main }
  RESET(F, 'RFILE2.DAT/SEEK'); {System dependent direct file access}
  REPEAT
    WRITE('Command - A)dd record, I)nspect, or Q)uit -->');
    READLN(COMMAND);
    CASE COMMAND OF
      'A':
        ADDREC;
      'I':
        INSPECT;
      'Q':
        BEGIN
        END;
      OTHERWISE
        WRITELN('Invalid command')
      END { Case }
  UNTIL COMMAND = 'Q';
  CLOSE(F)
END.
```

Sample run:

```
Command - A)dd record, I)nspect, or Q)uit -->A
Enter ID number-->1094
Enter initials-->BD
Enter last name-->CUMMINGS
Enter salary-->4.5
Record has been added.
Command -A)dd record, I)nspect, or Q)uit -->A
Enter ID number-->7783
Enter initials-->FG
Enter last name-->MINTON
Enter salary-->6.5
Record has been added.
Command - A)dd record, I)nspect, or Q)uit -->I
ID number to inspect>1094
    1094
BDCUMMINGS
 4.500000E+00

Command - A)dd record, I)nspect, or Q)uit -->I
ID number to inspect>7783
    7783
FGMINTON
 6.500000E+00

Command - A)dd record, I)nspect, or Q)uit -->Q

Ready
```

SUMMARY

The following table summarizes the efficiencies of the search strategies discussed in this chapter.

Summary of Search Efficiencies

Method	Efficiency
Sequential	Worst case : number of records Average: (number of records)/2
Binary	Worst case: $\log_2$ (number of records)
Linear hashing	Average successful: $(1/2)*(1 + 1/(1 - D))$ Average unsuccessful: $(1/2)*(1 + 1/(1 - D)^2)$ where density D = number of records/record space
Quadratic hashing	Average successful: $-(1/D)*\log_e(1 - D)$ Average unsuccessful: $1/(1 - D)$
Linked hashing	Average successful: $1 + D/2$ Average unsuccessful: D (where record space used in computation of D is that in primary hash area)
Indexed sequential (one directory level)	Worst case: number of index probes = size of index Number of file probes = number of records/size of index
Binary tree index	Worst case: Number of index probes proportional to $\log_2$ (number of records) *if* height-balanced
B-tree index of order N	Worst case requires $1 + \log_N$ ((number records + 1)/2) disk accesses for index
Trie index	Worst case requires as many disk accesses to search index as there are characters in target key

KEY TERMS

Key
Record
Field
Sequential search
Direct (random) access
Binary search
Volatile file
Binary tree search
Quantity dependent search
Density dependent search
Key-to-address transformation
Hashing function
Synonym
Collision
Randomized storage
Folding
Shift folding

Boundary folding
Character extraction
Linear hashing
Quadratic hashing
Linked hashing
Bucket hashing
Clustering
Track
Sector
Blocking
Index
Indexed sequential search technique
ISAM
Directory
Binary tree index
B-tree
Trie

EXERCISES

1. Suppose you know that the keys in a list are arranged in increasing order. How could the sequential search algorithm presented in this chapter be improved with this knowledge? Rewrite the Pascal procedure to incorporate this improvement.

2. Rewrite the binary search algorithm presented in this chapter with a list-splitting function other than halving. One possibility here would be to use an interpolation strategy which would examine the target's relative distance from the current low and high. Test run your program against a pure binary search and accumulate statistics to determine whether there is any significant difference between the two techniques.

3. Write a Pascal algorithm for the binary tree search.

4. Suppose you are given a list of data in increasing order of keys. Develop a Pascal algorithm which will load this list into an *optimal* binary search tree.

5. Write the algorithm to insert a key into a B-tree.

6. Discuss a key deletion strategy for B-trees. Write a procedure which implements your strategy.

7. Write an algorithm to insert a key and its data record into a trie.

8. Discuss a key deletion strategy for trie indexes. Write a procedure to implement your strategy.

9. Write procedures to insert a key into a list to be searched by

   a. Linear hashing
   b. Quadratic hashing
   c. Linked hashing
   d. Bucket hashing

10. Write procedures to search for a key via

   a. Quadratic hashing
   b. Bucket hashing

11. Devise strategies to delete keys from a list being maintained by each of the four hashing strategies in exercise (9). Write Pascal versions for each of these algorithms. Given your deletion strategy, what modifications would need to be made in the various search and insertion procedures of exercise (9) and (10)?

12. Develop a procedure to search a list via the ISAM method. Initially assume just one directory. Then alter the procedure so that it would work with one subdirectory.

13. Devise procedures to handle insertions into and deletions from a list maintained by the indexed sequential method. Do the strategies reflected by these procedures require any modifications in your answers to exercise (12)?

14. Carefully read your system reference material concerning the specifics of how disk file records are blocked. Then explain how this knowledge would influence your decisions in the construction of:

   a. An ISAM index structure
   b. A B-tree index structure
   c. A trie index structure
   d. A bucket hashing structure

15. What is a B-Tree of order n?
16. What is linked hashing?

PROGRAMMING PROBLEMS

1. The Wing-and-a-Prayer Airlines Company has the records of all its customers stored in the following form:

   - Last Name
   - First Name
   - Address
   - Arbitrarily long list of flights on which reservations have been booked

   Using a trie index, write a search and retrieval program that will allow input of a customer's last name (and, if necessary, the first name and address to resolve conflicts created by matching last names) and then output all flights on which that customer has booked reservations.

2. Assign relative record numbers to all records of the Fly-By-Night credit card company file and sort the records according to these numerical keys. Write a program based on the binary search procedure discussed in the text to quickly access any record whose relative record number is known. Create a separate directory of the relative record numbers and the customer's Social Security number, name, and address so that the binary search could also be based on the Social Security number, the name, or the address of the customer.

3. SuperScout Inc is a nationwide scouting service of college football talent to which the Bay Area Brawlers professional team subscribes. As the pool of college talent increases in size, SuperScout has found that its old record keeping system has deteriorated considerably in its ability to quickly locate the scouting record associated with a given player in its file. Rewrite their scouting record system using a trie to look up the record location of the data associated with a given player's name.

4. Using a large collection of randomly generated keys, write a series of programs which will test various hashing functions you develop. In particular, your programs should report statistics on the number of collisions generated by each hashing function. This information could be valuable in guiding future decisions about which hashing functions and techniques are most effective for your particular system.

5. Consider a student data record which consists of:

   - Student identification number
   - Student name
   - State of residence
   - Sex

   Choose an index structure to process a file of such records. Then write an **ACID** program to maintain such a file. ACID is a commonly used acronym meaning your program should have the capability to

■ Add a record
■ Change a record
■ Inspect a record
■ Delete a record

6. Suppose that data records for a phone book file consist of a key field, containing both name and address, and a field containing the phone number for that key. Devise an appropriate index for such a file. Then write a program which calls for input of:

   a. A complete key, or, if not available,
   b. As much of the initial portion of a key as the inquirer is able to provide.

   In the case of (a), your program should output the phone number corresponding to the unique key. In the case of (b), have your program output all keys (and their phone numbers) which match the initial portion which was provided.

7. Consider the following problem faced in the development of a compiler. The source program contains many character string symbols such as variable names, procedure names, etc. Each of these character string symbols has associated with it various attributes such as memory location, data type, etc. However, it would be too time-consuming and awkward for a compiler to actually manipulate character strings. Instead, each string should be identified with an integer which is viewed as an equivalent to the string for the purpose of compiler manipulation. In addition to serving as a compact equivalent form of a string symbol within the source program, this integer can also serve as a direct pointer into a table of attributes for that symbol. Devise such a transformation which associates a string with an integer which in turn serves as a pointer into a table of attributes. Test the structure(s) you develop by using them in a program which scans a source program written in a language like Pascal. You will in effect have written the symbol table modules for a compiler.

8. Hashing can be used effectively to solve the sparse matrix problem presented in Chapter 8. Use the row-column coordinates of a sparse matrix entry as arguments to a hashing function that determines that entry's position in a linear list. Apply this method in implementing one of the sparse matrix programming problems in Chapter 8.

9. The program discussed in the Program Design Considerations section of this chapter is presently only capable of adding records to the direct access file and then searching for these records by their integer identification number. Modify this program in any or all of the following ways.

   a. Alter the hashing function so that it accepts an alphabetic key.
   b. Add an error trap to the program which will catch an attempt to add a record for which a key already exists in the file.
   c. Add the capability to change a record that already exists in the file.
   d. Add the capability to delete a record exists in the file.

12

Data Structures and Data Management

"From each according to his ability, to each according
to his need."

KARL MARX (1818–1883)

12-1 Introductory Considerations

Any application of data structures has as a general goal the **management** of data within a computer system. **Computer system** in this context refers to the integrated whole consisting of central processing unit, main memory, and associated peripheral devices. In this concluding chapter, we shall not introduce any new data structures; rather, we will explore how combinations of the data structures we have already studied can be applied in two rather broad data management areas.

The first of these areas occurs typically in the writing of operating systems for multiuser machines and is called **garbage collection.** As used in this chapter, the term "garbage collection" means effectively recovering memory allocated to a user who no longer needs it. There is a hint of socialism to garbage collection algorithms. Each system user should get precisely what she or he needs at any given instant, but no more than is needed. As soon as a user's needs partially or completely vanish, the resources which were so generously doled out should be greedily reclaimed by the operating system in its big brother role.

The other general area we shall explore is more of a file-oriented problem known as **database management.** A **database** is essentially a collection of logically related files. Managing information in such a

365

collection is the subject of database management techniques which have arisen as solutions to the following types of problems:

1. In a large organization, each department maintains its own files. As a consequence, updates such as address changes frequently are made in one file but not in another. The data base solution is to store the data only once and give each department a pointer to that part of the data which it needs.
2. In an application such as a student records keeping system, the proverbial professional student takes more courses than allowed by the fixed length records which were thought to allow ample space when the system was originally designed. The database solution is to view records as dynamic entities.
3. A customer file is organized to search effectively by Social Security number. Unfortunately, a list of the names of all customers who live in California is needed. The database solution is to plan ahead and realize that the organization of a file may in fact require efficient access by more than just one **primary key**.

Such problems still arise far too often in data processing applications. The database approach is to consider not only the relationships between the records within a given file but also to broadly consider relationships between various files.

The problems of garbage collection and database management which are taken up in this chapter are merely meant to serve as illustrations of how data structures can be applied in the management of data. Definitive treatments of these problems are in fact the subject matter for advanced courses of study which have as their prerequisite a thorough knowledge of data structures. Our intention here therefore is not to present a comprehensive treatment of these problems but rather to give the curious reader a hint of what lies ahead.

12-2 Garbage Collection

We have briefly touched upon the problem of allocation and recovery of memory resources in Chapters 2 and 3. In Chapter 2, we developed procedures GETNODE and RETURNNODE for the purpose of allocating and recovering **fixed length** memory nodes to be used in list processing. In Chapter 3, we discussed a process called **compaction** which could be called upon at periodic intervals to relocate character strings in memory, thereby reorganizing memory in such a fashion that all free space is shifted to one large contiguous memory area. Prior to the compaction process, free space obtained from the deallocation of string storage is likely to be scattered in small **fragments** of various sizes throughout memory. Indeed, the problem solved by the compaction process is often termed the **fragmentation** problem.

The fragmentation problem occurs on a larger and more complicated scale in multiuser operating systems. Consider for instance the sequence of user requests portrayed in Figure 12-1. The complications presented by a multiuser environment will not allow this fragmentation problem to be solved by either of our two earlier strategies. The GETNODE/RETURNNODE scheme will fail because it deals with fixed-size nodes, and clearly user requests to an operating system will be for memory allocations of varying sizes. The compaction technique, on the other hand, would require a stoppage of user activity

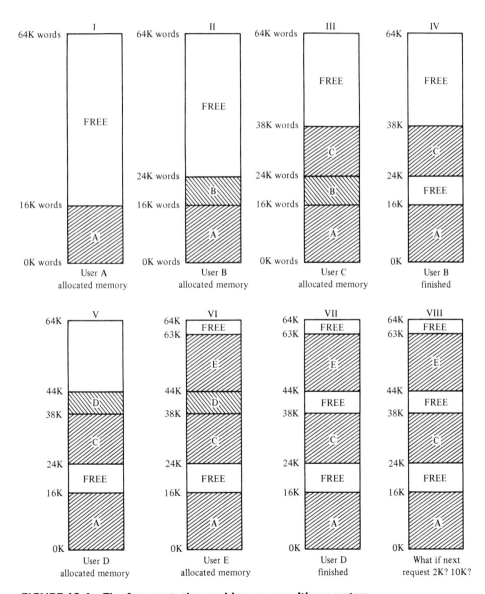

FIGURE 12-1 The fragmentation problem on a multiuser system.

while memory is reorganized in a way requiring large scale data movement. Hence compaction would not be dynamic enough to be used on the scale required by a multiuser operating system.

An initial approach to solving this problem is to generalize the algorithm behind the GETNODE/RETURNNODE procedures of Chapter 2, enabling them to handle variable length records. For instance, the free blocks pictured in the last memory snapshot of Figure 12-1 could be linked into an **available list** by allocating two words in each block to store the size of the block and a pointer to the next available block. (See Figure 12-2.) When a new user request is made of the list in Figure 12-2, the list could be searched for the first block whose size meets the request (or for the block whose size comes closest to meeting the request). Having determined the block to allocate to the user, it would be wise to check next whether or not the user actually requires the entire block. If not, it could be split—giving the user what is requested and keeping what remains of the block in the available block list. This strategy, applied to the available block list of Figure 12-2 for a request of 2K memory, yields the result displayed in Figure 12-3.

Unfortunately, this scheme will only lead to another problem when it comes time to garbage-collect the memory blocks no longer needed by users. Consider, for instance, what happens if the 2K memory block allocated in Figure 12-3 is returned by its user before any other changes are made in the available space structure. The new available space list now contains one additional 2K block as indicated in Figure 12-4.

Clearly what will happen as more and more of these relatively small blocks are returned is that the available list will have an inordinate number of very small blocks. This is not desirable because it will eventually make it impossible to fill the legitimate request of a user

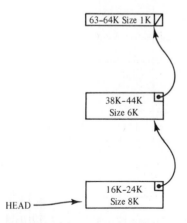

FIGURE 12-2   Available block list derived form snapshot VIII of Figure 12-1.

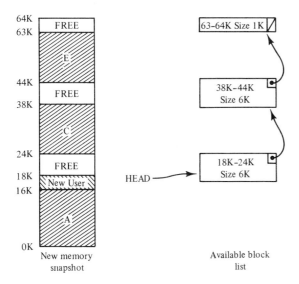

FIGURE 12-3 Honoring a 2K request from the available block list of Figure 12-2.

needing one large memory block. We will have small neighboring blocks, the sum of whose sizes may collectively surpass the total memory needed by the large request. However, their being partitioned into many small blocks instead of relatively few large blocks will make it impossible to fill the request. To remedy this problem, we must devise a method which will allow a block being returned to the

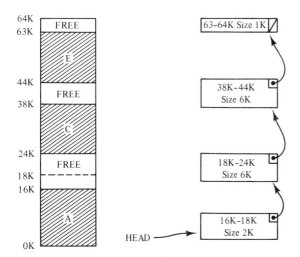

FIGURE 12-4 Available block list after returning the 2K block.

available list to be **coalesced** with any other block(s) in the list which are the physical neighbor(s) of the returning block.

Buddy Systems

A common method for doing this is to designate for each block one or two **buddy** blocks. A buddy must reside next to its corresponding block in memory. When a block is ready to be returned, we check the available space list for its buddy. If the buddy is also available, we coalesce the two before returning them as one block to available space. This is not quite as easy as it sounds, however. To determine the buddy of a given block, it will be necessary to impose certain restrictions upon block sizes and/or to store a fair amount of bookkeeping data in each block. We shall examine three buddy schemes:

1. Binary buddies
2. Fibonacci buddies
3. Boundary tag buddies.

They differ in the data structures used for their implementation. After stating the general algorithms in pseudocode we shall give a more detailed discussion of these data structures.

```
PROCEDURE ALLOCATE(S,P)

{ Given a request for a memory block of size S, return a pointer
  P to a memory block which meets the request with a minimum
  amount of waste }

CALL A SEARCH PROCEDURE TO SEARCH THE AVAILABLE BLOCK LIST(S)
        AND FIND A BLOCK WHICH SURPASSES THE SIZE REQUESTED WITH
        THE LEAST POSSIBLE AMOUNT OF EXCESS.

IF NO SUCH BLOCK CAN BE FOUND THEN
        CALL INSUFFICIENT-MEMORY

ELSE IF THE BLOCK FOUND CANNOT BE SPLIT INTO BUDDIES (ONE OF
        WHICH WOULD SATISFY THE SIZE REQUESTED) THEN
                RETURN THE POINTER FROM THE SEARCH PROCEDURE AS P

ELSE { The buddy system being used allows splitting }
        SPLIT THE BLOCK INTO TWO BUDDIES
        RETURN ONE BUDDY APPROPRIATELY TO AVAILABLE BLOCK  LIST(S)
        RETURN P AS THE POINTER TO THE OTHER BUDDY

ENDIF

RETURN
END ALLOCATE
```

The search procedure called upon to find a block in this procedure would be dependent upon the data structure used by a particular buddy system to store available blocks. Whether a block, once found, can be further split is determined by the restrictions the given buddy system imposes on block sizes.

A similar generic pseudocode algorithm to perform garbage collection on a returning memory block is presented below in recursive form. The recursion expresses the fact that, once a returning block has been coalesced with its buddy on the left or right, we have a larger block that may itself be a candidate for coalescing with another buddy.

```
PROCEDURE GARBAGECOLLECT(P,AVAIL)

{ Perform garbage collection on memory block being pointed to by
  P. AVAIL represents the available space structure used by the
  buddy system in question.}

{ Begin by recursively coalescing P with its buddies. }

CALL COALESCE(P,AVAIL)    { See procedure COALESCE below }

{ Upon return from COALESCE, P may well be pointing to a much
  larger block than it was before. The final step is now to
  attach this potentially larger block to the available space
  structure. }

CALL ATTACH(P,AVAIL)

RETURN
END GARBAGECOLLECT
```

PROCEDURE COALESCE(P,AVAIL)

{ This procedure will coalesce block pointed to by P with a
  buddy on its left or right. AVAIL represents the available
  block structure used by this particular buddy method }

{ The call to CHECK-BUDDIES below represents a call to a
  procedure which will determine whether buddies of P exist in
  the available space structure. If a left buddy of P is
  available, then a pointer to it is returned in LBUDDY.
  Otherwise LBUDDY is returned as NULL. A similar process
  is followed for the pointer RBUDDY. }

CALL CHECK-BUDDIES(P,AVAIL,LBUDDY,RBUDDY)

{ If both LBUDDY and RBUDDY come back as NULL, both of the
  conditional tests which follow will fail and an immediate
  return will result. Otherwise coalescing must occur on left
  and/or right. }

IF RBUDDY <> NULL THEN
     REMOVE RBUDDY FROM AVAIL STRUCTURE
     CHANGE APPROPRIATE FIELDS IN P TO COALESCE P WITH RBUDDY
        {Fields dependent upon buddy system being used }
     CALL COALESCE(P,AVAIL)
        {Recursively attempt to coalesce the new, larger P
         with its buddies }

ENDIF

IF LBUDDY <> NULL THEN
     REMOVE LBUDDY FROM AVAIL STRUCTURE
     CHANGE APPROPRIATE FIELDS IN LBUDDY TO COALESCE P & LBUDDY
        {Fields dependent upon buddy system being used }
     SET P TO LBUDDY { P points to new, larger block }
     CALL COALESCE(P,AVAIL)
        { Recursively attempt to coalesce the new, larger P
          with its buddies }
ENDIF

RETURN
END COALESCE

We will now explain in more detail the methodology of each of the
three previously cited buddy systems. From the generic procedures
ALLOCATE and GARBAGECOLLECT given above, it is clear that a
detailed exposition must describe both the data structure used to store
available blocks and the bookkeeping type of data that must be stored
within and about each memory block.

Binary Buddy System. The logic of this method requires that all blocks be of size 2^i for some i. Whenever a block is split, the resulting two buddies must be of equal size. That is, if a block of size 2^i is split, then the resulting buddies will each be of size $2^{(i-1)}$. As an example, let us suppose that we have 2^{16} ($= 64K$) words of memory to manage and that we wish to allocate no blocks smaller than 2^{10} ($= 1K$) words. Then, at any given time, we could potentially have free blocks of size 2 raised to the 10th, 11th, 12th, 13th, 14th, 15th, and 16th power. The available space structure in this case will consist of a **doubly linked list** of free blocks for each of the seven potential block sizes. Hence we would need head pointers:

```
AVAIL(1)--->Head of list for blocks of size 2¹⁰
AVAIL(2)--->Head of list for blocks of size 2¹¹
AVAIL(3)--->Head of list for blocks of size 2¹²
        .           .
        .           .
        .           .
AVAIL(7)--->Head of list for blocks of size 2¹⁶
```

Each block would need to contain the following bookkeeping information:

- A boolean flag to indicate whether or not it is free
- An integer field to store its size
- Left and right links used when it is a node in an AVAIL list

A graphic illustration of such a node is given in Figure 12-5.

Initially, all 2^{16} words of memory would be viewed as one free block, that is, AVAIL(7) would point to the beginning of memory and all other AVAIL pointers would be NULL. Now let us suppose that a sequence of user requests came in the order given below.

    a. Request for memory block of size 2^{14}
    b. Request for memory block of size 2^{13}
    c. Request for memory block of size 2^{14}
    d. Request for memory block of size 2^{14}
    e. Block from (a) no longer needed
    f. Block from (b) no longer needed

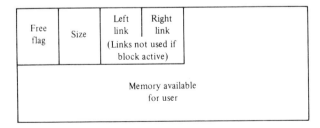

FIGURE 12-5 Bookkeeping information in block for binary buddy system.

The dynamic processing of these requests can best be described pictorially. In Figure 12-6, we have used tree diagrams to represent the splitting and coalescing that would occur as (a) through (f) are processed. Memory addresses in this figure are given as $0, 1, 2, \ldots$, 62, 63 where i represents the beginning of the $(i + 1)$st 1K memory block (of which there are 64 in all).

Three comments are needed to explain more fully the actions highlighted in Figure 12-6. First, the point of coalescing is that one available block of size $2N$ is always preferred to two available blocks of size N. The whole is greater than the sum of its parts. This is why, in returning the block from (b) in Figure 12-6, we coalesce two 8K blocks into a 16K block and then immediately take advantage of an available 16K left buddy to coalesce further into a 32K block.

Second, the binary splitting scheme means that, when a block is to be returned, the address of its buddy can be immediately determined. For instance, the block of size 2^{14} which begins at address 0 (relative to 1K blocks) has a right buddy of the same size which begins at address 16 (relative to 1K blocks). The location of this block's buddy is purely

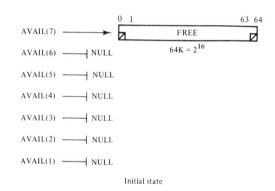

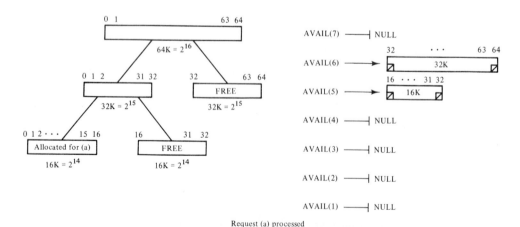

FIGURE 12-6 Processing requests using the binary buddy system.

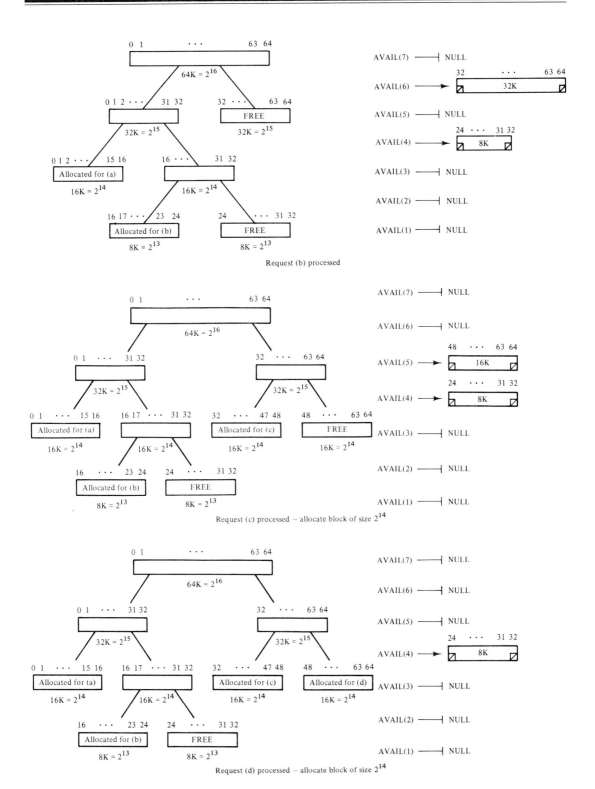

FIGURE 12-6 Continued.

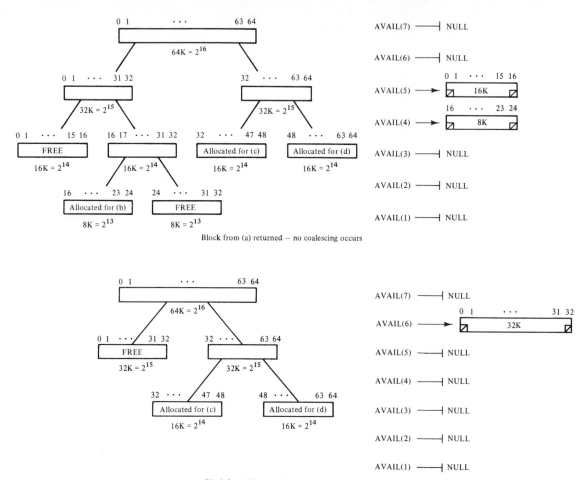

Block from (a) returned — no coalescing occurs

Block from (b) returned — coalescing occurs

FIGURE 12-6 Continued.

a function of the block's own size and location. In absolute terms, a block of size 2^i with starting address $n \times 2^i$ will have a right buddy with starting address $(n + 1) \times 2^i$ if n is even and a left buddy starting at address $(n - 1) \times 2^i$ if n is odd. This means that, as a block is being returned, a simple computation allows us to find its buddy, whose free flag would then be checked to determine whether or not coalescing is possible. Notice that, in a binary buddy system, a given block has either a left or a right buddy but not both.

Third, if the buddy of the block to be returned is free, the doubly linked nature of the available block lists becomes crucial. This is because we have essentially jumped into the middle of an available space list in accessing the buddy of the block to be returned. Without the double linking, we would not have the back pointer necessary to remove this buddy from the available list of which it is presently a part.

Of course, once a returning block has been coalesced with its buddy, we now have a new returning block which may recursively undergo further coalescing as indicated in our generic COALESCE procedure.

Fibonacci Buddy Systems. Let us begin a consideration of Fibonacci systems by analyzing the binary buddy system. Contradictory as this may seem, the rationale is that we must define the relationships between block sizes that must exist in a buddy system of this type. Examining the sequence of possible block sizes in the binary system,

$$2^1, 2^2, 2^3, \ldots, 2^{10}, 2^{11}, \ldots$$

we notice that every member of the sequence except the first is the result of adding the previous member to itself. Since any block size (except the smallest possible) may result from coalescing two smaller blocks, it becomes clear that any sequence of possible block sizes for a buddy system of this variety must have the property that any size element within the sequence is the sum of two preceding members of the sequence. In the binary buddy system, this sum is always obtained by adding the size of the immediately prior member of the sequence to itself. However, the binary system is a special case; all that is really required is that any size can be represented as the sum of two smaller sizes.

Perhaps the most famous sequence of numbers having this property is the Fibonacci sequence. The ith member of the Fibonacci sequence can be recursively defined as:

$$F_1 = 1$$
$$F_2 = 1$$
$$F_i = F_{(i-1)} + F_{(i-2)} \text{ for } i > 2$$

Hence, the initial members of the Fibonacci sequence are:

$$1, 1, 2, 3, 5, 8, 13, 21, 34, \ldots$$

Suppose, for instance, that we were managing 21K memory and were faced with the following requests for storage:

    a. Request for 7K
    b. Request for 7K
    c. Request for 2K
    d. 7K from (b) no longer needed
    e. 2K from (c) no longer needed
    f. 7K from (a) no longer needed

Figure 12-7 illustrates the allocation, deallocation, and resulting coalescing that would occur as these requests were processed; circled digits are used to indicate left buddy counts.

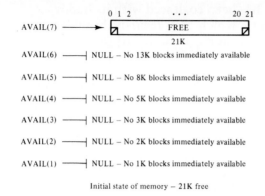

Initial state of memory – 21K free

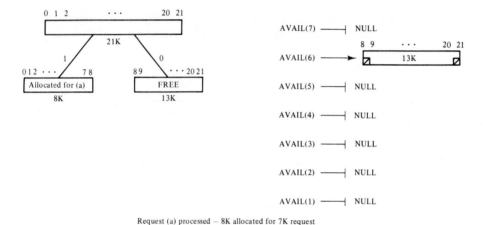

Request (a) processed – 8K allocated for 7K request

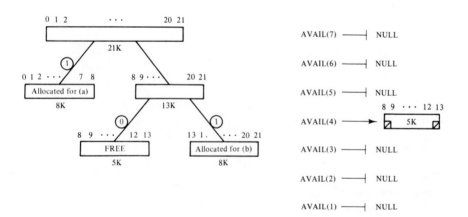

Request (b) processed – 8K allocated for 7K request

FIGURE 12-7   Processing requests using the Fibonacci buddy system. Circled digits represent left buddy counts.

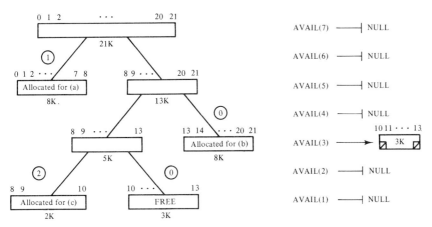

Request (c) processed – 2K allocated for 2K request

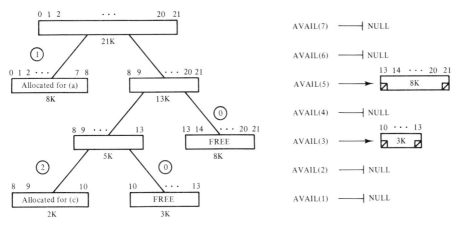

Request (d) processed – no coalescing

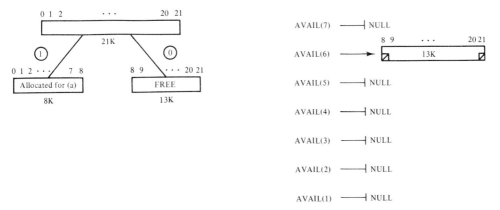

Request (e) processed – coalescing occurs up to 13K block

FIGURE 12-7 Continued.

Request (f) processed – coalescing occurs – one free 21K block results

FIGURE 12-7 Continued.

Naturally, some additional overhead is required when the Fibonacci buddy system is used. First, depending upon the implementation scheme, it may be necessary to store the Fibonacci numbers themselves in an array to allow quick access to data necessary to allocate, split, and coalesce blocks. The alternative would be to recompute the sequence each time it is needed. Second, unlike the binary system, it is not clear from a block's size and location whether it is the left buddy or right buddy of another block. Consequently, it becomes necessary to store some additional bookkeeping data within each block, in the form of a **left buddy count** field as indicated in Figure 12-8. The left buddy count maintains a record of how deep a given block is nested as the left buddy of other blocks. In Figure 12-7, the left buddy count is indicated by the circled digit appearing above each block. The algorithm for maintaining this left buddy count involves these steps:

1. As a block is split, the resulting left buddy has its left buddy count field increased by one. The resulting right buddy has its left buddy count field set to zero.
2. As coalescing occurs, the left buddy must always have its left buddy count field decreased by one.

Given the increase in overhead involved in the Fibonacci system, it is certainly a valid question to ask whether or not it offers any advantage over the binary system. Its primary advantage is that it allows for a greater variety of possible block sizes in a given amount of memory than its binary counterpart. For instance, in 64K words of memory the binary system would allow block sizes of 1K, 2K, 4K, 8K, 16K, 32K, and 64K—7 possibilities in all. The Fibonacci method would yield potential block sizes of 1K, 2K, 3K, 5K, 8K, 13K, 21K, 34K, and 55K—9 sizes in all. Clearly a greater variety of sizes will allow us to allocate memory in a fashion which minimizes the difference between what the user actually needs and what our block sizes force us to give.

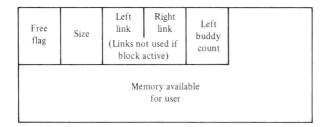

FIGURE 12-8 Bookkeeping information in a block for the Fibonacci buddy system.

In fact, if one uses a more generalized **kth Fibonacci sequence** defined by:

$$F_j = 1 \text{ for } j = 1, 2, \ldots, k$$
$$F_j = F_{(j-1)} + F_{(j-k)}$$

then it can be readily seen that, the larger k becomes, the finer our partitioning of block sizes will be. (Notice that by this definition, the binary buddy system is in fact generated by the 1st Fibonacci sequence). Of course, with each increase in k comes a corresponding increase in the overhead of bookkeeping information that must be balanced against the greater selection of block sizes. The reader is referred to J. A. Hinds' discussion for a more theoretic discussion of which k may be appropriate to choose in a given situation.*

Boundary Tag Buddies.   Both the binary and Fibonacci systems have the disadvantage of not allowing an arbitrary selection of block sizes thereby forcing the waste of some memory each time a user's request does not precisely match one of the specified block sizes. The boundary tag method overcomes this drawback but only at the expense of requiring even more bookkeeping data than either of the other methods.

The reason why the binary and Fibonacci schemes limit us to a finite number of block sizes and splitting possibilities is that, without such a limitation, it would be impossible to determine where a block's buddy begins. For instance, suppose that we were using the Fibonacci buddy system and were about to return a block of size 13K whose left buddy count field was found to be zero. Because of the limitations on the sizes into which a block may be split under the Fibonacci method, we know that this block must have a left buddy of size 8K with which it could possibly coalesce. Using the starting address of the block to be

---

returned and the fact that its left buddy has size 8K, the starting address of the left buddy can be obtained.

The problem of determining the size and starting location of a returning block's buddy is less complicated if the returning buddy has a right buddy instead of a left buddy. In this situation, the starting location and size of the returning block would tell us the starting address of the right buddy. Then, provided we have stored the bookkeeping information for that right buddy precisely at its starting location, the size field and free flag are immediately available for our inspection. The distinction between finding the size and starting location of left and right buddies in the binary and Fibonacci systems is highlighted in Figure 12-9.

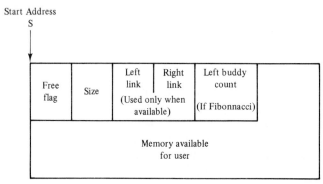

The bookkeeping information for this block's right buddy
can be accessed at memory address (S + size)

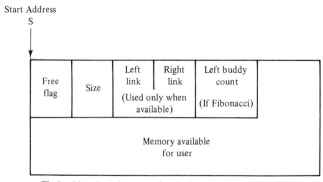

The bookkeeping information for this block's left buddy can be

accessed at memory address $\begin{cases} (S - Size) \text{ if binary system} \\ (S - \text{Fibonacci number preceding size}) \\ \quad \text{if Fibonacci system} \end{cases}$

FIGURE 12-9 Top: Determining size and start address of a right Fibonacci or binary buddy. Bottom: Determining size and start address of a left Fibonacci or binary buddy.

Figure 12-9 should make it apparent that, if we were willing to store duplicate copies of a block's size and free flag at its right boundary as well as its left boundary, then the problem of determining the starting address of a left buddy would not require a priori knowledge of what its size must be. Its size could be found by checking the bookkeeping information along the right boundary. The effect of this concept is that sizes can now be chosen arbitrarily to specifically meet a user's request. No longer would it be necessary to allocate 13K to meet an 11K request because the available choices of block sizes demanded it. This is the primary motivation behind the boundary tag buddy system. A block and the bookkeeping information within it would now appear as in Figure 12-10.

As is always the case, the boundary tag technique has advantages and disadvantages which must be carefully considered before choosing it to use in a particular context. The major advantage, of course is that it allows a user's request to be granted *precisely*, with no excess memory being allocated and therefore wasted. The logic of the method also implies that a given block is not a left or right buddy *per se*. Rather any block except one starting or ending at a memory boundary has *both* a left and a right buddy with which it could coalesce. The primary disadvantages of the boundary tag method are the additional bookkeeping information that must be stored and maintained within each block, and the fact that the available space structure now must be stored as one long doubly linked list instead of as a sequence of doubly linked lists for each of the respective block sizes allowed. This latter point means that, in determining whether a user's request can be met, the boundary tag method will require sequentially searching a single

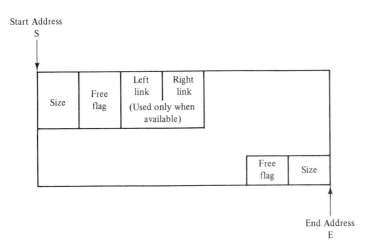

FIGURE 12-10 **Block and bookkeeping information for the boundary tag method.**

available space list — clearly a slower process than is required for either the binary or Fibonacci schemes. At this point, you are encouraged to trace through the actions diagrammed in Figure 12-11, highlighting the allocation and deallocation of memory as the following results are processed:

a. Initially all memory, 64K, is free
b. User requests 7K
c. User requests 9K
d. User requests 4K
e. Memory requested in (c) no longer needed
f. Memory requested in (b) no longer needed
g. Memory requested in (d) no longer needed

The three memory management methods discussed in this section provide an excellent illustration of the application of data structures at the operating system level. Notice in particular that all three methods require the use of one or more doubly linked lists to store available memory blocks. The elegance of this relatively simple data structure allows us to delete a given block from the middle of an available list without having to traverse the entire list to find a back pointer as we would be forced to do with a singly linked list. In the next section we shall consider how a broad knowledge of data structures may be applied in the management of files.

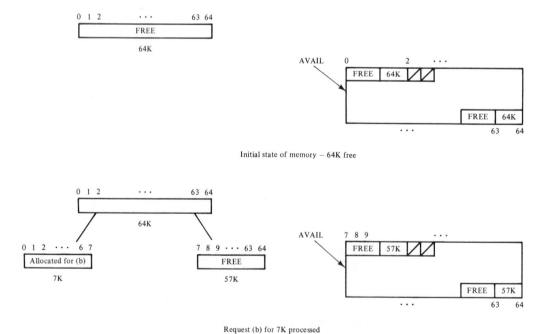

FIGURE 12-11 Processing requests using the boundary tag buddy system.

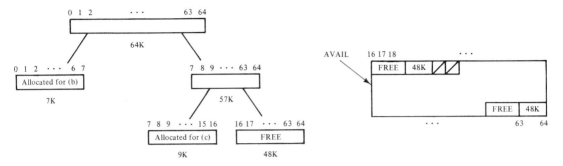

Request (c) for 9K processed

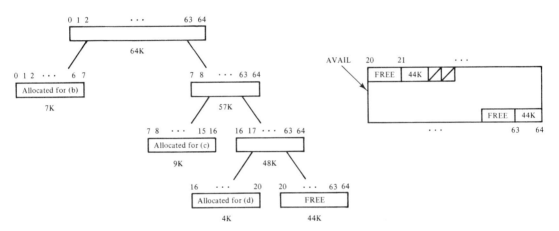

Request (d) for 4K processed

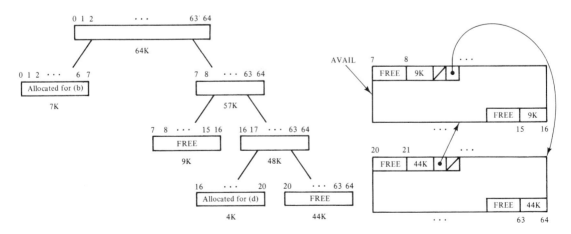

(e) Processed – no coalescing

FIGURE 12-11 Continued.

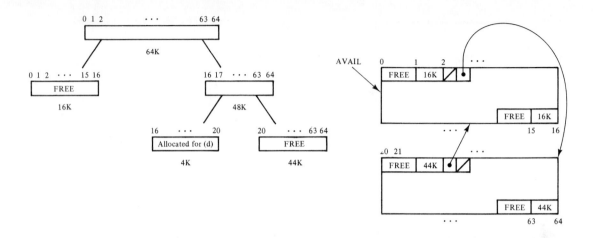

(f) Processed — returning block coalesces with right buddy

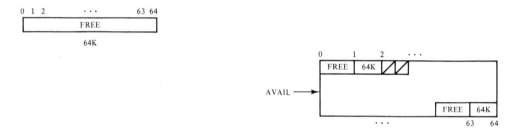

(g) Processed — coalescing occurs on both sides

FIGURE 12-11 Continued.

12-3 Database Management

In general, we may think of a file as a collection of parallel lists. For example, Figure 12-12 pictures the file of employee records for a hypothetical company. The vertical lines in this figure divide the file into separate lists, or **fields**, while the horizontal lines divide the file into separate occurrences of complete employee **records**.

The Data Duplication Problem

A **database** may be defined as a collection of **related** files. As an easy example of a database and the advantages it offers in comparison to normal file processing, consider the following **data duplication** problem. Suppose that our hypothetical company decides that, for privacy considerations, the payroll department should not have access to an employee's EDUCATIONAL-LEVEL or SPOUSE-NAME. Similarly, the

EMPLOYEE-NAME	ADDRESS	SALARY-RATE	TAX-CATEGORY	EDUCATIONAL-LEVEL	SPOUSE-NAME
Cowans, P.	N. 4th St.	9.34	A	12	Joyce
Jones, D.	E. 9th St.	8.45	B	16	Bert
Hiller, B.	S. 8th St.	7.09	A	14	Grace
Miller, S.	W. 3rd St.	6.45	C	12	Ernie
Smith, W.	E. 1st St.	9.12	A	16	Bertha

FIGURE 12-12 *Employee record file for hypothetical company.*

company's Committee on Planning Social Events should not have access to an employee's SALARY-RATE or TAX-CATEGORY. The non-database approach to this problem would be to create two separate unrelated files—one containing the information needed by payroll and the other containing the data needed by the social planning committee. However, note that this approach to the problem leads to the storage of the EMPLOYEE-NAME and ADDRESS fields in two separate files. The problems involved with such data duplication go well beyond mere considerations of the amount of disk space that is consumed in storing certain data items more than once. Just as serious is the question of accurately updating information which is stored in such a duplicate fashion. For instance, if an employee should move, the change of address would have to be made in two separate places and potentially by two separate individuals. Clearly there is the danger that this approach may result in one employee living at two different addresses—one for payroll and one for social planning.

The database approach to solving this data duplication problem would be to divide the file presented in Figure 12-12 into three *related* files as indicated in Figure 12-13. Note that, in Figure 12-13, three

Accounting Department Access Only		Common Access		Social Planing Access Only	
SALARY-RATE	TAX-CATEGORY	EMPLOYEE-NAME	ADDRESS	EDUCATIONAL-LEVEL	SPOUSE-NAME
9.34	A	Cowans, P.	N. 4th St.	12	Joyce
8.45	B	Jones, D.	E. 9th St.	16	Bert
7.09	A	Hiller, B.	S. 8th St.	14	Grace
6.45	C	Miller, S.	W. 3rd St.	12	Ernie
9.12	A	Smith, W.	E. 1st St.	16	Bertha

FIGURE 12-13 **Employee database derived from Figure 12-12.**

files replace the single file which appeared in Figure 12-12. One file, containing the EMPLOYEE-NAME and ADDRESS fields, is open to common access. A second file, containing the SALARY-RATE and TAX-CATEGORY fields, is open to payroll access only. A third file, containing the fields needed by social planning, is only open to access by those users. The relationship between records in the files of this database is extremely straightforward; records in the same relative position in different files are related to each other. Hence, a social planning committee member could use a search routine to find an employee's name in the common access file and then access the same position in the file limited to social planning use to determine the employee's EDUCATIONAL-LEVEL and SPOUSE-NAME. Note that any information updates, such as address changes, would have to be made only once and would be immediately known to all users entitled to that information.

The Variable Length Records Problem

Let us now consider a situation that arises in systems responsible for maintaining student records at a university. Each student's name must be related to a variable number of courses that the student has taken. If we attempt to store all the data in one file, we are faced with the variable length records that appear in Figure 12-14.

Clearly, the jagged edge traced on the right of the data in Figure 12-14 presents some data storage problems. How much storage do we allocate for each student's record to insure that we do not run out of course space for the proverbial professional student? At the same time, how do we hold wasted course space to a minimum? The answers to these two questions obviously conflict with each other. The professional student may require 100 course fields, but such an allocation will be a tremendous waste for most of our students.

A database perspective, on the other hand, would allow us to view this data as two separate files—a student name file and a course record file—with relationships existing between the records in each file. Here the relationship between student name records and course records would be **one-to-many** as opposed to the **one-to-one** type of relationship that existed in our previous example of an employee database. That is, each student is related to many course records, whereas

STUDENT	COURSE1	COURSE2	COURSE3	COURSE4	COURSE5	COURSE6
Egghead, I.	BOT422 A	MAT444 B	PHI309 A	CPS110 B		
Kopf, D.	MAT111 C	ENG201 D				
Smart, B.	PHI723 B	PSY388 A	ZOO910 A	CPS310 B	ENG222 B	MAT311 A

FIGURE 12-14 Variable length student records.

each employee was related to only one payroll record and one social planning record. The added complexity of the one-to-many relationship would require pointers to maintain the relationship between student and course files, as indicated in Figure 12-15. Essentially, this figure shows the courses taken by each student as a linked list with the head pointer being stored in the student name file.

The one-to-many relationship exemplified between the student and course files in the student database system of Figure 12-15 is an integral consideration in nearly all database management problems. In fact, as we shall see, more complex database relationships are usually implemented by decomposing them into several one-to-many relationships. A convenient way of representing such a one-to-many relationship was described by D. Kroehnke* and is illustrated for our student records database in Figure 12-16. In this figure, the double arrows pointing at the course file indicate that there may be more than one course record for each student record. The single arrow pointing towards the student file indicates that there is only one student record associated with each course record.

You may also have noticed that a one-to-many database relationship is really just a special example of the general tree that we have already studied in Chapters 6 and 7. To see this, compare the essentially equivalent information stored in the database of Figure 12-15 with the general tree of Figure 12-17.

	Student Name File			Course Record File		
	STUDENT	LINK		COURSE	GRADE	LINK
1	Egghead, I.	1	1	BOT422	A	4
2	Kopf, D.	2	2	MAT111	C	5
3	Smart, B.	3	3	PHI723	B	6
			4	MAT444	B	8
			5	ENG201	D	NULL
			6	PSY388	A	7
			7	ZOO910	A	9
			8	PHI309	A	10
			9	CPS310	B	11
			10	CPS110	B	NULL
			11	ENG222	B	12
			12	MAT311	A	NULL

FIGURE 12-15 *Student records database derived from Figure 12-14.*

*Kroehnke, D. 1977. *Database Processing*. Chicago: Science Research Associates.

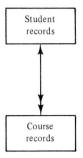

FIGURE 12-16   Notation for a one-to-many relationship.

Secondary Key Processing

As another example of how a one-to-many relationship may arise in database processing, consider the file of student records which appears in Figure 12-18. In this example, we have what seems to be a rather ordinary fixed record length file in which each student record consists of:

1. A student identification number
2. Student name
3. Sex of the student
4. Class of the student—FReshman, SOphomore, JUnior, or SEnior

Assume that the file is organized so that we may use one of the search procedures described in Chapter 11 to quickly locate a student using his or her identification number as a key.

The organization of the student records file in Figure 12-18 is adequate if all user requests are of the form "Find the data for the student who has ID number XXXXX". However, users are notorious for coming up with requests which the organization of the file was not designed to handle. Examples of such requests for the file of Figure 12-18 would include:

1. Find all female students
2. Find all sophomore students
3. Find all students who are male AND juniors
4. Find all students who are female OR seniors

These requests represent attempts to access the records in the file by a **non-unique secondary key.** That is, each of the preceding requests uses a field (or fields) other than the usual **primary key** of IDNUMBER as the key by which records are to be accessed. Moreover, the access being requested is via secondary key fields for which many records may share the same value, so these secondary key fields are termed *non-unique.* The non-unique nature of these key fields means that

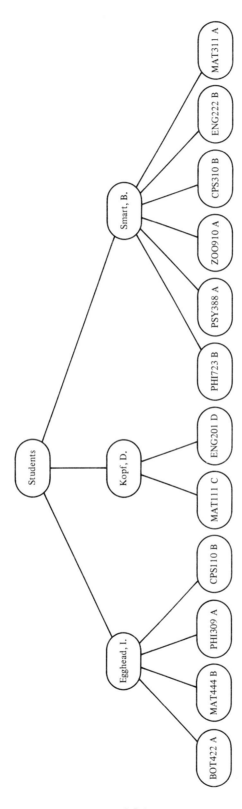

FIGURE 12-17 General tree representation of Figure 12-15.

	IDNUMBER	NAME	SEX	CLASS
1	34762	JONES,T.	M	JU
2	37938	GARNER,D.	M	SE
3	12387	EVANS,K.	F	FR
4	27127	HOYT,L.	F	SO
5	93791	HAYES,P.	M	JU
6	35261	MURPHY,G.	F	SO
7	59795	ZEMAN,G.	F	SO
8	23719	MILLER,B.	M	FR
9	64272	DAVIS,K.	M	SE
10	48262	AARON,H.	M	FR
11	58799	RUTH,B.	F	JU
12	97271	GEHRIG,L.	M	SO
13	59143	COSELL,H.	F	FR
14	87927	BURKE,J.	F	SE
15	28098	SMITH,P.	M	JU
16	47819	WOLF,B.	F	SE

FIGURE 12-18   Student records organized by IDNUMBER field.

each secondary key in effect defines a one-to-many relationship between key value and the records in the file. For instance, the one-to-many relationships existing in the file of Figure 12-18 are highlighted in Figure 12-19.

Implementing One-to-many Relationships in Database Systems

Given the organization of the file in Figure 12-18, the only strategy that can be used to handle secondary key requests is to plod sequentially through the file, checking each record to see if it meets the criteria specified. However, in databases with large numbers of records, this sequential plodding approach may well be too slow to be practical. Users want their requests handled immediately; forcing them to wait minutes for a response from the system is a good way to become unemployed. The key to effective database management is to:

1. Plan ahead: foresee the types of secondary key requests that are likely to be made for a given database
2. Then build the one-to-many relationships represented by these secondary keys into the structure of the files that make up the database

We will concentrate on the second of these two steps. This is not to say that the first step is less important. However, the analysis of what a user wants from a system is not *per se* a data structures consideration and is more appropriately studied in systems analysis. The second question of how to build one-to-many relationships into the files that compose a database is most commonly approached using one of two strategies: multilink files or inverted files.

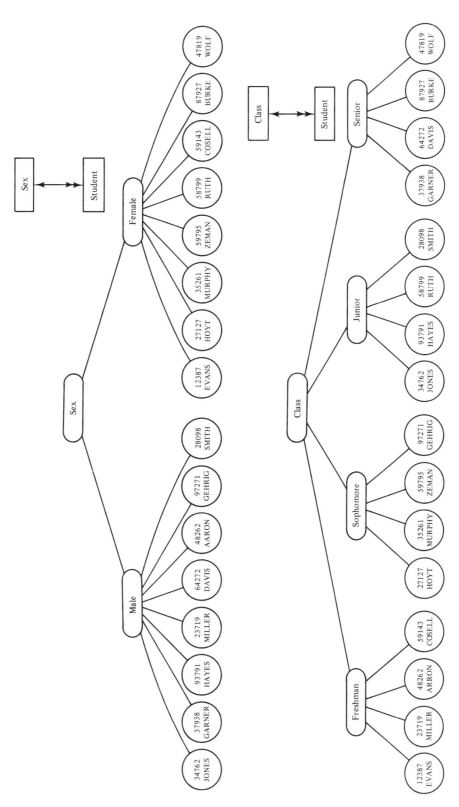

FIGURE 12-19 One-to-many relationships in the records shown in Figure 12-18.

393

In the World of Applications...

An article entitled *R[elational]DBMS: Is Now the Time?*, which appeared in the March 1984 issue of *Datamation*, gives an excellent profile of the impact that relational database management systems are about to have. According to Michael Stonebreaker of Relational Technologies, Inc., "Relational database is an answer. Now what is the question?" Perhaps the question is how to design user-oriented data management systems that hide the complexities of the data structures behind the scenes from those users who have absolutely no desire to deal with them. This idea of *data abstraction* has been the goal of the relational model since it was first put forth by Ted Codd of IBM more than 10 years ago–to allow the user to view the data as a simple table of records divided into fields.

What kept the relational model from having anything more than a theoretical impact until the 80's? The answer lies in the fact that the simplicity of the data organization as seen by the naive user must be matched by a detailed complexity in the underlying data structures when the system is designed. This complexity means that relational systems have tended to be slow—particularly on small computers. However, Peter Tierney of Relational Technologies sees much progress being made now, and more in the future. The article quotes Tierney as saying, "There are no technical barriers [to increasing speed]. We know we can increase the speed by a factor of two in the next six months."

Multilink Files. The **multilink file** strategy requires that, for each secondary key field by which we anticipate accessing the file, a link field must be established in the record structure of the file. This link field is then used to link together all those records that share a given value for the secondary key in question. Essentially this means that each secondary key gives rise to multiple linked lists—one list for each value that the key may take on. These linked lists weave their way through the database, allowing users to access efficiently only those records in which they are interested. There is no need to sift through and discard records that have a secondary key value other than the one being sought, because such records are not included in the linked list that is being followed through the file. A multilink implementation for the student database of Figures 12-18 and 12-19 is given in Figure 12-20. In database terminology, a multilink implementation strategy is also called a **chained pointer** database. (Refer back to Figure 1-1 on page 3.)

Some comments are in order concerning the relative advantages and disadvantages of a multilink file, considering what we already know about its underlying data structure, the linked list. First, we have extremely efficient sequential processing of those records satisfying a single secondary key value; we can just traverse the corresponding linked list. The number of file accesses required is the number of records which satisfy that particular key value.

	ID NUMBER	NAME	SEX	SEXLINK	CLASS	CLASSLINK
1	34762	JONES,T.	M	2	JU	5
2	37938	GARNER,D.	M	5	SE	9
3	12387	EVANS,K.	F	4	FR	8
4	27127	HOYT,L.	F	6	SO	6
5	93791	HAYES,P.	M	8	JU	11
6	35261	MURPHY,G.	F	7	SO	7
7	59795	ZEMAN,G.	F	11	SO	12
8	23719	MILLER,B.	M	9	FR	10
9	64272	DAVIS,K.	M	10	SE	14
10	48262	AARON,H.	M	12	FR	13
11	58799	RUTH,B.	F	13	JU	15
12	97271	GEHRIG,L.	M	15	SO	NULL
13	59143	COSELL,H.	F	14	FR	NULL
14	87927	BURKE,J.	F	16	SE	16
15	28098	SMITH,P.	M	NULL	JU	NULL
16	47819	WOLF,B.	F	NULL	SE	NULL

MALE-HEAD-POINTER = 1　　SO-HEAD-POINTER = 4
FEMALE-HEAD-POINTER = 3　JU-HEAD-POINTER = 1
FR-HEAD-POINTER = 3　　　SE-HEAD-POINTER = 2

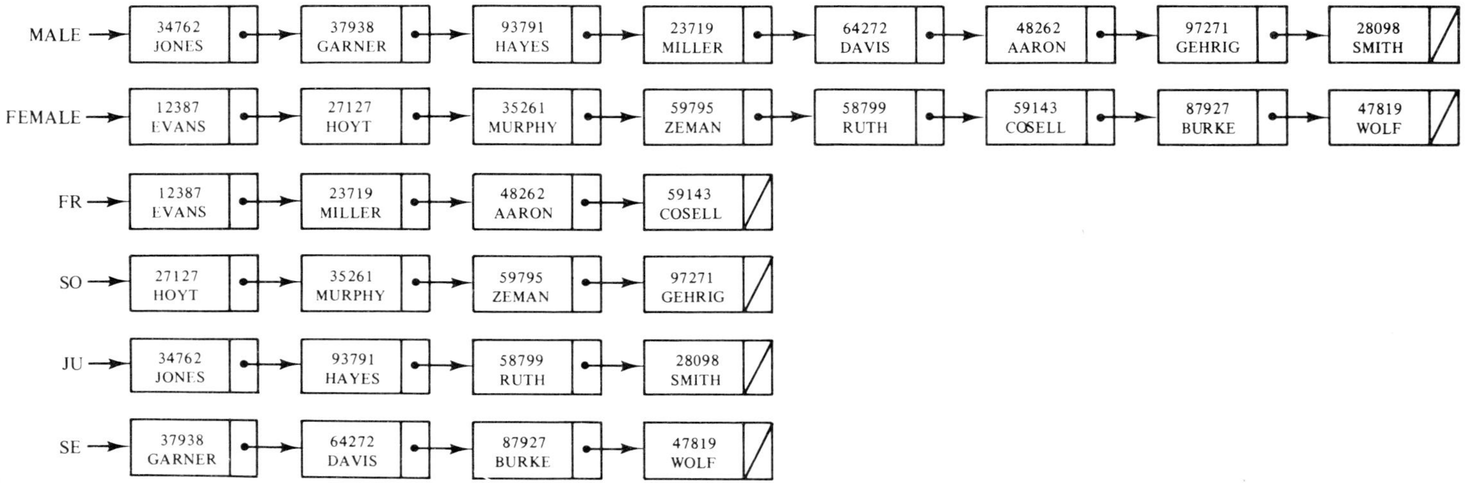

FIGURE 12-20　Top: physical representation of multilink student database from Figure 12-18. Bottom: logical representation of multilink student database.

Second, although in the example of Figure 12-20 we have not maintained the multiple lists in any particular order, such ordering (e.g., alphabetically by student name) would not be difficult to maintain given the ease and efficiency of insertions and deletions in a linked list. One consideration, however, would be whether to maintain the various one-to-many relationships as doubly linked lists. The motivation for this is that a deletion would usually require accessing the record to be deleted by its primary key and then removing it from all the one-to-many relationships in which it participates. If each one-to-many relationship is a linked list, this means that we would be deleting from the middle of a linked list without having traversed the entire list up to that point. This is precisely the situation in which a doubly linked list gives us the backward pointer we need without requiring the list traversal needed for a singly linked list.

Third, changes in a secondary key value for a record are merely a matter of a deletion from one list followed by an insertion into another list. Hence, a demotion from junior to sophomore for HAYES, P. in Figure 12-20, though trying from a personal viewpoint, would be quite trivial for our multilink database.

The preceding advantages of a multilink file are, as with any data structure, offset by disadvantages that must be carefully considered for each application. The first of these disadvantages is that the storage of links within the record itself makes it quite difficult to add a new one-to-many relationship after the database has been built. This would be the case, for instance, if we maintained a STATE-OF-RESIDENCE field in the student database of Figure 12-20 but had not built the corresponding 50 linked lists for states into the original database. If the administration of the university belatedly decided that they now wanted to process students by STATE-OF-RESIDENCE, the database would have to be rebuilt from scratch instead of being dynamically altered to reflect this new one-to-many relationship. In practice, since users frequently make such after-the-fact requests, this disadvantage can often be very serious, again emphasizing the need for careful prior planning in database design.

A second disadvantage of the multilink method involves the way in which queries involving boolean combinations of secondary key values must be processed. For instance, suppose the data base of Figure 12-20 were to be queried for all students who were FEMALE OR SENIORS. Any algorithm to process this request in a multilist structure would require a complete traversal of both the FEMALE *and* the SENIOR lists. The records of those students who are *both* FEMALE *and* SENIOR would actually be accessed twice via such an algorithm. In the worst possible case, in which the N members of the SENIOR class coincided with the N FEMALE students at our hypothetical university, we would actually require $2 \times N$ disk accesses to determine this N member set.

The two disadvantages cited above should be kept in mind as we begin the following discussion of inverted files. Inverted file implementations of one-to-many relationships are able to circumvent both of these drawbacks at the expense of using a structure which is slightly more difficult to maintain.

Inverted Files. The essential idea behind inverted files is to *not* place in the data records themselves the bookkeeping information necessary for efficient secondary key processing. Remember that the placement of such bookkeeping information in the data records of a multilink file led to both of the inefficiencies which were cited for that method. Instead, the inverted file method locates this data-about-data in small files which are maintained apart from the actual data records. These small **inverted files** are, in effect, indexes which contain the relative record positions of those records sharing identical values for a given secondary key. For instance, inverted files for the database of Figure 12-18 and 12-19 are given in Figure 12-21.

Given a secondary key query, we would have to search the appropriate inverted file for that particular secondary key value. Once found, we have at our disposal the list of all positions in the actual data file where we will find records satisfying the query. Hence, inverted files invert a problem such as searching for all students who are JUNIORS into the problem of searching a much smaller file for the key value JU and then simply accessing all of the records we find associated with that key value. Searching the inverted file for a particular key value is highly efficient because the file contains only relative record positions and no real data. Hence the inverted files themselves

INVERTED FILE FOR SEX FIELD

VALUE	POSITIONS OF RECORDS HAVING THIS VALUE
M	1 2 5 8 9 10 12 15
F	3 4 6 7 11 13 14 16

INVERTED FILE FOR CLASS FIELD

VALUE	POSITIONS OF RECORDS HAVING THIS VALUE
FR	3 8 10 13
SO	4 6 7 12
JU	1 5 11 15
SE	2 9 14 16

FIGURE 12-21 Inverted files for database of Figure 12-18.

are small, allowing large portions to reside in main memory at any given time. Moreover, the lists of relative record positions pictured in Figure 12-21 could be stored by any of the list storage techniques that we have discussed in earlier chapters, such as dense linear arrays, linked lists, or trees. In choosing what type of list implementation to use to maintain the relative record positions, one would consider such factors as the frequency of insertions and deletions and whether or not it was important to traverse the records satisfying a query in a particular order (for example, alphabetically by student name).

The inverted file approach resolves both of the inefficiencies mentioned in our previous discussion of multilink files. First, should we wish to add an inverted file for a many-to-one relationship after a database is already built, it requires just one sequential pass through the actual data records to build the appropriate inverted file. Since the data records themselves contain no bookkeeping information, they do not need to be reconstructed, as they would in the multilink implementation. Second, the problem of accessing certain records twice for some boolean queries of the database is alleviated by the fact that we need only look at the inverted files to find the appropriate records. Moreover, the determination occurs at main memory speeds since large portions of the inverted files may be brought into main memory for efficient processing.

The disadvantages of the inverted file approach lie primarily in the added complexity it introduces. Each inverted file adds another file to the overall database. This file may be another physical file, in which case there are the problems typically associated with file input/output, such as finding available buffer space in main memory and minimizing the number of times the file must be opened and closed. On the other hand, if the inverted file merely represents a logical remapping of a small portion of the same file which stores the data records, then extreme care must be taken to insure that we do not confuse bookkeeping data and actual data. Moreover, inverted files are more difficult to maintain than their multilink counterparts. Consider, for instance, the problem of deleting a record whose primary key equals a specified input. To do this, we must:

1. Search the actual data file for the primary key
2. Determine the values this record takes on for various secondary key fields
3. Remember these values and the record position of the actual data record
4. For each inverted file, search for the key value and record position in (3) and appropriately delete this record position from the list of record positions.

Although this process could occur at high speed if search strategies and list representation techniques are wisely chosen, it is still considerably more complex than deletion from multilink lists.

More Complex Database Relationships and Their Implementation

Two relationships in addition to the one-to-many relationship are recognized in common database terminology: the **simple network** and the **complex network**. The term *network* in this context is only loosely affiliated with the concept of networks covered in Chapter 9. In this context a simple network is nothing more than a restricted graph consisting of several one-to-many relationships, and a complex network is essentially equivalent to a full-blown, directed graph as discussed in Chapter 9. In terms of implementation, it turns out that both simple and complex networks are decomposed into multiple one-to-many relationships. These one-to-many relationships are then implemented by one of the techniques that we have already discussed. The process of decomposing a graph into a **spanning forest** of trees (that is, one-to-many relationships) was covered in 9-3 and should be reviewed at this time.

As an example of a simple network relationship, let us again consider a university record keeping system in which course records are classified both by their level (FReshman, SOphomore, JUnior, or SEnior) and by the department in which they are offered. In the figures which follow, we will assume that the university has only three departments, designated as departments 1, 2, and 3, and eight courses, designated as A, B, C, D, E, F, G, and H respectively. Then the two one-to-many relationships in this database—those of course level to course and department to course—are represented in Figure 12-22. Notice that the structure which emerges in Figure 12-22 is a graph which is not quite a tree. Rather each course node has, in a sense, two parents—one course level parent and one department parent.

Formally, we would say that a simple network is a collection of several one-to-many relationships whose resulting representation as a graph is *acyclic* in the sense that this term was defined in Chapter 9. Working more intuitively from the picture presented in Figure 12-22, we could say that a simple network is a near-tree in which a child may

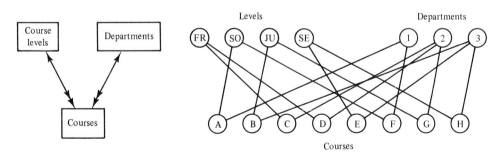

FIGURE 12-22   Simple network relationship among course levels, departments, and courses.

have multiple parents but only one parent of any given type. This intuitive definition should make it immediately evident how the simple network of Figure 12-22 could be implemented as a spanning forest of trees. Such a spanning forest is given in Figure 12-23. Notice that, in the spanning forest of Figure 12-23, each course node actually appears twice. It should be clear from what we have already said about avoiding data duplication that these course nodes would not actually be stored in two separate physical locations. For instance, the fact that course B appears as subordinate to both course level JU and department 3 in Figure 12-23 merely means that both the course level JU node and the department 3 node have logical pointers to the actual physical location of the data for course B.

In contrast to a simple network, a **complex network** in database terminology corresponds to what we have previously described as a (possibly cyclic) directed graph in Chapter 9. For instance, consider the relationship that would exist between students and current course offerings in our university records keeping system. Each student is enrolled in one or more courses; hence we have a one-to-many relationship running from student records to current course offering records. Conversely, each current offering is being taken by many students, so there is also a one-to-many relationship running from current course offering records to student records. A situation such as this, where we have one-to-many relationships running in both directions, is called a **many-to-many relationship,** or **complex network.** An example of a complex network for a university offering courses A, B, and C and with students SMITH, JONES, MURRAY, BACH, and LEWIS is given in Figure 12-24. The double-headed arrows running in both directions in this figure indicate that we have one-to-many relationships running in both directions.

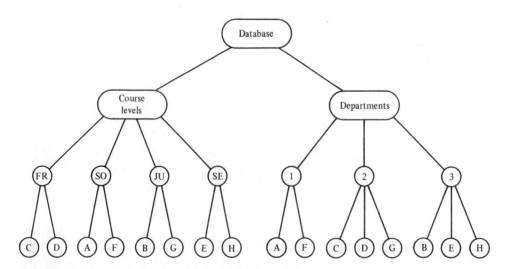

FIGURE 12-23   Spanning forest of trees for Figure 12-22.

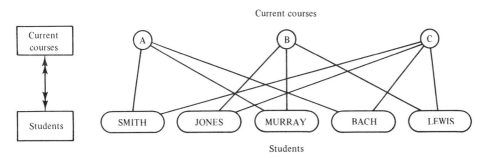

FIGURE 12-24   Complex network of current course offerings and students.

We note that the complex network of Figure 12-24 could in fact be represented by the adjacency matrix (see Chapter 9) of Figure 12-25. However, the current trend in database terminology is generally to avoid any direct reference to the notion of adjacency matrices. Instead, the database approach to representing a complex network such as that appearing in Figure 12-24 is to first decompose it into its spanning forest of trees. One such decomposition for the complex network of Figure 12-24 is given in Figure 12-26. Once decomposed, the spanning forest of trees is essentially nothing more than a collection of one-to-many relationships, each of which may be represented via the techniques already discussed in this chapter.

Two remarks are in order concerning the spanning forest in Figure 12-26. The first is merely a reiteration of what was said about spanning forests of simple networks. That is, one should not assume, because a particular course offering or student name appears at more than one node in a spanning forest, that the course or student in question is actually stored more than once in the database. The spanning forest only represents the logical arrangement of data in the database, not the physical arrangement. Second, we would note that, although the database environment avoids direct mention and use of adjacency matrices such as that appearing in Figure 12-25, the actual implementation of a spanning forest of trees via multilink or inverted file techniques is in fact functionally equivalent to a sparse matrix representation of an adjacency matrix which allows direct access by both row and column. Hence, in many ways, database management is really just an application of the data structures we have already studied hidden under a veneer of slightly different terminology.

	SMITH	JONES	MURRAY	BACH	LEWIS
A	1	0	1	1	0
B	0	1	1	0	1
C	1	1	0	1	1

FIGURE 12-25   Adjacency matrix for complex network of Figure 12-24.

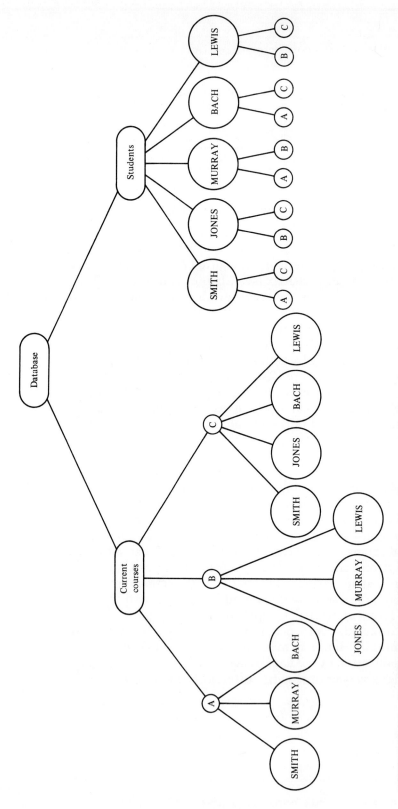

FIGURE 12-26   Spanning forest of trees for complex network of Figure 12-24.

12-4 Database Management Systems

A **database management system** (hereafter referred to as a **DBMS**) is essentially software which establishes and maintains the relationships between the records and files in a database and allows users to make queries of the database based on the relationships that are represented therein. Up to this point, the emphasis of this chapter has been to describe how the authors of a DBMS might go about implementing the various relationships within a database. However, the current trends in database technology indicate that a diminishing percentage of the people involved with databases will actually be writing such systems. This is because of the emergence of a large number of general purpose DBMS's which will actually build the implementation of a database for the user, provided the user can accurately describe the database in the language accepted by the DBMS. This means that we are now beginning to see three groups of people involved with the development and usage of general purpose DBMS's:

1. The authors of the system. This group is actually involved in the development of algorithms to build and maintain the multilink and/or inverted files that underlie the entire database.
2. The naive end users of the system. This group simply makes queries of the system and then watches it all happen with little understanding of why it is happening.
3. The sophisticated end users of the system. Perhaps a better term to describe this group would be *database designers*. They are concerned with communicating to the general purpose DBMS a description of their database so that the DBMS can build the necessary structures to maintain the system.

It is to this last group that our remarks in the closing portion of this chapter are directed. The database designer must thoroughly understand the structures upon which a general purpose DBMS is based. She or he need not be concerned with the actual implementation of such structures since the DBMS will do that automatically. Instead, based upon a knowledge of the capabilities and limitations of the structures used by the DBMS, the database designer can effectively use the DBMS to build and maintain a variety of databases.

Three primary database models exist—the hierarchical model, the CODASYL model, and the relational model. In the remainder of this chapter we intend to give a brief description of how a database designer could use each of these models to represent the types of database relationships described in the previous section: the one-to-many relationship, the simple network, and the complex network. We stress that our discussion is not meant to be a full treatment of any of the three models; there are complete books written about each of them cited in the bibliography at the end of the chapter. It is rather our intent to provide an introduction which could serve as the basis for further study about more sophisticated database design.

The Hierarchical Model

The hierarchical model was the earliest of the three, so, as one might expect, it is also the most limited of the three. Its best-known implementation is in the IMS (Information Management System) marketed by IBM. The basic building block made available to the database designer using the hierarchical model is the tree, that is, the one-to-many relationship. This means that the language of the particular hierarchical DBMS being used allows the designer to specify the one-to-many relationships that are wanted in the database. Automatically, the necessary links or inverted files are built and maintained by the DBMS; this is no longer a concern of the designer.

However, should the designer using the hierarchical model wish to build more complex database relationships such as simple and complex networks into the database, it is the responsibility of the designer to decompose such relationships into several one-to-many relationships, just as we did in Figures 12-23 and 12-26. The designer is additionally able to specify which of the multiple occurrences of an item in such a decomposition are to be physical occurrences and which are to be logical pointers.

The crucial limitation of the hierarchical model is that, as a model, it is too tightly tied to the implementation schemes for databases. That is, since DBMSs generally use multilink files and inverted files, which can only directly represent one-to-many relationships, the hierarchical model forces its designer to work solely in terms of the one-to-many relationship. In a sense, the only real independence between the hierarchical model and its underlying implementation is that it is inconsequential to the model whether multilink or inverted files are used.

The CODASYL Model

Developed under the auspices of the Data Base Task Group of the *Conference on Data Systems Languages*, the CODASYL model offers the designer a slightly more versatile modeling tool. The CODASYL model uses the notion of a **set** to describe one-to-many and simple network relationships. CODASYL sets are analagous to trees as we have described them. Each set has an **owner** (the parent) and **members** (the children). By declaring sets in the language of the CODSYL model, the designer is able to specify the one-to-many relationships that the DBMS should build and maintain. For instance, with declarations of the form:

```
SET IS COURSELEVEL-COURSE
   OWNER IS COURSELEVEL
   MEMBER IS COURSE
```

and

```
SET IS DEPT-COURSE
   OWNER IS DEPT
   MEMBER IS COURSE
```

the designer could establish the simple network relationship given in Figure 12-22. Notice that, conceptually, the CODASYL model and the hierarchical model are very similar. That is, though different terminology is used, a CODASYL set is still essentially a hierarchical tree. The primary conceptual difference between the two is that the CODASYL model does not force the designer to think of members as existing twice within the database (either physically or logically) when a simple network relationship is specified. In graphic terms, it could be said that the hierarchical model forces the designer to specify a simple network in terms of its spanning forest, that is, in terms of Figure 12-23. The CODASYL model, on the other hand, allows the designer who is defining a simple network to work directly from a mental image of what a simple network really is—not a spanning forest but rather what appears in Figure 12-22.

Like the hierarchical model, the CODASYL model gives no means for directly defining a complex network. However, the method that the CODASYL model designer uses to implement such a network is somewhat different from the decomposition into trees forced upon the designer using the hierarchical model. Instead, the CODASYL model allows the designer to define (sometimes artificially) **intersection records** to act as a pseudolink between the records in a many-to-many relationship. As an example of intersection records, let us consider how the CODASYL designer might define the complex network of Figure 12-24. He or she would look for some data item that the current course records and the student records share in respective one-to-many relationships. Such an item could perhaps be TIME. For courses, TIME would mean the time(s) at which sections of the course are offered. For student records, TIME would mean the time(s) at which a student is in class. Notice that, by this definition of TIME, it is essentially an item which is shared in a one-to-many relationship by both course offering records and student records. Hence it could be used to go from a given student to the many courses being taken by the student and conversely from a given course to the many students in that course. This method of defining a complex network in terms of an intersection record is highlighted in Figure 12-27. Again, the multiple occurrences of certain items in Figure 12-27 represent logical occurrences only.

Course Offering Records   Intersection Records   Student Records

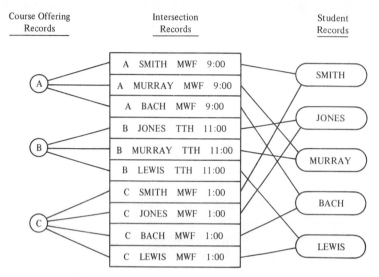

FIGURE 12-27   Using intersection records to define a complex network.

The Relational Model

First formulated by E. F. Codd,* the relational model is a radical departure from the hierarchical and CODASYL models in that it is *completely* abstracted form the underlying implementation scheme. The designer using the relational model describes the database in terms of **relations.** A relation is simply a table of rows and columns. To a certain degree, a relation looks like what has traditionally been called a file. Each column corresponds to a field name and each row to a record. Figure 12-28 gives a relation in which each row represents a student record, and the columns represent NAME, SEX, and CLASS respectively.

Initially, it may seem contradictory that something as simple as a relation allowing no variable length rows could in fact lead to the most general, flexible database model yet developed, but this is indeed the case. The power of the method comes from the fact that the database designer is free to define virtually any relation which is needed to specify a particular relationship within a database. Moreover, Codd has supplied a collection of general purpose operations upon relations (called the **relational algebra** and **relational calculus**) which allows the designer to build a variety of new relations from existing old ones. As an example of how a relation can be used to reflect a one-to-many relationship in a database, consider the STUDENT-COURSE relation appearing in Figure 12-29. This is essentially the relational model

---

*Codd, E. F. 1970. A relational model of data for large shared data banks. *Communications of the Association for Computing Machinery* 13: (6).

NAME	SEX	CLASS
Egghead, I.	M	FR
Kopf, D.	F	SO
Smart, B.	M	SO

FIGURE 12-28 Student record relation.

embodiment of the one-to-many relationship which initially appears in Figure 12-14. Codd's relational algebra would then allow us to draw from the relation of Figure 12-29 new relations which, for instance, could isolate all the rows of the relation belonging to one particular student. Note that the multiple occurrences of NAMEs within the relation of Figure 12-29 are really of no concern at the database design level. The occurrences represent logical occurrences only; their physical placement in the database is an implementation concern.

As examples of how relations may be used to define simple and complex networks, Figure 12-30 shows relations for the simple and complex networks that originally appeared in Figures 12-22 and 12-24 respectively. Note again the difference between the relations of Figure 12-30 and their implementations. As relations consisting of rows and columns, they unambiguously contain all of the necessary information to describe a simple or complex network. Consequently, they are ideal from the database design perspective. Underneath the elegant simplicity of describing a database in terms of relations must

NAME	COURSE
Egghead, I.	BOT422 A
Egghead, I.	MAT444 B
Egghead, I.	PHI309 A
Egghead, I.	CPS110 B
Kopf, D.	MAT111 C
Kopf, D.	ENG201 D
Smart, B.	PHI723 B
Smart, B.	PSY388 A
Smart, B.	ZOO910 A
Smart, B.	CPS310 B
Smart, B.	ENG222 B
Smart, B.	MAT311 A

FIGURE 12-29 Relation for one-to-many STUDENT-to-COURSE relationship of Figure 12-14.

COURSE
LEVEL	COURSE	DEPT
FR	C	2
FR	D	2
SO	A	1
SO	F	1
JU	B	3
JU	G	2
SE	E	3
SE	E	3

COURSE	STUDENT
A	SMITH
A	MURRAY
A	BACH
B	JONES
B	MURRAY
B	LEWIS
C	SMITH
C	JONES
C	BACH
C	LEWIS

**FIGURE 12-30   Top: relation for the simple network of Figure 12-22.
Bottom: relation for the complex network of Figure 12-24.**

still lie an implementation scheme which relies on a collection of data structure techniques to insure that the designer's perception of rows and columns can in fact be represented with tolerable efficiency.

The relational model would seem to represent the ultimate in a DBMS, completely unshackling the designer from any considerations or limitations derived from the underlying implementation scheme. This evolution toward complete generality is not a trivial matter. Codd first proposed his model in 1970; only recently have practical relational DBMS's become available in the marketplace. There seems to be little doubt, however, that is is the DBMS of the future.

SUMMARY

In this chapter we have attempted to give an overview of how a general knowledge of data structures may be applied in two specific areas—memory management and database management. The problem of memory management is typically encountered by an operating system that must allocate and then reclaim or **garbage collect** appropriately sized blocks of memory among its many users. Three memory management techniques were discussed: the binary buddy system, the Fibonacci buddy system, and the boundary tag buddy system. The database management problem more typically applies to huge amounts of data stored in various related files. Three general database models exist—the hierarchical model, the CODASYL model, and the relational model. Underlying the conceptual framework of the model, there are two primary implementation techniques: multilink or inverted files. Most commercially available database management systems use one or potentially a combination of these techniques.

KEY TERMS

Garbage collection
Database management
Primary key
Secondary key
Compaction
Fragmentation
Binary buddy system
Fibonacci buddy system
Boundary tag buddy system
Kth Fibonacci sequence
Field
Record
Data duplication problem
Variable length records problem
One-to-many relationship

Multilink files
Chained pointer database
Inverted files
Simple network
Complex network
Spanning forest
Acyclic graph
DBMS
Database designer
Hierarchical model
CODASYL model
Relational model
Intersection records
Relations

GENERAL DBMS BIBLIOGRAPHY

Atre, S. 1980. *Database: structured techniques.* New York: Wiley.

Auerbach Publishers. 1981. *Practical database management.* Reston, VA: Reston.

Date, C. J. 1974. *An introduction to database systems.* Reading, MA: Addison-Wesley.

Ellzey, Roy S. 1982. *Data structures for computer information systems.* Chicago: Science Research Associates.

Flores, Ivan. 1977. *Data structures and management.* Englewood Cliffs, NJ: Prentice-Hall.

Johnson, Leroy, and Rodney Cooper. 1981. *File techniques for database organization in COBOL.* Englewood Cliffs, NJ: Prentice-Hall.

Katzan, Harry. 1975. *Computer data management and database technology.* New York: Van Nostrand, Reinhold.

Martin, James. 1975. *Computer database organization.* Englewood Cliffs, NJ: Prentice-Hall.

————. 1976. *Principles of database management.* Englewood Cliffs, NJ: Prentice-Hall.

Sprowles, Clay R. 1976. *Management data bases.* Santa Barbara, CA: Wiley/Hamilton.

EXERCISES

1. Write Pascal algorithms ALLOCATE and GARBAGECOLLECT specifically for the binary buddy system.
2. Write Pascal algorithms ALLOCATE and GARBAGECOLLECT specifically for the Fibonacci buddy system.
3. Write Pascal algorithms ALLOCATE and GARBAGECOLLECT specifically for the boundary buddy system.
4. In processing secondary keys via the multilink and inverted file methods, it is possible to not store the actual data for each secondary key in each record. That is, the possible secondary key values could be stored once in a separate table instead of being stored repeatedly in each individual record. Discuss the pros and cons of doing this.
5. What are the advantages of double linking in multilink files?
6. Discuss the relative advantages and disadvantages of multilink files vis-a-vis inverted files.
7. Develop a general Pascal algorithm for record deletion in an inverted file database.
8. Discuss the relative advantages and disadvantages of the three buddy systems discussed in this chapter.
9. What sort of memory management algorithms and structures could be used to implement the NEW and DISPOSE procedures for

arbitrary length records in a language which (like Pascal) offers dynamic memory management?

10. In the boundary tag buddy system, one long doubly linked list of available blocks is maintained. When a user request is received, this list must be searched for a suitable block. A question arises as to whether this search should continue until the first block which meets the user's request is encountered (a **first fit** strategy) or until it is certain that the block to be allocated for the user is the one that comes closest to meeting the request (a **best fit** strategy). Discuss the relative advantages and disadvantages of the first fit and best fit methods.

11. For each of the following diagrams, first determine whether it represents a simple or a complex network. Then decompose it into a spanning forest of trees.

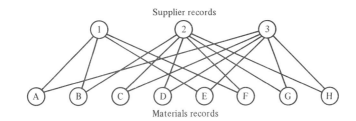

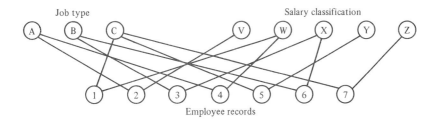

PROGRAMMING PROBLEMS

1. Passenger records for the Wing-and-a-Prayer Airlines Company consist of

>Last name
>First name
>Street address
>State of residence
>ZIP code
>Phone number
>First class or tourist class preference
>Smoker or nonsmoker seating preference

A passenger's last name is the primary key to his or her record, with first name and street address used when necessary to guarantee uniqueness. State of residence, first class or tourist class preference, and smoker or nonsmoker seating preference are to be regarded as secondary keys. In addition, each passenger possesses arbitrarily many:

    a. Records of flights taken during the past year, with the mileage for each of these flights, and

    b. Records of future flights on which reservations have been booked.

Design a database organization and then write a program that will allow a Wing-and-a-Prayer agent to:

    a. Add a passenger record to the database

    b. Add a future flight reservation record for a specified passenger

    c. Cancel a future flight reservation for a specified passenger

    d. Change a passenger record or future flight reservation for a specified passenger

    e. Inspect all future flight reservations for a specified passenger

    f. Determine whether a specified passenger qualifies for a "frequent flyer" discount; that is, whether she or he has flown more than 3000 miles during the past year

    g. Purge from the database records all flights that occurred more than one year ago

    h. Search for passengers having a specified secondary key value (such as all passengers living in Utah)

    i. Allow secondary key searches to be built out of boolean combinations of secondary key values (such as all passengers who prefer to travel first class AND in a non-smoking section)

2. Simulate a multiuser operating system environment for each of the three buddy systems discussed in this chapter by declaring a large array and randomly generating user requests for pieces of this array. Have your program accumulate statistics as to how each of the three methods performs on percentage of requests that could be met, average amount of memory not in use, average amount of wasted memory (that is, given to a user in excess of the amount requested), average time to process a request, etc.

3. Suppose that a student record at a university contains fields for student identification number, student name, sex, class, and state of residence. Sex, class, and state of residence are to be regarded as secondary keys. Additionally, each student possesses arbitrarily many grade records, each consisting of the name of the course taken and the grade received. Design a database organization and then write a program which will allow a user to:

    a. Add a student record to the database

    b. Add a course record for a specified student

c. Change a student record or course record for a specified student
d. Delete a specified student from the database, along with all of his or her course records.
e. Inspect the record of a given student
f. Search for those students having a specified secondary key value
g. Make secondary key searches using boolean combinations of secondary key values

A

Direct Access Files in Pascal

The original standard for Pascal developed by Kathleen Jensen and Niklaus Wirth made no provision for direct (random) access files. From the perspective of learning structured programming concepts, this is not a serious omission. From the perspective of applying data structure concepts in the real world, however, it is a major omission. This is because most programs with a database orientation involve storing large amounts of data in files and then accessing it by a search strategy which guarantees a quick response time. Without direct access, a tedious sequential search is the only method possible. Hence, what has emerged is that most implementors of Pascal compilers have developed their own procedures for directly accessing records which reside in a disk file.

A general picture which applies in all of these various implementations is given in Figure A-1. A record from a direct access file may be acted upon (for instance, updated) only when it has been fetched as the currently available record in the main memory buffer associated with that file. (Actually, applications programmers may think of the currently available record and the file's buffer as

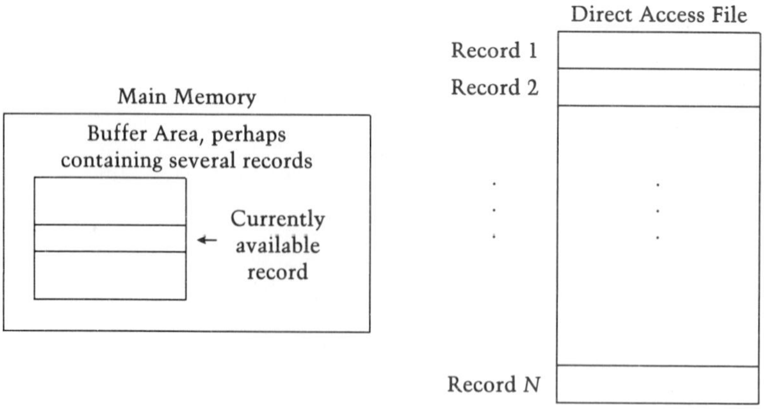

FIGURE A-1   General Direct Access File Set-Up.

coinciding, though this is an oversimplification that can affect the efficiency of the search technique being considered. See Chapter 11 for a discussion of this point.) Hence the problem of programming in Pascal with direct access files becomes one of being able to:

1. Fetch in the Ith record from the file as the currently available record in main memory (where I is an arbitrary positive integer less than or equal to the number of records in the file),
2. Update the currently available record in main memory,
3. Write the currently available record in memory to the Ith position in the file.

Step (2) above may typically be accomplished by using standard Pascal's up-arrow notation for a file variable. For example,

```
F^. IDNUMBER := 4918;
```

will assign the value 4918 to the IDNUMBER field of the record currently available in main memory. Note that this assignment is only made in memory; nothing is altered in the file until this record is written out to the appropriate file position.

Thus, it is only steps (1) and (3) above which require special non-standard Pascal procedures. Once such procedures exist, search algorithms which apply to arrays may also be appropriately applied to direct access files. Hence, a direct access file may be conceptually thought of as a large array which resides on disk.

In the examples which follow, we assume that F is a Pascal file variable associated with records of an appropriate type (other than TEXT). For each implementation of Pascal specified, we describe how to open, fetch, and update records for direct access file processing. If you do not see your system specified, the examples should nonetheless provide points of comparison which will help you to understand the local documentation describing similar facilities for your environment.

Oregon Software's (OMSI) Pascal-1 and Pascal-2

- To open a file for direct access:

```
RESET(F,filename specified with '/SEEK' switch)
```

- To fetch Ith record as currently available record:

```
SEEK(F,I)
```

- To write currently available record to Ith file position:

```
SEEK(F,I);
        .
        .        (Appropriate updating)
        .
PUT(F)
```

DEC's VAX-Pascal

- To open a file for direct access:

```
OPEN(F,ACCESS_METHOD=DIRECT,ORGANIZATION=RELATIVE)
```

- To fetch Ith record as currently available record:

```
FIND(F,I)
```

- To write currently available record to Ith file position:

```
LOCATE(F,I);
PUT(F);
```

   or

```
UPDATE(F)    { if file already positioned at Ith record }
```

UCSD and TURBO Pascal

- To open a file for direct access:

```
RESET(F,filename)
```

   (However, keep in mind that records are numbered beginning
   at 0 in these implementations.)

- To fetch Ith record as currently available record:

```
SEEK(F,I);
GET(F)
```

■ To write currently available record to *I*th file position:

```
SEEK(F,I);
PUT(F)
```

ALCOR Pascal and TRS-80 Model IV Pascal

■ To open a file for direct access:

```
OPENRAND(F,recordlen,filename,status)
```

where recordlen = number of bytes in record
     filename = name of file
     status   = error status code

■ To fetch *I*th record as currently available record:

```
READRAND(F,I,recordarea,status)
```

where recordarea = identifier for main memory area where
     record to be stored, usually F˄
     status   = error status code

■ To write currently available record to *I*th file position:

```
WRITERAND(F,I,recordarea,status)
```

where recordarea and status are defined as in fetch operation.

B

Analysis of Algorithms

B-1 Introductory Considerations

The types of efficiency results that are cited throughout the text usually require non-trivial mathematical techniques for their formal proofs. We provide here the formal results for some algorithms discussed in the text. Our purpose in doing so is to whet the appetite of those readers whose curiosity demands this type of rigor. None of the proofs presented in this appendix are essential to understanding the material in the main body of the text.

Algorithms

An **algorithm** is a set of precise instructions needed to solve a problem on a computer. It may be characterized by five properties:

   a. **Finiteness.** No matter how fast a machine is, an algorithm requiring infinitely many steps will take forever to solve the problem. Therefore the total number of steps in the algorithm must be finite.
   b. **Preciseness.** Each step in the algorithm must be precisely stated.
   c. **Uniqueness.** Each step in the algorithm has a unique outcome. This outcome depends only on the preceding steps of the algorithm.
   d. **Input.** To solve any problem, there must be some input into the algorithm.
   e. **Output.** The algorithm produces an output which is the solution to the original problem.

In order to further explain these properties of an algorithm we shall describe in detail a method for finding the square root of a number. The corresponding Pascal program is also given for further clarity.

The Newton Method for Finding Square Roots

To find the square root of a number N by the Newton method, divide the number by an estimate E. Add E to the result of the division, and multiply the new quantity by 0.5. (In other words, take the average of E and the quotient.) This now becomes the new estimate which replaces the old estimate E. Now repeat the whole process again until a desired accuracy for the square root is obtained. For most square roots 30 iterations of this method are more than sufficient.

Algorithm for Computing $\sqrt{N}$

1. Read N.
2. Set estimate E equal to some initial guess. Any guess other than 0 will work.
3. Divide N by E and save the result.
4. Add E to the result of step (3) and save the result.
5. Divide the result of step (4) by 2 and save the result.
6. Set E equal to the result of step (5). E is now closer to $\sqrt{N}$.
7. Test whether E is sufficiently accurate.
8. If the answer in (7) is yes, you are done; otherwise repeat steps (3) through (8).

We shall now see if we have satisfied all the five properties (a) through (e) of an algorithm.

Finiteness.   Since the method converges to the desired accuracy in about 30 steps, there are only finitely many steps.

Preciseness.   Each step of the algorithm except (7) is precisely defined. Step (7) asks whether E is sufficiently accurate. This is not precise. What is "sufficiently accurate"? For some people's purposes $\sqrt{2}$ = 1.4 meets the criterion, while others, needing more accurate measurements, may be dissatisfied even with $\sqrt{2}$ = 1.4142.

Therefore, to make Step (7) more precise, we must state *precisely what is sufficiently accurate.* Let us therefore restate step (7) as

7. Is $N - E^2$ within the interval $(-.001, +.001)$?

Uniqueness.   With the modified step (7), each step of the algorithm definitely produces a unique output which only depends on the preceding steps.

Input.   The algorithm receives input which in this case is the number whose square root is desired.

Output.   The algorithm produces output, which in this case is the square root of the input number.

Pascal Program for Computing $\sqrt{N}$

```
PROGRAM COMPUTE(INPUT, OUTPUT);

  VAR
    N: REAL;

  FUNCTION SQUAREROOT(A: REAL): REAL;

    VAR
      ESTIMATE: REAL;

    BEGIN
      WRITELN('ENTER YOUR ESTIMATE');
      READLN(ESTIMATE);
      {COMPUTE NEW ESTIMATE}
      WHILE ABS(ESTIMATE * ESTIMATE - N) > 0.0001 DO
        BEGIN
        ESTIMATE := 0.5 * (A / ESTIMATE + ESTIMATE)
        END {WHILE} ;
      SQUAREROOT := ESTIMATE
    END {SQUAREROOT} ;

  BEGIN {COMPUTE}
    WRITELN('ENTER THE NUMBER');
    READLN(N);
    WRITELN('THE SQUAREROOT OF', N: 10: 3, 'IS=', SQUAREROOT(N): 20: 4)
  END.
```

B-2   Efficiency of an Algorithm

It is difficult to say what a good algorithm is. Many people regard clarity, simplicity and over-all execution time as criteria of a good algorithm. Perhaps the single most important criterion in choosing an **efficient** algorithm is the objective issue of **execution time,** or the **run time,** of the algorithm. An algorithm is called *efficient* if its run time is as small as it can be for the problem it is intended to solve.

Since the run time of an algorithm is a function of the size of the input data, one way to determine the run time would be to run the algorithm on a *specific* computer for a *specific* size of input data and measure the corresponding run time. The problem with this approach is that the results will depend upon the skill of the programmer, the machine language of the computer used, the type of test data, and the type of high-level language used. As an example, one of the authors once used a BASIC program to bubble-sort 1000 random numbers (discussed later in this appendix) first on TRS-80 Model III, and then on the IBM PC. TRS-80 took 1 hour of run time as opposed to less than 30 minutes on the IBM PC.

To avoid these environmental diversities, computer scientists have agreed to accept the eventual or asymptotic run time as a fundamental criterion of the *efficiency* of an algorithm. There are usually three cases that are considered in measuring the efficiency of an algorithm—the **worst case**, the **best case**, and the **average case.**

In the preceding Pascal program for $\sqrt{N}$, for example, the WHILE loop may be executed no more than once if the ESTIMATE entered is already within 0.0001 of the real square root. That will be the best case performance of this algorithm. If, on the other hand, the initial estimate given to find the square root of 1000000 is 0.001, then the performance of the algorithm may deteriorate to the worst case. It is usually the worst-case efficiency which is regarded as a better measure of the performance of an algorithm.

Asymptotic Measurements—Big O

Let f and g be functions defined on a common domain A, where A is an unbounded set of real numbers. Then we say that $f(x)$ is of order $g(x)$, written as

$$f(x) = O(g(x))$$

if and only if there exists a constant $k > 0$ such that

$$|f(x)| \le k|g(x)|$$

for $|x| \ge N$, where N is an arbitrarily large positive integer.

For example, if we let A be the set of all integers then

$$|2 \sin z| \le |z-1|$$

for $|z| > 3$. Therefore this function $f(z)$ is of order $O(z - 1)$. (In fact, it is also $O(1)$. Why?) In relation to algorithms, our set A will be the set of all positive integers.

As a second example, let us determine the order of a function that is the sum of the first n integers. Recall that the sum of the first n integers for $n \ge 1$ is

$$\sum_{i=1}^{n} i = \frac{n(n + 1)}{2}$$

Now

$$\left|\sum_{i=1}^{n} i\right| = |1/2(n^2 + n)| \le 1/2(n^2 + n^2) \quad \text{for } n \ge 1.$$

which is $O(n^2)$.

The Bubble Sort and its Efficiency

To gain further insight into the efficiency of an algorithm, we shall analyze a common sorting algorithm called the **bubble sort**. It is introduced with the pointer sort in Chapter 1 and later briefly described in Chapter 11. We shall compute the worst-case efficiency of the bubble sort.

Given a table of n objects such as integers, the bubble sort first finds the *largest* integer among them and puts it in the nth slot in the table as shown in Figure B-1:

1	95	1		
2	10	2		Second pass will be
3	85	3		applied to these numbers
4	102	4		
5	7	5	102	Largest in 5th slot

FIGURE B-1   First Pass of Bubble Sort.

The second pass of the algorithm is applied to the numbers in slots 1 through $n - 1$, finding the second largest, which is then put in the $(n - 1)$th slot. This is shown in Figure B-2. This process is repeated until, after $n - 1$ passes, the array of numbers is completely sorted, as shown in Figure B-3. We can now completely specify the algorithm as follows:

1. Put the numbers in an array $A(N)$,
2. Start the counter L at $N - 1$,
3. Find the largest among the first $L + 1$ integers and exchange it with the number in the $(L + 1)$st slot in the array,
4. If the counter L has reached 1 you are done. Otherwise reduce L by 1 and repeat steps (3) and (4).

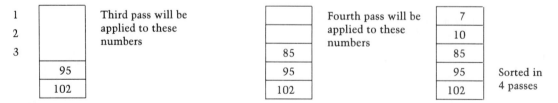

FIGURE B-2   Second Pass of Bubble Sort.

FIGURE B-3   Third and Fourth Passes of Bubble Sort.

Step (4) of the algorithm requires that the largest among L numbers be found. This can be further broken down as follows:

4. a. $K = 1$,
   b. Compare $A(K)$ with $A(K+1)$; swap $A(K)$ and $A(K+1)$ if $A(K) > A(K+1)$,
   c. Increment K and repeat step (b) until $K = L$.

The following is a Pascal version of this algorithm which can be applied to an array of size no more than 1000.

```
PROGRAM SORTDEMO(INPUT, OUTPUT);

  TYPE
    XA = ARRAY [1..1000] OF INTEGER;

  VAR
    N, I: INTEGER;
    P: XA;

  PROCEDURE BUBBLESORT(A: XA;
                       N: INTEGER);

    VAR
      S, L, I, J, K: INTEGER;

    BEGIN
      WRITELN('ENTER SIZE OF ARRAY TO BE SORTED');
      READLN(N);
      WRITELN('ENTER', N, 'NUMBER ONE PER LINE')'
      FOR I := 1 TO N DO
        READLN(A[I]);
      {BEGIN THE LOOP FOR MAIN PASSES}
      FOR L := 1 TO N -1 DO
        BEGIN
        I := N - L;
        {SET THE LOOP FOR FINDING LARGEST}
        FOR K := 1 TO I DO
          BEGIN

          IF A[K] > A[K + 1] THEN
            BEGIN {SWAP}
            S := A[K];
            A[K] := A[K+ 1];
            A[K + 1] := S
            END {IF}
          END {INNER FOR}
        END {OUTER FOR}
    END {BUBBLESORT} ;
```

```
BEGIN {MAIN}
  READLN(N);
  FOR I := 1 TO N DO
    READ(P[I]);
  BUBBLESORT(P, N);
  {NOW WRITE OUT THE SORTED ARRAY}
  FOR I := 1 TO N DO
    WRITELN(P[I])
END.
```

Analysis of the Bubble Sort. The bubble sort in the worst case makes $n - 1$ comparisons and the same number of swaps in the first pass; $n - 2$ comparisons in the second pass, and so on until it makes one comparison and swap in the $(n - 1)$th pass. Therefore, for an input of size $n > 1$, the maximum number of swaps K is

$$K = (n - 1) + (n - 2) + \cdots + 1$$
$$= 1/2\, n(n - 1) < 1/2(n^2 + n) < 1/2(n^2 + n^2)$$

Therefore the worst case run-time efficiency of the bubble sort is proportional to n^2. That is, the bubble sort is an $O(n^2)$ algorithm. Hence, if n is very large and the machine on which the data are being sorted is relatively slow, then the bubble sort may indeed by very inefficient.

The Binary Search and its Efficiency

As a second example, consider the problem of searching for a data value in an ordered table of N data values. For the sake of this example, we assume that the data values in the table are N names arranged alphabetically. This problem naturally arises in data processing activities handling large sorted files, and was discussed in Section 11-2.

One algorithm that easily comes to mind is simply searching the table from beginning to the end until the match is made. However, this search doesn't take advantage of the sorted nature of the table. A sequential search like this would obviously be a poor choice if N is very large. In fact, if the name we are looking for is the last one in the table, then we will need to make N comparisons before we find it. Thus, the worst-case efficiency of the sequential search algorithm is $O(N)$.

Now consider the following more efficient algorithm known as a **binary search,** in which we designate by NAME the data value to be searched.

1. Set FIRST $= 1$ and LAST $= N$.
2. Compute $R = ($FIRST $+$ LAST$)/2$ using integer division.
3. Compare NAME with Rth value in the table.
4. If there is a match in step (3) the algorithm ends.

5. If NAME $>$ Rth value then set FIRST $=$ $R + 1$ and go to step (2).
6. If NAME $<$ Rth value then set LAST $=$ $R - 1$ and go to step (2).

Efficiency of the Binary Search   Step (2) divides the search area in half with each cycle of the loop. Therefore, we would be able to conclude the search in at most k steps where

$$2^k \geq N$$

which gives

$$k = \log_2 N$$

Therefore, the worst case efficiency of the binary search is $O(\log_2 N)$. Notice what a significant gain in efficiency results when N is large. For example, if $N = 10,000$, then a sequential search requires 10,000 comparisons, compared to only 14 in the binary search, since $2^{14} >$ 10,000.

The Indexed Sequential Search and Its Efficiency

Section 11-4 describes an indexed sequential search strategy in which the choice of an optimal index played a key role. Briefly recall that such an index divides a disk file into regions, indicating which region each record is in. After finding the record number in the index, the system can bring the appropriate segment into main memory and search it for the desired record. We shall now compute the efficiency for this type of search.

Let N be the number of records being searched, m the amount of time required for one access to the index, and d the amount of time for one access to the actual file. Then the optimal choice for I, the size of the index, is given by

$$I = \sqrt{dN/m}$$

To prove this, we notice that in the worst case, the amount of time spent searching the index will be mI. Similarly, the worst-case time for searching the file once an index pointer is followed is given by $d(N/I)$. Hence, we wish to minimize the expression $(mI + dN/I)$. Applying calculus techniques, we differentiate this expression with respect to I, and by setting the resulting expression equal to zero we obtain

$$m - dN/(I^2) = 0$$

This yields $I = \sqrt{dN/m}$. The second derivative test verifies that this choice of I is indeed a minimum.

If both the index and the data file reside on the same storage medium, $\sqrt{N}$ is the optimal choice for the index size since $m = d$.

SUMMARY

In almost all aspects of computing, the average run time efficiency of an algorithm is crucial to know. A program that initially runs slowly can quite often be made to run faster by appropriate refinement of the algorithm. In addition to the execution time of an algorithm, the space needs of all the variables in the algorithm must also be considered. However, the availability of increasingly cheaper memory has made space needs a less important consideration than the run time of an algorithm.

C

Program Testing, Verification and Debugging

The Program Design Considerations sections found at the end of each chapter in this book have emphasized techniques which should help make your programs error-free. However, even well-designed systems must be thoroughly tested and verified before being released to users. The importance of this testing and verification phase cannot be overemphasized. As an example, consider the figures presented in Figure C-1, which summarize the percentages of total project time devoted to testing in several computerized systems developed for Air Force space missions.[1] The general rule of thumb that emerges from this figure is that the testing phase of a large project can (and should) consume roughly half of the time scheduled for the project. Of course, assignments in a data structures course may not be of the same magnitude as an Air Force space mission, but the message is clear. If you fail to schedule a considerable amount of time to verify the correctness of your program, your users (or instructor) will inevitably find bugs in it!

How exactly does one verify the correctness of a large program? Appendix B on the formal analysis of algorithms suggests one approach. That is, construct formal mathematical proofs of your algorithm's correctness. Though progress is being made in applying this type of formal mathematical approach, the problems of most "real world" systems remain too complex to allow this method to be

SAGE	47%
NAVAL TACTICAL DATA SYSTEM	50%
GEMINI	47%
SATURN V	49%

FIGURE C-1 **Percentage of Time Devoted to Testing in Space Missions.**

---

[1]Boehm, B.W. 1970. Some Information Processing Implications of Air Force Space Missions: 1970–1980. Memorandum RM-6213-PR, p. 136. Santa Monica, CA: The Rand Corporation. As cited in R.W. Jensen and C.C. Tonies. 1979. Software Engineering. Englewood Cliffs, N.J.: Prentice-Hall, p. 330.

employed efficiently in most practical situations. Consequently, the most often employed method of verifying a program's correctness is to test it thoroughly.

If testing is deemed so important as to take 50% of your time, it must clearly require more than a haphazard approach. Hence, we counsel against strategies such as creating your test data "on the fly" or creating test data by random techniques. Testing must be planned to be convincing. The plan that we shall briefly describe in this appendix is called **modular testing**. Modular testing is the natural outgrowth of the principles of modular design which have been emphasized throughout the text. The various steps involved in program development may now be summarized:

1. Define the interrelationships between modules in your system via a modular structure chart.
2. Develop each module's logic and eventually its (Pascal) code. This development should proceed in a top-down fashion.
3. Test each module as it is developed.
4. After the testing in step (3), merge the modules into a complete system. Since all modules have been tested individually, there is now a much smaller chance that errors will arise in the final system.

The third step here is the key from a testing/verification perspective. Testing at the modular level involves:

1. Developing short **driver** procedures which artificially call the modules you have written.
2. Developing short **stub** routines which (again artificially) report the values computed or otherwise obtained by any modules called by the module being tested.
3. Designing **test cases** which exercise all the logical possibilities the module may encounter. Be aware that such test cases consist of more than just strategically chosen input data. Each set of input data must also include its **expected result** (sometimes called the **test oracle**) if it is truly to convince anyone of the module's correctness.

It is in the area of designing test cases that program verification begins to mix methods of science and art. Every mathematician knows that we can never actually prove anything by testing examples (that is, input data). So, how can we verify a module's correctness by merely concocting examples? One proposed answer is to classify possible input data into **equivalence classes**. Test cases within one such equivalence class are all viewed as testing the same set of possible conditions. Hence, a finite set of well-chosen equivalence classes can be sufficient to verify an infinite number of possible inputs. Deciding what such equivalence classes should be is the point at which this process becomes more of an art than a science. Perhaps the best way to illustrate this concept is to actually design equivalence classes and corresponding test cases for an example from Chapter 1— PROCEDURE PTRSORT2 on page 21. This procedure and its driver testing program are reproduced here for your convenience.

```
PROGRAM POINTERSORT(INPUT, OUTPUT);

        {Logically sort an array by manipulating pointers
         instead of actually moving data. In this version, Pascal
         dynamic memory allocation is used.}

  CONST
     ARRAYSIZE = 100;
     MAXNAMELEN = 20;
     MAXADDRESSLEN = 60;

  TYPE
    CUSTREC =
      RECORD
        NAME: PACKED ARRAY [1..MAXNAMELEN] OF CHAR;
        ADDRESS: PACKED ARRAY [1..MAXADDRESSLEN] OF CHAR
      END;
    PTRTOCUSTREC = ^CUSTREC;

  VAR
     POINTER: ARRAY [1..ARRAYSIZE] OF PTRTOCUSTREC;
     I, NUMREC: INTEGER;

PROCEDURE PTRSORT2(N: INTEGER);

 {Apply pointer sort logic to list of N records}

  VAR
     I, J: INTEGER;
     TEMP: PTRTOCUSTREC;
     NOEXCHANGES: BOOLEAN;
  BEGIN
     I := 0;
     REPEAT {Loop to control passes through array}
       NOEXCHANGES := TRUE;
       I := I + 1;
       FOR J := 1 TO N - I DO {Number of comparisons}

         {The next line compares names being pointed to}

         IF POINTER[J]^.NAME > POINTER[J + 1]^.NAME THEN

         { But will only exchange pointers }
```

```
          BEGIN
          TEMP := POINTER[J];
          POINTER[J] := POINTER[J + 1];
          POINTER[J + 1] := TEMP;
          NOEXCHANGES := FALSE
          END
     UNTIL (I = N - 1) OR NOEXCHANGES
  END; {PTRSORT2}

  BEGIN {Main}
    WRITE('HOW MANY RECORDS-->');
    READLN(NUMREC);
    WRITELN('ENTER NAMES AND ADDRESSES ON SEPARATE LINES:');
    FOR I := 1 TO NUMREC DO
      BEGIN
      NEW(POINTER[I]); {Request heap space}
      READLN(POINTER[I]^.NAME);
      READLN(POINTER[I]^.ADDRESS)
      END;
    PTRSORT2(NUMREC);
    WRITELN;
    WRITELN('NAMES HAVE NOW BEEN SORTED.');
    WRITELN;
    WRITELN('NAME                    ADDRESS');
    FOR I := 1 TO NUMREC DO
      WRITELN(POINTER[I]^.NAME, POINTER[I]^.ADDRESS)
  END.
```

Our criterion for choosing equivalence classes of test data for this program is based on two factors:

a. The size of *N*—the number of items to be sorted
b. The ordering of the original data

Figure C-2 presents a partitioning of test data into equivalence classes for this example.

SIZE OF *N*	ORDER OF ORIGINAL DATA
N = 1	Not applicable
N = 2	Ascending
N = 2	Descending
N midsize and even	Ascending
N midsize and even	Descending
N midsize and even	Randomized
N midsize and odd	Ascending
N midsize and odd	Descending
N midsize and odd	Randomized
N = physical array size	Ascending
N = physical array size	Descending
N = physical array size	Randomized

FIGURE C-2   Partitioning of Test Data.

Hence the module should be run for a minimum of 12 test cases, one for each of the classes dictated by the table in Figure C-2. Ideally, a few subcases should be run for each of the randomized cases. We cannot overemphasize the importance of testing seemingly trivial cases such as $N = 1$ and $N = 2$. These lower boundary conditions are typically examples of data which may cause an otherwise perfectly functioning loop to be incorrectly skipped. Similarly, it is important to test the upper boundary condition in which N reaches the physical array size.

The main goal of program testing is to find errors. Though at first glance this statement may seem counterproductive, we note that it is better for errors to be detected at the testing stage than when the software product is actually in use (or when your instructor is assigning a grade). Given this negative premise of testing, you must also know how to debug your programs when testing achieves its goal of finding errors. If testing can be categorized as an art, debugging could facetiously be described as bordering on black magic. However, you should be reminded of some general guidelines which apply to the debugging of all programs:

1. Typing is no substitute for thinking. Don't be too quick to make changes in your source program. Instead, when an error occurs, take your test cases and hand trace them through the logic currently present in your module. Here the advantage of modular testing becomes apparent. Such hand tracing is nearly impossible if you are dealing with an entire system; with a mere one module it is quite manageable.

2. Make use of various debugging tools which are provided with most compilers. These tools allow you to scatter tracer output and breakpoints throughout your program in a convenient, on-line fashion. The time spent learning how to use such tools will be repaid many times over.

3. Don't assume that, once you've repaired your program for the test case which generated the error, all previous test cases will now work correctly. You now have a new program, and all of your carefully designed test cases need to be applied again.

4. Of course, leave time to debug. This avoids "band-aid" patches and encourages alternatives which may actually improve the design of your program.

If you are interested in finding out more about this dark side of computer science, we suggest you consult:

- *The Art of Software Testing.* Glenford Myers. 1979. New York: John Wiley and Sons.
- *Modern Structured Programming: Logic, Style, and Testing.* R. Schneyer. 1984. Santa Cruz, CA: Mitchell Publishing.

D

Hints and Solutions

Chapter 1 Solutions

1. ```
{Global declarations }

CONST

    N = 100;

TYPE

  ARR = ARRAY[1..N] OF INTEGER;

VAR

 LARGE, SMALL : INTEGER;

 PROCEDURE LARGESMALL (A:ARR);

 VAR

   I : INTEGER;

 BEGIN

    LARGE := A[1];
    SMALL := A[1];

    FOR I := 2 TO N DO

    BEGIN
       IF LARGE < A[I] THEN LARGE := A[I];
       IF SMALL > A[I] THEN SMALL := A[I]
    END {FOR};

    WRITELN(' THE LARGEST ELEMENT IN THE ARRAY = ', LARGE);
    WRITELN(' THE SMALLEST ELEMENT IN THE ARRAY =', SMALL)
END {LARGESMALL};
```
```

3. { Global declarations }

```
CONST

  N = 100;

TYPE

  ARR : ARRAY[1..N] OF INTEGER;

  PROCEDURE REVERSE (VAR A : ARR );

  VAR

  B : ARR;
  I : INTEGER;

  BEGIN

  FOR I := 1 TO N DO
    B[I] := A[I];

  FOR I := 1 TO N DO
    A[I] := B[N+1-I]

  END {Reverse};
```

Chapter 2 Solutions

1. The POINTERSORT in Chapter 1 is essentially a bubble sort applied to the indices of an array. There is therefore movement of data. In a linked list, there is no movement of the stored data.

3. The Pascal version of the procedure GETNODE is the procedure NEW. For this refer to the complete program in the "Program Design Considerations" section at the end of this chapter.

5. First initialize a singly linked list using the procedure NEW and an appropriate record structure. Read the first data item and insert it in the list. Read the next data item, and then walk through the list from the beginning, comparing the new item to every other data item, and insert it into its correct place in the list. Repeat this process for the remaining data items, inserting them into their alphabetically correct places. When done, simply walk through the linked list printing every node.

```
7. PROGRAM READANDINSERT(INPUT);

   TYPE

     RECPOINTER = ^SPACEREC;
     SPACEREC =
       RECORD
         DATA : ARRAY [1..20] OF CHAR;
         FLINK : RECPOINTER;
         BLINK : RECPOINTER
       END {RECORD};

   VAR
    NEXT, HEAD : RECPOINTER;

   PROCEDURE INSERTNODEDOUBLE (VAR POINT1, POINT2 : RECPOINTER);
    { Insert a node pointed to by POINT1 into a doubly linked
      list just before the node pointed to by POINT2 }

   VAR
    PREV : RECPOINTER;
    HOLD : ARRAY [1..20] OF CHAR;
    I : INTEGER;

   BEGIN
     PREV := POINT2^.BLINK;
     POINT1^.FLINK := POINT2;
     POINT1^.BLINK := PREV;
     PREV^.FLINK := POINT1;
     POINT2^.BLINK :=POINT1
   END {INSERTNODEDOUBLE};

   BEGIN {Main program }

     NEW(HEAD);
     FOR I := 1 TO 20 DO
       READ (HOLD[I]);
     HEAD^.DATA := HOLD;
     HEAD^.FLINK := HEAD;
     HEAD^.BLINK := HEAD;
     { Get the next data item }
     FOR I := 1 TO 20 DO
       READ (HOLD[I]);
     {Get the new node }
     NEW(NEXT);
     NEXT^.DATA := HOLD;
     { Insert it }
     INSERTNODEDOUBLE(NEXT,HEAD)
   END { READANDINSERT }.
```

9. This node can be queried to determine the statistical status of the list. This informationn can be used to design a more efficient algorithm at the expense of the small memory slot occupied by this node.

11. {Global declarations}

```
TYPE

  AREC = ^POINTRC;
  POINTREC =
     RECORD
        DATA : INTEGER;
        NEXT : AREC
     END { RECORD };

PROCEDURE INSERTSINGLYCIR (VAR HEAD,PREV,POINT,LIST : AREC );

VAR
 PREV : AREC;

BEGIN
     { Insert a node pointed to by POINT after the node pointed
       to by PREV }

   IF PREV = NIL THEN

   BEGIN
      HEAD := POINT;
      POINT^.NEXT := HEAD
   END
   ELSE
   BEGIN
      POINT^.NEXT := PREV^.NEXT;
      PREV^.NEXT := POINT
   END
END { INSERTSINGLYCIR };
```

13. In addition to containing statistical information about the status of the list, the PREFIRST node means that the list can be regarded as if it is never empty. Insertions and deletions into and from an empty list need not be considered.

15. It is not necessary to maintain two pointers PREV and NEXT in searching the position of a node to be deleted or inserted.

Chapter 3 Solutions

1. { Global declarations }

```
CONST N = 100;

VAR
    LENGTH : ARRAY[1..N] OF INTEGER;
    INDEX : ARRAY[1..N] OF INTEGER;
    WORK :  ARRAY[1..1000] OF CHAR;

PROCEDURE  ASSIGNWORKSPACE(VAR I,J: INTEGER);
{ Assign a string J beginning at the position INDEX [J] in
the workspace WORK to another string I.   The length of the
J string is LENGTH[J] }

BEGIN
            INDEX[I] := INDEX[J];
            LENGTH[I] := LENGTH[J]
END { ASSIGNWORKSPACE };
```

3.
```
PROCEDURE WORKCONCATENATE (VAR I,J,M,NEW : INTEGER);
{ This procedure concatenates two strings presently
existing in the work space WORK and stores the concatenated
string beginning at the free portion of the work space. The
free portion of the work space begins at the position M. As
in the solution of exercise 1, LENGTH, INDEX and WORK are suitable
arrays  declared  in  the  calling  program.   LENGTH[T] and
INDEX[T]  give  respectively  the  length and  the  starting
position of the string T in the work space WORK }
{   Assume  that WORK is large enough to hold I, J  and  I + J
strings  }
{   String NEW= string I + string J }

VAR
     L,N : INTEGER;
BEGIN     {  First copy of the string I  }

    FOR L := INDEX[I] TO LENGTH[I] DO
        WORK[M+L-1] := WORK[L];
    { Now copy the J string }
    FOR N := INDEX[J] TO LENGTH[J] DO
        WORK[M+INDEX[I]+N-1] := WORK[N];
    INDEX[NEW] := M;
    LENGTH[NEW := LENGTH[I] + LENGTH[J]
END {  WORKCONCATENATE };
```

5. { Global declarations }

```
CONST

    N = 1000;
TYPE
    STRINGARRAY = ARRAY [1..N] OF CHAR;

VAR

 MAINSTR : STRINGARRAY;
 L, M : INTEGER;

PROCEDURE  FINDPAT(PATSTR : STRINGARRAY;
                VAR FOUND : BOOLEAN );

VAR

   FLAG, CONTINUE : BOOLEAN;
   I, J : INTEGER;

   {  This procedure finds the first occurence of
      the pattern string PATSTR of length M inside
      the main string MAINSTR of length L.
      If the string is found, the boolean flag FOUND
      is returned as TRUE. Otherwise FOUND is
      returned as FALSE  }
BEGIN
   FLAG := TRUE;
   FOUND := FALSE;
   CONTINUE := TRUE;
   IF L > M THEN {  PATSTR too long  }
        FOUND := FALSE;
   I := 0;
   WHILE FLAG AND (I <= M-L) DO
   BEGIN
        I := I+1;
        J := I;
        WHILE J <=L AND CONTINUE DO
        BEGIN
            IF  PATSTR[J]<>MAINSTR[J]   THEN
                    CONTINUE := FALSE;
            IF  CONTINUE  THEN
                    J := J+1
        END { WHILE };
            { If J = L + 1 the match is found }
        IF J = L+1 THEN
        BEGIN
            FOUND := TRUE;
            FLAG := FALSE
          END { IF }
      END { WHILE}
  END { FINDPAT };
```

[Handwritten annotations: arrows pointing to "M" labeled "L" and to "L" labeled "m"; "THIS PROGRAM IS VERY FLAWED"]

7.   { Global declarations }

TYPE

        STRINGPTR = ^STRINGNODE;
        STRINGNODE =
            RECORD
                DATA : CHAR;
                LINK : STRINGPTR
            END;

VAR

        MAINH : STRINGPTR;

PROCEDURE FINDPATLINK (VAR FOUND : BOOLEAN;
                                   PATH : STRINGPTR);

VAR

        FLAG : BOOLEAN;
        M1, P1, P2 : STRINGPTR;

BEGIN

{ This procedure searches a linked string
   headed by PATH inside another linked string headed by
   MAINH. Strings are maintained by singly linked lists }

        FOUND := FALSE;
        FLAG := TRUE;
        P1 := MAINH^.LINK;
        WHILE FLAG AND (P1 <> NIL) DO
        BEGIN
          P2 := PATH^.LINK;
          M1 := P1;
          WHILE (M1^.DATA = P2^.DATA) AND
                (P2 <> NIL) AND (P1 <> NIL) DO
          BEGIN
            M1 := M1^.LINK;
            P2 := P2^.LINK
          END { WHILE };
          IF P2 = NIL THEN   { String found }
          BEGIN
                FOUND := TRUE;
                FLAG := FALSE
          END {IF};
          P1 := P1^.LINK
        END {OUTER WHILE }
    END { FINDPATLINK };

9. Solution to exercise (5) with minor modifications can be adapted.

11. Use the solution to exercise (5) to first find the substring PATSTR of length L inside the main string MAINSTR of length N. If L > N, no deletion occurs. If L = N, then the whole string is deleted. If L < N, and PATSTR is found beginning at position J in MAINSTR then the following coding can be used to finish the problem:

```
FOR M := J TO N-L DO  MAINSTR[M] := MAINSTR[L+J];
FOR M := N-L+1 TO N DO MAINSTR[M] := ' ';
```

13. In a manner of the solution of exercise (7), first find where the substring (PATSTR) begins inside the mainstring (MAINSTR). Suppose the substring PATSTR begins at node J of the mainstring MAINSTR. Reassign the pointers so that the node (in MAINSTR) which points to J now points to the node J+L+1 in MAINSTR.

15. Refer to Section 3-4, under the heading "Problems with the Linked List Method", for a thorough discussion of these problems.

Chapter 4 Solutions

1. Using the Pascal version, adapt the procedure REMOVE given in this chapter for the linked list method. Needed changes are minor.

3. ```
{ Global declarations }

TYPE

  STACKPOINTER = ^TOPPOINTER;
  TOPPOINTER =
    RECORD
       DATA : INTEGER;
       LINK : STACKPOINTER
    END;

PROCEDURE PUSH(VAR HEAD, TOP : STACKPOINTER; ITEM : INTEGER);
{ HEAD points to the top of the STACK. TOP
  points to the first data item on the stack.
  ITEM is pushed on top of the stack maintained via a
  linked list. }
VAR
 P : STACK POINTER;
```
```

```
    BEGIN
    {  First get an empty node pointed to by P  }
       NEW(P);
       P^.DATA := ITEM;
       P^.LINK := TOP;
       TOP := P;
       HEAD^.LINK := TOP;
    { Now update the count in the prefirst node  }
       HEAD^.DATA := HEAD^.DATA+1
    END { PUSH };
```

5. In the linked list implementation of a circular queue, the pointers HEAD and REAR should satisfy the following conditions:

```
    Empty queue --------> REAR = HEAD
    One-entry queue ----> REAR = HEAD^.LINK
    Full queue ---------> Handled by GETNODE or NEW
                          procedures.
```

7. One of the two versions of the procedure REMOVE given in this chapter can be adapted for any language with or without recursion capabilities.

9. While implementing a circular queue of maximum size MAX, one location must be sacrificed. At the expense of one memory location, we now have the following stipulations:

```
    FRONT = REAR ---> One-entry queue
    (REAR MOD MAX) + 1 = FRONT ---> Empty queue
    (REAR MOD MAX) + 2 = FRONT ---> Full queue
```

Chapter 5 Solutions

1. A stack is a data structure with the storage scheme that the last data item to be put in is first one to be taken out. The acronym LIFO (last-in-first-out) stands for that rule.

3. Stack priority table

Character	*	/	+	−	(	)	#
Stack Priority	2	2	1	1	0	undefined or infinity	0

5. A recursive procedure calls on itself, just as an image of you standing between two parallel mirrors duplicates itself infinitely many times.

Chapter 6 Solutions

1. A full binary tree is a binary tree in which all the leaf nodes are at the same level and every nonleaf node has two child nodes.

3. The inorder traversal of a binary tree processes the left child, the root, and the the right child respectively; therefore the tree can be originally loaded so that the items less than the root go on the left subtree, and those which are greater than the root go on the right subtree. If for example the data loaded on the tree are alphabetic in nature, then the inorder traversal of this tree would yield this data in ascending sorted order.

5.

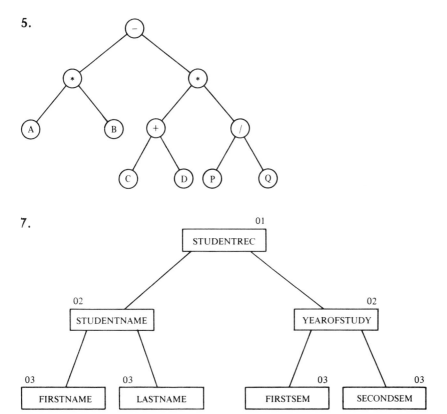

7.

9. If the data being entered into the tree are fairly random, or unsorted, the tree can be expected to have just about equal numbers of left and right subtrees each with almost equal numbers of nodes. This is the best situation as far as the fullness of the tree is concerned. If, however, the data are almost sorted, then in the worst case situation there may not be any left subtree (as in the case of alphabetized data) or any right subtree (as in the case of numerical data sorted in decreasing order).

11. {Global declarations}

```
TYPE

    NODEPOINTER = ^ TREE;
    TREE =
      RECORD
        DATA : CHAR;
        BLINK : NODEPOINTER;
        LLINK : NODEPOINTER;
        RLINK : NODEPOINTER
      END;

PROCEDURE DELETEBINTREE( VAR ROOT, P : NODEPOINTER);
{ This procedure deletes a node pointed to by P from
a binary tree pointed to by ROOT }

VAR
   X, Q, QPARENT : NODEPOINTER;

BEGIN

  IF(P^.LLINK^.RLINK = NIL AND P^.LLINK <> NIL) THEN
  BEGIN               { Case 1 }
     X := P;
     P := X^.LLINK;
     P^.RLINK := X^.LLINK;
     DISPOSE (X)
  END
  ELSE
  IF (P^.LLINK^.RLINK <> NIL) AND( P^.LLINK <> NIL) THEN
  BEGIN
     X := P;
     Q := X^.LLINK^.RLINK;
     QPARENT := X^.LLINK;
    { Q will eventually point to a node to replace P}
    { QPARENT will point to Q's parent. The following loop
      forces Q as deep as possible along the right branch
      leaving P^.LLINK }
     WHILE Q^.RLINK <> NIL DO
     BEGIN
        Q := Q^.RLINK;
        QPARENT := QPARENT^.RLINK
     END {WHILE};

       { Having found node Q to replace P, adjust pointers
         to appropriately link it into the tree }

     Q^.RLINK := X^.RLINK;
     P := Q;
     QPARENT^.RLINK := Q^.LLINK;
     Q^.LLINK := X^.LLINK;
     DISPOSE (X)
  END { IF }
```

```
      ELSE { Case 2 }
      IF (P^. LLINK = NIL) AND (P^. RLINK <> NIL) THEN
      BEGIN
         X := P;
         P := X^. RLINK;
         DISPOSE (P)
      END
      ELSE {Case 3 - Node pointed to by P has no children }
      BEGIN
         X := P;
         P := NIL;
         DISPOSE (X)
      END
   END { DELETEBINTREE };
```

Chapter 7 Solutions

1. A tree structure, in an abstract sense, represents hierarchical relationships between data objects.
3. The reference to TLPOINT would need to be modified. It can be replaced by a test on LLINK being NIL.
5. The main difficulty is when all the threads are arranged, there are some nodes to which no thread points.
7.
```
{ Global declarations }

TYPE

   POINTER = ^TERNARYNODE;
   TERNARYNODE =
      RECORD
         LSIBLING : POINTER;
         CHILDREN : POINTER;
         RSIBLING : POINTER;
         DATA : CHAR { or other appropriate type }
      END;

 PROCEDURE TERNARYPOSTORDER (ROOT : POINTER);
{ Achieve postorder traversal of a general tree
  represented via ternary tree representation }

   BEGIN

      IF ROOT <> NIL THEN
      BEGIN

          TERNARYPOSTORDER(ROOT^. LSIBLING);
          TERNARYPOSTORDER(ROOT^. CHILDREN);
          TERNARYPOSTORDER(ROOT^. RSIBLING);
      END
   END { TERNARYPOSTORDER}
```

9. Follow the guidelines of the solution to exercise (11) in Chapter 6. Assignment of threads should be a minor matter.

11. See the tree in the solution to exercise (13). It is height balanced but not full.

13.

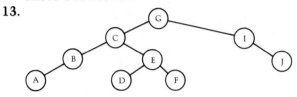

Chapter 8 Solutions

1. For a two-dimensional array, storage in row major form implies that, in the actual linear storage allocated for the array, all the elements within a row are stored contiguously. That is, two-dimensional array elements would appear in linear storage as:

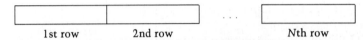

Column major implies that the elements of a column would be stored contiguously. For higher-dimensioned arrays, left subscript major storage is the analog of row major storage; that is, all entries for a fixed setting of the leftmost subscript are grouped contiguously. Similarly right subscript major is the analog of column major.

3. The term *sparse* in relation to a multi-dimensional array refers to a relatively high percentage of zeroes being stored in the array. The sparse matrix problem is the problem of representing such an array in computer memory without having to store all of these zeroes.

5. The linear list is:

   19 64 23 61 71 17 99 90 44 84 81 8 8 36 57 18 32 12 10 12 61 96 15 34

7. Picture a three-dimensional array as multiple occurrences of a two-dimensional array. Each row in each occurrence has a non-zero band of entries just as each row of an ordinary two-dimensional band matrix array has a non-zero band.

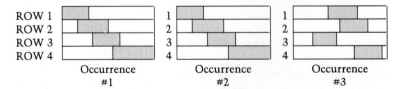

Shaded Regions Represent Non-Zero Bands

The entries within the non-zero bands must be stored in one long linear list. The non-zero band in the first row of the first occurrence would be stored first, then the non-zero band in the second row of the first occurrence, and so on. The arrays FIRSTNONZERO, LASTNONZERO, and SUM described in the text's treatment of the generalized dope vector method would now be two-dimensional arrays instead of one-dimensional arrays. Hence the bookkeeping data about the new three-dimensional structure must now be stored in two-dimensional structures with the following interpretations:

```
FIRSTNONZERO[I,J] = the column position of the first
                    non-zero entry in the Jth row of
                    the Ith occurrence
LASTNONZERO[I,J] =  the column position of the last
                    non-zero entry in the Jth row of
                    the Ith occurrence
SUM[I,J] =          the total number of entries in non-
                    zero bands which are stored prior
                    to the band in the Jth row of the
                    Ith occurrence.
```

Under these conventions, the procedures SPARSE(I,J) and PUT(V,I,J) in Chapter 8 can be easily converted to procedures SPARSE(I,J,K) and PUT(V,I,J,K) which will apply in the three-dimensional case.

9. Given the solution described for exercise (8), the efficiency ratio would be

$$\frac{NROW + NCOL + 5N}{NROW \times NCOL}$$

11. An arbitrary range of ordinal values such as

$$-4, \ldots, 4$$

would have to be mapped into the range

$$1, \ldots, 9$$

by adding 5 to each coordinate before applying the translation techniques discussed in this chapter.

13. Suppose we have declared

```
CONST L = 10;
      M = 15;
      N = 20;
VAR A : ARRAY[1..L,1..M,1..N] INTEGER;
```

Then the entry A(I,J,K) can be found at the position

```
(I - 1)*M*N + (J -1)*N + K
```

in the linear storage list with this three-dimensional structure stored in the left subscript major form. In the right subscript major form this formula would be

$$(K - 1)*L*M + (J - 1)*M + K$$

Chapter 9 Solutions

1. A tree is a particular kind of graph representing a hierarchical relationship.
3. The indegree of a source node is zero.
5. No.
7. No.
9. A spanning forest is the decomposition of a graph (or network) into a collection of disjoint trees according to a particular traversal scheme for visiting the nodes of the graph. A depth-first search and a breadth-first search yield respectively a depth-first spanning forest and a breadth-first spanning forest.

11.

Node	Indegree	Outdegree
A	1	2
B	2	1
C	1	1

13. The program is a trivial matter. The sum in each row represents the outdegree of the corresponding node. There are 2 paths of length 3 between A and B. These are $A \rightarrow C \rightarrow D \rightarrow B$ and $A \rightarrow B \rightarrow A \rightarrow B$.

15.
```
PROGRAM DOESPATHEXIST (INPUT, OUTPUT);

CONST
  N = 100;

TYPE
  ARR = ARRAY [1..N, 1..N] OF INTEGER;

VAR
  P, Q, X : INTEGER;
  FLAG : BOOLEAN;
  M1 : ARR;
PROCEDURE POWER(VAR M : ARR); EXTERNAL;
PROCEDURE ENTERMATRIX(VAR M : ARR; SIZE : INTEGER); EXTERNAL;
PROCEDURE FINDPATH(VAR M : ARR;
                   I, J : INTEGER;
                   PATHEXISTS : BOOLEAN);

  VAR
    KPOWER : ARR;
    K : INTEGER;
```

```
      BEGIN
           {Determine if there is a path between I and J nodes
            in the graph represented by the N by N adjacency
            matrix M}

         PATHEXISTS := FALSE;
         { Check first for the easiest possible case}
         IF M[I, J] <> O THEN
            PATHEXISTS := TRUE
         ELSE
         BEGIN
         K := 2;
         WHILE K < N + 1 DO
           BEGIN
           POWER(M, K, KPOWER);
            { This call returns in KPOWER the matrix M
              raised to the power K}
           IF KPOWER(I, J) <> O THEN
              PATHEXISTS := TRUE
           ELSE
             K := K + 1
           END {WHILE}
        END { ELSE }
   END {FINDPATH};

BEGIN {MAIN}
   ENTERMATRIX(M1, X); {This procedure reads an adjacency
                        matrix of size X}

   FOR P := 1 TO X DO
   BEGIN
     FOR Q := 1 TO X DO
     BEGIN
       FINDPATH (M1, P, Q, FLAG);
       IF FLAG THEN
         WRITELN ( ' The path between node', '(',P:3,')',
                     'and node','(',Q:3,') exists')
     END {Inner FOR }
   END { Outer FOR }
END { DOESPATHEXIST }.
```

17. {Global declarations }

```
CONST
   N = 100;

TYPE
  ARR = ARRAY [1..N, 1..N] OF INTEGER;
   ARRAYBOOLEAN = ARRAY [1..N] OF BOOLEAN;

 VAR
  MAT : ARR;
  INCLUDED : ARRAYBOOLEAN;
```

```
PROCEDURE FINDMIN(VAR J : INTEGER; I : INTEGER);

{ This procedure finds a node J not on the tree, having
  minimum edgeweight with a node I already on the tree }

VAR  FLAG : BOOLEAN;
 LO, K, I1, I2, COL,: INTEGER;
 SUB, ROW : ARRAY [1..N] OF INTEGER;

BEGIN

  FLAG := FALSE;
  FOR I2 := 1 TO N DO
   BEGIN
      ROW[I2] := 0;
      SUB[I2] := 0
   END { FOR };

  K := 1;
  WHILE INCLUDED[K] DO
  BEGIN
    FLAG := TRUE;
    LO := MAXINT;
    FOR I1 := 1 TO N DO
    BEGIN
      IF(LO > MAT[K, I1]) AND (MAT(K, I1) <> 0) THEN
      BEGIN
        LO := MAT[K,I1];
        COL := I1
      END {IF}
    END {FOR}
    SUB[COL] := LO; {Keeps track of what Col LO is }
    ROW[K] := LO; {Keeps track of what row it belongs to}
    K := K+1

  END {WHILE};
{Now find nonzero minimum in SUB and its position in SUB.
  The position of minimum in SUB pinpoints J }
  WHILE FLAG DO
  BEGIN
    LO := MAXINT;
    FOR I1 := 1 TO N DO
    BEGIN
      IF (SUB[I1] <> 0) AND(LO > SUB[I1]) THEN
      BEGIN
        LO := SUB[I1];
        J := I1
      END {IF}
    END {FOR};
    { Now identify I from the array ROW }
    FOR I2 := 1 TO N DO
```

```
    BEGIN
      IF ROW[I2] = LO THEN
          I:=I2
    END {FOR}
  END {WHILE}

  END {FINDMIN};
```

19. Matrix PATH follows:

	1	2	3	4	5
1	0	800	1210	310	200
2	800	0	410	612	1000
3	1210	410	0	1022	1410
4	310	612	1022	0	400
5	200	1000	1410	400	0

21. Follow the guidelines of the procedure DF-SEARCH. The logic and the code for breadth-first search steps are mirror images of DF-SEARCH.

23. A x B is given in the text. B x A follows:

$$B \times A = \begin{bmatrix} 10 & 18 & 27 \\ 16 & 25 & 38 \\ 30 & 58 & 83 \end{bmatrix}$$

Notice that A x B is not equal to B x A.

25. The only procedure that can conceivably present some challenge is FINDMIN. For FINDMIN refer to the solution of exercise (15).

Chapter 10 Solutions

1. All practical data processing requires accessing records quickly and efficiently. Search algorithms are most efficient only when the records are sorted according to some specified keys. If the records in a file are not sorted, searching for a particular record would require checking every record until the match is made. This is unnecessarily wasteful of precious computer time especially if the file to be searched is very large.

Consider for example a file consisting of 1000 unsorted records. To find a record in this file we may, in the worst case, need to make 1000 comparisons. If the same file is sorted on some key, then a binary search algorithm can pinpoint the record in less than 10 comparisons.

3. The insertion sort derives its name from the fact that in its ith iteration it inserts the ith record in its correct place among the first i records.

5. In the process of sorting, the method creates a heap. A heap by definition is a full binary tree with the property that a parent node is always greater than or equal to both of its child nodes.

7. The shell sort is named after its inventor, Dr. D. L. Shell.

9. When the array to be sorted consists of a small number of data items (usually ≤ 100), and the array is almost sorted, then the bubble sort may prove to be slightly better than the quick sort.

11. The shell sort will work for any set of increments as long as the last one is 1. Modify the procedure SHELLSORT given in the text with this information.

13. There is no special magic about the relatively prime values of the increments. Other choices would work also. Choosing values of increments as powers of 2, such as 16, 8, 2, 1 would not be advisable because the keys compared on one pass would be compared again. Keeping increments relatively prime avoids this problem.

15. If n is the size of the array to be sorted, then the average and worst case efficiency of the heap sort is $O(n \log_2 n)$.

17. The bubble sort, the insertion sort, the selection sort, and the merge sort are stable. The quick sort, the shell sort and the heap sort are not stable.

Chapter 11 Solutions

1. In the case where the TARGET is not present in the list, the search could be terminated as soon as a KEY greater than the TARGET is encountered.

3. ```
{Global declarations}

TYPE
  POINTER = ^NODEPOINTER;
  NODEPOINTER =
    RECORD
        DATA : CHAR; {Or any other appropriate type }
        KEY : INTEGER;
        LCHILD : POINTER;
        RCHILD : POINTER
      END;

VAR
 ROOT : POINTER;

PROCEDURE BINARYTREESEARCH(TARGET : INTEGER;
                          VAR ITEM : CHAR;
                          VAR FOUND : BOOLEAN);
VAR
 P : POINTER;
```
```

```
BEGIN
  FOUND := FALSE;
  P := ROOT;
  REPEAT
     IF TARGET < P^.KEY THEN
         P := P^.LCHILD
     ELSE
     IF TARGET > P^.KEY THEN
         P := RCHILD
     ELSE
      BEGIN
            ITEM := P^.DATA;
            FOUND := TRUE
      END
  UNTIL FOUND OR P = NIL
END {BINARYTREESEARCH};
```

5. Given below is the general sketch of a solution in Pascal. Since a B-tree index presupposes a file-oriented system, the specific implementation would depend upon the intricacies of the file-handling statements in the high-level language selected. Note that the solution assumes (as indicated in the text) that each B-tree node includes:

   a. A count of the number of key-pointer pairs in the node
   b. A back-pointer to the node's parent

```
{Global declarations}

TYPE
 BTREE = ^TREEPOINTER;
 TREEPOINTER =
   RECORD
       { Proper B-tree node structure }
   END;
VAR
 N : INTEGER;

PROCEDURE SEARCH(NEWKEY1 : INTEGER;
                VAR L : BTREE); EXTERNAL;

PROCEDURE INSERT(NEWKEY2 : INTEGER;
                 L1 : BTREE); EXTERNAL;

PROCEDURE SPLIT(L2 : INTEGER); EXTERNAL;

PROCEDURE INSERTBTREE(NEWKEY : INTEGER);
VAR
 PARENT : BTREE;
```

```
BEGIN
{ The call to SEARCH returns a pointer P to the bottom-
  level node in which NEWKEY belongs. }

    SEARCH(NEWKEY,P);

{ The next call, depending upon the list structure in the
  node  pointed to by P, is responsible for inserting the
  key-pointer pair for NEWKEY into the B-tree node
  indicated by P. }

    INSERT(NEWKEY,P);

{ Finally, if the preceding insert caused the B-tree node
  to overflow, we must, perhaps repeatedly, split a node
  and pass a key up to the parent node. }

    WHILE COUNT(P) > N-1 DO
    BEGIN
        SPLIT(P); { Split node P into 2 }
        INSERT(SPLITKEY,PARENT);{ Pass splitting key to
                                  parent }
        P := PARENT
    END { WHILE }
END {INSERTBTREE};
```

7. Given below is the general sketch of a solution in Pascal. Since
a trie index presupposes a file-oriented system, a specific implementation would depend upon the intricacies of the file-
handling statements in the chosen language.

```
{Global declarations}

CONST
  N = 100;
  M = 100;

TYPE
  TREENODE = ^POINTERNODE;
  POINTERNODE =
    RECORD
        { Proper trie node structure }
    END;
    ARR1 : ARRAY[1..M] OF CHAR;

VAR
 M : INTEGER;
 ROOT : TRIENODE;
 TRIENODE : ARRAY [1..N, 1..28] OF TREENODE;
FUNCTION  SEEKINDEX(INDEX : INTEGER): INTEGER; EXTERNAL;
{ SEEKINDEX reads a file of indexes associated with
  the main record file, and returns the position
  of a record in the main file.}
```

```
PROCEDURE INSERTTRIE(VAR NEWKEY : ARR1);
    { TRIENODE represents an array of nodes as
      pictured in Figure 11-25. }

VAR KEY : ARR1;
    I : INTEGER;
    Q, R, P : TREENODE;

BEGIN

 I := 1;
 P := ROOT;
WHILE (TRIENODE[P,POS(NEWKEY[I])] <> NIL)
      AND (TRIENODE[P,POS(NEWKEY[I])] > NIL DO
BEGIN

 { The preceding WHILE assumes existence of function
   POS which returns ordinal position of character
   NEWKEY[I] relative to indexing of TRIENODE, and
   that negative values are used to point to actual
   data records. }
   P := TRIENODE[P,POS(NEWKEY[I])];
   I := I+1

END {WHILE}
IF TRIENODE[P,POS(NEWKEY[I])] = NIL THEN
   TRIENODE[P,POS(NEWKEY[I])] := SEEKINDEX (I)
                {Data record position for NEWKEY }

ELSE
BEGIN
  R := TRIENODE[P,POS(NEWKEY[I])];
{ Fetch KEY pointed at by R from data record file.}
  WHILE KEY[I+1] = NEWKEY[I+1] DO
  BEGIN
     NEW(Q);
     TRIENODE[P,POS(NEWKEY[I])] := Q;
     P := Q;
     I := I+1
  END { WHILE};
  NEW(Q);
  TRIENODE[Q,POS(KEY[I+1])] := R;
  TRIENODE[Q,POS(NEWKEY[I+1])] := SEEKINDEX(I)

          { Data record position for NEWKEY }

 END {ELSE}
END {INSERTTRIE};
```

9. {Global declarations}

```
CONST
  N = 100;

TYPE
  ARR1 = ARRAY [1..N] OF INTEGER;
  ARR2 = ARRAY [1..N] OF CHAR; { or any other appropriate type}
VAR
 KEY : ARR1;
 DATA : ARR2;
FUNCTION HASH(NEWKEY1 : INTEGER):INTEGER; EXTERNAL;

PROCEDURE INSERTLINEARHASH(NEWKEY : INTEGER; ITEM : CHAR);
   { Insert NEWKEY and associated DATA in ITEM
     into linearly hashed structure. }
VAR J:INTEGER;

BEGIN
   J := HASH(NEWKEY);
   WHILE KEY[J] <> 0 DO
    J := (J MOD RECORDSPACE) + 1;
   KEY[J] := NEWKEY;
   DATA[J]:=ITEM
END { INSERTLINEARHASH};
```

The insertion procedures for the other methods would be similarly handled with appropriate modifications being made in the WHILE loop to take care of collision processing.

11. The key in any deletion strategy for a hashed file is to use separate flags to distinguish locations which are

EMPTY AND NEVER ACTIVE
vs.
EMPTY BUT PREVIOUSLY ACTIVE

Without such a distinction, the search procedure cannot determine whether or not it should stop upon coming to an empty record.

13. The key to these procedures is to keep the file itself physically ordered by key values. As an insertion into a sequential search block overflows that block, the final item in the block must be moved out to an overflow area. As this occurs, a pointer to that overflow area must be inserted within the block itself. In this regard the method is similar to linked hashing and the resolution of a full bucket in bucket hashing. Deletions may be handled by simply inserting an empty flag in the area occupied by the key to be deleted. As the file is periodically re-built, these flagged records may be physically removed from the file.

15. There are five properties which must be satisfied for a data structure to be a B-tree of order n. These are listed in Section 11-4 under the heading "B-tree Indexing."

Chapter 12 Solutions

1. Follow the guide given by the generic PROCEDURE ALLOCATE(S,P) and PROCEDURE GARBAGECOLLECT(P,AVAIL) in the text. In particular note that, for the binary buddy system, whether a returning block has a left or right buddy (clearly it cannot have both) is simply a function of the block's starting address.

3. Again follow the general strategy of the generic procedure given in the text. In particular, note that for the boundary tag method:

    a. There are no limitations on block sizes which may be allocated
    b. When coalescing occurs, this is the only one of the three methods in which a given block can have both left and right buddies.

5. If a record to be deleted is accessed directly without a list traversal, deletion is *immediately* possible because of the back pointer.

7. Four steps are involved—search for the key to be deleted, determine the secondary key values of the record associated with this key, store these secondary key values along with the position of the record to be deleted, and finally delete this record position from the list associated with each of the secondary key values.

9. Since Pascal's NEW and DISPOSE procedures must handle requests for blocks of greatly varying yet precise sizes, aspects of the boundary tag method could be applied. The binary and Fibonacci systems would not apply because of the fixed-block sizes which are needed. Another strategy might be to maintain multiple linked lists of blocks for each type of record in the Pascal program. By this strategy, a generalization of the GETNODE and RETURNNODE procedures from Chapter 2 could be used.

11. The first is a complex network; the second is simple.

Glossary
of Terms*

*Numbers in brackets at the end of each entry refer to the chapter in which the term is first discussed.

acyclic graph   A directed graph in which there are no paths from any one node back to itself. [9]

adjacency matrix   A method of representing the physical structure of a graph by a matrix that holds information about connections between nodes in the graph. [9]

algorithm   The concise instructions that manipulate related data items. A collection of steps that solve a specified problem in a finite number of steps. [1]

arc   A directed path between two nodes of a graph. [9]

array   A collection of a specific number of variable data elements, individual members of which may be accessed by specifying numeric coordinates. [1]

assignment   The copying of one variable into another. [3]

available list   A linked list containing nodes that are presently not in use for active data storage. [2], [12]

AVL-rotation   A process by which a tree is maintained in a form close to full, thereby ensuring rapid insertions and searches. Developed by Adelson-Velskii and Landis. See also **height-balanced tree.** (7)

backward arc   Indicates that it is possible to follow arcs through a graph to arrive at one's origin. [9]

band matrices   Matrices in which the nonzero entries tend to cluster around the diagonal of the matrix. [8]

binary buddy system   A memory allocation system in which all blocks are of a size 2^i for some i. When a block is split, the resulting blocks must be equal in size. Available space is kept track of using a doubly linked list. [12]

binary search   A method used to search an ordered list. The search begins in the middle of a table and determines whether the argument is in the upper or lower half of the table, and continues to halve that portion of the table in which the argument being sought is located until the argument is found. [11]

binary tree   A finite set of elements arranged into a hierarchical structure consisting of a root and two disjoint subtrees, in which each node has at most two nodes descending from it. [6]

binary tree index   A binary tree which stores nodes containing a key and a pointer to a record associated with that key. [11]

binary tree representation of a general tree   Requires that each node have only two pointer fields. The first pointer indicates the leftmost child of the node, and the second pointer identifies the next sibling of the node. [7]

456

binary tree search Implements the binary search method through use of a binary tree structure. [11]

blocking The positioning of records into contiguous regions on a track of a disk so that a fixed number are brought into main memory when a record in that block is requested. [11]

boundary folding When producing a hash position, every other number in a key is reversed before being added into the total. [11]

boundary tag buddy system A garbage collection scheme that allows arbitrary selection of block sizes, thereby saving memory from being wasted. Information on block sizes and location of adjacent blocks is stored at the boundaries of each block. [12]

B-tree A generalized tree that can dynamically handle insertions and deletions without deterioration in search efficiency. Its main application is as an index into a file. [11]

bubble sort Compares each element of an array with its successor, swapping the two if they are not in the proper order. [1]

bucket hashing Transforms a key to a position representing a "bucket"—a physically contiguous region of locations. After having hashed to the bucket, records are accessed sequentially. [11]

chained pointer database A database relationship in which the use of a secondary key is handled by linking together all those records that share a given value for the secondary key. [12]

child A descendant of a preceding node in a tree. [6]

circular linked list A linked list in which the last node in the list points to the first node in the list, eliminating the need for null pointers. [2]

clustering A problem arising when a hashing function is biased toward placement of keys into a single region within a storage space. [11]

CODASYL model A database management system that uses the notion of a set to describe one-to-many and simple network relationships. [12]

collision A problem arising in hashing when two items hash to the same position. [11]

column major A method by which multidimensional arrays are stored in a linear sequence in memory by columns. [8]

compaction A process by which character strings are relocated in memory, resulting in a shift of available free space into one large contiguous memory region. [12]

complex network A directed graph where there are many-to-many relationships between records. [12]

concatenation The joining together of two character strings. [3]

cross arc During a depth-first search, used to connect nodes on different trees within the spanning forest of a graph. [9]

cycle A path in a directed graph of length at least 1 that originates and terminates at the same node in the graph. [9]

database A collection of logically related data files on which operations are performed. [12]

database management The process of managing a collection of logically related files. [12]

data duplication problem A problem arising in database management that occurs when the same information is stored more than once in separate files, and must be kept current in all locations. [12]

data structure A way of organizing data that considers not only the items stored but also their relationships to each other. Requires efficient algorithms for accessing the data both in main memory and on secondary storage devices. Efficiency is intrinsically linked to the structure of the data being processed. [1]

DBMS Database management system. [12]

deletion (1) A procedure that removes a node from a linked list or tree. [2] (2) A procedure that removes a portion of a designated string from a larger string. [3]

density-dependent search A search method whose efficiency is dependent on the ratio of the number of records currently in the list compared to the total record space available. [11]

depth of a tree The maximum level of any node in a tree. [6]

digraph A graph in which an edge between two nodes is directionally oriented. Also known as a **directed graph.** [9]

diminishing increment sort A synonym for shell sort. [10]

direct (random) access The ability to access any location in a storage medium without first having to access prior locations. [11]

directory The index that stores file locations. [11]

DISPOSE A Pascal verb which dynamically deallocates (frees up) the memory space used by a record. [2]

dope vector Contains information that helps to interpret the actual data in an array. [8]

doubly linked list A linked list in which each node contains two pointers, one to its predecessor and another to its successor, thus allowing traversal of the list both backwards and forwards. [2]

dummy header A node in a linked list that points to the first node containing valid data. It is used to simplify code for insertions and deletions at the beginning of a linked list. [2]

edge A directed connection between two nodes of a graph. [9]

execution time A measure of the efficiency of an algorithm determined by the number of operations that must be performed. [1], [10]

external sorting The sorting of data that resides on a secondary storage device. [10]

extraction Removing any digits or characters that are likely to bias the hash value of a key before hashing. [11]

Fibonacci buddy system A garbage collection scheme that allows for a large variety of possible block sizes within a given memory space by allocating blocks of a size in the Fibonacci sequence. [12]

Fibonacci numbers Numbers that are the sum of the preceding two numbers in a sequence. For example, 1, 1, 2, 3, 5, 8, 13 . . . [12]

field A subdivision of a record that contains an elementary data item. [2]

FIFO First-in-first-out. Used in describing a queue. [4]

fixed length method String variables are allocated to handle the maximum possible string length that is envisioned for an application. [3]

folding A hashing method by which noninteger keys are transformed into integers suitable for further hashing action. [11]

fragmentation A problem that occurs when allocation and deallocation of memory breaks free space up into smaller, less useful portions. [12]

garbage collection The effective recovery of memory that is no longer in use. [12]

generalized dope vector method A method of efficiently representing sparse band matrices by maintaining a separate array indicating which entries are nonzero. [8]

general tree A tree in which each node may have any number of descendant nodes. [7]

graph A many-to-many relationship between objects in a database, represented as a collection of nodes and edges joining them. [9]

graph traversal An algorithm that determines the possible ways of visiting the nodes of a graph. [9]

hashing function Acts upon a given key in such a way as to return a position in the list where the key can be placed. [11]

heap sort A two-phase sort procedure that uses a full binary tree structure. [10]

height-balanced tree Maximizes the speed with which insertions and searches are handled by decreasing the depth to which one must search for an item in a tree. It involves maintaining full trees. See **AVL-rotation.** [7]

hierarchical model A database model that limits its users to specifying one-to-many relationships. Many-to-many relationships can be implemented only be decomposition into one-to-many relations. [12]

incidence matrix A method of representing the physical structure of a graph by a matrix that holds information about the connections between nodes in the graph. Also called an **adjacency matrix.** [9]

indegree The number of arcs entering a node. [9]

index A list of keys and locational information around which a file is organized. [11]

indexed sequential access method   A partial index is built that leads to an appropriate region, where a sequential search is then undertaken. [11]

infix notation   In an arithmetic expression, the arithmetic operator appears between the two operands to which it is being applied. Infix notation often requires the use of parentheses to specify a desired order of operation. [5]

inorder predecessor   The node that, in an ordered list, comes before the node being examined. [7]

inorder successor   The node that, in an ordered list, follows a node being examined. [7]

inorder traversal   An algorithm that moves through a tree in such a fashion that an ordered list results. [6]

insertion   (1) A procedure which adds a node to a linked list or tree. [2], [6]. (2) A procedure by which a given string is added into the middle of another string. [3]

insertion sort   In the ith pass, inserts the ith element in its correct place. [10]

internal sorting   Retains all the data to be sorted in main memory. [10]

intersection record   A record used in the CODASYL model to link one-to-many relationships having that record in common into a many-to-many relationship. [12]

inverted file method   Locates information about the data in small files that are maintained apart from the actual data records. These files are indexes containing relative record positions of those records sharing identical values for a given secondary key. [12]

ISAM   Indexed sequential access method. [11]

key   A data item that identifies a record. [11]

key-to-address transformation   An algorithm that acts on a given key in such a way as to return a position in a list where the key can be placed. A synonym for **hashing.** [11]

LABEL   In Pascal, a statement position identifier that can be referred to by other statements. [1]

left buddy count   Maintains a record of how deep a given block is nested as the left buddy of other blocks. [12]

LIFO   Last-in-first-out. Used in describing a stack. [4]

Linear hashing   When a collision occurs while hashing, proceed down a list in sequential order until a vacant position is found. [11]

linked hashing   Requires a storage area divided into two parts—a prime hash area and an overflow area. Initially, a hashing function translates keys into the prime area. Collisions are resolved by linking into the overflow area. [11]

linked list   A structure in which each data node contains not only a data field but also one pointer to the next field in the list. The pointer system in the linked list structure eliminates the need for a lot of movement of data. Thus, insertions and deletions become more economical in terms of processing time. [2]

linked list method Stores character strings in linked lists, and thereby allows for dynamic string allocation with no limit on string length and also for efficient insertions and deletions. [3]

many-to-many relationship Each node or record in a database may be related to many other nodes or records without any limitation on the type of relationship. The relationship need not be hierarchical. See **one-to-many relationship.** [12]

matrix A two-dimensional array in which the position of a data element must be specified by giving two coordinates. [8], [9]

merge sort Most commonly used in external sorting. A file is divided into two subfiles. These files are compared, one pair of records at a time, and merged by writing them to other files for further comparisons. [10]

minimum spanning tree A subcollection of the nodes and edges of a network that results in a tree of minimum total edge weight. [9]

mod The remainder of dividing an integer P by an integer Q. For example, 5 mod 2 = 1. [4]

multidimensional array An array of dimension higher than one. Each data element must be specified by giving one coordinate for each dimension. [8]

multilinked list A linked list structure that has links for each of several orders in which the list is to be traversed. [2]

multilink files A database relationship in which the use of a secondary key is handled by linking together all those records that share a given value for a secondary key. [12]

network A graph with a value placed on the path between two nodes, such as a distance between two places. [9]

NEW A Pascal verb used to dynamically allocate memory space for the next record. [2]

one-dimensional array A specific number of consecutive memory locations. This number is the size of the array. [2]

one-to-many relationship Each node or record in a file is hierarchically related to many other nodes or records in a database. [12]

outdegree The number of arcs exiting a node of a digraph. [9]

parsing The process of collapsing any of various different expressions into one unique form, which simplifies its eventual evaluation. [5]

Pascal record A logically related group of heterogeneous data fields. [1]

path A sequence of arcs connecting two nodes of a digraph. [9]

pattern matching The process of searching a given string for an occurrence of another string. [3]

pointer variable   In Pascal, a variable whose value is the address in memory of some other variable. [1]

polyphase merge sort   A merge sort using multiple channels. [10]

pop   Removing the top entry from a stack. [4]

postfix notation   In the determination of an arithmetic expression, the need for parentheses is eliminated because the operator is placed directly after the two operands to which it applies. Also called **reverse Polish notation.** [5]

postorder traversal   A recursive tree traversal in which each node is processed after its children. [6]

prefix notation   In an arithmetic expression, the operator is placed directly before the two operands to which it applies. [5]

preorder traversal   A recursive tree traversal in which each node is processed before its children. [6]

primary key   The field by which a file is most commonly accessed. Primary keys are usually unique. [12]

push   Adding a new entry onto a stack. [4]

quadratic hashing   Resolves collisions by proceeding to locations $\text{HASH(KEY)} + 1\hat{\ }2, \text{HASH(KEY)} + 2\hat{\ }2, \text{HASH(KEY)} + 3\hat{\ }2, \ldots$ until an available position is found. [11]

quantity dependent search   A search method, the efficiency of which is dependent on the quantity of data stored. [11]

queue   A first-in-first-out (FIFO) list structure in which insertions are limited to one end of the list, whereas deletions may occur only at the other end. [4], [5]

quick sort   A pivotal item near the middle of the array is chosen, then moves are made such that items placed on one side of the pivot are smaller than the pivot and those placed on the other side are larger. This procedure is applied recursively until the whole array is sorted. [10]

randomized storage   Sorting and accessing elements in a list by the use of a hashing function. [11]

rank   The number of dimensions of an array. [8]

record   A group of related data items. [1], [11]

recursion   A conditional call by a procedure or function to itself. [5]

relational model   A database management system that describes the database in terms of tables called relations. [12]

relations   A table of rows and columns in which each row corresponds to a record and each column to a field name. [12]

reverse Polish notation   See **postfix notation.** [5]

root   The highest level of a tree. It is the only node in a tree to which a direct pointer exists. [6]

row major   The method by which multidimensional arrays are stored in a linear sequence in memory by rows. [8]

secondary key A key other than the primary key on which one may sort a file or search for an item. [12]

sector A predefined pie-shaped slice on a circular magnetic disk. [11]

SEEK A nonstandard but common random file access verb in Pascal. [11]

selection sort Successive elements are selected from a file or array and placed in their proper position. [10]

sequential search Involves beginning with the first record in a list and examining each subsequent record until the record being sought is found. [11]

shell sort An array is divided into smaller segments that are then separately sorted using an insertion sort. [10]

shift folding A hashing method by which noninteger keys are broken up and added into a total, which is used as a hash key. [11]

shortest path An algorithm used on graph structures that proceeds by choosing from nodes not yet selected, that node closest to the source node, and keeping track of those in an array. On completion of the algorithm, the data in the array determine the shortest path from the given source node to all other nodes. [9]

simple network A collection of several one-to-many relationships whose resulting representation as a graph is acyclic. [12]

singly linked list A linked list in which each node contains only one link field pointing to the next node in the list. [2]

sink node A node in a digraph that has no arcs exiting from it. [9]

source node A node in a digraph that has no arcs entering it. [9]

spanning forest A set of trees obtained by decomposing a graph with a depth-first search. [9]

sparse matrix An array with a low percentage of nonzero entries. [8]

stack A last-in-first-out (LIFO) list structure in which both insertions and deletions occur at only one end of the list. [4], [5]

string length The number of characters in the string, with all trailing blanks removed. For example, "TOOT   " takes up 6 spaces. Its actual length is 4. [3]

strongly connected A digraph in which there exists, for any two nodes, a bi-directional path between them. [9]

substring operations Procedures that allow a user to examine, insert, or delete a portion of a string. [3]

subtree A subset of a tree that is itself a tree. [6]

symmetric matrix A matrix in which the ith row and the ith column are always identical. An incidence matrix for an undirected graph is an example. [9]

synonyms Describes two keys that hash to the same position. [11]

ternary tree representation of a general tree Requires that each node of a general tree have three pointer fields; one for its left sibling, one for its children, and one for its right sibling. [7]

threaded tree Eliminates the need for recursive traversal through a tree by making use of previously null pointers to point to preceding or succeeding nodes. [7]

topological sort   An algorithm to establish an ordered relationship among the nodes of a graph that ensures its adjacency matrix has only zeroes below the main diagonal [9]

track   One of the concentric circles of storage into which a magnetic disk is divided. [11]

tree   A data structure that represents a hierarchical order of precedence between related items. [6]

trie   A method of handling keys that are variable length strings. Each node of the trie consists of an array of pointers (one for each possible character) that point either to another node in the trie or to the actual data record for the key. [11]

upper triangular matrix   A matrix in which all entries below the main diagonal are zeroes. [9]

variable length records problem   A database storage allocation problem that occurs when the lengths of records are not fixed. [12]

vector   A one-dimensional array. [2]

volatile file   A file that undergoes frequent insertions and deletions. [11]

weakly connected   A digraph in which there exists between any two nodes an unidirectional path. [9]

workspace/index table method   One large memory workspace is allocated, and all strings are stored in it. Information about this string storage is kept in a separate index table. [3]

Index